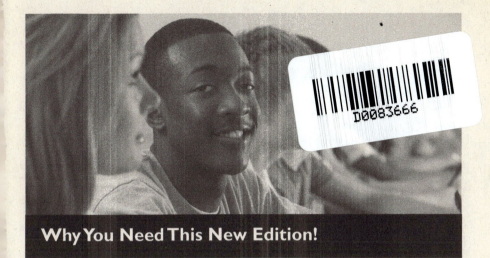

Why You Need This New Edition!

If you're wondering why you should buy this new edition of *The Simon & Schuster Short Prose Reader,* here are six good reasons!

- **New topics for debate**—"Can Money Buy Happiness?" and "How Real Is Reality TV?" (Ch. 10)—offer compelling opportunities for both discussion and written responses.
- The **updated appendix**, Writing with Sources, includes the most recent changes in the MLA documentation style, as well as new guidance for using a research notebook and additional examples for integrating secondary-source material.
- Additional instructions and practice in writing and using **summaries** (Ch.1 and throughout) will help you to understand and remember what you read.

- Updated links to **Web sites** (throughout) encourage you to find additional information online about the readings and their authors.
- **Thirteen new readings,** including selections by Rita Dove, Cynthia Crossen, Sue Shellenbarger, and Nancy Masterson Sakamoto, along with **two new student essays,** offer fresh content to complement the many favorites (including selections by Russell Baker, Brent Staples, Gloria Naylor, Judith Viorst, Isaac Asimov, Suzanne Britt, Elizabeth Berg, Mike Royko, Stephen King, and Jade Snow Wong) that have been retained from previous editions.
- Numerous revised prompts and updated topics are offered for **Writing Step by Step** and **Other Writing Ideas**, along with several innovative activities and new exercises for **Gaining Word Power** and improving **Editing Skills**.

The Simon & Schuster

SHORT PROSE READER

Sixth Edition

ROBERT W. FUNK
Eastern Illinois University

SUSAN X DAY
University of Houston

LINDA S. COLEMAN
Eastern Illinois University

ELIZABETH McMAHAN
Illinois State University

Prentice Hall

Boston Columbus Indianapolis New York San Francisco Upper Saddle River
Amsterdam Cape Town Dubai London Madrid Milan Munich Paris Montreal Toronto
Delhi Mexico City Sao Paulo Sydney Hong Kong Seoul Singapore Taipei Tokyo

Senior Sponsoring Editor: Virginia L. Blanford

Marketing Manager: Thomas DeMarco

Senior Supplements Editor: Donna Campion

Senior Media Producer: Stefanie Liebman

Project Coordination, Text Design, and Electronic Page Makeup: Laserwords/Amy L. Saucier

Senior Art Director, Cover: Pat Smythe

Cover Designer: Dutton & Sherman Design

Cover Illustration/Photo: Alamy

Photo Research: Bill Smythe Group/Lynne Shulhafer

Text Permissions: Glenview/Virginia Creeden

Senior Manufacturing Buyer: Mary Ann Gloriande

Printer and Binder: R.R. Donnelley-Harrisonburg

Cover Printer: R.R. Donnelley-Harrisonburg

For permission to use copyrighted material, grateful acknowledgment is made to the copyright holders on pp. 366–367, which are hereby made part of this copyright page.

Library of Congress Cataloging-in-Publication Data

The Simon & Schuster short prose reader / [compiled by] Robert W. Funk . . . [et al.]. 6th ed.
   p.—cm.
  Includes bibliographical references and index.
  ISBN-13: 978-0-205-82599-8
  ISBN-10: 0-205-82599-0
  1. College readers. 2. English language—Rhetoric—Problems, exercises, etc. 3. Report writing—Problems, exercises, etc.
I. Funk, Robert. II. Title: Simon and Schuster short prose reader.
  PE1417.S453 2010
  808'.0427—dc22

                    2010044159

Copyright © 2012, 2009, 2006 by Pearson Education, Inc.

5 6 7 8 9 10—RRD-H—18 17 16 15 14

ISBN-13: 978-0-205-82599-8
ISBN-10: 0-205-82599-0

Contents

1

Active Reading

The Reading-Writing Connection

3

Strategies for Conveying Ideas: Narration and Description

4

Strategies for Making a Point: Example and Illustration

5

Strategies for Clarifying Meaning: Definition and Explanation

6

Strategies for Sorting Ideas: Classification and Division

7

Strategies for Examining Two Subjects: Comparison and Contrast

8

Strategies for Explaining How Things Work: Process and Directions

9

Strategies for Analyzing Why Things Happen: Cause and Effect

10

Strategies for Influencing Others: Argument and Persuasion

Appendix: WRITING WITH SOURCES   343

Thematic Contents

Social Issues

Work

Humor

Entertainment and Leisure

Editing Skills: Contents

Chapter 3 Strategies for Conveying Ideas: Narration and Description

Thomas, "Rain of Fire"

Royko, "Jackie's Debut: A Unique Day"

McGrath, "Walking Away"

Lewis, "Road Work"

Combining sentences

Punctuating conversation

Quotation marks inside quotations

Choosing *there*, *their*, or *they're*

Chapter 4 Strategies for Making a Point: Example and Illustration

Berg, "My Heroes"

Staples, " 'Just Walk On By' "

Meier, "One Man's Kids"

Jones, "The Working Poor"

Semicolons between sentences

Commas around interrupters

Using subordination

Commas in series

Chapter 5 Strategies for Clarifying Meaning: Definition and Explanation

Naylor, "Mommy, What Does 'Nigger' Mean?"

Asimov, "What Is Intelligence, Anyway?"

Baron, "The Noun Game"

Gonzalez, "Viva Spanglish!"

Hyphens

Using the right tense

Using noun clauses

Using coordination

Chapter 6 Strategies for Sorting Ideas: Classification and Division

Viorst, "Friends, Good Friends— and Such Good Friends"

Zimring, "Confessions of an Ex-Smoker"

Elkind, "Types of Stress for Young People"

Lantigua, "The Latino Show"

Using pronouns consistently

Avoiding sexist language

Transitions

Using apostrophes

Chapter 7 Strategies for Examining Two Subjects: Comparison and Contrast

Sakamoto, "Conversational Ballgames"

Britt, "Neat People vs. Sloppy People"

O'Shaughnessy, "A Whole New Ballgame"

Seal, "The Trouble with Talent"

Commas after dependent elements

Using apostrophes

Choosing *its* or *it's*

Using dashes

Preface

Good readers are usually good writers, and good writers are always good readers. Researchers tell us that reading and writing are complementary processes that involve the use of language to create meaning. This text is designed to reinforce this relationship and to encourage reading by students who want to improve their writing. The selections are short and lively, not too difficult, but rich enough to provide ideas for thought and discussion. The instructional apparatus accompanying each reading has two main goals:

1. To encourage students to use writing as a means of exploring the readings.
2. To call attention to strategies used in the essays that students can employ in their own compositions.

The Simon & Schuster Short Prose Reader is a flexible resource. The numerous readings, activities, and writing topics give instructors the freedom to select from a broad range of assignments and approaches.

NEW TO THE SIXTH EDITION

Features new to this edition include the following:

- The updated appendix on **Writing with Sources** now includes the most recent changes in the MLA documentation style; it also provides instructions for using a research notebook and additional examples for integrating secondary-source material.
- New topics for debate: Sets of readings on "Can Money Buy Happiness?" and "How Real Is Reality TV?" enhance Chapter 10, Argument, with trendy subjects that will appeal to students of all ages.
- Numerous revised prompts and updated topics for **Writing Step by Step** and **Other Writing Ideas**, along with several innovative activities and new exercises for **Gaining Word Power** and improving **Editing Skills**.
- Additional help in understanding and writing **summaries** (Chapter 1 and throughout the book).
- Updated links to **Web sites** where students can find additional information about the readings and their authors.

- **Thirteen new readings**, including selections by Rita Dover, Cynthia Crossen, Sue Shellenbarger, and Nancy Masterson Sakamoto, along with **two new student essays**. Many favorites by Russell Baker, Brent Staples, Gloria Naylor, Judith Viorst, Isaac Asimov, Suzanne Britt, Elizabeth Berg, Mike Royko, Stephen King, and Jade Snow Wong have been held over from previous editions.

These additions strengthen the key features that have made the first five editions of *The Simon & Schuster Short Prose Reader* a popular and successful text.

THE READING SELECTIONS

The readings are brief, accessible, and easy to teach. They cover a wide range of topics and viewpoints to involve students with ideas and issues that relate to their own experience and also expand their understanding of people, places, and ideas. A special effort has been made to appeal to a cross section of students by including a number of essays by women and writers from diverse cultural backgrounds and a recurrent focus on the world of work. Many of the selections are standard pieces that have been used successfully in writing classes; others are new readings that have never been anthologized before.

ORGANIZATION

The readings are grouped according to their major pattern of organization and presented as strategies for approaching a given writing task. The introduction to each strategy explains the point, the principles, and the pitfalls of using this particular pattern. An Images and Ideas page begins each introduction with a relevant visual accompanied by questions that draw connections between the image and the chapter's rhetorical strategy. This opening material is followed by four published essays (ten in Chapter 10) and a student essay that illustrate the strategy.

WRITING STEP BY STEP

Writing Step by Step is a distinctive guided-writing feature in the *Simon & Schuster Short Prose Reader*. Realizing that many of today's students have scant exposure to expository essays, we decided to help them understand specifically how the form works. After each reading, we provide a sequence of specific directions that guide students in writing a short essay imitating the reading's structure and purpose. This directed writing can be used to provide inexperienced readers of nonfiction and novice writers with a successful composing experience.

One of the most popular innovations in this reader, **Writing Step by Step** helps compensate for the modern habit of acquiring information in fragments and bits rather than from written paragraphs. The exercise assists students in seeing how ideas are developed in coherent organizational schemes. It also supports writing instructors in their efforts, because the essays produced from following **Writing Step by Step** instructions belong uniquely to each student: They can't be downloaded from Internet sources.

OTHER INSTRUCTIONAL FEATURES

Two **introductory chapters** present a concise explanation of the interrelated processes of reading and writing. Chapter 1 gives specific directions for learning how to become active readers, including a sample reading that has been annotated by an active reader. Chapter 2 describes the process of writing in response to reading. It includes a sample student essay and a brief reading to respond to and write about.

The **prereading apparatus** includes three instructional aids: (1) a brief thinking/writing activity (Preparing to Read) that gets students ready to read by evoking thoughts and feelings on the subject of the reading; (2) a short biographical headnote that provides a context for reading; and (3) a list of Terms to Recognize that defines potentially unfamiliar words in the selection.

The **postreading apparatus** includes a selection of activities that instructors can assign, as needed, to help students increase their skills in reading and writing:

1. *Responding to Reading*—a journal-writing or possible in-class assignment that asks students to record their reactions to an issue or idea in the selection they have just read. This brief activity promotes fluency and may be used as the basis for the essay assignments that follow.
2. *Considering Content*—a series of questions that assist students in becoming focused, attentive readers. Answering these questions assures basic comprehension.
3. *Considering Method*—several questions that help students to identify successful strategies in the reading and to examine rhetorical choices that the author made.
4. *Writing Step by Step*—described in the previous section of this Preface, the Writing Step by Step assignment helps students perceive and imitate the rhetorical strategies used in the reading.

5. *Other Writing Ideas*—additional writing assignments that relate to the rhetorical mode or subject matter of the reading. These assignments, which include a mix of personal and academic topics, focus on Collaborative Writing, Using the Internet, and Writing about Reading. New to the sixth edition, several assignments give students practice in summarizing material.

6. *Gaining Word Power*—an exercise that examines words and phrases from the reading selection and promotes active vocabulary building.

7. *Editing Skills*—an exercise that assists students in checking and improving the essay they have just written. Each editing section focuses on a different skill, one that pertains to some grammatical, mechanical, or rhetorical feature of the reading selection.

8. *Web sites*—URLs to Web sites related to each reading. We describe the relevant content of each site, and frequently suggest how the student can use the site to develop material for the writing assignments. These citations encourage students to see Web sites as resources for writing rather than collections of unprocessed information.

This extensive apparatus gives teachers and students a wide variety of choices for exploring the reading-writing connection.

OTHER IMPORTANT FEATURES

- A comprehensive appendix on **Writing with Sources**, which includes a sample documented student essay and offers guidance for locating and evaluating secondary sources, using a research notebook, incorporating paraphrases and quotations, avoiding plagiarism, and documenting sources according to the latest MLA style.

- A table of **Thematic Contents** that groups the reading selections according to several common themes. With these suggested groupings, instructors can correlate reading assignments or organize their courses according to issue-centered units.

- A guide to **Editing Skills** and their locations within chapters. With these references, instructors can direct individual students to sections addressing their particular editing problems.

INSTRUCTIONAL SUPPLEMENT

Instructors using the sixth edition of *The Simon & Schuster Short Prose Reader* will receive pedagogical advice and support from an online **Instructor's Manual**, which includes responses to all the postreading questions in the text, answers to the vocabulary and editing skills exercises, teaching tips and background information on the readings, guidance for implementing the writing assignments, and suggestions for making connections among the readings in the book.

ACKNOWLEDGMENTS

We want to extend appreciation and thanks to the many people who have helped us in producing this book, especially our editors and the editorial staff at Pearson Education: Matthew Wright, Ginny Blanford, and Tanya Nguyen. We are indebted to the students in our writing classes for field-testing the assignments and for providing us with inspiration and insights as well as sample essays. We are also grateful for the excellent ideas and suggestions provided by our reviewers: Amy Hundley, Merced College; Peggy R Porter, Houston Community College-Northwest; Andrew S. Tomko, Bergen Community College; and Andrena Zawinski, Laney College. And of course we must thank Bill, Brian, Casey, and Danny for the many ways they make our work easier and our lives happy.

Robert Funk
Susan X Day
Linda S. Coleman
Elizabeth McMahan

CHAPTER 1

Active Reading

Most people who write well also read well—and vice versa. The two skills are so intertwined that they are often taught together, as we do in this textbook. Reading gives you not only information and amusement, but also a sense of how sentences work and how paragraphs are best organized. Most of the time, you get this sense without really paying attention: It just seeps into your mind with the rest of the material. In this textbook, we ask you to make the reading-writing connection more consciously than you may have done before. By looking carefully at good writing, you will better understand the content as well as the techniques the writers use. And by being aware of yourself as a reader, you will develop useful strategies for attracting and keeping the attention of your own readers.

LEARNING TO BE AN ACTIVE READER

Did you ever finish reading something, look up from the page, and realize that you didn't take in anything at all? That you passed your eyes over the print, but you might as well have stared out the window? At such times, you know that you have been an extremely passive reader. On the opposite end of the spectrum, you've probably had the experience of being swept away from reality while reading, so involved in the printed word that the rest of your world fades. Much of your college reading won't be able to carry you off that completely. By learning to be an **active reader,** though, you will be able to handle your reading assignments competently—remembering more and using what you have learned more effectively. The main idea is to stay involved with the reading through interaction—bringing mental and emotional energy to the task.

KEEPING A JOURNAL

One good way to become an interactive reader is to keep a journal about your reading. In a journal, you can experiment with ideas and express your responses with greater freedom than you can in formal writing assignments. Before each reading selection in most chapters of this book, we ask you a Preparing to Read question, which you may answer in your journal as well as in class discussions. This activity starts you thinking about the ideas you will find in the essay that follows. After each selection, we give you a Responding to Reading suggestion to consider in your journal, encouraging you to write about your personal reactions. You will see as this chapter goes along how your two journal entries fit into your role as an active reader.

PREVIEWING THE READING

If you're the type who simply plunges into a reading assignment, you're missing something. Study skills experts emphasize the value of previewing the reading, getting your mind ready for full comprehension. **Previewing** involves more than merely counting the number of pages you have to go: No one needs to remind you to do that! The trick is to develop a mental set that makes your brain most receptive to the material.

Title

Try stopping after you read the **title** and asking yourself what it suggests to you. The sample essay we use in this chapter is named "Handled with Care." Where have you heard such a phrase before? What image does it bring to your mind? The title often gives you a clue about what's ahead.

Author and Other Publication Facts

With some assignments, you will recognize the author's name. Bob Greene is the writer of "Handled with Care," and you may know that he was a long-time columnist for the *Chicago Tribune*. You may also know that his columns often comment on culture and politics and the connections between them. Again, the author's name provides clues about the essay that follows. You may know something about the time period when it was written (as you would if the byline reads "Mark Twain"). Similarly, if the byline reads "Dave Barry," you can expect something humorous about modern life.

Even when you don't recognize the author, you can take note of other publication facts. The date of publication, if you have it, gives you an idea of how current the information is. If the reading is reprinted, as the ones in this textbook are, consider where it originally appeared and whether that means anything to you. If an essay first showed up in *U.S. News and World Report*, you can assume it will have a conservative political slant; if it came from *The Nation*, it will probably have a liberal viewpoint. If it came from a city newspaper, like the *Chicago Tribune*, you can't be so sure about the political perspective, since most big newspapers attempt to cover the spectrum.

Visual Features and Supplements

Page through the reading, notice its design, and look at parts that stand out from the ordinary print, such as headnotes, headings, photos, diagrams, boxed material, summaries, and questions after the reading. Your textbooks, like most of the successful Web pages you visit, are specially designed to include lots of these helpful materials. Unfortunately, many students skip them, thinking they're not as important as the rest. Actually, they are there to focus attention on what *is* important in the reading. Or they may give you information that assists you in understanding the reading; for example, the headnote paragraphs before essays in this textbook give a little biographical information about the writer. The Terms to Recognize section lists some difficult words from the essay and their definitions, so you won't have to look them up in the dictionary right away. In this list, we provide only the definition that fits the way the term is used in the reading; the term probably has other meanings as well.

Some reading material doesn't include any obvious help. It's just straight print. But you can benefit from the only visual clue: paragraph indentations. Read the first sentence of each paragraph. This survey will probably give you ideas about the content and organization of the reading.

Responses and Predictions

"This preview stuff just slows me down," you may be thinking. "I don't have time for it." Let us assure you, the first stage does seem slow, but it makes later stages faster and more efficient. It also markedly increases your memory for what you read.

The main thing you're doing as you preview is responding to clues and making predictions about what the reading contains. It may seem like a guessing game, but actually you are clearing the brush from pathways in your brain, making the way easy for the information to get through. By guessing what to expect, you are directing your attention, focusing on the material so that it won't be fighting through a tangle of thoughts about why you squabble with your roommate and what you'll have for lunch.

Instead, let your mind wander through the associations and experiences you already have with the material suggested by your preview. What people, events, and feelings in your own life did you stumble across in your preview? If you are from Chicago, you are able to visualize the setting of the essay and may even be able to predict Bob Greene's overall style. Or the title, "Handled with Care," may have reminded you of a delicate package that happened to reach you intact, miraculously, through the mail.

A FIRST READING

Now is the time to plunge in. Try to place yourself in a setting that aids concentration. This setting varies from person to person, and you probably know your ideal situation. You can't always get it, but at least don't undermine yourself by choosing a spot where you know you'll be distracted or where you know you'll be lulled to sleep. Sitting up at a table or desk is a good idea because the position suggests that you are going to work.

You'll need a pencil, pen, or pad of sticky notes to read interactively. Make it a habit. Mark words and terms that you need to look up later. Write questions—or just question marks—in the margins near material you don't quite understand. Write your spontaneous responses (*Yes! No! Reminds me of Aunt Selma! What!? Prejudiced crap!*) in the margins. Underline sentences that you think may contain the main ideas and phrases that impress you with the way they are worded. We provide one reader's markings of "Handled with Care" in this chapter.

STAYING AWARE OF CONVENTIONS

Conventions are the traditional ways of doing things: For example, we have conventional ways of beginning and ending telephone conversations, and we expect everyone to follow them. If a friend closed a phone conversation by saying, "Pick me up at 9:15," and immediately hung up, you would think it strange not to have any of the usual sign-off words. The same type of expectation goes for writing **conventions,** some of which we outline here. Stories and poems don't have to follow these conventions, but nonfiction works like essays, textbooks, and manuals do. You can enhance your reading by looking for conventional features as you go along. They provide clues to the author's purpose and help to break down complicated readings into manageable chunks.

Subject

Each piece of writing is expected to deal with one subject or topic. This should be fairly clear to you near the beginning, perhaps even from the title ("Why We Crave Horror Movies," in Chapter 9, is about exactly that). Once you identify the subject, you can be pretty sure the whole reading will stay on that topic.

Main Idea or Thesis

We expect a reading not only to have a subject but also to say something *about* the subject. That is the **thesis** or main idea. Frequently, the main idea comes up early in the reading, clearly expressed in one sentence. At other times, you must put together the main point piece by piece as you read. It may finally be stated in a sentence at the end, or it may not be stated directly at all. As you read, underline sentences that seem to add to your understanding of the author's main point.

Supporting Material

Writers must prove their main points by providing convincing **supporting material.** This can be in the form of logical reasoning, emotional appeal, examples, evidence from experts, specific details, facts, and statistics. Different main points and different readers lend themselves to different types of supporting material: for example, your math textbook uses mostly logical reasoning and examples, while an essay about capital punishment might use all the forms we listed. While you read an assignment, ask yourself: *What forms of supporting material does this author use and are they appropriate for the intended audience?*

Patterns of Organization

The conventions of subject, thesis, and supporting material deal with the content of the reading. You also need to look at *how* the content is presented. After each selection in the following chapters, you will see questions called Considering Content and Considering Method. The method questions ask you to consider the techniques the author used to present material, including organization.

We organize the chapters in this book according to **patterns of development** that are the most conventional ways to organize writing: patterns such as comparison and contrast, cause and effect, and narration. Each chapter explains one basic pattern, although in practice, most authors combine several strategies to support and develop their central pattern. As you read an essay, notice how the writer uses patterns to arrange ideas.

Paragraphs

As a reader, you will also notice how writers package their meaning in units of thought called **paragraphs.** Paragraph indention usually signals the introduction of a new topic or a new aspect of a current topic. In other words, writers start new paragraphs to show that they are moving on to another topic or subtopic. Paragraphs in prose essays tend to be longer than paragraphs in newspapers and magazines, where journalists break their paragraphs frequently to make narrow columns of type easier to read.

Transitions

Another element of a writer's method involves how he or she makes connections between ideas. These connections are called **transitions.** A common place for a transition is between two paragraphs (at the end of one and/or at the beginning of the next one), where the author shows the logical relationship between them. Recognizing transitions helps you direct your thought process in the way the author wants you to. For example, a paragraph that begins "Furthermore, ..." lets you know that you should expect material that adds to and agrees with the material before it. A paragraph that begins "On the other hand, ..." lets you know that you should expect material that contradicts or shows the opposite of the material before it. By noticing transitions, you prepare the appropriate mindset for understanding what comes next.

A SAMPLE ESSAY

Handled with Care

••

BOB GREENE

The day the lady took her clothes off on Michigan Avenue, people   1
were leaving downtown as usual. The workday had come to an end; men
and women were heading for bus and train stations, in a hurry to get home.

She walked south on Michigan; she was wearing a white robe, as if   2
she had been to the beach. She was blond and in her thirties. As she passed
the Radisson Hotel, Roosevelt Williams, a doorman, was opening the door
of a cab for one of the hotel's guests. The woman did not really pause while
she walked; she merely shrugged the robe off, and it fell to the sidewalk. She
was wearing what appeared to be the bottom of a blue bikini bathing suit,
although one woman who was directly next to her said it was just underwear. She wore nothing else.

Williams at first did not believe what he was seeing. If you hang   3
around long enough, you will see everything: robberies, muggings, street
fights, murders. But a naked woman on North Michigan Avenue? Williams
had not seen that before and neither, apparently, had the other people on
the street.

It was strange; her white robe lay on the sidewalk, and by all   4
accounts she was smiling. But no one spoke to her. A report in the newspaper the next day quoted someone: "The cars were stopping, the people on
the buses were staring, people were shouting, and people were taking pictures." But that is not what other people who were there that afternoon
said. The atmosphere was not carnival-like, they said. Rather, they said, it
was as if something very sad was taking place. It took only a moment for
people to realize that this was not some stunt designed to promote a product or a movie. Without anything telling them, they understood that the
woman was troubled, and that what she was doing had nothing to do with
sexual titillation; it was more of a cry for help.

The cry for help came in a way that such cries often come. The   5
woman was violating one of the basic premises of the social fabric. She was
doing something that is not done. She was not shooting anyone, or breaking a window, or shouting in anger. Rather, in a way that everyone understood, she was signaling that things were not right.

The line is so thin between matters being manageable and being out   6
of hand. One day a person may be barely all right; the next the same person
may have crossed over. Here is something from the author John Barth:

> She paused amid the kitchen to drink a glass of water; at that instant,   7
> losing a grip of fifty years, the next-room-ceiling plaster crashed. Or he
> merely sat in an empty study, in March-day glare, listening to the uni-
> verse rustle in his head, when suddenly a five-foot shelf let go. For ages
> the fault creeps secret through the rock; in a second, ledge and railings,
> tourists and turbines all thunder over Niagara. Which snowflake triggers
> the avalanche? A house explodes; a star. In your spouse, so apparently
> resigned, murder twitches like a fetus. At some trifling new assessment,
> all the colonies rebel.

The woman continued to walk past Tribune Tower. People who saw   8
her said that the look on her face was almost peaceful. She did not seem to
think she was doing anything unusual; she was described as appearing
"blissful." Whatever the reaction on the street was, she seemed calm, as if
she believed herself to be in control.

She walked over the Michigan Avenue bridge. Again, people who were   9
there report that no one harassed her; no one jeered at her or attempted to
touch her. At some point on the bridge, she removed her bikini bottom.
Now she was completely undressed, and still she walked. "It was as if people knew not to bother her," said one woman who was there. "To tell it,
it sounds like something very lewd and sensational was going on. But it
wasn't like that at all. It was as if people knew that something very . . .
fragile . . . was taking place. I was impressed with the maturity with which
people were handling it. No one spoke to her, but you could tell that they
wished someone would help her."

Back in front of the Radisson, a police officer had picked up the   10
woman's robe. He was on his portable radio, advising his colleagues that
the woman was walking over the bridge. When the police caught up with
the woman, she was just standing there, naked in downtown Chicago, still
smiling. The first thing the police did was hand her some covering and ask
her to put it on; the show was over.

People who were there said that there was no reaction from the peo-   11
ple who were watching. They said that the juvenile behavior you might
expect in such a situation just didn't happen. After all, when a man walks
out on a ledge in a suicide attempt, there are always people down below
who call for him to jump. But this day, by all accounts, nothing like that
took place. No one called for her to stay undressed; no one cursed the
police officers for stopping her. "It was as if everyone was relieved," said a

woman who saw it. "They were embarrassed by it; it made them feel bad. They were glad that someone had stopped her. And she was still smiling. She seemed to be off somewhere."

The police charged her with no crime; they took her to Read Mental   **12**
Health Center, where she was reported to have signed herself in voluntarily. Within minutes things were back to as they always are on Michigan Avenue; there was no reminder of the naked lady who had reminded people how fragile is the everyday world in which we live.

MARKING THE TEXT

Here is an example of how a student reader marked the Bob Greene essay.

Handled with Care

Like a package with breakables in it

● ●

BOB GREENE

—Emotion— shock value!

The day the lady took her clothes off on Michi-   **1**
gan Avenue, people were leaving downtown as usual. The workday had come to an end; men and women were heading for bus and train stations, in a hurry to get home.

Time of day important?

She walked south on Michigan; she was wearing   **2**
a white robe, as if she had been to the beach. She was blond and in her thirties. As she passed the Radisson Hotel, Roosevelt Williams, a doorman, was opening the door of a cab for one of the hotel's guests. The woman did not really pause while she

Why?

walked; she merely shrugged the robe off, and it fell to the sidewalk. She was wearing what appeared to be the bottom of a blue bikini bathing suit, although one woman who was directly next to her said it was just underwear. She wore nothing else.

What difference would that make?

Williams at first did not believe what he was see-   **3**

Contrast with other outrageous events

ing. If you hang around long enough, you will see everything: robberies, muggings, street fights, murders. But a naked woman on North Michigan Avenue? Williams had not seen that before and

neither, apparently, had the other people on the
street.

*Papers were
wrong—misre-
ported the event!*

*Transition:
expand on
"cry for help"*

Who is?

*Supporting materi-
al from expert—
more examples*

It was strange; her white robe lay on the sidewalk, and by all accounts she was smiling. But no
one spoke to her. A report in the newspaper the
next day quoted someone: "The cars were stopping, the people on the buses were staring, people
were shouting, and people were taking pictures."
But that is not what other people who were there
that afternoon said. The atmosphere was not
carnival-like, they said. Rather, they said, it was as
if something very sad was taking place. It took only
a moment for people to realize that this was not
some stunt designed to promote a product or a
movie. Without anything telling them, they understood that the woman was troubled, and that what
she was doing had nothing to do with sexual titillation; it was more of a cry for help.

The cry for help came in a way that such cries
often come. The woman was violating one of the
basic premises of the social fabric. She was doing
something that is not done. She was not shooting
anyone, or breaking a window, or shouting in
anger. Rather, in a way that everyone understood,
she was signaling that things were not right.

The line is so thin between matters being manageable and being out of hand. One day a person
may be barely all right; the next the same person
may have crossed over. Here is something from the
author John Barth:

She paused amid the kitchen to drink a glass
of water; at that instant, losing a grip of fifty
years, the next-room-ceiling plaster crashed. Or
he merely sat in an empty study, in March-day
glare, listening to the universe rustle in his head,
when suddenly a five-foot shelf let go. For ages
the fault creeps secret through the rock; in a second, ledge and railings, tourists and turbines all
thunder over Niagara. Which snowflake triggers
the avalanche? A house explodes; a star. In your

*Subject—an
unusual event* 4

Main point?

*People had
sympathy*

5

*more overt
"violations"?*

Thesis? 6

7

?

?

spouse, so apparently resigned, murder twitches like a fetus. At some trifling new (assessment,) all the colonies rebel.

The woman continued to walk past Tribune Tower. People who saw her said that the look on her face was almost peaceful. She did not seem to think she was doing anything unusual; she was described as appearing "blissful." Whatever the reaction on the street was, she seemed calm, as if she believed herself to be in control.

Because she was acting out her cry for help?

She walked over the Michigan Avenue bridge. Again, people who were there report that no one harassed her; no one jeered at her or attempted to touch her. At some point on the bridge, she removed her bikini bottom. Now she was completely undressed, and still she walked. "It was as if people knew not to bother her," said one woman who was there. "To tell it, it sounds like something very (lewd) and sensational was going on. But it wasn't like that at all. It was as if people knew that something very . . . fragile . . . was taking place. I was impressed with the maturity with which people were handling it. No one spoke to her, but you could tell that they wished someone would help her."

| Def. of maturity

| A quiet response/

Back in front of the Radisson, a police officer had picked up the woman's robe. He was on his portable radio, advising his colleagues that the woman was walking over the bridge. When the police caught up with the woman, she was just standing there, naked in downtown Chicago, still smiling. The first thing the police did was hand her some covering and ask her to put it on; the show was over.

People who were there said that there was no reaction from the people who were watching. They said that the juvenile behavior you might expect in such a situation just didn't happen. After all, when a man walks out on a ledge in a suicide attempt, there are always people down below who call for him to jump. But this day, by all accounts, nothing

| Contrast with what was expected

8

9

10

11

People identified with her? Feared for her? for themselves?

like that took place. No one called for her to stay undressed; no one cursed the police officers for stopping her. "It was as if everyone was relieved," said a woman who saw it. "They were embarrassed by it; it made them feel bad. They were glad that someone had stopped her. And she was still smiling. She seemed to be off somewhere."

The police charged her with no crime; they took her to Read Mental Health Center, where she was reported to have signed herself in voluntarily. Within minutes things were back to as they always are on Michigan Avenue; there was no reminder of the naked lady who had reminded people how fragile is the everyday world in which we live.

12

Because? Surprising? Main point? See ¶ 6.

CLARIFYING MEANING

Put yourself in the student reader's place to see what happens next after reading and marking the text.

Using the Dictionary

First, use a dictionary to look up terms and words you marked as unfamiliar on the first reading. In this textbook, some will be defined just before the selection. Be sure to look up even words you *think* you know but are a bit fuzzy on. What exactly does *assessment* mean in paragraph 7? Although we often use the word to mean *evaluation*, in this case it means *taxation*, which makes more sense in the context.

You may use specialized dictionaries to look up unfamiliar references in the selection. For example, Greene writes that John Barth is an author. If you looked in a biographical or literary dictionary, you would find that Barth is a contemporary author who sees the world as absurd, as making no real sense. This detail helps you understand the quotation. Many writers make references to names from mythology, philosophy, and literature that you will need to look up. The reference librarian will show you where the specialized dictionaries are kept.

Reading Aloud

Return to the spots where you drew a question mark, and read those passages slowly aloud. Hearing your voice find the proper way to read a sentence may shed the necessary light on its meaning.

Discussing

Having a conversation about your reading will usually help you understand it. Another person who has read the same selection will probably have different reactions and may be able to clarify points that stumped you. Even someone who has not read the selection may be a good sounding board to discuss the ideas with.

Rereading

At some point, you will need to go back and reread the whole assignment, especially if you are going to be tested on it or intend to write a formal essay about it. With difficult material, the second read-through will be more comfortable and will allow you to notice things you missed the first time.

MAKING INFERENCES AND ASSOCIATIONS

Bob Greene's essay is a good example of one that isn't completely spelled out for you. You have to make judgments about what he writes, inferences or conclusions about the meaning.

Reading Between the Lines

You can train yourself to infer knowledge that lies below the surface meaning of the words. To *infer* means to arrive at an idea or a conclusion through reasoning. When you infer, you balance what the writer says with your own ideas and hunches about what is left unsaid. This process may sound difficult, but making **inferences** is a skill that can be learned.

Developing Inference Skills

Here are some suggestions for improving your ability to read between the lines:

Read Beyond the Words.   Fill in details and information to complete the writer's suggestions. Use the writer's hints to discover the meanings that often lie beneath the surface. But don't go too far: You should be able to point to words and phrases that support what you have inferred.

Question Yourself as You Read and After You Finish.   You might use questions like these: Why did the author include these details? What does this example mean? How am I supposed to react to this sentence?

Draw Conclusions and Speculate on Outcomes.   In reflecting on Bob Greene's essay, for example, you might ask yourself these questions: Is the article saying that people are more sensitive than we usually assume—or less sensitive? Is the message of the selection positive or negative? Would people have reacted differently if the woman had not been young, blonde, and attractive? What truths about our society does this incident suggest?

Make Associations Between the Reading and Your Own Experience. For instance: Have you ever witnessed a "cry for help"? Was it like the one Greene describes or different? How did you and other people respond?

Your own observations and reflections add richness to the selection's meaning. Our Responding to Reading exercises will assist you in developing your personal reaction.

Responding to Tone

To get a complete understanding of an author's meaning, you need to pay attention to the **tone** of the writing. Tone means the attitude a writer conveys toward the topic and sometimes toward the readers. The language, sentence structure, and selection of details will tell you if the writer is serious or humorous, critical or sympathetic, friendly or hostile, passionate or indifferent, sarcastic or sincere— or any of numerous other attitudes. Most writing will appeal to your emotions in one way or another, and the author's feelings are likely to affect you the most.

WRITING TO UNDERSTAND AND RESPOND

If you write out your Responding to Reading assignment, you have already begun the interactive process that will set the selection firmly in your memory. Study skills experts point out that we have four modes of verbal communication: We listen, we read, we speak, and we write. Different people learn best through different modes, but college learning often emphasizes only the first two: listening to course lectures and reading textbooks. When you add the other two modes to your study habits, you more than double your learning potential. Speaking in class and discussing the material with friends and classmates are important. Writing about what you have heard and read is equally important.

Writing a Summary

A real sign that you have understood something is that you can translate it into your own language. Summarizing a reading is an effective way to sort out the basic information and fix those points in your mind. A summary will also give you a concise overview that you can study and use at a later date.

A summary is a shortened version of a piece of writing. Your objective is to accurately communicate the essential message of the reading in fewer words. Before starting a summary, review the selection, paying particular attention to the marks and notes you made when you did your active reading. Then jot down the most important points, using your own words. If you have trouble expressing some of these ideas, go back and reread those sections again. Use this list of main points to prepare a draft of your summary, keeping these suggestions in mind:

1. Cite the title and author of the work as you begin.
2. Stick to the main ideas; include important supporting details but leave out those that merely expand the major points.
3. Express the main ideas and key supporting details in your own words.
4. Keep them in the same order as in the original.
5. Quote from the original material only to clarify an important or difficult idea.
6. Don't introduce your own views or make comments about the material.

Compare your draft summary one last time with the original and write up the final version.

Here is a sample summary of the article "Handled with Care":

In "Handled with Care," newspaper columnist Bob Greene writes about an incident when a woman removed her clothes while walking down Michigan Avenue in Chicago. People see all kinds of violent and outrageous behavior on the streets in Chicago, but this was something different. Although a newspaper report later claimed that by-standers stared, shouted, and took pictures, other witnesses said the crowd's reaction was mature and controlled. They quickly realized the woman was not part of some publicity stunt; they seemed to understand that she was violating social convention because she needed help. According to Greene this episode reflects the thin line "between matters being manageable and being out of hand." The smallest thing can sometimes cause a person to break down. Greene thinks the onlookers understood this distinction and respected the woman's condition, instead of looking at her as a freak. She seemed peaceful, so no one bothered or harassed her, although they wanted someone to help her. Eventually the police came. They also treated her gently and took her to a mental health facility instead of arresting her. After the woman was taken away, Michigan Avenue quickly went back to normal. The woman had reminded people of how unsteady everyday life can be.

Other Ways to Respond in Writing

You could also use your journal to write a letter to the author of the selection. What would you say to the author if you could? Do you have any questions you'd like to ask about the reading? Perhaps you could explain any personal significance the selection had for you.

One way to combine summary with personal response is to write an email or text message to a good friend about the article or story you've just read. Assume that your friend hasn't read the same piece, so you need to fill her in briefly about the main points before you give her your personal point of view on the subject or your emotional response to the article or essay. You might consider relating the reading to some shared experience or conversation you and your friend have had. Go ahead and send your email or text—your friend will probably enjoy it.

WEB SITE

www.csbsju.edu/academicadvising/help/list.htm
Visit this site to gather additional strategies for effective reading and studying.

CHAPTER 2

The Reading-Writing Connection

The connections between reading and writing are strong: In both activities you use language to create meaning. In Chapter 1, you learned how writing can help you to understand and remember what you read; in this chapter, you will learn how reading and responding to essays can help you to improve your writing.

WRITING IN RESPONSE TO READING

The basic principle of this book is that reading and writing go together. Each chapter follows a four-part pattern that you will discover works well in many of your college classes: (1) read a selection, (2) examine the content, (3) analyze the techniques, and (4) write something of your own that relates to the reading.

When you read, you get ideas for your own writing. Reading can supply you with topics to write about and show you how to write about them. Even when you already have a topic, reading can help you to come up with material to develop that topic. Reading will also provide you with models to follow. By studying the strategies and techniques that professional writers use, you can learn methods and procedures for writing effectively on many different subjects and in many different writing situations.

BUILDING AN ESSAY

Writing an essay is a lot like building a house. A writer fits separate pieces of meaning together to make an understandable statement. If you want to write well, you need to learn the basic skills of constructing an essay.

Despite differences in education and personality, most writers follow a remarkably similar process of *prewriting*, *planning*, *writing*, *revising*, and *editing*. Whether building a single paragraph or a ten-page article, successful writers usually work through several stages, which go roughly like this:

1. Find a subject; gather information. (Prewriting)
2. Focus on a main idea; map out an approach. (Planning)

3. Prepare a rough draft. (Writing)
4. Rework and improve the draft. (Revising)
5. Correct errors. (Editing)

If you follow these operations, you will learn to write more productively and more easily. But keep in mind that this sequence is only a general guide. The steps often overlap and loop around. The important point to remember is that writing is done in stages; successful writers take the time to build their essays step by step and to polish and finish their work the way a good carpenter sands rough surfaces.

Finding Ideas

One of the most difficult challenges of writing is coming up with a topic. Even when you are responding to a reading, you still have to decide what to say about it. In this textbook and in most classes, you will be given some direction toward a topic; the job from there on is up to you. Rather than wait for inspiration to strike, you can go after the ideas you need by doing some **prewriting.** Here are three methods that experienced writers use to generate material for writing.

1. **Freewriting.**   Write without stopping for five or ten minutes. Don't pause to consider whether your ideas are any good; just get down as many thoughts as you can within the time limit. If you're freewriting on a computer, turn down the contrast to write without seeing the screen, or turn the monitor off. After the time is up, read through your freewriting and highlight anything that strikes you as interesting or important. Then do some more freewriting on one or two of these points. Here is an example of freewriting done by student Tara Coburn in response to "Handled with Care," the article by Bob Greene that you read in Chapter 1:

> Basic themes of Greene's essay. People watched a break in normalcy with maturity, saw the fragility of life, a lesson with tones of sadness, embarrassment, sympathy, but then forgot it. Compared with the lesson of the fragility of life when the situation is personal. The reaction of the people on Michigan Avenue was formed by their detachment from the woman. If they'd known her, someone would have spoken to her, helped her, the world would not have gone back to normal, the incident would not have been forgotten. Their lesson was fleeting but when there is a tear in the social normalcy of your daily life and someone you love shows you the fragility of life, it is more real.

At this point, Tara stopped and looked at what she had written. She liked the idea that surfaced in the last sentence and decided that she had a topic she could develop into an essay. She put the freewriting aside for a while—to let the ideas work around in her mind before she moved on to the next stage in the process.

2. **Brainstorming.** As an alternative to freewriting, you can ask yourself a question and list as many answers as you can. For example: *What have I done that's unexpected or out of the ordinary?* or *When is it all right to get involved with someone in trouble?* Challenge yourself to make the list as long as you can. If necessary, ask yourself a new question: *When is it a bad idea to help someone in trouble?* In making this list you have already started writing. Think of it as a bank of raw material on which you can draw.

In order to develop ideas for her topic, Tara Coburn posed this question to herself: *When did the fabric of my life begin to tear?* And then she brainstormed a list of responses to that question:

part of my world, my fabric, was belief in my dad

thought he could do anything

helped us build a snowman

finished the ice cream

fix anything

even our cat brought him things

build anything—bed, chairs, room

not a book smart guy

tear happened gradually

getting older, tired, looking older

can't fix everything—computer

as strong as everything seemed, it was fragile

not a cry for help, more a sign that he can't help anymore

like the people on Mich. Ave., it's a sign it's my turn to come forward

3. **Questioning.** Write a broad topic—such as *Helping People in Trouble*—at the top of a sheet of paper. Then write the headings *Who? What? When? Where? Why? How?* down the page. Fill in any thoughts about the topic that occur to you under these headings. If you can't think of anything for one heading, go to the next, but try to write something under each heading.

The goal is to think creatively about the topic as you try to come up with material to use in writing.

Devising a Working Thesis

At this stage, you need to collect the ideas that you came up with in prewriting and organize them. One way to focus your material is to ask yourself, *What point do I want to make?* The answer to that question will lead you to your main idea, or working **thesis.** Once you decide what point you want to make, then you can go through your prewriting material and decide which details to use and which ones to toss.

As you learned in Chapter 1, a thesis says something *about* the subject of a reading. As a reader, your job is to discover the writer's thesis; as a writer, your job is to provide a clear thesis for your readers. Look at the difference between a **subject** and a thesis in these examples:

Subject: Helping strangers
Thesis: I think we are responsible for helping people in trouble.

Subject: Doing something socially unacceptable
Thesis: As soon as I got to college, I set out to prove that I was an adult and beyond the control of my parents.

Here is an example of the thesis statement that Tara Coburn devised from her freewriting and her brainstorming list:

> When I saw that my dad's strength was limited, I began to realize that life was fragile and fleeting and that I would have to learn to be strong and do things for him and for myself.

You may change or refine your thesis as the paper develops, but having an idea of what you want to say makes the actual writing considerably easier.

Making a Plan

Having a plan to follow makes you less likely to wander from your main point. An outline of your major points will provide you with a framework for your first draft; it can help you shape and arrange your thoughts and keep you from making organizational missteps. There is no need for complete sentences or balanced headings in your outline. Just make a list of your main points in the order that you plan to cover them. The following brief plan is based on the thesis you just read:

SOMEONE TO HELP

1. Opening
   - Yarn ankle bracelet—first clue that life is fragile
   - My social fabric—my belief in my dad
2. Always thought Dad could do anything
   - Helped us with the giant snow bunny
   - Lifted its head—not as easy as it looked then
3. Dad always did the hard work
   - Cranked the ice cream
   - Even the cat came to him
   - Built furniture, almost everything around me
4. Realized he was getting older
   - Hair and beard turned white
   - Couldn't fix the computer—but I could
   - I became the fixer—my chance to grow stronger
5. Closing
   - People on Michigan Ave—strangers didn't know what to do
   - I love my dad—I can step forward to help him
   - Helping makes me grow and become stronger

Composing a Draft

If you have an outline or plan to work from, you shouldn't have any trouble producing the first draft of your paper. Don't fret about trying to write a brilliant **introduction.** Skip it if you can't come up with anything inspired, and start right in on the first main point. You can always come back and add an introduction when you revise.

Some people write the first draft from start to finish without bothering to search for the best word or the right phrase. If that's your method, fine. But many successful writers stop to reread what they have written, especially when they get stuck; rereading helps them to regain momentum and bring back fluency. The main goal is to get your ideas down on paper in a reasonably complete draft. Then you are ready for the important next step: revising.

Improving the Draft

Set your first draft aside, at least overnight, so you can look at it in a new light. This process of looking at your draft *again* is called **revising,** and it literally means "re-seeing." In fact, you want to try to see your work now with different eyes—the eyes of a reader.

When revising your draft, concentrate on making major improvements in content and organization. Such improvements might include enlarging or narrowing the thesis, adding more examples or cutting irrelevant ones, and reorganizing points to improve logic or gain emphasis. Tackling the simple problems first may seem reasonable, but you will find that dealing with a major difficulty may eliminate some minor problems at the same time—or change the way you approach them. If you try to do the fine-tuning and polishing first, you may burn up valuable time and energy and never get around to the main problems.

Targeting the Readers

Most of the writing you do has an **audience**—the person or group of people who will read what you've written. Keeping these readers in mind will help you decide not only what to say but also how best to say it.

You already have considerable reader awareness: You would not write a letter applying for a job in the same way you write a thank-you note to dear Aunt Marie. But writing a class assignment presents a special problem in audience. You know you're writing for your instructor and perhaps other members of the class, but you also know that they are going to read your paper no matter what. In order to develop your writing abilities, you need to get beyond the captive, limited audience of an instructor and your classmates and learn how to write for readers who have different expectations and interests.

Although they often have specific, well-defined audiences, many successful writers still find it useful to imagine an audience that is reasonably informed and generally attentive, readers who will keep reading as long as the writing is interesting and worthwhile. For example, when we write the chapters of this book we think about the students who have been in our classes over the years. If you can picture such an audience, you'll have an easier time deciding what to revise and how to improve your paper. Having other people read your drafts and give you their reactions will also teach you a lot about the importance of audience.

Getting Feedback

Writers routinely seek the help of potential readers to find out what is working and what is not working in their drafts. Someone else can often see places where you *thought* you were being clear but were actually filling in details in your head, not on the page.

The ideal people to help you evaluate your first draft are the members of your own writing class. They will be familiar with the assignment and will understand why you are writing the paper and for whom. In many writing classes, students work together on their papers. Meeting in small groups, they read photocopies of each other's drafts and respond to them; sometimes they post their drafts on a class Web site or submit them electronically on a computer bulletin board. If your instructor doesn't set up a peer review system, try to get several readers' reactions to your drafts. You can meet together outside of class or use an Internet mailing list. Here are some questions to use in asking for feedback:

Have I made my thesis clear to the reader?

Does the *introduction* get the reader's attention?

Are there any points that the reader might not understand?

Do I need to give the reader more reasons and examples?

Have I shown the reader how every point relates to the thesis?

Does the *conclusion* tie everything together for the reader?

Polishing the Final Draft

When you are satisfied with the changes you've made to improve content and organization, you can move on to matters of spelling, word choice, punctuation, capitalization, and mechanics. This is the **editing** stage, and you cannot skip it. Readers become quickly annoyed by writing that is full of errors.

Here are some additional tips that will help you polish and correct your final draft:

1. Let your work sit for a day to clear your head and increase your chances of spotting errors.

2. Read your draft out loud, listening for anything that sounds unclear or incomplete or awkward.

3. Don't try to do everything at once; save time to take a break when you need one.

4. Slow down when you edit: Look at each word and punctuation mark individually and watch for mistakes that you know you usually make.

5. Ask a reliable reader to check over your draft one more time before you turn it in.

SAMPLE STUDENT ESSAY

The essay that follows was written by Tara Coburn, a first-year student at Eastern Illinois University. She was responding to some of the ideas expressed in "Handled with Care" by Bob Greene. The comments in the margin call your attention to important features of organization and development.

Someone to Help

When I was eight, I had a favorite red yarn
ankle bracelet that I wore for an entire year. I
tugged on it one day to show that it was strong
enough to last another year, and it broke. It was a
clue that the things we count on in life are fragile.
In his essay "Handled with Care," Bob Greene
describes how the sudden appearance of a naked
woman on busy Michigan Avenue taught the people walking in the street a similar lesson—that "the
line is so thin between matters being manageable
and being out of hand." Part of my world—my
"social fabric"—was based on my childhood belief
that my father could do anything. When I began
to see that my dad's strength was limited, his
weakness reminded me that life is fragile and
fleeting and that I would have to learn to be
strong on my own.

As a child, no matter how big the problem, I
always thought, "Dad can do it." One winter, the
other neighborhood children and I had a grand
plan to build a giant snow bunny. We somehow
managed to lift the bottom and middle balls into
place, but the head was far too heavy for us to
boost up six feet onto a half-finished snow bunny.
My very first thought was to ask my dad, and he
tramped out into the snow to check the situation.
At the time, he seemed to lob the snow bunny's
head effortlessly into place, but thinking back I realize how heavy that big ball of snow must have been.

Dad was always the one we called on to do the
hard work. When the homemade ice cream was getting to the final stages of freezing, we called Dad to
kneel down and crank the final turns that no one
else could manage. His reputation as a Mr. Fix-it was
renowned, even to our cat, Mousie. When she had
played too roughly with the mouse or snake from
the backyard, she'd drop the dead animal at his feet
with a look that said, "Daddy, I broke my toy. Will
you make it play again?" My dad built much of the

Introductory paragraph: opens with a specific example, relating main idea to the reading and moving into the thesis.

Thesis: last sentence of first paragraph.

First body paragraph begins with topic sentence and develops it with an extended example.

Second body paragraph begins with topic sentence and develops it with several examples.

1

2

3

world I lived in, from the chairs in the living room to the bed I slept in. Being surrounded by things he built is probably the reason my ideas about him were so important to me.

The tears in my social fabric appeared gradually as I realized that my dad was getting older. When I came home from college for the first time, I noticed that his beard had started to turn from red to white; he was becoming an old man. Not only was his appearance changing, but the arrival of our household's first computer also revealed that my dad cannot fix everything. Now when he says to me, "The computer's little doodad is spinning and I can't make it stop!" his frustration is obvious. But his inability has given me the chance, for once, to be the fixer. I always relied on him, but as he gets older and I learn more, I can let him rely on me. The fragility I now see in my dad has given me the chance to be stronger.

The people on Michigan Avenue did not step forward to help the naked woman. One passerby remarked, "No one spoke to her, but you could tell that they wished someone would help her." The crowd felt sorry for the woman, but they were strangers and didn't know how to respond. My dad's turn from strong to fragile was not a cry for help; it was just a sign that he cannot always help me as he once did. But because I know and love my father, I can step forward to help him. And by helping him I have grown strong and have learned to help myself.

*Side notes:*

Paragraph ends by summing up the significance of the examples.

Third body paragraph begins with topic sentence and develops it with two specific examples. **4**

End of paragraph sums up the point and connects it to the main thesis.

Conclusion returns to Greene's essay to make a point through contrast. **5**

Closing sentences reinforce the thesis.

RESOURCES FOR WRITERS ON THE INTERNET

You can find a lot of advice on the writing process at Web sites and online services. They vary widely in quality, presentation, and amount of detail. The following are some of the most helpful and usable:

- **http://web.uvic.ca/wguide/Pages/StartHere.html**
  The University of Victoria's Hypertext Writer's Guide will help you through the basics of the writing process and answer questions about essays, paragraphs, sentences, words, and documentation.
- **www.powa.org**
  Paradigm Online Writing Assistant offers useful advice on writing various types of papers. It contains sections on discovery, organization, editing, and other topics.
- **http://owl.english.purdue.edu/owl**
  The Online Writing Lab (OWL) at Purdue University has printer-friendly handouts, interactive PowerPoint presentations, and hypertext workshops about the process and mechanics of writing—one of the most extensive collections of advice about writing on the Web.

RESPONDING TO A READING

Now that you have seen samples of close reading and of writing in response to reading, it's time to try these skills yourself. Use the advice in Chapters 1 and 2 as you practice.

PREPARING TO READ

Are you a successful writer? Do you like to write? Did you have any experiences in English or other classes that affected your attitude toward writing? What were they?

••

Learning to Write

••

Russell Baker

The winner of a Pulitzer Prize for journalism, Russell Baker began his career as a writer for the Baltimore Sun *and moved to the* New York Times *in the 1950s, where he wrote the "Observer" column from 1962 to 1998. He currently hosts the* Masterpiece Theater *series on PBS. Baker is known for his humorous observations of everyday life, but in this excerpt from his autobiography* Growing Up *(1982), his lighthearted tone gives way to a serious description of an important personal event.*

TERMS TO RECOGNIZE

notorious (*para. 1*)	known widely and usually unfavorably, disreputable
prim (*para. 1*)	formal and neat, lacking humor
listless (*para. 2*)	without energy, boring
ferocity (*para. 2*)	fierce intensity, savagery
irrepressible (*para. 2*)	impossible to control or hold back
essence (*para. 3*)	the most important ingredient or element, fundamental nature
antecedent (*para. 4*)	the word that a pronoun refers to
exotic (*para. 6*)	rare and unusual
reminiscence (*para. 8*)	a thing remembered, a memory
contempt (*para. 10*)	scorn, disrespect
ridicule (*para. 10*)	mockery, teasing
ecstasy (*para. 11*)	bliss, delight, joy

When our class was assigned to Mr. Fleagle for third-year English   1
I anticipated another grim year in that dreariest of subjects. Mr. Fleagle was notorious among City students for dullness and inability to inspire. He was said to be stuffy, dull, and hopelessly out of date. To me he looked to be sixty or seventy and prim to a fault. He wore primly severe eyeglasses, his

wavy hair was primly cut and primly combed. He wore prim vested suits with neckties blocked primly against the collar buttons of his primly starched white shirts. He had a primly pointed jaw, a primly straight nose, and a prim manner of speaking that was so correct, so gentlemanly, that he seemed a comic antique.

I anticipated a listless, unfruitful year with Mr. Fleagle and for a long time was not disappointed. We read *Macbeth*. Mr. Fleagle loved *Macbeth* and wanted us to love it too, but he lacked the gift of infecting others with his own passion. He tried to convey the murderous ferocity of Lady Macbeth one day by reading aloud the passage that concludes

> . . . I have given suck, and know
> How tender 'tis to love the babe that milks me.
> I would, while it was smiling in my face,
> Have plucked my nipple from his boneless gums. . . .

The idea of prim Mr. Fleagle plucking his nipple from boneless gums was too much for the class. We burst into gasps of irrepressible snickering. Mr. Fleagle stopped.

"There is nothing funny, boys, about giving suck to a babe. It is the— the very essence of motherhood, don't you see."

He constantly sprinkled his sentences with "don't you see." It wasn't a question but an exclamation of mild surprise at our ignorance. "Your pronoun needs an antecedent, don't you see," he would say, very primly. "The purpose of the Porter's scene, boys, is to provide comic relief from the horror, don't you see."

Later in the year we tackled the informal essay. "The essay, don't you see, is the . . . ." My mind went numb. Of all forms of writing, none seemed so boring as the essay. Naturally we would have to write informal essays. Mr. Fleagle distributed a homework sheet offering us a choice of topics. None was quite so simpleminded as "What I Did on My Summer Vacation," but most seemed to be almost as dull. I took the list home and dawdled until the night before the essay was due. Sprawled on the sofa, I finally faced up to the grim task, took the list out of my notebook, and scanned it. The topic on which my eye stopped was "The Art of Eating Spaghetti."

This title produced an extraordinary sequence of mental images. Surging up out of the depths of memory came a vivid recollection of a night in Belleville when all of us were seated around the supper table— Uncle Allen, my mother, Uncle Charlie, Doris, Uncle Hal—and Aunt Pat served spaghetti for supper. Spaghetti was an exotic treat in those days.

Neither Doris nor I had ever eaten spaghetti, and none of the adults had enough experience to be good at it. All the good humor of Uncle Allen's house reawoke in my mind as I recalled the laughing arguments we had that night about the socially respectable method for moving spaghetti from plate to mouth.

Suddenly I wanted to write about that, about the warmth and good feeling of it, but I wanted to put it down simply for my own joy, not for Mr. Fleagle. It was a moment I wanted to recapture and hold for myself. I wanted to relive the pleasure of an evening at New Street. To write it as I wanted, however, would violate all the rules of formal composition I'd learned in school, and Mr. Fleagle would surely give it a failing grade. Never mind. I would write something else for Mr. Fleagle after I had written this thing for myself.   7

When I finished it the night was half gone, and there was no time left to compose a proper, respectable essay for Mr. Fleagle. There was no choice next morning but to turn in my private reminiscence of Belleville. Two days passed before Mr. Fleagle returned the graded papers, and he returned everyone's but mine. I was bracing myself for a command to report to Mr. Fleagle immediately after school for discipline when I saw him lift my paper from his desk and rap for the class's attention.   8

"Now, boys," he said, "I want to read you an essay. This is titled 'The Art of Eating Spaghetti.'"   9

And he started to read. My words! He was reading *my words* out loud to the entire class. What's more, the entire class was listening. Listening attentively. Then somebody laughed, then the entire class was laughing, and not in contempt and ridicule, but with openhearted enjoyment. Even Mr. Fleagle stopped two or three times to repress a small prim smile.   10

I did my best to avoid showing pleasure, but what I was feeling was pure ecstasy at this startling demonstration that my words had the power to make people laugh. In the eleventh grade, at the eleventh hour as it were, I had discovered a calling. It was the happiest moment of my entire school career. When Mr. Fleagle finished he put the final seal on my happiness by saying, "Now that, boys, is an essay, don't you see. It's—don't you see—it's of the very essence of the essay, don't you see. Congratulations, Mr. Baker."   11

WEB SITE

www.albany.edu/writers-inst/webpages4/archive/olv6n2.html
Read a transcript of a 1991 interview with Russell Baker, who talks about his life and his writing career.

SUGGESTIONS FOR WRITING

1. Baker's experience in eleventh-grade English changed the way he thought about himself. Have you ever had such an eye-opening experience—some event you really want to write about, some incident you want to "recapture and hold" for yourself? Write an essay in which you describe what happened.

2. Write an essay about the most important thing that happened to you in school. It could be either a positive or negative experience—one that taught you something about yourself or about school or about the subject you were studying.

3. USING THE INTERNET. Take a look at the list of common myths about writing at **http://wire.rutgers.edu/i_myth.html**. Then get together with a small group of classmates and talk about how each of you feels about writing. Compare notes on what you like and don't like about writing. Which of the myths do you still believe in? Discuss the kinds of writing that you have done, and tell each other about previous writing experiences. Then write an essay explaining your thoughts and feelings about writing. If you changed your attitude (as Baker did), tell about that change.

4. Write an essay describing your writing process: how you get started, how you go about getting ideas, what you like to write about, where you like to write, whether you like background music or need quiet, whether you make an outline or plunge right in, how long it takes to complete an assignment, whether you work in stages, how many drafts you write, whether you write by hand or use a computer, how much correcting and recopying you do, and so on. Think carefully about the way you write, and describe it in as much detail as you can. Conclude your essay by explaining what you think you could do to make your writing process more efficient.

CHAPTER 3

Strategies for Conveying Ideas: *Narration* and *Description*

IMAGES AND IDEAS

Source: AP Wide World Photos   *Source:* Robert Funk

For Discussion and Writing

Look at the two photographs reproduced here. First, give each one a title that you think expresses the mood or atmosphere of the picture. The title will probably be a general word or phrase that describes an emotion or state of mind.

Next, choose one of the pictures to write about. One purpose is to present a detailed description of the picture to someone who has never seen it. The description should carefully differentiate this photo from other ones like it— that is, if your readers were to look at five winter scenes, they could pick out this particular one. In your description, get across the feeling or state of mind you used in your title. Be sure to use words that are very specific and have strong associations. Your description should be at least one paragraph long.

Now consider changing your approach. Create a caption for the photograph. Write another paragraph telling a story of what events led to the scene or what led to the viewer's witnessing of the scene. Use your imagination to provide the details of the story.

He falls back upon the bed awkwardly. His stumps, unweighted by legs and feet, rise in the air, presenting themselves. I unwrap the bandages from the stumps, and begin to cut away the black scabs and the dead, glazed fat with scissors and forceps. A shard of white bone comes loose. I pick it away. I wash the wounds with disinfectant and redress the stumps.
—Richard Selzer, "The Discus Thrower"

That powerful paragraph, written by a surgeon good with words as well as with scalpels, combines description and narration. Dr. Selzer, narrating an experience in treating a terminally ill patient, uses description to make his account of this brief event vividly, compellingly real. Simply put, a narrative is a story; **narration** is the telling of a story. The preceding passage is taken from a longer narrative (with a beginning, a middle, and an end) that makes a point. As you can see, the strength of narrative and descriptive writing lies in the use of vivid language and in the selection of precise details.

THE POINT OF NARRATION AND DESCRIPTION

Although the selections in this chapter combine several writing strategies, they are primarily narratives that make a point using descriptive details to add clarity, liveliness, and interest. You will notice that most of the readings throughout this text use both narration and description to help them develop many different kinds of essays.

Using Narratives

Consider how often we use narrative in everyday speech. If you want to convince your daughter to avoid becoming pregnant as a teenager, you'll probably tell her the story of your high school friend who made that mistake and missed her chance to become the architect she always wanted to be. We tell stories because they are convincing—they have the ring of truth to them—and most people are able to learn from the experience of others. So, narrative is a good strategy to consider if you are writing to persuade, to make a point.

If you are going to write a narrative essay, be sure your story has a point. You wouldn't tell a joke without a punch line, and only mothers and close friends will hold still for stories without a purpose.

Much more frequently, you will use short narratives as part of a longer essay. Notice in your reading how often writers begin essays with a brief narrative to catch our interest and lead us into the topic. Once the writers have our attention, they may move to other strategies to develop their ideas and present the material, but a good story makes an effective lure.

Using Description

Essays of pure description are rare, but descriptive details provide one of the most common ways of adding interest and clarity to your writing. **Description** can put a picture in the minds of readers, helping them to see what you mean. Most writing would seem dull and lifeless without descriptive details, like this sentence:

> The firefighter rescued a child.

Although the action referred to is exciting, the sentence is blah. But add some descriptive details, and the sentence gains meaning and interest:

> The exhausted firefighter, a rookie on the force, staggered from the flames with the limp body of an unconscious child cradled in his arms.

You can, of course, include too much description. But use any details that come to you while writing your first draft. Then, when you revise, decide whether you've gone too far and eliminate any that seem overdone or unnecessary. Of course, add more details if you think you have too few.

THE PRINCIPLES OF NARRATION AND DESCRIPTION

Good narrative and descriptive writing depends, as does most other writing, on making choices. In narratives, the main choices involve deciding which events to include and which ones to leave out. In descriptions, the choices involve selecting words that appeal to the senses—usually to sight, but also to touch, taste, hearing, and smell.

Organizing the Events

If you've ever listened to a boring storyteller, you know how important a concise and effective framework is to a narrative. Organizing a narrative seems easy because the story almost always proceeds in **chronological order** (according to the time in which events happened). But a poor storyteller (or a writer who fails to revise) will get things out of order and interrupt the tale with "Oh, I forgot to mention that Marvin got fired just before his cat got lost and his dog was run over." Or the storyteller will get hung up on a totally unimportant detail:

> The moment I saw him—I think it was at the senior prom—or was it at the homecoming dance—or it could have been the party at Yolanda's—oh, wait, I don't think it was at a party at all, it was at a football game—or no, a basketball game. . . .

even though the point of the story has nothing to do with where or when it happened.

Get your story straight in your mind before you begin, or else straighten it out when you revise. Eliminate any dull or unnecessary material, and then go to work on making it interesting.

Including Specific Details

All good writing is full of specific *details*, but a narrative will simply fall flat without them. Recall the paragraph we quoted by Dr. Richard Selzer. We could summarize that paragraph in a single sentence:

> After the patient fell back awkwardly in bed, I removed the bandages, cleaned, disinfected, and rebandaged the ends of his amputated legs.

What did we leave out? The details—in this case mostly descriptive details—and what a difference they make in allowing us to visualize the doctor's performance.

Selecting Descriptive Words

Effective description depends heavily on the use of specific details, but also crucial are the words you choose in presenting those details. Consider this sentence quoted from Dr. Selzer's paragraph:

> I unwrap the bandages from the stumps, and begin to cut away the black scabs and the dead, glazed fat with scissors and forceps.

Look at what happens when we substitute less specific, less descriptive words in that same sentence:

> I take the bandages off the amputated legs, and begin to remove the dead tissue with my instruments.

The meaning is the same, and most of us would probably have written it that way, but it's clear that the force of Dr. Selzer's sentence lies in his word choice: *unwrap, stumps, cut away, black scabs, glazed fat, scissors, forceps.*

Good description stems from close observation, paying close attention to the sights, sounds, textures, tastes, or smells around you. Then you must search for exactly the right words to convey what you experience to your readers. Try to think of words that go beyond the general to the specific:

GENERAL ←—————————————→ **SPECIFIC**

a drink	a soft drink	a diet cola	a stale diet Coke
move	run	run fast	race headlong
weather	rain	cold rain	cold, blowing rain

You get the idea. As you read, be alert for words that convey **images**, which let you know how something looks or feels or moves or tastes or smells or sounds.

When you revise, try to replace the following useful but run-of-the-mill verbs with words that are more specific and more interesting:

is (are, was, were, etc.)   go   get   has

come   move   do   make

Notice the difference a livelier word choice makes:

O'Malley moved on to second base.
O'Malley slid into second base.

I'm going to do my homework.
I'm going to struggle with my homework.

Lapita made a chocolate mousse.
Lapita whipped up a luscious chocolate mousse.

Keep a vocabulary list and try to use the new words in speaking and writing. The theory is that if you use a word three times, it enters your vocabulary. Part of becoming a good writer (as well as a good speaker) depends on increasing the number of words you have at your command, so get to work on it.

THE PITFALLS OF NARRATION AND DESCRIPTION

The narratives included in this chapter, written by experienced authors, will not show you the many things that can go wrong in this kind of writing. Descriptions and narratives are among the easiest kinds of writing to do, but they are probably the most difficult to do well. You need to find someone who will read your draft, not only for enjoyment, but also with the promise of helping you improve it. It's always hard to see the flaws in our own writing. It's especially hard with narratives and descriptions. But you can do a good job if you are willing to work at it and can find a reliable person to help you in revising.

As you rewrite, ask yourself—and ask your helper to answer—the following questions:

1. Is the point of my narrative clear? It may not be stated directly, but readers should be able to see *why* I'm telling this story.
2. Are the events in order? Are there any gaps? Any backtracking?
3. Are there enough details to be clear and interesting?
4. Are there any unnecessary details that I should take out?
5. Do the descriptions provide an image (a picture, a sound, a smell, a taste, an atmosphere, an action)?

Respond to the questions as honestly as you can—and have your helper do the same. Then keep revising until you are both happy with the results.

WHAT TO LOOK FOR IN NARRATION AND DESCRIPTION

As you read the essays in this chapter, pay attention to these characteristics:

1. *Look at the way the essay is put together.* Probably the events are told chronologically, as they happened, but if not, try to figure out why the writer departed from the usual method of organization.
2. *Decide what point the narrative makes.* Its purpose may be simply to entertain the readers, but more often it will illustrate or make a point. Look for an underlying meaning that you discover as you think about the story and the author's reasons for telling it.
3. *Consider the elements of the narrative.* Think about why these particular events, people, and descriptions are included. If they are not crucial, try to decide what they add to the story and what would be lost if they were left out.
4. *Notice the descriptive details.* Underline any sentences or phrases that appeal to your senses or put a picture in your mind.
5. *Pick out good descriptive words.* Most of these you will already have underlined. Add them to your vocabulary list.

PREPARING TO READ

Have you ever been involved in a serious accident or caught in a burning building or been especially frightened by something? Describe how you felt at the time. Were you terrified—or did everything happen too fast? Record the thoughts and feelings you experienced once the incident was over.

••

Rain of Fire

••

EVAN THOMAS

Evan Thomas, a graduate of Harvard and the University of Virginia Law School, has been assistant managing editor of Newsweek *magazine since 1991 and the lead writer on many major news stories. His vivid reporting on the September 11th disaster helped win for* Newsweek *the National Magazine Award for General Excellence in 2002. The following selection appeared in* Newsweek *(December 31, 2001/January 7, 2002) as Part IV of an extensive article entitled "The Day That Changed America." If you want to find out how Virginia DiChiara made it down those seventy-eight flights of stairs, read the whole gripping article.*

TERMS TO RECOGNIZE

moseying (*para. 1*)	moving slowly and aimlessly
translucent (*para. 4*)	clear, letting light through
prosaic (*para. 6*)	everyday, ordinary
suffused (*para. 8*)	spread throughout
cacophony (*para. 8*)	harsh, nerve-jangling sound

A self-described workaholic, Virginia DiChiara was normally out of her 1 house and on her way to work by 7 A.M. But the morning of September 11 was so brilliantly beautiful that DiChiara decided to dawdle. She let her two golden retrievers play in the yard, cooked herself some eggs, poured herself a cup of coffee. "I was just moseying along," she says. "I didn't feel like rushing." She left her Bloomfield, N.J., home at 7:40, a 40-minute delay that would end up saving her life.

It was a little after 8:40 when she entered the lobby of the North 2 Tower of the World Trade Center. Together with a Cantor Fitzgerald co-worker, she rode the elevator up to the 78th floor, where she crossed a lobby to take a second elevator the rest of the way to her office on the 101st floor. The elevator door opened and she pressed the button for 101. It was 8:46 A.M.

As the elevator doors closed, Flight 11 plowed into the northern face   3 of Tower I some 20 floors above. The elevator went black and "bounced around like a ball," DiChiara recalls. "I remember seeing two lines shooting around the top of the elevator"—electrical cables that had come loose and were spitting current—and "everybody started screaming." In front of her was a man named Roy Bell, who later said that the sound of impact was "deafening," like someone banging a 2-by-2-foot sheet of aluminum with a hammer "six inches from your head." The right wall of the elevator car crashed into Bell, breaking several of his fingers and flinging him to the left side. Miraculously, the elevator doors remained open about a foot. Within seconds, Bell "just sprinted" out of the elevator, he recalls. "Inside was not where you wanted to be."

DiChiara had crouched down behind Bell. She saw Bell go through,   4 and thought, "I don't hear any screaming, so I know he's not on fire . . . I'm outta here." She decided to go for it. But as she gathered herself, huge blue flames—translucent teardrops of fire, a foot in diameter—began falling in a steady curtain. DiChiara dropped her bag, covered her face with her palms and squeezed through the door, her elbows pushing the black rubber guards on the elevator doors. Left behind was her Cantor co-worker. DiChiara never saw her again; at times she feels guilty that she made it out and her co-worker did not.

DiChiara was aflame when she emerged from the elevator. "I   5 remember hearing my hair on fire," she says. (She later joked, "I must have put on some extra hair spray.") With her hands she tapped out the fire. "I got it out, I got it," she said to herself. Then, feeling something else, she looked back and saw flames rising from her shoulder. In that instant, she remembered the old lesson from grade school: stop, drop, and roll. She threw herself to the carpeted floor and rolled over and over, frantically patting out the flames. "I remember getting up and just looking at myself," she says. "'OK, everything's out.' And then sort of laughing, almost like a hysteria, like a little giggle, like, 'Oh my God, let me do it again just in case I missed it.' I was so scared, like there was an ember on my body that was still going to go up."

DiChiara crawled some 20 feet down the hallway and sat with her   6 back propped against a wall. She was wearing a sleeveless cotton shirt that day, and her arms and hands were seared with third-degree burns.

In shock, she did not feel the pain—yet. Improbably prosaic thoughts crossed her mind. In the briefcase she'd left on the elevator were some airplane tickets recently purchased for a vacation jaunt to the Florida Keys, as well as a wad of cash. Should she go back and retrieve it? "No," she thought to herself. "Just stay right where you are."

Then she spotted a co-worker, Ari Schonbrun, head of global accounts receivable at Cantor. "Ari!" she called out. He turned around and looked at her. "Virginia! Oh my God!" he said. "Ari, I'm badly burned," Virginia told him. She was gradually realizing how grave her condition truly was, and beginning to feel it as well. "I'm in so much pain," she said. Schonbrun was horrified. "The skin was peeled off her arms," he says. "You knew this woman was in trouble." DiChiara read his expression. "I knew by the look on his face that I was bad," she says. Schonbrun told her, "Virginia, take it easy. We're going to get help. Don't worry. You're going to be fine." She begged, "Whatever you do, don't leave me." Schonbrun reassured her, "I'm not going to leave you. I'll be with you." 7

The hallways were smoky, suffused with the nauseating smell of burned jet fuel, littered with debris, and completely dark save for some outdoor light filtering in from windows at the end of the hall. Schonbrun gently guided DiChiara toward a small security office behind the elevator banks where the lights still worked. About a dozen people were huddled there, including two security guards. DiChiara lay down on the floor, on the verge of passing out. A woman sitting nearby was crying. One of the security guards was furiously dialing for help on the office phone but couldn't get through. The other guard had a radio, but she was paralyzed, crying. Schonbrun told her, "You've got to calm down. You've got to get on that radio and get us help." The guard tried, but the only sound coming over the radio was a cacophony of screams. 8

Singed by his narrow escape through the elevator doors, Bell had also made it to the security office. His doctors would later tell him that the few seconds between his exit and DiChiara's made the difference between his second-degree and her third-degree burns. Suddenly, a man appeared saying that he was a fire warden. There was a stairwell in the middle of the tower that they could use, he announced. Schonbrun leaned over DiChiara and laid out the options: either they could wait for someone to rescue them, or they could start heading down by foot. 9

For DiChiara, there was no choice. No way was she going to sit there and wait. Gritting her teeth, she got up and headed for the stairwell. 10

RESPONDING TO READING

Everyone has seen on television the visual images of the horrific events of September 11, 2001. The previous selection recounts the experience of one woman caught up in that tragedy. What did you get from the reading that you did not get from seeing the visuals?

CONSIDERING CONTENT

1. Why was Virginia DiChiara late going to work on September 11, 2001? Was she a person who was often late?
2. How did she know her hair was on fire? How did she extinguish the flames on her clothing?
3. How did DiChiara discover how severe her burns were? Why do you suppose she did not immediately know how gravely she was injured?
4. What help did the survivors get from the security guard's radio?
5. Why did DiChiara decide to struggle down seventy-eight flights of stairs instead of waiting for rescue?
6. What does Thomas show us about her character, throughout the narrative, that aids her in making that life-saving decision?

CONSIDERING METHOD

1. How is this selection organized?
2. What is the author's **purpose?** Who is the intended **audience?**
3. At the end of paragraph 2, Thomas includes this small detail in a sentence all by itself: "It was 8:46 A.M." Why do you think he made that stylistic choice?
4. In paragraph 7, Thomas writes, "In shock, she did not feel the pain—yet." What does he achieve with the use of that dash?
5. How does the writer engage our emotions in this narrative?
6. The piece is packed with specific details. Point out three or four that you find particularly effective and explain why you think Thomas included them.
7. What makes the concluding paragraph effective?

WRITING STEP BY STEP: DESCRIBING A CATASTROPHE

Think about a catastrophe that you witnessed or were involved in—a flood, a fire, an auto wreck, an earthquake, a tornado, or a hurricane. Jot down as many specific details as you can remember. Then write a short narrative describing the experience. Use "I" in referring to yourself and "we" if others join you in the action. Or, write about the experience of someone else caught up in a major ordeal, the way Evan Thomas writes about Virginia DiChiara's struggles in the previous essay. Collect material through interviewing the other person, with your narrative purposes in mind.

A. Begin, as Thomas does, with a brief explanation of how you got involved—what you were doing, who (if anyone) was with you, and what led up to the catastrophe.

B. Then recount the events from beginning to end. Before you begin, make a detailed list of everything that happened and all the specific details you can recall. Next, decide which actions to include and which to leave out.

C. You do not need a thesis statement in a personal narrative. Let your readers infer what your point is.

D. Include any interesting thoughts that went through your mind (as Thomas does in para. 6). Use quotation marks, since you are, in effect, quoting yourself. If other people are involved, quote directly anything memorable that they said.

E. Use plenty of description (like "lines shooting around the top of the elevator," "translucent teardrops of fire, a foot in diameter," "frantically patting out the flames"), as well as pertinent specific actions ("She let her two golden retrievers play in the yard, cooked herself some eggs, poured herself a cup of coffee," "One of the security guards was furiously dialing for help on the office phone but couldn't get through"). Put pictures in your readers' minds. Lively verbs help create striking images—*moseying, plowed, bounced, shooting, banging*.

F. Avoid telling your readers what to feel. Let them experience your emotions through your forceful recounting of the events.

G. Experiment with several very short sentences for emphasis.

H. Write a concluding sentence or a short concluding paragraph that brings the account to a definite close. Don't let your narrative just trail off at the end.

OTHER WRITING IDEAS

1. In his account of the survivors trapped on the 78th floor, Evan Thomas shows them experiencing many varying emotions—fear, panic, hysteria, courage, self-discipline, determination, resolve. Think of a time when you felt one of these emotions and write a narrative account analyzing the experience. Describe where you were, what happened, and how you reacted. You might conclude by explaining how you feel about the occurrence now, as you reflect on it.

2. COLLABORATIVE WRITING. Write a narrative to support or disprove some familiar proverb or saying, such as "Home is where the heart is,"

"Crime doesn't pay," or "Virtue is its own reward." Get together with several classmates before you begin writing to help one another decide what saying would make a good choice and what story might provide convincing illustrations.

3. USING THE INTERNET. Visit the Chicago Historical Society's Web site on the Great Chicago Fire and read several of the accounts in the anthology of fire narratives (**www.chicagohistory.org/fire/ witnesses/library.html**). Using the information you've acquired, write a narrative recounting your imaginary escape from the Great Chicago Fire of 1871. Or, if you prefer, narrate the progress of a single lucky person who fled the conflagration and survived. You can follow the chronology of that person's account, but try for the immediacy that Evan Thomas captures in his reporting of Virginia DiChiara's miraculous escape. Supply your own specific events, vivid descriptions, and action verbs.

4. WRITING ABOUT READING. Analyze the writing strategies used in Thomas's essay. Use the five points on page 35 in the introduction of this chapter to guide you in your analysis.

GAINING WORD POWER

Thomas uses a number of precise descriptive word choices in this narrative. Several appear in the Terms to Recognize section preceding the selection. Here are some others:

DiChiara decided to *dawdle*. (para. 1)

Flight 11 *plowed* into the northern face of Tower I. (para. 3)

DiChiara was *aflame*. (para. 5)

Her arms and hands were *seared*. (para. 6)

One of the security guards was *furiously* dialing for help. (para. 8)

We repeat these sentences below, minus the italicized words. Fill in each blank with your own definition of the missing word.

DiChiara decided to _____.

Flight 11 _____ into the northern face of Tower I.

DiChiara was _____.

Her arms and hands were _____.

One of the security guards was _____ dialing for help.

What is lost or changed in the second set of sentences? Which sentences do you prefer?

EDITING SKILLS: COMBINING SENTENCES

Writing lots of short sentences with little variety produces a choppy effect that sounds a bit childish. In order to make your writing fluent, you need to take those choppy sentences and combine them into a single sophisticated one. It works like this:

Choppy sentences:

She had two golden retrievers.

She let them play in the yard.

She cooked herself some eggs.

She poured herself a cup of coffee.

If you combine those sentences, you get one of Evan Thomas's well-crafted sentences:

She let her two golden retrievers play in the yard, cooked herself some eggs, poured herself a cup of coffee.

Here is another example:

Choppy sentences:

She threw herself to the floor.

The floor was carpeted.

She rolled over and over.

She was frantic.

She patted out the flames.

Thomas wrote his sentence this way:

She threw herself to the carpeted floor and rolled over and over, frantically patting out the flames.

EXERCISE

Now you try it. Here are some short sentences to combine into a single effective one. Begin the first one with *if*.

You may like to travel.

You may want to travel alone.

You are a woman.

I have some tips for you.

My friend is a woman
She travels alone a lot.
She has given me good advice.

You may be on a train or plane.
You choose your departure times.
You choose your arrival times.
Check the time of your arrival at your destination.
Be sure your arrival will be during daylight hours.

The station or airport may be far from your hotel.
You need to find the best way to get there.
Taxis are expensive.

You should travel light.
You should take only two bags.
One bag should be on wheels.
You will probably have to carry your own luggage.

Now examine the narrative you just wrote. If you find limp or choppy sentences, combine them into pleasing ones.

🌐 **WEB SITE**

http://911digitalarchive.org/gallery_index.php
Click on "Stories" to read compelling personal narratives written by people who were involved in the tragedy of September 11th.

PREPARING TO READ

Did you ever have an experience that changed the way you look at the world—perhaps while traveling, or getting to know a stranger, or suffering a serious illness, or being inspired by a teacher?

••

Jackie's Debut: A Unique Day

••

MIKE ROYKO

Born in Chicago, Mike Royko (1932–1997) attended Wright Junior College there. He wrote a syndicated column for the Chicago Tribune *and was awarded the Pulitzer Prize. His columns often ridiculed human greed, vanity, and stupidity. The piece reprinted here is perhaps not typical, since it focuses on an uplifting event—a step toward reversing the usual pattern of ignorant prejudice. It appeared in the* Chicago Daily News *on Wednesday, October 15, 1972, the day after Jackie Robinson died. If you enjoy this article about Jackie Robinson, you might want to read Robinson's autobiography,* I Never Had It Made.

TERMS TO RECOGNIZE

scalpers (*para. 3*)	people selling tickets at higher than regular prices
Ls (*para. 4*)	elevated trains
caromed (*para. 11*)	hit and bounced
chortling (*para. 12*)	chuckling and snorting with laughter

All that Saturday, the wise men of the neighborhood, who sat in chairs on the sidewalk outside the tavern, had talked about what it would do to baseball. I hung around and listened because baseball was about the most important thing in the world, and if anything was going to ruin it, I was worried.

Most of the things they said, I didn't understand, although it sounded terrible. But could one man bring such ruin? They said he could and would. And the next day he was going to be in Wrigley Field for the first time, on the same diamond as Hack, Nicholson, Cavarretta, Schmidt, Pafko, and all my other idols. I had to see Jackie Robinson, the man who was going to somehow wreck everything. So the next day, another kid and I started walking to the ball park early.

We always walked to save the streetcar fare. It was five or six miles, but I felt about baseball the way Abe Lincoln felt about education. Usually, we could get there just at noon, find a seat in the grandstands, and watch some batting practice. But not that Sunday, May 18, 1947. By noon, Wrigley Field was almost filled. The crowd outside spilled off the sidewalk and into the streets. Scalpers were asking top dollar for box seats and getting it.

I had never seen anything like it. Not just the size, although it was a new record, more than 47,000. But this was 25 years ago, and in 1947 few blacks were seen in the Loop, much less up on the white North Side at a Cub game. That day, they came by the thousands, pouring off the north-bound Ls and out of their cars. They didn't wear baseball-game clothes. They had on church clothes and funeral clothes—suits, white shirts, ties, gleaming shoes, and straw hats. I've never seen so many straw hats. Big as it was, the crowd was orderly. Almost unnaturally so. People didn't jostle each other.   4

The whites tried to look as if nothing unusual was happening, while the blacks tried to look casual and dignified. So everybody looked slightly ill at ease. For most, it was probably the first time they had been that close to each other in such great numbers.   5

We managed to get in, scramble up a ramp, and find a place to stand behind the last row of grandstand seats. Then they shut the gates. No place remained to stand.   6

Robinson came up in the first inning. I remember the sound. It wasn't the shrill, teen-age cry you now hear, or an excited gut roar. They applauded, long, rolling applause. A tall middle-aged black man stood next to me, a smile of almost painful joy on his face, beating his palms together so hard they must have hurt.   7

When Robinson stepped into the batter's box, it was as if someone had flicked a switch. The place went silent. He swung at the first pitch and they erupted as if he had knocked it over the wall. But it was only a high foul that dropped into the box seats. I remember thinking it was strange that a foul could make that many people happy. When he struck out, the low moan was genuine.   8

I've forgotten most of the details of the game, other than that the Dodgers won and Robinson didn't get a hit or do anything special, although he was cheered on every swing and every routine play. But two things happened I'll never forget. Robinson played first, and early in the game a Cub star hit a grounder and it was a close play. Just before the Cub reached first, he swerved to his left. And as he got to the bag, he seemed to slam his foot down hard at Robinson's foot. It was obvious to everyone that he was trying to run into him or spike him. Robinson took the throw and got clear at the last instant.   9

I was shocked. That Cub, a home-town boy, was my biggest hero.   10
It was not only an unheroic stunt, but it seemed a rude thing to do in front
of people who would cheer for a foul ball. I didn't understand why he had
done it. It wasn't at all big league. I didn't know that while the white fans
were relatively polite, the Cubs and most other teams kept up a steady
stream of racial abuse from the dugout. I thought all they did down there
was talk about how good Wheaties are.

Later in the game, Robinson was up again and he hit another foul   11
ball. This time it came into the stands low and fast, in our direction. Somebody in the seats grabbed for it, but it caromed off his hand and kept coming. There was a flurry of arms as the ball kept bouncing, and suddenly it
was between me and my pal. We both grabbed. I had a baseball.

The two of us stood there examining it and chortling. A genuine   12
major-league baseball that had actually been gripped and thrown by a Cub
pitcher, hit by a Dodger batter. What a possession! Then I heard a voice
say: "Would you consider selling that?" It was the black man who had
applauded so fiercely. I mumbled something. I didn't want to sell it.

"I'll give you $10 for it," he said.   13

Ten dollars. I couldn't believe it. I didn't know what $10 could buy   14
because I'd never had that much money. But I knew that a lot of men in the
neighborhood considered $60 a week to be good pay. I handed it to him,
and he paid me with ten $1 bills. When I left the ball park, with that
much money in my pocket, I was sure that Jackie Robinson wasn't bad for
the game.

Since then, I've regretted a few times that I didn't keep the ball. Or   15
that I hadn't given it to him free. I didn't know, then, how hard he probably
had to work for that $10. But Tuesday I was glad I had sold it to him. And if
that man is still around, and has that baseball, I'm sure he thinks it was
worth every cent.

RESPONDING TO READING

Read again Royko's last paragraph. Explain in your journal why he wishes, as an
adult, that he had given the baseball to the man who bought it from him. Do
you think you would feel the same way?

CONSIDERING CONTENT

1. What made the old men of the neighborhood say that Jackie Robinson
   would ruin the game of baseball?
2. How did young Royko and his friend get to Wrigley Field, and why did
   they choose that way to get there?

3. What does he mean when he says, "I felt about baseball the way Abe Lincoln felt about education" (para. 3)?
4. Why was he surprised to see so many black people at the game?
5. Why were the black people wearing their good clothes?
6. When the young narrator says, "It wasn't at all big league" (para. 10), what does he mean?

CONSIDERING METHOD

1. How does Royko get the readers' attention in the opening paragraph?
2. How does he let us know that the "wise men of the neighborhood" are not truly wise—that he is being sarcastic? What small detail in the sentence gives us the clue?
3. Why does Royko tell most of the narrative through the thoughts of himself as a young boy?
4. In paragraph 3, why does he give the exact date—Sunday, May 18, 1947?
5. When you think about all the details he could have included in describing the crowd at the baseball game, why do you think he chose to relate how the black people were dressed?
6. In paragraph 10, Royko tells us something he learned later in life. How does he handle this shift in time so that we scarcely notice it?
7. In paragraphs 12 and 13, why does Royko give us the exact words of the man who wants to buy the baseball?
8. Explain why the final paragraph makes a good conclusion.

WRITING STEP BY STEP: AN EYE-OPENING CHILDHOOD EXPERIENCE

Using Mike Royko's column as an example, write a narrative essay about a childhood experience that suddenly let you see some less than admirable aspect of the adult world. Royko, after making it clear that he grew up in a white section of the city, lets us see how the vicious action of his former hero on the Cub team opened his eyes to racial prejudice.

Think of a similar experience in your own past that will allow you to show the unfairness of some human behavior or the pain caused by some human weakness. Perhaps you could tell about your accidental discovery of disloyalty or cheating by someone you admired and trusted. Or you could tell the story of the first time you observed adult violence or adult cruelty. Write this assignment as a cautionary tale for an audience of high school seniors.

A. Think about the story and the insight you gained from it. Write out the meaning of the incident as a thesis statement, but do not include it in the essay. Just keep it in mind as a guide in selecting details.

B. Jot down the events you want to cover, leaving lots of space between them. Next, go over the events, and fill in the spaces with all the details you can think of about each event. Then, go through the whole sheet again, and carefully decide just which events and which details you want to use in your narrative. Select only the most descriptive details that will allow your readers to experience the event as you did.

C. Use *I* in telling your story. Consider narrating it from the point of view of yourself as a child, as Royko does. Try to remember how you actually saw things when you were young and innocent and tell the story that way. See Royko's paragraphs 1, 10, and 14 for good examples.

D. Begin, as Royko does, by briefly setting the scene. Be sure to work in the time, either here or later (as Royko does in para. 3).

E. Don't give away the point of your story, but try to work in a teaser (or a *delay*) as he does in his opening. The men are talking about what "it" would do to baseball, but we readers have no clue what "it" means and read on to find out.

F. In your conclusion, try to let your readers understand what you learned from the incident, but don't tell them straight out. See Royko's last three paragraphs, in which he tells us how he felt as a child and how he feels now as a man—and both are positive feelings. He lets us see how wrong racial prejudice is and at the same time reminds us of how proud blacks could feel about Jackie Robinson's success.

G. If exactly what people say is important to the story, put the speech in direct quotations, as Royko does in paragraphs 12 and 13.

OTHER WRITING IDEAS

1. Did you ever do something quite wrong in response to peer pressure? Tell the story of how this happened and how you felt about it at the time—and how you feel about it now.

2. USING THE INTERNET. Enter the name of Ida Wells–Barnett or Wilma Rudolph into your search engine, and you will find the story of another African American who, like Jackie Robinson, led the way in the fight against racial segregation. After reading about one of these women, write a narrative for a group of middle school students telling the story of her stand against injustice.

3. COLLABORATIVE WRITING. With a group of classmates, have a brainstorming session in which you discuss difficult ethical and moral decisions each of you has faced and how you responded. For many, deciding whether to cheat, steal, or tattle creates their first moral crisis. Then, tell the story of a tough decision you had to make and what happened as a result.

4. WRITING ABOUT READING. Write a summary of Royko's narrative for readers who aren't familiar with this selection. Instead of using first-person pronouns (*I, me, we, us*) as Royko does, write your summary in the third person (*he, him, they, them*).

GAINING WORD POWER

Following is the vocabulary entry for the word *unique*, which appears in Mike Royko's title. It comes from the *Webster's New World Dictionary*, third college edition, published by Simon & Schuster. Can you make sense of it?

u|nique (yoo nēk´) *adj.* [[Fr < L *unicus*, single < ONE]] 1 one and only; sole *[a unique* specimen*]* 2 having no like or equal; unparalleled *[a unique* achievement*]* 3 highly unusual, extraordinary, rare, etc.: a common usage still objected to by some—**u|nique´ly** *adv.*—**u|nique´ness** *n.*

All dictionaries are unique, but here's how to read this entry from the *New World.*

1. The boldfaced word itself tells you how to spell it, and the thin line (between the *u* and the *n*) shows where it divides into syllables. Some dictionaries use centered dots instead.
2. The syllables inside the parentheses (some dictionaries use slash marks) let you know how to pronounce the word. If you don't understand the symbols, check inside the front or back cover or at the bottom of the page.
3. The boldfaced abbreviation tells you the part of speech. Notice that further down in the entry you'll see other forms of the same word that are different parts of speech (*uniquely* **adv**. and *uniqueness* **n**.). Sometimes those other parts of speech have different meanings listed.
4. Those weird notations inside the double brackets give the *etymology* of the word—that is, they tell us how it came into our language. The entry reads this way: "The word *unique* comes to us from the French, derived from the Latin *unicus*, meaning *single*, derived from *unus*, meaning *one*." Check the explanatory notes in your dictionary to learn how to figure out the etymologies.
5. Various meanings are numbered. Some dictionaries list the most common meaning first; others begin with the oldest meaning, which would often be the least common. So, again, check your dictionary's explanatory notes. The *New World* lists meanings from oldest to newest.
6. All dictionaries give warnings about usage. If you look up the word *ain't*, you will find it labeled *slang* or *nonstandard*, perhaps even with a

warning that some people have strong objections to it. In the entry for *unique*, the third meaning of "highly unusual, extraordinary, rare, etc." is followed by a caution that this is "a common usage still objected to by some." Those *some* often include English teachers, so avoid writing *most unique* or *quite unique* or *very unique*. Remember the etymology.

Now, to practice what you just learned, look up the word *debut* from Royko's title, and answer the following questions:

1. How many syllables does it have?
2. What different ways can it be correctly pronounced?
3. What parts of speech can it be?
4. What language did it come from?
5. What are two meanings of the word?
6. Are there any usage labels or warnings?

EDITING SKILLS: PUNCTUATING CONVERSATION

When adding conversation to your narrative, you know, of course, to use quotation marks around other people's words. But you also need to notice how other marks are used with those quotation marks. Look at the punctuation in these sentences from Royko's essay:

Then I heard a voice say: "Would you consider selling that?"
"I'll give you $10 for it," he said.

The words telling who is talking—called a tag—need to be separated from the quotation. When the tag comes *before* the quotation, you can use either a comma or a colon to separate. When the tag comes *after* the quoted words, use a comma.

Sometimes you may want to put the tag in the middle:

"I don't want to sell it," I mumbled; "it's mine!"
"Go away!" I yelled, "or I'll call a cop."
"I'm going home," I told Joe, "before I lose this ball."

If you start a new sentence after the tag, you need a semicolon or a period, just as you would in any other writing.

And don't stack up punctuation. If you use an exclamation mark or a question mark, omit the comma or period.

Notice that periods and commas go before the ending quotation marks. But with question marks (and exclamation marks), you have to decide whether the tag is a question (or an exclamation) or whether the quoted words are.

"Oh, well," Jamal said, "it takes all kinds!"
Can you believe Jamal said, "It takes all kinds"?

Finally, whenever you change speakers, begin a new paragraph.

As you read your way through the selections in this text, pay attention to the way quoted material is punctuated.

EXERCISE

Now, for practice, put the necessary punctuation in the following sentences:

Oh, heaven help us Marvin exclaimed I forgot to do our income taxes

We'd better get started on them fast then responded Rosa

Marvin groaned You get the receipts together while I try to find the calculator

How am I supposed to know where to find the receipts asked Rosa

Surely roared Marvin you've been keeping them all together some place

Rosa was silent during a long pause, then asked Was I supposed to

Marvin slapped his palm against his forehead and yelled We're doomed

Don't worry, honey soothed Rosa they never send you to Leavenworth on a first offense

Go back and look at the essay you just wrote: Did you punctuate the conversations accurately? Check all your quotations carefully, and make any necessary corrections.

🌐 WEB SITES

www.negroleaguebaseball.com
The online home of Negro League history
www.blackbaseball.com
The Negro League's Web site

Both sites provide historical background and perspectives that relate to the topic of Royko's essay.

PREPARING TO READ

Would you endure almost constant pain and risk permanent injury or even perhaps death to play a professional sport?

••

Walking Away

••

BEN MCGRATH

Ben McGrath is one of the youngest staff writers at the New Yorker *magazine, where he frequently profiles athletes and east-coast politicians. He has also written for the* New York Times, Slate, *and the* New York Observer, *among other publications. He lives in Manhattan.*

TERMS TO RECOGNIZE

tolerance (*para. 2*)	the degree to which someone can suffer without being harmed or damaged
perpetual (*para. 3*)	continuing, never ending
analogy (*para. 3*)	something that seems similar between two situations or processes
ulna (*para. 5*)	the inner bone of the lower arm, on the opposite side of the thumb
unceremoniously (*para. 5*)	in a rough or sudden way, without showing respect or politeness
compensate for (*para. 7*)	to replace or balance the effect of something bad
degenerative (*para. 8*)	gradually getting worse and unstoppable
zeal (*para. 9*)	eagerness to do something

On a Tuesday afternoon a few weeks ago, the New York Giants running back Tiki Barber shuffled to the door of his apartment, on East Sixty-ninth Street, and apologized for the mess inside. His two-year-old son, Chason, had a playdate, and Legos, wooden horses, and used tissues were all over the floor. Tuesday is a professional football player's day off, and Barber had just woken up from a nap. He was wearing a hooded gray sweatshirt, gray sweatpants, and thick wool socks, and walked without seeming to lift his feet. He rubbed the top of his head a lot, like someone who'd just bumped into a street sign.

1

Pain tolerance is an essential requirement of his profession. "You get   2
hit in ways that you can't even make up," he said. "It doesn't look bad. It
just looks routine. But you'll get up and you'll say, 'God, I feel like my ribs
are broken.' And that's how it was for me this week against Dallas." The
Giants had just lost their fourth game in a row, to the Cowboys, and stood
at 6-6, with their playoff chances in jeopardy. "We're in the red zone and I
take a shot in my side: 'Ughh—that's going to kill me tomorrow.' And I knew
it. I woke up yesterday morning and I couldn't even sit up." He was not
exactly sitting up now. He had shut himself off in the den, to block out the
noise made by Chason and his friend, who were attacking toy guitars. He
was stretched out on a brown sofa, with one hand behind his head and the
other arm folded across his midsection.

He is, among his peers, small: about five feet nine and two   3
hundred and five pounds. He has a shaved head, thick eyebrows, a
boxer's jaw, not much of a neck, and a soft, nasal voice that makes him
sound as though he had a perpetual cold, which enhanced, that day, the
over-all effect of a kid staying home sick from school. "It's like someone's
hitting you with a baseball bat," he continued. "That's really what it is,
with the helmets and the pads. The way that our equipment has improved
over the years, guys are getting less and less scared of contact." He
paused, unhappy with the analogy. "It's hard to describe, because there's
nothing else like it. Um, I'm trying to think. I'm sure there are things—like,
if you fall off a ladder, that's probably what it would feel like. Or get in a
car accident."

Barber is thirty-one, and several weeks earlier he had revealed that he   4
planned to retire at the end of the season, his tenth. He was already, by a
large measure, the most accomplished offensive player in the history of the
Giants. He was also, at the moment, second in his conference in rushing,
and had amassed more total yards in the preceding three seasons than any
player in the league. He was quitting at the top of his game. When the news
broke, David Letterman invited Barber on his show, and, speaking on behalf
of puzzled Giants fan—football fans—everywhere, he said, "Before we get to
this supposed retirement . . . are you really going to retire?"

Barber felt that he'd been fortunate to last as long as he had without   5
suffering any injuries that would be considered major by football standards.
(A fractured ulna in his left arm, late in the 2000 season, did not prevent
him from playing in the playoffs.) An N.F.L. career usually lasts about three
or four years. Running backs, who take more hard hits than players at any
other position—as many as two dozen a game, and often from multiple

bodies, and multiple angles, simultaneously—typically fare less well. On average, their bodies give out, or they're unceremoniously cut, after just two and a half years.

"You see this big-ass scar?" Barber said, pulling the leg of his sweats up and exposing a six-inch seam across his left kneecap. "I got that from riding my bike when I was twelve. And it's funny, because at the N.F.L. Combine they go over us with a fine-tooth comb, like they're inspecting a precious piece of equipment. They would see this scar and they would think I had surgery."   6

He almost had surgery once, during his rookie season, when he tore the posterior cruciate ligament, or P.C.L., in his right knee. ("That didn't hurt—it just felt weird.") One of the team doctors recommended an operation, but Barber consulted a number of veterans, and many of them advised against it: surgery, they said, only begets more surgeries; better not to start so soon. (Jim Otto, a center with the Oakland Raiders in the nineteen-sixties and seventies, has had forty-eight knee operations.) Barber built up the surrounding muscles to compensate for the damaged ligament, but he still can't lock his right knee, and standing up straight wears him out. His natural stance involves crossing his right leg in front of his left, and placing his hands on his hips for balance, like a catalogue model.   7

Barry Word, a former Kansas City Chiefs running back, recently sent Barber an e-mail saying, "It gets worse." Word, who is forty-two, played only six seasons and retired in 1994. "My knees, my feet, my shoulders, my wrist—I ache," he told me. "Sometimes I have a difficult time walking." Like nearly forty percent of all retired football players, he has degenerative arthritis.   8

"The short-term zeal and passion that comes from being an athlete, it's immeasurable," Barber said, with only halfhearted conviction. "Sure, you're mortgaging your future health to do it, but I think most guys will tell you it was worth it. And I'm not talking monetarily—because for a lot of those old guys it certainly wasn't worth it monetarily—but I think just the chance to be a hero. Football is America's game. Everybody says baseball is. But, nah, football is. Football defines a day of the week for six months of the year."   9

RESPONDING TO READING

Now that you have read the selection, write a paragraph describing what kind of person you think Tiki Barber is and how he feels about playing football. In another paragraph, note any ways in which he is different from what you expected of a professional football player.

CONSIDERING CONTENT

1. Why is Tuesday a professional football player's day off? What does he do the rest of the week?
2. Why is Barber's decision to quit puzzling to the fans (para. 4)? How does he explain it? Do you understand why he's quitting?
3. Why didn't Barber have surgery? What did he do instead?
4. Barber refers to the "N. F. L. Combine," which he says goes over the players with a fine-tooth comb. What does he mean by calling it a Combine?
5. Do you agree with Barber's comments in paragraph 9? Do you think most players would agree that playing pro football is worth the health risks?

CONSIDERING METHOD

1. Do you know who Tiki Barber is? Does the author assume that you do?
2. Why does McGrath include the details about Barber's son and his play-date? What contrast do these details provide, and what does that contrast contribute to your understanding of Barber's condition?
3. Look at the physical description of Barber. How many traits does the author describe? Which senses does he involve? Why is description such an important part of this article?
4. The author names the injury that Barber had as a rookie—a tear to "the posterior cruciate ligament, or P.C.L, in his right knee"—but doesn't give any description. Why not? Has he given you enough information?
5. Why does McGrath include the information about the other N. F. L. players, Jim Otto and Barry Word?

COMBINING STRATEGIES

McGrath employs several strategies in writing about Tiki Barber's decision to quit football. The author combines description with illustrations and examples (see Chapter 4) and cause-and-effect analysis (see Chapter 9). Choose one description and one example and explain how each appeals to your emotions and to your understanding of Barber's situation.

WRITING STEP BY STEP: QUITTING A JOB

Did you ever quit a job or give up an activity because it was too painful, stressful, difficult, or unhealthy? If so, write an essay describing the conditions that led you to walk away. Use specific details that will let your readers share your experience.

A. Begin by giving your readers some background about the job or activity. Where did this happen? When did you start? How long did you continue?

B. At the end of your introduction, let your readers know that you will be explaining why you quit the job or activity.

C. Next, tell why you took the job or began the activity in the first place. What benefits and positive outcomes did it seem to offer? Did other people influence you?

D. Then describe what happened to change our mind. Were there a number of troublesome incidents or annoying details that drove you to distraction? Was there a single event or occurrence that sealed the deal for you? This section will probably take several paragraphs. You may want to jot down a list of points to help you organize this part of your essay.

E. Include the comments and experiences of fellow workers/participants, if they help to explain your decision. You can even quote these people directly (as McGrath did in para. 8).

F. Is there anything that could have made you stay or might make you come back? If so, write a paragraph that describes the changes that would improve conditions and keep people from quitting.

G. Write a closing that sums up how you feel now about your decision to quit. Do you regret what you did? Would you do it again?

OTHER WRITING IDEAS

1. Write about a job or activity that turned out to be better than you expected. Perhaps it was a job you were forced to take or a team you were pressured to join, but you then discovered that it was fun and rewarding. You can use several of the strategies outlined in the Step-by-Step writing above.

2. COLLABORATIVE WRITING. Get together with classmates or friends and trade stories about the most stressful vacation you ever took (or the most stressful picnic or wedding or trip to the zoo or any activity that you would expect to be pleasurable but wasn't). Then help one another write individual accounts of a disappointing experience.

3. USING THE INTERNET. The long-term consequences of concussions and head injuries in sports, particularly in football, have become the focus of recent public discussion. Use the Internet to find out what the potential problems are, and for an audience of high school athletes, summarize the main concerns. You can find a list of pertinent articles at **www.suite101 .com/reference/football_players_and_concussions**.

4. WRITING ABOUT READING. Writers use concrete descriptions and examples to make abstract feelings easier to understand. What feelings

does McGrath convey with his use of descriptive details and specific instances? Identify five or six and evaluate their effectiveness. What feelings did they suggest to you?

GAINING WORD POWER

Since the brief definitions in the Terms to Recognize list are sometimes limited or incomplete, look up the following words in a college-size dictionary:

tolerance   perpetual   analogy   unceremoniously   degenerative

Now use these words to fill in the blanks in the following sentences:

1. Dr. March drew an _____ between the movement of light and the movement of water.
2. A _____ disease involves the gradual deterioration in the function or structure of tissues or organs.
3. The _____ noise of the idling semis keeps some of the motel guests awake.
4. Many older people have a limited _____ of cold.
5. The usher grabbed my arm and hauled me _____ to my feet.

EDITING SKILLS: QUOTATION MARKS INSIDE QUOTATIONS

Once in a while, when you have enclosed conversation or quoted material in quotation marks, you may need quotation marks around something within the passage. You can't use regular quotation marks inside quotation marks because your reader would never be able to tell what ended where. So inside regular double quotation marks, you use single quotation marks around any words that also need quotation marks.

Notice that in his second paragraph, McGrath quotes Tiki Barber at length, and within that quotation Barber verbalizes what a player might say to himself after taking a hard hit:

"It looks routine. But you'll get up and you'll say, 'God, I feel like my ribs are broken.' And that's how it was for me this week against Dallas."

Here is a similar example from the same paragraph, this time of Barber quoting himself:

"We're in the red zone and I take a shot in my side: 'Ughh—that's going to kill me tomorrow.' And I knew it."

On your keyboard, you may have an opening single quotation mark. Check the keys beside the numbers at the top. The closing mark is one you use all the time: the apostrophe. It can also serve as the left-hand quotation mark if you don't have a special key for an opening mark.

Here are some other uses of quotation marks, including some instances where single marks are used inside double ones:

1. To enclose words used as words:

> It's all right to begin a sentence with "and" as long as you don't do it too often.

(You can use italics or underlining to indicate words used as words, if you prefer.)

2. To enclose titles of short works—short stories, poems, essays, chapters of books, or song titles:

> Edgar Allan Poe's story "The Pit and the Pendulum"
>
> Robert Frost's poem "The Road Not Taken"
>
> Richard Selzer's essay "The Discus Thrower"
>
> Bob Dylan's song "Mr. Tambourine Man"

But underline or put in italics the titles of longer, separately published works:

> Alice Walker's novel <u>The</u> <u>Color</u> <u>Purple</u>
>
> Arthur Miller's play <u>Death</u> <u>of</u> <u>a</u> <u>Salesman</u>
>
> Steven Spielberg's movie *Jurassic Park*
>
> Georges Bizet's opera *Carmen*

3. To enclose quoted material within a quotation:

> "What did your instructor do when you didn't turn in your term paper?"
>
> "I went into her office with my paper in my hand, and she said, 'I hope you just got out of the hospital; otherwise, you just failed the course.'"

EXERCISE

In the following sentences, insert regular quotation marks and single quotation marks where needed. You may use italics in some cases if you prefer.

1. Proofread carefully to be sure you have not confused its and it's.
2. Reggie said to me, You be there on time or I'm leaving without you, Squirt.
3. Then I said to Reggie, You call me Squirt again and I'm not going anywhere with you ever again!

4. Serena wrote an analysis of Sandra Cisneros's short story Woman Hollering Creek.
5. I liked this poem, Kesha observed, but when Frost says The woods are lovely, dark, and deep, what does deep mean?

Now go through your writing for this class (your essays and your journal entries), and see whether you've been using quotation marks correctly. Then make up a sentence of your own using single quotation marks inside regular quotation marks.

🌐 **WEB SITE**

www.nj.com/sports/njsports/index.ssf/2010/02/as_is_football_is
_far_too_dang.html
In his blog, reporter Sid Dorfman claims that "As is, football is far too dangerous to play." Read his article to see if you agree.

PREPARING TO READ

Think of the last time you were personally, emotionally affected by something that happened outside your own country or community. What was the experience or news that touched you? How did you react? Do you know why this particular happening moved you emotionally?

••

Road Work

••

STAFF SERGEANT JACK LEWIS

The following selection appeared in the anthology Operation Homecoming: Iraq, Afghanistan, and the Home Front, in the Words of U.S. Troops and Their Families *(2006). This collection of eyewitness accounts, private journals, short stories, letters, and other writings grew out of a series of workshops sponsored by the National Endowment for the Arts and conducted by a group of distinguished American writers.*

TERMS TO RECOGNIZE

monstrous (*para. 1*)	exceptionally large, enormous
hypnotically (*para. 8*)	in a sing-song, trancelike way
dervish (*para. 10*)	member of a Moslem sect that engages in a whirling dance to bring about a mystic trance
capered (*para. 15*)	leaped or jumped around
superficially (*para. 15*)	not seriously, on the surface
animated (*para. 15*)	active, energized
sedate (*para. 30*)	administer a calming drug
Gauloise (*para. 33*)	a French brand of cigarette, made with dark tobacco from the Middle East
IEDs (*para. 37*)	improvised explosive devices

Iraqi civilians are not only caught in the crossfire when hostilities erupt between American troops and insurgents, they are the victims of military-related accidents as well. In February 2005, forty-one-year-old U. S. Army Reserve Staff Sergeant Jack Lewis witnessed the aftermath of a late-night crash involving a nineteen-ton Stryker armored vehicle (call sign "Rattlesnake Six-Seven") and a small car. While Lewis had seen shocking acts of violence and bloodshed during his deployment with Tactical Psychological Operations Detachment 1290, 1-25 SBCT (Stryker Brigade Combat Team), nothing had struck him as hard emotionally as the suffering caused by this collision.

—Editors, *Operation Homecoming*

I never heard the boom-CRUNCH, only imagined it later. There was 1
strong braking, followed by a great deal of shouting. Our Stryker moaned
through its monstrous air brakes and then bumped, heaved, and finally
ground itself to a halt.

"Six-Seven's in the ditch!" 2

"Did they roll it?" 3

"No, they're up. I think they're disabled." 4

"Where's the colonel? Is the colonel's vehicle okay?" 5

The colonel's vehicle was okay. 6

The major said that we would need a combat lifesaver. It wasn't com- 7
bat. There were no lives left to save. But I dug out the CLS bag, because you
never know, do you? And walked across a pitch dark highway.

Somebody was wailing in Arabic, hypnotically, repetitiously. 8

A single car headlight was burning, a single shaft of light beaming 9
across the road like an accusing finger. When tactical spotlights suddenly
illuminated the little car, we found the source of the wailing.

He was an older man with a silver beard, a monumental, red-veined 10
nose, and a big, thick wool overcoat. He was hopping like a dervish, bowing
rapidly from the waist and throwing his arms to the sky, then to his knees,
over and over again in a kind of elaborate dance of grief.

Down the road a hundred meters or so, Six-Seven's vehicle comman- 11
der and air guards had dismounted and were standing around in the ditch.
Nobody had started smoking yet.

I walked to the car with an Air Force sergeant and moved the older 12
man aside as gently as possible. He was built like a blacksmith, powerful
through the neck and shoulders.

It's hard to describe what we found in the car. It had been a young 13
man, only moments earlier that night. A cop or a fireman or a soldier would
have simply said, "It's a mess in there." I used to be a fireman. I'm a soldier
now. It was as bad a mess as I've seen.

I'm not a medic. We didn't have one with us. It's still my responsibil- 14
ity to preserve life. So I squeezed into the crumpled passenger area, sat on
the shattered glass, and tried to take the pulse from his passenger-side arm
(nothing) and his neck (nothing). I thought about CPR, but only for a
moment. His left arm was mostly torn off, and the left side of his head
was flattened.

Up on the highway, CIs walked around, gave and took orders. By the 15
car, the victim's father still capered madly, throwing his arms around, crying
out to God or anyone. I asked him, in my own language, to come with me,
to calm down, to let me help him. I put my arm around him and guided the
old Arab to the road. I sat him on the cold ramp of our Stryker and tried to

assess his injuries. It seemed impossible that he could be only as superficially scratched up as he appeared. His hand was injured, bruised or possibly broken, and he had a cut on his left ear. I wrapped a head bandage onto him and tied it gently in back. It looked like a traditional headdress with a missing top. Every few seconds he would get animated, and I would put my hand firmly on his shoulder. He would not hold still long enough for me to splint his arm.

"Why can't he shut up?"   16

"You ever lose a kid?" This is a pointless question to ask a soldier   17
who's practically a kid himself.

We moved him into the Stryker, assuring him that no, we weren't   18
arresting him. But he didn't care. Whenever he started to calm down, he
would look toward the car and break into wails. I sat next to him, put my
arm around his shoulder, tried to keep him from jumping around enough to
hurt himself or a soldier. I held him tightly with my right arm. By the next
morning, my shoulder would be on fire.

Forty minutes later a medic arrived.   19

"What's his status, sergeant?"   20

"He has a cut on his left earlobe. I think his hand is broken." (I think   21
his heart is broken.)

"Roger. Okay, I got this."   22

"Thanks." (Bless you for what you do every day, doc.)   23

I got out of the way, letting the old guy go for the first time in   24
almost an hour. He started wailing again almost immediately. While the
medic worked on him, the colonel's interpreter came over and fired a few
questions at the man. It sounded like an interrogation.

They had been on their way back to Sinjar, just a few miles away. The   25
younger man had been taking his father back from shopping. They were
minutes from home.

We didn't find any weapons in the car—either piece of it. There was   26
no propaganda, nor were there false IDs. If we had stopped these people at
a checkpoint, we would have thanked them and let them go on.

The young man had been a student. Engineering. With honors.   27
Pride of the family. What we like to think of as Iraq's future.

Finally, I had to ask, "What does he keep saying?"   28

The terp looked at me, disgusted, resigned, or maybe just plain tired.   29
"He says to kill him now."

The colonel came over and asked the medic if he could sedate the   30
man with morphine.

"No, sir. Morphine won't help."   31

"Well, can't you give him something to calm him down? I mean, this   32
is unacceptable."

I walked away and lit a Gauloise. A sergeant came up next to me,   33
smoking. I didn't say anything. After a few moments in the black quiet, I
overheard him say, "It wasn't anyone's fault. It was just an accident."

"I know." Inhale. Cherry glow. Long exhale. "Why we gotta drive in   34
blackout—here—I don't get."

"If Six-Seven had turned their lights on a couple of seconds   35
earlier . . . ."

"Yeah. I know." And he went to help carry the young man's remains   36
into the sudden light show of ambulances and police jeeps, surrounded by
young Arabic men with steely eyes.

The supersized staff sergeant who mans the .50 cal on our truck   37
walked down the road to kick a little ass and get Six-Seven's recovery
progress back on track. Within a few minutes, they had it hooked up. It
would be two weeks before that Stryker would roll outside the wire again,
this in an environment where trucks totaled by IEDs are welded back
together and sent again into harm's way in mere hours.

I went and sat on the back gate of the Stryker. I felt the cold creep   38
into me.

The old man sat next to me, perhaps too tired to continue his tirade   39
against cruel Fate, careless Americans, war and its accidents.

I haven't lost a full-grown son, just a little daughter. A baby. And she   40
wasn't torn from me in a terror of rending steel, stamped out by a sudden
monster roaring out of the night. She went so quietly that her passing
never woke her mother. I like to think she kissed her on the way out, on
her way home.

But still, sitting on the steel tail of the monster that killed his son, I   41
think I knew exactly how one Iraqi man felt.

"Just kill me now."   42

We sat and looked straight into the lights.   43

RESPONDING TO READING

Were you surprised at the author's reactions to this event? What caused his
strong emotional response to the father's grief? How do you think you would
have reacted? Explain.

CONSIDERING CONTENT

1. Why do you think Sgt. Lewis wanted to tell this story? For whom was he writing? Do you think you're part of the audience Lewis had in mind?

2. What do you learn about the Iraqis? What is the point of saying they didn't have any weapons, propaganda, or false IDs (para. 26)?

3. Why does the author include the details about the young man who was killed? What does he mean when he says, "What we like to think of as Iraq's future" (para. 27)?

4. What do you discover about the author's personal life? How does this information shape your understanding of the story?

5. What kind of person is Sgt. Lewis? Do you think you would like to meet him?

CONSIDERING METHOD

1. Take note of the verbs that Lewis uses in the second sentence of the opening paragraph of his narrative: *moaned, bumped, heaved,* and *ground to a halt.* What sights and sounds do these verbs convey?

2. Why does the author enclose two comments in parentheses (paras. 21 and 23)?

3. What do you make of the comments of the others on the scene (the young soldier, the medic, the colonel, the staff sergeant)? How do their reactions and attitudes compare to Lewis's?

4. In what ways does the author use dialogue (or spoken conversation) to advance the narrative? Is it effective?

5. Reread paragraph 36 with attention to the descriptive language. Find another paragraph that uses vivid description and point out specific words that bring the scene to life.

6. Consider the last two lines in the narrative. How do they make you feel? Why do you think the author ended his narrative in this way?

WRITING STEP BY STEP: BEING HELPFUL

Write an essay in which you tell the story of how you helped another person and realized that you benefited as well. Brainstorm a list of situations and choose the best example to write about. Remember that your own story doesn't have to be solemn: it could be humorous, or you could have been unsuccessful in your efforts.

A. Set the stage for your story in the opening paragraph by describing where you were when you encountered the challenge, problem, disagreement, or conflict that you helped with.

B. Then briefly explain the events that gave rise to the situation, including just enough background details to let your readers understand how the trouble arose.

C. Next, describe the person (or people) you helped. Use concrete details, as Lewis does in telling us about the Iraqi father.

D. Identify other people who played a part in this story. Use dialogue, as Lewis does, to give your readers a sense of how these other people felt and reacted.

E. Explain what you did to help the person in trouble (as Lewis does in paras. 15 and 18).

F. Mention any obstacles or difficulties you encountered in trying to help out.

G. End on a note of reflection: Explain how you felt about your actions and how you benefited from helping someone else. You could also conclude with a thesis statement about the value of helping others.

OTHER WRITING IDEAS

1. Narrate an event in which you hid your true feelings about what took place. Some possibilities: a going-away party for someone you disliked, a weekend trip you didn't want to take, an interview for a low-paying job, a blind date, a conversation in which you held a minority opinion, an ex-girl/boyfriend's wedding. Make it clear why you didn't show your true feelings and how you felt about keeping them hidden.

2. COLLABORATIVE WRITING. Discuss with a group of friends or class-mates whether the old saying "There is no education like adversity" is true. After you decide how you feel about the matter, think of an incident that illustrates your belief and use it to make your point in a narrative.

3. USING THE INTERNET. "Road Work" is included in the book *Operation Homecoming*, an anthology of eyewitness accounts, private journals, short stories, and other writings by U.S. military personnel stationed in Iraq and Afghanistan. The Public Broadcasting System featured the project in its "America at the Crossroads" series. Visit the PBS Web site at **www .pbs.org/weta/crossroads/about/show_operation_homecoming _writings.html** to read other essays and stories written by troops about their wartime experiences. Choose one selection and write a summary of what you read and explain how you reacted to the story.

4. WRITING ABOUT READING. Near the end of his essay Lewis says, "I think I knew exactly how one Iraqi man felt." Do you think he really did? Write an essay explaining what Lewis meant by this comment and analyzing why he was able to empathize with the Iraqi father.

GAINING WORD POWER

Lewis uses several striking *similes* to enhance his descriptions:

> a single shaft of light beaming across the road like an accusing finger
>
> hopping like a dervish
>
> built like a blacksmith

Similes use *like* or *as* to compare things that are usually not seen as similar. A simile catches the reader's attention by pointing out a resemblance that is surprising or imaginative.

EXERCISE

Come up with a simile to describe each of these scenes or qualities and use it in a sentence. If you can, add another sentence or two to extend and explain the comparison.

> *Example*: a person's personality
> My roommate is like an empty candy wrapper. At first you think he's full of
> personality, but then you find out there's nothing there.

1. The sound of a school cafeteria
2. People waiting in a long line at a supermarket or bank
3. The effect of eating a big meal
4. Driving in a heavy downpour
5. The feeling of meeting someone's parents for the first time

Now look through the essay you have just written and see if you can improve the descriptions by adding a simile or two.

EDITING SKILLS: CHOOSING *THERE, THEIR,* OR *THEY'RE*

Words that sound alike, called **homophones,** can be treacherous. In speech, we don't think about which one to select, but in writing we have to make a choice. Because homophones are often common words, such as *there, their,* and *they're,* we can't avoid using them. And because the meanings are quite different, we really do have to get them right or our readers will be confused.

First, look at the use of the word *there* in these sentences from "Road Work":

There was strong braking, followed by a great deal of shouting. *There* were no lives left to save.

In these sentences *there* is just a fill-in word; it doesn't have much meaning. We use *there* to begin sentences like these when we want to say that something or someone exists or existed. The same spelling goes for the use of the word to indicate a place:

It's a mess in *there*.

Now look at the use of *their* in these passages from the same essay:

They had been on *their* way back to Sinjar, just a few miles away.

If Six-Seven had turned *their* lights on a couple of seconds earlier . . .

The word *their* is a possessive, showing ownership or belonging. In the first example it refers to "they" (the Iraqi man and his son); in the second example, it refers to the men in "Six-Seven" (the armored vehicle).

Finally, take a look at this sentence:

No, *they're* up. I think *they're* disabled.

In these examples, *they're* sounds just like the others, but you can substitute the words *they are* for it. *They're* is a contraction, just like *don't* for *do not* and *she's* for *she is*. If you can substitute *they are*, you know you have the right word. If you can't, you need *there* or *their*.

All right, let's review:

There are numerous sound-alike words in English.

You have to know the differences in *their* meanings if you want to use them correctly.

They're often common words that we use a lot.

EXERCISE

Fill the blanks in the following sentences with *there*, *their*, or *they're*.

1. _____ are no solutions to this problem.
2. Your cousins have arrived, and _____ going to stay for dinner.
3. When George Eliot and Jane Austen wrote _____ great novels, _____ were few creative opportunities for women besides writing.

4. The team members should have known that _____ luck wouldn't hold. But _____ definitely looking forward to next season.

5. Although it wasn't _____ fault, the twins are sure to get blamed, and _____ not happy about it.

Look over the essay you have just written to see if you used *there*, *their*, or *they're*. Did you choose the right one? Go over some past papers, too, to see how accurate you are in using these three homophones. Copy three to five sentences in which you use one and justify your choice in each case. (For more about homophones, see Chapter 4, p. 96.).

13

☙ WEB SITE

www.afsc.org/Iraq/ht/display/ContentDetails/i/19235
Maintained by the American Friends Service Committee, this site focuses on the civilian side of the war in Iraq by posting personal stories of Iraqis and Iraqi refugees.

STUDENT ESSAY USING DESCRIPTION AND NARRATION

Domestic Abuse

Kelly Berlin

*Kelly Berlin grew up in a farming community in east central Illinois. She attended
Eastern Illinois University, where she wrote this essay for her freshman composition class.
At that time she was planning to major in business.*

It was the summer of my freshman year, and I had been baby-sitting   1
my two-year-old niece, Briana, at my sister's house every weekday for the
past couple of months. It was late in the afternoon on a Friday, so I couldn't
wait for my sister Kim to come home from work. Since she was already a
half an hour late, I decided to take a shower so I wouldn't be late for my date
later that evening. I was in the bathroom blow-drying my hair when my sister
and her boyfriend Scott came home.

My sister and Scott had been dating a couple of years, despite the   2
disapproval of my family. Scott, even though he had a child, was not a good
"father figure" for my niece. Scott was a regular drinker and smoker, and his
appearance did nothing for him. He was over six feet tall with big, bulging
muscles; he wore tight clothes; and he had long, shaggy hair. My sister, on
the other hand, standing only five-feet-five-inches tall, was slender with
long, curly brown hair and a beautiful white smile.

I finished blow-drying my hair and was going to ask my sister to take   3
me home, but I heard her and Scott fighting in the bedroom. I went into the
living room to watch television with my niece and to keep her mind off the
shouting. I started to become worried because the yelling became more
intense. All of a sudden, I heard a loud noise—not a boom, but more like a
crack, a board breaking. The shouting stopped.

"Briana, stay here!" I left my niece in the living room and ran into the   4
bedroom. "Scott, what in the hell did you do to her? Get away from her!"
My sister was lying limp on her bed with her face down.

"It's none of your business. Get out of here," he yelled at me with a   5
fierce look in his eyes.

I was shaking but yelled back at him with just as much determination   6
and strength. "Bullshit, if it's not my business. She's my sister. Don't think
I'm just going to sit here while you push her around!" I turned, looked at my
sister, and asked gently, "Kim, are you all right?"

"Yeah," Kim told me in a shaky voice. "I'll be all right. But my legs   7
hurt because I hit the foot board when he pushed me down."

"Scott, leave NOW!" I said with all the authority I could manage.   8

"Shut up, Kelly. This isn't your house, and I'll leave whenever   9
I please."

My sister pleaded with him. "Scott, please leave me alone. Just leave   10
me alone."

He stormed out of the bedroom and out of the house like a raging bull.   11
I helped my sister sit up and looked at her legs. She had two long, wide bruises
forming across her upper thighs from where they hit the foot board. I told her
to stay on her bed while I checked on Briana and called my mom for help.

My mom arrived about ten minutes later, and I told her what had   12
happened. She was furious and was determined to do something about it.
We called the police to report the incident and file charges. When the police
arrived at the house, I described the scene and signed my name to the
papers to file charges. Then, they took photographs of my sister's bruises
and recorded her statement. But she wouldn't sign the papers. She had
decided not to press charges. Well, I was confused, but I thought I could
still press charges against him. I was wrong. I hadn't actually seen Scott
push my sister. I had only heard them fighting and had found her lying on
the bed. We tried to convince my sister to press charges against Scott,
but she refused. She believed that he'd just gotten carried away, that he
wouldn't do it again. We tried to make her realize that he could very
well do it again, but she wouldn't believe us.

As it turned out, my sister was mistaken. Scott continued to beat her
and control her life, and she continued to refuse to press charges. Finally, she
realized he was not going to stop, so she left Scott. At one time, she put a
restraining order on him, which kept him away temporarily. And fortunately,   13
he lost his license due to DUIs, so he had no legal transportation to get to her
house. Now, the only time he harasses her is when he's high on drugs. But as
time and experience have taught my sister, she now calls the police herself.

CONSIDERING CONTENT AND METHOD

1. Do you think the topic is well chosen? Is the focus narrow enough?
2. What descriptive details does the writer include? Do you think they are
   effective? If so, why? If not, why not?
3. Do you like Kelly's use of direct conversation in telling the story? What
   does it add to the account?
4. What is the point of this narrative essay? Does the writer state it directly
   or merely imply it? If it is stated directly, tell where.
5. What suggestions would you make to the author to improve this essay?

Strategies for Making a Point:
Example and *Illustration*

Source: Ken Karp\Pearson Education/PH College

For Discussion and Writing

What qualities of the father and daughter relationship are illustrated by this photograph? Make a list of three or four qualities that best define your relationship with one of your parents and provide several examples of memories or experiences that illustrate each of those qualities. Then write a paragraph or two in which you describe the relationship with this parent, using the examples to make your description clear and convincing.

There's an old saying that a picture is worth a thousand words. It may be true. But we can't always communicate with pictures. Most of the time we have to convey our ideas with words—often with written words. You will find that your skills in describing and narrating can be put to good use in providing examples and illustrations to make a point.

Did you ever read a passage that seemed hard to get the meaning of—that remained fuzzy in your mind no matter how many times you plowed through it? Here's an example of the kind of writing we mean:

> A democratic plan of education includes more than the mere transmission of the social heritage and an attempt to reproduce existing institutions in a static form. The democratic school is also required to indoctrinate individuals with the democratic tradition which, in turn, is based on the agitative liberties of the individual and the needs of society.

If a person spoke those words to you, you could say, "What was that again?" or "Could you give me an example, please?" or "What do you mean by *agitative liberties*?" But you can't question the written page, so the meaning of whatever that writer had in mind is lost.

The difference between an **illustration** and an **example** is not clear cut. Some people use the terms to mean the same thing; some people use illustration to mean several short examples or a fairly long example, such as a brief narrative used within an essay. We don't think it makes a whole lot of difference what you call them—just be sure to use them.

THE POINT OF EXAMPLE AND ILLUSTRATION

Good writers use examples or illustrations to make their writing clear and to make it convincing. As a bonus, concrete examples make writing interesting.

Using Examples to Explain and Clarify

The paragraph about democratic education shows how vague writing is that uses only general statements. Here's another illustration to let you see how examples help in explaining ideas. We have deliberately taken the examples out of the following paragraph. See how much you can get out of it:

> You should define what you mean when any abstract, ambiguous, or controversial terms figure importantly in your writing. Serious miscommunications can occur when audience and writer do not share the same idea about what a word or phrase means, either *connotatively* or *denotatively*.

That's not too clear, is it? But read it now with the examples that were included in the original:

> You should define what you mean when any abstract, ambiguous, or controversial terms figure importantly in your writing. Serious miscommunications can occur when audience and writer do not share the same idea about what a word or phrase means, either *connotatively* (by its associations) or *denotatively* (by its direct meaning). Consider, for instance, the connotations of these words: *daddy, father, old man.* All denote *male parent,* but their understood meanings are quite different. Also, the phrase *good writing* seems clear, doesn't it? Yet three English teachers can argue endlessly about what constitutes good writing if teacher A thinks that good writing is honest, direct, and completely clear; if teacher B thinks that good writing is serious, formal, and absolutely correct; and if teacher C thinks that good writing is flashy, spirited, and highly entertaining.

Several of the examples in that paragraph are definitions; the others explain the need for definitions. All the examples add clarity and meaning to the passage.

Using Examples and Illustrations to Convince

Examples and illustrations are essential in making a point—that is, as evidence to convince your readers that what you say is right. Take a look at this passage from an article about marriage laws and customs in the nineteenth century:

> Lawmakers passed a hodgepodge of bills setting the terms of the marriage contract. Before Americans could marry, they had to ask the government's permission. Thirty states prohibited people with physical or mental disabilities—epileptics or the "feebleminded, idiotic, imbecilic, or insane"—from marrying. (In many states, women over 45 were exempted from this rule.) Four states disqualified paupers or inmates in public institutions for the indigent. Washington and North Dakota didn't issue marriage licenses to people suffering from advanced tuberculosis. Most states banned interracial marriage; white citizens of Florida could not marry anyone of "one-eighth or more Negro blood." California's white residents couldn't legally marry "a Negro, mulatto, Mongolian, or member of the Malay race."

> —*Wall Street Journal*, 25 Feb. 2004

The general claims in the first two sentences are backed up with a series of specific examples.

If you want to convince readers that they should run out and rent *Batman Forever,* you have to provide examples to explain why. You will need to discuss the thrill-packed plot, the wonderful gizmos and toys (including a Batmobile that climbs walls), the deadpan jokes, the uproarious physical humor of Jim Carrey, and Chris O'Donnell's spirited performance as Robin. The more illustrations of this sort you can provide, the more persuasive your essay will be.

THE PRINCIPLES OF EXAMPLE AND ILLUSTRATION

The success of a piece of writing often depends on how well you choose your supporting evidence.

Select Appropriate Examples

You must be sure, first of all, that the examples actually do illustrate the point you want to make. If, for instance, you are explaining how you feel about people who borrow a book and then write their own comments in the margins, be sure to focus on your feelings—of interest, outrage, violation, loss, or whatever you felt. Do not slide off the subject to discuss the interesting philosophy course you bought the book for and the time you accidentally left the book on a lunchroom counter and were quite sure you had lost it forever only to have the guy who sat behind you in class return it, saying he found it when he happened to stop in for a late lunch in the same greasy spoon that afternoon. When people do that sort of free associating in conversation, we tend to suffer through it, even as our eyes glaze over. But it will not do in writing.

Give Plenty of Examples

Keep in mind, though, that you need to supply enough examples to make your ideas clear and convincing. Say you want to persuade your readers that becoming a vegetarian is the key to a long life in a healthy body. If you offer only the single illustration of your uncle Seymour who never ate meat, never had a cold, always felt frisky, and ran in the Boston Marathon to celebrate his seventy-ninth birthday, you are not likely to sway many readers. They'll just think, "Well, wasn't he lucky?" You need either to dig up more examples—perhaps even some statistics about low-fat diets and heart disease—or else change your thesis to focus on Uncle Seymour's personal recipe for keeping fit. There's nothing wrong with using one long illustration, if that single illustration really does prove your point.

Include Specific Information

Finally, you need to develop your examples and illustrations with plenty of specific, graphic details. If you say that riding motorcycles is dangerous, you need to follow up with examples more specific than "Every year many people are injured in motorcycle accidents" and "The person on the motorcycle can't always tell what motorists are going to do." Instead, describe what happens when an automobile unexpectedly turns left in front of a motorcyclist traveling 40 miles an hour. Mention the crushed noses, the dislocated limbs, the fractured femurs, the broken teeth, and the shattered skulls that such accidents cause. As a general rule, if you use an **abstract word,** like *dangerous,* follow it soon with a specific example, like "His splintered kneecap never did heal properly."

THE PITFALLS OF EXAMPLE AND ILLUSTRATION

If you are writing an essay developed almost entirely through the use of examples, you need to make sure those examples are connected smoothly when you furnish several in a row. Notice how the italicized **transitions** introduce the examples in this paragraph defining a psychological term:

> People who use reaction formation avoid facing an unpleasant truth by acting exactly opposite from the way they truly feel. *For example,* you may have known somebody who acts like the life of the party, always laughing and making jokes, but who you suspect is trying to fool everybody—including herself—into missing the fact that she is sad and lonely. *Another example* of reaction formation involves the person who goes overboard to be open-minded, insisting, "I'm not prejudiced! Why some of my best friends are _____!"
>
> —Ronald Adler and Neil Towne, "Defense Mechanisms"

Here are some other transitional expressions that you may find useful:

such as	that is	in the following way
namely	in this case	as an illustration
for instance	in addition	at the same time

It's quite possible to use too many transitions. Ask the friend or classmate who helps you edit your first draft to let you know if you've put in more than you need.

As you prepare to revise your essay, ask yourself (and your editorial helper) the following questions:

1. Does each of my examples really illustrate the point I'm trying to make?
2. Have I included enough examples to be convincing?
3. If I'm using a single illustration in some paragraphs, is that convincing?
4. Do any of my illustrations begin to prove the point and then stray from it?
5. Are any of my examples too short or my illustrations too long?
6. Have I used enough specific details?

WHAT TO LOOK FOR IN EXAMPLE AND ILLUSTRATION

As you study the essays in this chapter, focus on the way examples and illustrations are used.

1. In the paragraphs that have a **topic sentence** (the sentence that tells what the paragraph is about), look at the examples or illustrations and decide how convincing they are—that is, how well they explain, support, or enlarge on that idea.

2. Look for concrete, specific, sometimes visual details in the examples and illustrations themselves. Ask yourself what would be lost if these were omitted.

3. Underline the transitional terms used to introduce the examples and illustrations and keep a list of them in your journal.

PREPARING TO READ

List three people, living or dead, that you consider heroes, and write a sentence explaining why you think each is a hero.

....

My Heroes

....

ELIZABETH BERG

Elizabeth Berg worked as a registered nurse for 10 years before becoming a full-time writer, although she has written since she was a child. (She received her first rejection letter at age 9.) She has published a book a year since her first novel, Durable Goods, *in 1993, and many have become bestsellers.* Range of Motion *(1995) was made into a cable-TV movie with Rebecca deMornay in 2000. Berg's themes include the emotional effects of physical illness and "the power and salvation of female friendship." In 1999, Berg published a book of advice on the art and business of writing,* Escaping into the Open: The Art of Writing True.

TERMS TO RECOGNIZE

straight-laced (*para. 10*)	excessively strict
bowed (*para. 11*)	stooped or yielded in defeat
sophisticated (*para. 12*)	refined, worldly wise
intent (*para. 12*)	firmly focused
luxuriating (*para. 13*)	basking, enjoying
relinquish (*para. 15*)	give up, let out of one's control
precipitated (*para. 16*)	caused

My eight-year-old daughter, Jenny, was given a school assignment not 1
too long ago to write about a hero. "So who did you pick?" I asked her. I
was imagining some possibilities: Rosa Parks, Christa McAuliffe, Sara Lee.
But Jenny answered, "Laura."

"Who?" I asked. 2

"Laura," she said again. 3

"You mean your friend from across the street?" I asked. 4

"Yeah!" she said. 5

I was a little mystified. "How come you picked her?" I asked. 6
"Because," Jenny answered in the ultrapatient voice of Instructor to the
Hopeless, "she is my hero."

"Oh," I said. "I see."   7

I must confess that at first I was disappointed. I thought that if her   8
hero was only her friend, she had failed to appreciate the magnificent contributions that real heroes have made to the world. I thought I'd better go
out that afternoon and buy some books about famous scientists, artists,
athletes, world leaders. That would wise her up. Also, I'd have a look at
what they were teaching in her school—didn't she have an appreciation for
Martin Luther King?

But then I thought about who I would say my heroes are, and I real-   9
ized that if I told the truth, they wouldn't be famous, either. For although it
is undeniable that there have been outstanding people in history who have
set glorious examples and inspired me mightily, the people who inspire me
most tend to be those who touch me personally, and in quiet ways.

For example, I had an eighth-grade English teacher named Mrs. Zinz.   10
She was demanding and rather straight-laced, I thought, but she taught us
certain critical skills for reading and writing. She was concerned not only
with what we learned but also with what we were becoming: She put a pre-
mium on honesty and tried to get us to understand why it was important.
She insisted that we always do our best, and in her class, we almost always
did. She told me that I was a terrific creative writer and encouraged my
every effort.

As payment for all her good work, I, along with my evil best friend,   11
tortured her. We laughed at her in class, tried to pit our other teachers
against her by telling them how unfairly she graded, and once, in a moment
of extreme obnoxiousness, called her on the telephone over and over, only
to hang up when she answered. Mrs. Zinz was no dummy. She knew who
was calling her. In turn she called my mother, who insisted that I call Mrs.
Zinz and apologize. With my face aflame, and between clenched teeth, I
muttered a grossly insincere "Sorry." She accepted my apology warmly and
with a style so graceful that I was infuriated all the more. And though I
sulked every day in her class for the rest of the year, she never bowed by
reacting to it. I got an A for the term. I moved soon after that and lost track
of Mrs. Zinz. I never did apologize in any legitimate way to her. Ironically,
she is still an inspiration to me, a lesson in how not to lower yourself to
someone else's level, even when that person is doing everything she can to
make you crazy. She is, in that way, a hero.

My grandfather, known to me as "Papa," was also a hero of mine.   12
For one thing, he made all of us grandchildren laugh all of the time. He told
riddles that were viewed by us as the essence of sophisticated humor. When
he greeted us, he shook our hands enthusiastically and at great length,

shouting, "How do! How do!" We used to line up to sit on his lap and watch him pop his dentures in and out of his mouth, an astounding feat that thrilled and terrified us—especially before we realized that the teeth were false. He was unfailingly warm and kind and knew how to make a friend out of a stranger; he loved people. I saw him as a man who felt light inside, happy; and feeling that way is no small task in a world that often seems intent on taking back two for every one you get.

Then there is my mother-in-law, Sylvia, who at the age of retirement   13
went back to school to pursue a lifetime dream: getting a college diploma. She bumped her bifocals into microscopes, suffered verbal abuse at the hands of an insensitive computer instructor, got used to being the last one to finish every exam, and worried about homework on weekends when she could have been luxuriating in the fact that she had nothing to do. She says that she learned an awful lot, but if you ask me, it's she who did the teaching. I am honored that our family has her love of learning to inspire us.

Beyond that, there are people who are heroes to me because of what   14
they do: mail carriers, who, on days when I stay inside hiding from the cold or heat, subject themselves to hours of it; nurses, who care for those who can't care for themselves every second of every day. I admire stay-at-home mothers for their patience and their creativity in the face of almost no thanks or recognition, and working mothers for the way they juggle an awesome load of responsibilities.

There are people with chronic illness, for whom getting through each   15
day is heroic. There are people who have been married for sixty years, who have lessons to teach us all. There are those who are strong enough in heart and in spirit to speak up when something feels wrong to them, to go against the majority, and oftentimes to risk themselves for the sake of others. And then there are those whom I admire most of all: people who seem to have found the secret of calm and can relinquish the race for the pleasure of seeing what's around them, right here, right now.

I was thinking about all this when I saw Jenny and Laura come into   16
the house. I wanted to know a little more about what had precipitated Jenny's calling Laura a hero. Was it her sharing her brand-new toys? Being there to listen, to soothe, to make better a bad situation in the way that only good friends can? Well, as it happens, no. Jenny told me that Laura was her hero because Laura had saved her from drowning in a creek. "*What?*" I yelled.

Laura rolled her eyes. "Jenny, the water was only about an inch deep."   17
Jenny shrugged and said, "So? You still saved me."

Laura and I let pass a certain look between us. Then she and Jenny   18
went outside again to play.

If you're smart, I thought, you gratefully take your heroes where you   19
find them. As it happens, they are everywhere. So what if the water was only
an inch deep? Someone was there, caring about Jenny and showing that she
did, a safe hand stretched out to another who was in trouble. This seemed
heroic indeed, and later that night when I was tucking her in, I told Jenny
that I thought her choice was perfect. "I know," she yawned. "Good night."

RESPONDING TO READING

How did you define "hero" before reading Berg's essay? (For help, look at the
examples you gave in Preparing to Reading.) Did the Berg essay change your
idea of what a hero is? Why or why not?

CONSIDERING CONTENT

1. Identify the three names Berg imagines as possible heroes for her
   daughter in paragraph 1. Why are these women heroes? Why does Berg
   include Sara Lee?
2. Berg's essay revolves around the understanding of the word *hero* by the
   daughter, which eventually expands the mother's thinking about the
   concept. What is the mother considering a *hero* at the beginning of
   the story? How does she expand on the concept by the end?
3. What kind of mother is Elizabeth Berg? List the details that back up
   your answer.
4. Why did the author and her friend torture Mrs. Zinz when they were in
   eighth grade?
5. "If you're smart, I thought, you gratefully take your heroes where you
   find them" (para. 19). What does this mean? Why is taking your heroes
   where you find them *smart*?

CONSIDERING METHOD

1. What are the three specific examples of heroes given by Berg? What do
   they have in common? What groups of people does Berg consider heroic?
2. This essay first appeared in *Parents* magazine in 1992. Name several of the
   statements and ideas that would appeal to the audience of this magazine.
3. Find instances where Berg uses direct quotations and dialog. Think
   about how these sections could be rephrased without direct quotations.
   What effect does using exact spoken words have?
4. What is Jenny's response to her mother's compliment in the end? What
   parent-child dynamics are underlined? Why do you think Berg closed
   this way, instead of with a restatement of her concept of heroism?

5. Would you recommend this essay to a good friend? Explain why or why not.

WRITING STEP BY STEP: EVERYDAY HEROES

A. Think of two to four people in your life whom you could consider *heroes*, using Berg's concept. These could be people from your school, your home town, your ethnic subculture, your family, or your social group.

B. Introduce your essay by naming some famous or highly recognized people that you consider heroes. You can include people who are highly recognized mostly within their own field—for instance, a chess player or computer programmer or fashion designer. These people should not be personal acquaintances of yours.

C. Write a transition paragraph that highlights the difference between famous heroes and everyday heroes. Explain what makes someone an everyday hero for you.

D. Develop a paragraph or two about each of the people who are your examples of everyday heroes. Be sure to provide vivid details. Leave no doubt about why you admire each one.

E. In this development, include at least one brief narrative, as Berg does for Mrs. Zinz, Papa, and Sylvia. Consider using direct quotations.

F. Close your essay with an incident or an episode rather than a summary or restatement.

OTHER WRITING IDEAS

1. Berg writes about getting "a lesson in how not to lower yourself to someone else's level" (para. 11). Write an essay on this topic, including examples of situations in which people either did lower themselves to someone else's level or refused to do so. You might decide to give examples of both giving in and resisting.

2. COLLABORATIVE WRITING. Write a collaborative essay on the previous topic, with a team of three or four. Each person should contribute an example. Work as a group to put the examples into an essay, organizing them to work smoothly together and adding an introduction and a conclusion.

3. USING THE INTERNET. In paragraph 10, Berg writes about an English teacher who "insisted that we always do our best, and in her class, we almost always did." Berg endorses the idea that people, even children, tend to rise to the expectations that others hold. Write an essay giving examples (or one long illustration) of this tendency. For inspiration, read the material on *self-fulfilling prophecy* at **http://members.fortunecity .com/nadabs/prophecy.html**.

4. WRITING ABOUT READING. Write a summary of Berg's article. Your goal is to demonstrate that you have read and understood this selection. Review the guidelines for writing a summary given in Chapter 1, pp. 13–14.

GAINING WORD POWER

Sometimes little words can mean a lot. What, for instance, does the word *wise* mean in this sentence?

That would wise her up.

Get together with several of your classmates and see how many other meanings of the word *wise* the group can come up with. Then look it up in a dictionary. Did you think of most of them? What are the differences among the words *wise, intelligent, smart,* and *brainy*?

Now, think about the word *set*. See how many sentences the group can write using *set* with a different meaning in each one. Do at least five. Then check the dictionary to see how many meanings there are. Surprising, isn't it, how much meaning can be packed into such a simple little word?

EDITING SKILLS: SEMICOLONS BETWEEN SENTENCES

If you tend to write mainly short, simple sentences, you may need to add some variety. If you have two sentences *that are closely related in meaning*, you can put them together—separated by a semicolon. For example,

He was unfailingly warm and kind and knew how to make a friend out of a stranger; he loved people.

Remember that the semicolon indicates a close relationship in meaning; it can't just go between any two sentences. Also, each of the sentences must be complete in most standard English writing for a semicolon to work between them. When you read older material, like novels by Jane Austen or Charles Dickens, you may see a fragment on one side of a semicolon and a complete sentence on the other, but that is not usually done these days.

EXERCISE

Dave Barry, a popular humorist, once described the new Jolly Green Giant this way: "He no longer looks like the 'Ho, Ho, Ho' guy; he now looks like Paul McCartney on steroids." Why do you think Barry chose a semicolon between his two sentences?

Go through the essay you just wrote to see whether you have any short, closely related sentences that come one right after the other. If so, try taking out the period, putting in a semicolon, and making the second sentence's capital letter lowercase.

A word of caution: Be sure to use a *semicolon* in joining sentences. A comma definitely will not do in most cases.

🌐 WEB SITE

www.elizabeth-berg.net
On her Web site Elizabeth Berg says, "You'll find things I might share with you if you were my friend": recipes, anecdotes, photos, quotations, jokes, podcasts—as well as information about all her books and her recent public appearances.

PREPARING TO READ

Do you feel safe when you go out alone at night? Are there certain sections of town that you would refuse to enter alone after dark? Does the fear, or lack of fear, in any way relate to your gender, your age, or the color of your skin?

"Just Walk On By": A Black Man Ponders His Power to Alter Public Space

Brent Staples

Born in 1951 in Chester, Pennsylvania, Brent Staples is a journalist who also holds a Ph.D. in psychology from the University of Chicago. His memoir, Parallel Time: Growing Up in Black and White *(1994), tells the story of his childhood in Chester, a mixed-race, economically declining town. He is currently on the editorial board of the* New York Times. *The selection reprinted here was first published in* Ms. *magazine in September 1986.*

TERMS TO RECOGNIZE

uninflammatory (*para. 1*)	not likely to cause violence or excitement
unwieldy (*para. 2*)	hard to manage or to deal with
indistinguishable (*para. 2*)	not clearly different from
elicit (*para. 3*)	draw forth
warrenlike (*para. 5*)	narrow and crowded like a rabbit hutch
bandolier (*para. 5*)	a belt holding bullets, draped across the chest
lethality (*para. 6*)	being lethal or deadly
bravado (*para. 6*)	pretended courage or false confidence
ad hoc (*para. 7*)	for this case only
labyrinthine (*para. 7*)	like the winding, confusing passages in a maze
berth (*para. 9*)	a safe distance
skittish (*para. 9*)	jumpy, easily frightened
constitutionals (*para. 10*)	walks to improve one's health

My first victim was a woman—white, well dressed, probably in her early 20s. I came upon her late one evening on a deserted street in Hyde Park, a relatively affluent neighborhood in an otherwise mean, impoverished section of Chicago. As I swung onto the avenue behind her, there seemed to be a discreet, uninflammatory distance between us. Not so. She cast back a worried glance. To her, the youngish black man—a broad six feet two inches with a beard and billowing hair, both hands shoved into the pockets of a bulky military jacket—seemed menacingly close. She picked up her pace and was soon running in earnest. Within seconds she disappeared into a cross street.

That was more than a decade ago. I was 22 years old, a graduate student newly arrived at the University of Chicago. It was in the echo of that terrified woman's footfalls that I first began to know the unwieldy inheritance I'd come into—the ability to alter public space in ugly ways. It was clear that she thought of herself as the quarry of a mugger, a rapist, or worse. Suffering a bout of insomnia, however, I was stalking sleep, not defenseless wayfarers. As a softy who is scarcely able to take a knife to a raw chicken—let alone hold one to a person's throat—I was surprised, embarrassed, and dismayed all at once. Her flight made me feel like an accomplice in tyranny. It also made it clear that I was indistinguishable from the muggers who occasionally seeped into the area from the surrounding ghetto. I soon gathered that being perceived as dangerous is a hazard in itself: Where fear and weapons meet—as they often do in urban America—there is always the possibility of death.

In that first year, my first away from my hometown, I was to become thoroughly familiar with the language of fear. At dark, shadowy intersections, I could cross in front of a car stopped at a traffic light and elicit the *thunk, thunk, thunk, thunk* of the driver—black, white, male, female—hammering down the door locks. On less traveled streets after dark, I grew accustomed to but never comfortable with people crossing to the other side of the street rather than pass me. Then there were the standard unpleasantries with policemen, doormen, bouncers, cabdrivers, and others whose business it is to screen out troublesome individuals *before* there is any nastiness.

I moved to New York nearly two years ago and I have remained an avid night walker. In central Manhattan, the near-constant crowd covers the tense one-on-one street encounters. Elsewhere, things can get very taut indeed.

After dark, on the warrenlike streets of Brooklyn where I live, I often see women who fear the worst from me. They seem to have set their faces on neutral, and with their purse straps strung across their chests bandolier-style, they forge ahead as though bracing themselves against being tackled. I understand, of course, that the danger they perceive is not a hallucination. Women are particularly vulnerable to street violence, and young black males are drastically overrepresented among the perpetrators of that violence. Yet these truths are no solace against the alienation that comes of being ever the suspect, an entity with whom pedestrians avoid making eye contact.

It is not altogether clear to me how I reached the ripe old age of 22   6
without being conscious of the lethality nighttime pedestrians attributed to me. Perhaps it was because in Chester, Pa., the small, angry industrial town where I came of age in the 1960s, I was scarcely noticeable against a back-drop of gang warfare, street knifings, and murders. I grew up one of the good boys, had perhaps a half-dozen fistfights. In retrospect, my shyness of combat has clear sources. As a boy, I saw countless tough guys locked away; I have since buried several, too. They were babies, really—a teen-age cousin, a brother of 22, a childhood friend in his mid-20s—all gone down in episodes of bravado played out in the streets. I chose, perhaps uncon-sciously, to remain a shadow—timid, but a survivor.

The fearsomeness mistakenly attributed to me in public places often   7
has a perilous flavor. The most frightening of these confusions occurred in the late 1970s and early 1980s, when I worked as a journalist in Chicago. One day, rushing into the office of a magazine I was writing for with a deadline story in hand, I was mistaken for a burglar. The office manager called security, and with the speed of an ad hoc posse, pursued me through the labyrinthine halls, nearly to my editor's door. I had no way of proving who I was. I could only move briskly toward the company of someone who knew me.

Relatively speaking, however, I never fared as badly as another black   8
male journalist. He went to nearby Waukegan, Ill., a couple of summers ago to work on a story about a murderer who was born there. Mistaking the reporter for the killer, police officers hauled him from his car at gunpoint and but for his press credentials would probably have tried to book him. Such episodes are not uncommon. Black men trade tales like this all the time.

Over the years, I learned to smother the rage I felt at so often being   9
mistaken for a criminal. Not to do so would surely have led to madness. I now take precautions to make myself less threatening. I move about with care, particularly late in the evening. I give a wide berth to nervous people on subway platforms during the wee hours. If I happen to be entering a building behind some people who appear skittish, I may walk by, letting them clear the lobby before I return, so as not to seem to be following

them. I have been calm and extremely congenial on those rare occasions   9
when I've been pulled over by the police.

And on late evening constitutionals I employ what has proved to be   10
an excellent tension reducing measure: I whistle melodies from Beethoven
and Vivaldi and the more popular classical composers. Even steely New
Yorkers hunching toward nighttime destinations seem to relax, and occasionally they even join in the tune. Virtually everybody seems to sense that a
mugger wouldn't be warbling bright, sunny selections from Vivaldi's "Four
Seasons." It is my equivalent of the cowbell that hikers wear when they are
in bear country.

RESPONDING TO READING

Why don't we expect muggers to be whistling melodies from Beethoven and
Vivaldi? In your journal write a brief explanation of the possible reasons.

CONSIDERING CONTENT

1. How does the author describe his physical appearance in the opening
   paragraph? What categories of readers would be drawn in by the opening paragraph?
2. Why does the woman take him for "a mugger, a rapist, or worse"?
3. What does the writer mean when he says "that being perceived as dangerous is a hazard in itself"? What illustrations does he offer to prove his point?
4. What kind of hometown background did Brent Staples have? What
   kind of person did he turn out to be?
5. At the end of paragraph 6, he speaks of three young men he was close
   to—"all gone down in episodes of bravado played out in the streets."
   Although he doesn't tell us how any of them died, can you guess? Give
   examples of the kind of "episodes of bravado" that may have cost them
   their lives.
6. How did Staples learn to deal with the problem of being a large, young
   African American man in the city?
7. Why would hikers in bear country wear cowbells? Explain how that
   wilderness situation is similar to Staples's urban situation.

CONSIDERING METHOD

1. Explain how the brief narrative in the opening paragraph catches our
   interest.
2. The thesis of this selection is implied, not directly stated. Write out in
   your own words a statement of the author's main point.

3. This essay first appeared in *Ms.* magazine, a publication that focuses on women's issues. What did the author probably assume about his audience? How did it affect his choice of examples?

4. How does description help to make Staples's illustrations interesting and convincing in paragraphs 1 and 5?

5. Using words that sound like the noise they describe is called **onomatopoeia** (for example, the *thunk, thunk, thunk, thunk* of the car door locks in para. 3). Explain why that word choice is effective. Can you think of other examples of words that sound like what they mean?

6. This essay is developed through example and illustration, yet Staples does not tell us how the three young men died (para. 6.) Why not?

7. Explain what makes the conclusion particularly satisfying.

WRITING STEP BY STEP: MISTAKEN STEREOTYPES

Stereotypes are oversimplified groupings of people by race, gender, politics, athletic ability, ethnic origin, and so on. Staples was stereotyped because he was a young black male, and as Staples says, "young black males are drastically overrepresented among the perpetrators of . . . violence." Although there is usually some grain of truth behind stereotypes, they tend to be negative and unfair. Women, for instance, are stereotyped as weak, passive, fickle, scatterbrained, and indecisive. Men, on the other hand, are supposed to be strong-minded and assertive, but dense and unfeeling. Stereotypes are unfair because they lump lots of people into a category whether or not the characteristics fit every individual.

A. Think of a stereotype that includes you. Choose one that you think is unfair to you; your essay will explain how you are different.

B. Begin, as Staples does, with a brief narrative, a story that illustrates how you *seem* to fit the type although you actually do not.

C. In the next paragraph, define the stereotype by giving examples of several characteristics people expect you to have—or not to have. For instance, if you are a male football player, people may take you for a clumsy hulk who can barely read and write.

D. Next, explain why people would tend to place you in this stereotype.

E. Then, explain why you don't fit the stereotype and tell about some influence while you were growing up that helped you to avoid the typical pattern of behavior. Provide concrete examples, as Staples does in paragraph 6 when he tells about his childhood among the gangs in Chester, Pennsylvania.

F. In conclusion, explain how you felt about being stereotyped and how you have learned to cope with the mistaken views of people who took you for a different kind of person than you truly are.

OTHER WRITING IDEAS

1. Write the paper outlined in the previous section but instead illustrate how you are the perfect example of a stereotype. You may want to think of a positive stereotype—or else make your essay humorous.

2. COLLABORATIVE WRITING. With a small group of classmates discuss phobias, those irrational fears that most of us have—fears of spiders, of snakes, of high places, of flying, of closed spaces. Which ones do you have? Choose your worst or your most embarrassing phobia and tell in an essay how it limits your activities, how it makes you feel, how you think you got it, and what you do to control it. Or, choose one phobia from your group's collection and develop an essay of example together.

3. USING THE INTERNET. Use Internet sources to find out about treatments for phobias. Write an essay explaining two or three different ways that people can overcome these irrational fears.

4. WRITING ABOUT READING. In paragraph 5, the author says, "Women are particularly vulnerable to street violence, and young black men are drastically overrepresented among the perpetrators of that violence." Do you agree with this comment? Write a response to this idea.

GAINING WORD POWER

The following words appear in the reading but are not included in the Terms to Recognize. Look up each one in your dictionary and use it in a sentence of your own.

1. affluent (para. 1)
2. menacingly (para. 1)
3. dismayed (para. 2)
4. taut (para. 4)
5. vulnerable (para. 5)
6. solace (para. 5)
7. entity (para. 5)
8. attributed (para. 7)
9. precautions (para. 9)
10. congenial (para. 9)

EDITING SKILLS: COMMAS AROUND INTERRUPTERS

An **interrupter** is just what it sounds like—a word or group of words that interrupts or breaks into the flow of a sentence, like the italicized words do here:

I understand, *of course*, that the danger they perceive is not a hallucination.

You need a comma before and after the interrupter as a signal to your readers that the interrupter is an addition that can be removed without changing the meaning of the sentence. The first comma signals the start of the interruption; the second comma signals the end of the interruption. It would be quite misleading in that sentence, with its flow interrupted, to use only one comma. But if you move the *of course* to the beginning or to the end of the sentence so that it no longer interrupts the flow, then a single comma is fine:

> *Of course,* I understand that the danger they perceive is not a hallucination.
> I understand that the danger they perceive is not a hallucination, *of course.*

The principle remains the same, even when the interrupter is longer:

> One day, *rushing into the office of a magazine I was writing for with a deadline story in hand,* I was mistaken for a burglar.

Remember: Put commas *around* interrupters—one before and one after.

EXERCISE

We've omitted the commas from around the interrupters in the following sentences. Figure out where they belong, and put them back in.

1. Suffering a bout of insomnia however I was stalking sleep, not defenseless wayfarers.
2. After dark on the warrenlike streets of Brooklyn where I live I often see women who fear the worst from me.
3. I chose perhaps unconsciously to remain a shadow—timid, but a survivor.
4. The office manager called security and with the speed of an ad hoc posse pursued me through the labyrinthine halls, nearly to my editor's door.
5. Relatively speaking however I never fared as badly as another black male journalist.

Now check the essay you've just written to be sure that you have punctuated interrupters correctly.

🌐 WEB SITE

www.pbs.org/blackpress/modern_journalist/staples.html
Video and audio clips of Brent Staples from the Public Broadcasting System.

PREPARING TO READ

Do men or women make better schoolteachers? Or does gender matter?
Does the age of the students make any difference?

••

One Man's Kids

••

D ANIEL R. M EIER

*Daniel Meier received a master's degree from the Harvard Graduate School of
Education in 1984. He taught first grade at schools in Brookline and Boston,
Massachusetts, before getting his Ph.D. at the University of California at Berke-
ley. He now teaches early childhood education at San Francisco State University.
His articles about teaching and his reviews of children's books have appeared in a
number of educational journals. The essay reprinted here appeared in 1987 in the
"About Men" series of the* New York Times Magazine.

TERMS TO RECOGNIZE

complying (*para. 4*)	agreeing to someone else's request or command
singular (*para. 5*)	exceptional, unusual, distinguished by superiority
consoling (*para. 6*)	offering comfort and advice
intellectual (*para. 7*)	guided chiefly by knowledge or reason rather than by emotion or experience
hilarity (*para. 7*)	spirited merriment, cheerfulness
complimentary (*para. 12*)	given free as a courtesy or a favor

I teach first graders. I live in a world of skinned knees, double-knotted   1
shoelaces, riddles that I've heard a dozen times, stale birthday cakes, hurt
feelings, wandering stories, and one lost shoe ("and if you don't find it my
mother'll kill me"). My work is dominated by 6-year-olds.

It's 10:45, the middle of snack, and I'm helping Emily open her   2
milk carton. She has already tried the other end without success, and
now there's so much paint and ink on the carton from her fingers that
I'm not sure she should drink it at all. But I open it. Then I turn to help
Scott clean up some milk he has just spilled onto Rebecca's whale
crossword puzzle.

While I wipe my milk- and paint-covered hands, Jenny wants to know   3
if I've seen that funny book about penguins that I read in class. As I hunt for
it in a messy pile of books, Jason wants to know if there is a new seating
arrangement for lunch tables. I find the book, turn to answer Jason, then
face Maya, who is fast approaching with a new knock-knock joke. After
what seems like the 10th "Who's there?" I laugh and Maya is pleased.

Then Andrew wants to know how to spell "flukes" for his crossword.   4
As I get to "u," I give a hand signal for Sarah to take away the snack. But
just as Sarah is almost out the door, two children complain that "we
haven't even had ours yet." I stop the snack mid-flight, complying with their
request for graham crackers. I then return to Andrew, noticing that he has
put "flu" for 9 Down, rather than 9 Across. It's now 10:50.

My work is not traditional male work. It's not a singular pursuit.   5
There is not a large pile of paper to get through or one deal to transact. I
don't have one area of expertise or knowledge. I don't have the singular
power over language of a lawyer, the physical force of a construction
worker, the command over fellow workers of a surgeon, the wheeling and
dealing transactions of a businessman. My energy is not spent in pursuing,
climbing, achieving, conquering, or cornering some goal or object.

My energy is spent in encouraging, supporting, consoling, and prais-   6
ing my children. In teaching, the inner rewards come from without. On any
given day, quite apart from teaching reading and spelling, I bandage a cut,
dry a tear, erase a frown, tape a torn doll, and locate a long-lost boot. The
day is really won through matters of the heart. As my students groan, laugh,
shudder, cry, exult, and wonder, I do too. I have to be soft around the edges.

A few years ago, when I was interviewing for an elementary-school   7
teaching position, every principal told me with confidence that, as a male,
I had an advantage over female applicants because of the lack of male
teachers. But in the next breath, they asked with a hint of suspicion why I
chose to work with young children. I told them that I wanted to observe
and contribute to the intellectual growth of a maturing mind. What I really
felt like saying, but didn't, was that I loved helping a child learn to write her
name for the first time, finding someone a new friend, or sharing in the
hilarity of reading about Winnie the Pooh getting so stuck in a hole that
only his head and rear show.

I gave that answer to those principals, who were mostly male,   8
because I thought they wanted a "male" response. This meant talking about
intellectual matters. If I had taken a different course and talked about my
interest in helping children in their emotional development, it would have
been seen as closer to a "female" answer. I even altered my language, not

once mentioning the word "love" to describe what I do indeed love about teaching. My answer worked; every principal nodded approvingly.

Some of the principals also asked what I saw myself doing later in my 9 career. They wanted to know if I eventually wanted to go into educational administration. Becoming a dean of students or a principal has never been one of my goals, but they seemed to expect me, as a male, to want to climb higher on the career stepladder. So I mentioned that, at some point, I would be interested in working with teachers as a curriculum coordinator. Again, they nodded approvingly.

If those principals had been female instead of male, I wonder 10 whether their questions, and my answers, would have been different. My guess is that they would have been.

At other times, when I'm at a party or a dinner and tell someone that 11 I teach young children, I've found that men and women respond differently. Most men ask about the subjects I teach and the courses I took in my training. Then, unless they bring up an issue such as merit pay, the conversation stops. Most women, on the other hand, begin the conversation on a more immediate and personal level. They say things like "those kids must love having a male teacher" or "that age is just wonderful, you must love it." Then, more often than not, they'll talk about their own kids or ask me specific questions about what I do. We're then off and talking shop.

Possibly, men would have more to say to me, and I to them, if my 12 job had more of the trappings and benefits of more traditional male jobs. But my job has no bonuses or promotions. No complimentary box seats at the ball park. No cab fare home. No drinking buddies after work. No briefcase. No suit. (Ties get stuck in paint jars.) No power lunches. (I eat peanut butter and jelly, chips, milk, and cookies with the kids.) No taking clients out for cocktails. The only place I take my kids is to the playground.

Although I could have pursued a career in law or business, as several 13 of my friends did, I chose teaching instead. My job has benefits all its own. I'm able to bake cookies without getting them stuck together as they cool, buy cheap sewing materials, take out splinters, and search just the right trash cans for useful odds and ends. I'm sometimes called "Daddy" and even "Mommy" by my students, and if there's ever a lull in the conversation at a dinner party, I can always ask those assembled if they've heard the latest riddle about why the turkey crossed the road. (He thought he was a chicken.)

RESPONDING TO READING

What do you think about Meier's choice of career? Do you think it's reasonable and appropriate? Why or why not?

CONSIDERING CONTENT

1. Why did Meier write this essay? What point do you think he wanted to make?

2. Meier says, "My work is not traditional male work" (para. 5)? What does he mean by that statement? Do you agree?

3. What is a "singular pursuit"? Why does the author use that phrase to describe "male work"?

4. Why did the principals who interviewed Meier have "a hint of suspicion" about him (para. 7)?

5. What kind of answers did Meier give in his job interviews (para. 8)? What kind of answers did he avoid? Why didn't he mention the word "love"?

6. The author says that men and women respond differently to him when he talks about his job (para. 11). What are the differences?

7. How does Meier feel about his job? Do you think he is being defensive or apologetic about it?

CONSIDERING METHOD

1. In the first paragraph the author says, "My work is dominated by 6-year-olds." What examples does he give to explain and support this general statement?

2. Why does Meier open his essay the way he does? Why doesn't he state his thesis until paragraph 5?

3. Find the series of words that Meier uses to describe "male work" (end of para. 5) and the words he uses to describe what he does (beginning of para. 6). What is he saying about the difference between his work and "male work"?

4. What does the author mean when he says, "In teaching, the inner rewards come from without" (para. 6)? What examples does he give to make his meaning clear?

5. What is the effect of the series of phrases that begin with "No" in paragraph 12? Why are the positive comments in parentheses? Why is the last sentence in the paragraph not in parentheses?

WRITING STEP BY STEP: QUALITIES FOR SUCCESS

Think of a workplace that you know well—a place where you have a job now or had one in the past. If your primary work is being a student, then school is your workplace.

A. First identify and briefly explain your role at the workplace ("I am a cashier, salesperson, and general trouble shooter at Posh Pups, a pet grooming and pet supply store").

B. Then name three or four personal qualities that make for success in that job. ("To work at Posh Pups, you need to be loyal and good at math and to like people as much as you like animals.")

C. Think about the order in which you want to present these qualities. You might start with a less important quality and build up to the most important one. Or you may see that two of them are related and need to be placed in back-to-back paragraphs. Make a scratch outline to help you decide how to arrange your main points and examples.

D. For each quality you name, give at least one example of how it is important in the job. Think of a specific time when each quality was needed. Tell the story of how you or your co-workers showed a particular quality (or, unfortunately, showed a lack of it).

E. If an example is long and detailed, give it its own paragraph, as Meier does in paragraphs 2, 3, and 4 of his essay. If some of your examples are only a sentence or two, try to expand them with more details that will give your readers the sights, sounds, and feel of your work.

F. Close with a summarizing statement of how you feel about this job. Or offer a recommendation to anyone who might consider going into this line of work. Try to reinforce your thesis idea without simply repeating it.

G. When you revise, look at the transitions between your paragraphs. Try to fill in any gaps between your main points. Also check to see that you used transitions to lead into your examples. Ask your instructor or your classmates to help you improve the flow of your ideas.

OTHER WRITING IDEAS

1. Select one of the following general statements, or compose one of your own. Make it the central idea of an essay full of examples and illustrations. Draw examples from your reading, your conversation, your observations, and your own experience.

   a. Action heroes in the movies today are pretty much alike.

   b. Being a good parent is probably the hardest job there is.

   c. The stereotypical female (or male) is not easy to find in our society anymore.

   d. Being a teenager can be difficult (or easy or perplexing or a lot of fun).

   e. Jealousy is a destructive emotion.

2. COLLABORATIVE WRITING. Discuss with your classmates some superstitions that you or members of your family or community have held. Frequently, these superstitions have to do with success or bad luck in sports, performances, weather, or work. Do they have any validity? How did they develop? Write an essay of example about the role that superstition plays in your life or in the life of someone you know.

3. USING THE INTERNET. Search the Web for information about the workforce of grade school teachers today. Are there more men than there used to be? Can you find information about what discourages or attracts males to grade school teaching? Integrate information you find with information from Meier to write an essay giving examples of pluses and minuses for men considering the teaching field.

4. WRITING ABOUT READING. Summarize the main points that Meier makes about work and its rewards.

GAINING WORD POWER

In paragraph 12 Meier uses the word *complimentary*. There is a word that's pronounced the same but has a different spelling and a different meaning—*complementary*. Do you know what each word means? English has many of these sound-alike words, and it's important to know the differences among them. They won't cause you any trouble in speaking, but they will change the meaning of your writing if you choose the wrong one.

Here is a list of words from Meier's essay. Using your dictionary, find a sound-alike word for each item in the list and write down its meaning. Then use the word you found in a sentence.

fare	right	male	principal	seen	whether
new	won	course	through	two	hole

EDITING SKILLS: USING SUBORDINATION

Writers often combine two or more ideas in a sentence by using **subordination.** When one idea is subordinate to or dependent on another, it is less important. Take a look at these sentences from Meier's essay to see how the subordinate ideas are introduced by words that make them sound less important:

Although I could have pursued a career in law or business, I chose teaching instead.
Then, *unless* they bring up an issue such as merit pay, the conversation stops.
If I had taken a different course and talked about my interest in helping children in their emotional development, it would have been seen as close to a "female" answer.

As you can see, each of these sentences has two parts. Notice that the second part, after the comma, can stand alone as a sentence: That part is called **independent.** If you read the first part alone, it does not sound complete. The first part is called **dependent** for this reason. The opening words—*Although,* *unless,* and *If*—make the first statement of each sentence dependent. These words are called *subordinating conjunctions*; they indicate that the first idea is not as important as the rest of the sentence. (You will also notice that when the dependent part comes first, a comma separates it from the independent part.)

Subordinating conjunctions are familiar words; we use them a lot. Here are some of the most common ones: *since, because, if, even if, unless, although, even though, though, as long as, after, before, when, whenever, while, until,* and *wherever.* Skillful writers use subordination to give variety to their sentences and to keep readers' attention focused on the main ideas.

EXERCISE

Imitate the following sentences. Each one begins with a dependent statement followed by an independent one. You don't have to imitate each sentence exactly; just follow the dependent-independent pattern and use the same subordinating conjunction as the model sentence. Put in the commas, too.

Model: If we want clean air, then we will have to drive more fuel-efficient cars.

Imitation: If you like lasagna, then you should try the new Italian restaurant on Division Street.

1. While I was eating my lunch, a friend walked in.
2. Wherever I go in this city, I run into old friends.
3. Before you gather up your books, be sure your notes are complete.
4. Although Selma is a good athlete, she sometimes swears at the umpire.
5. Unless she sees the error of her ways, Selma may get tossed off the team.

Write at least one more imitation of each of the preceding sentences.

WEB SITE

www.edutopia.org/male-teacher-shortage
This article—"Male Call: Recruiting More Men to Teach Elementary School"—discusses the reasons for the lack of male teachers in elementary and middle schools. The online comments in response to the article are especially interesting.

PREPARING TO READ
What income do you think marks the federal poverty line for a couple? For a family of four? What is the minimum wage in your state these days? Write down your estimates before reading the next essay.

••

The Working Poor

••

TIM JONES

Tim Jones is a writer for the Chicago Tribune. *He has covered media topics including Oprah Winfrey's Texas trial for disparaging beef and Hormel Foods's efforts to stop the use of* Spam *as a word for unwanted email. He often writes stories about areas where national economics and public media interconnect.*

TERMS TO RECOGNIZE

tapping (*para. 2*)	taking advantage or making use of
think tank (*para. 3*)	a group organized for the purpose of researching a problem
sparsely (*para. 6*)	thinly, lightly
severance (*para. 7*)	termination of employment
vise (*para. 14*)	clamping tool that holds material between two jaws
emphysema (*para. 14*)	a serious lung disease that makes breathing difficult

McArthur, Ohio. The food line begins to form during the sunrise chill, more than two hours before the metal gates to the Care United Methodist Outreach pantry open. Hundreds of people like Theresa Ware arrive early because they fear the boxes of food stacked in neat rows will be gone by the time they push their rusty grocery carts to the head of the hours-long line. Ware keeps an eye on her watch because she can't afford to be late for work, not even if the reason is to pick up food. "This is a have-to case for us. It's humiliating," said Ware, 49, who makes $7.50 an hour working the afternoon shift at a nursing home. This recent visit was one of two food pantry stops she and her unemployed husband, Rocky, make every month. "We shouldn't have to do this," she said.   1

Theresa and Rocky Ware toil in the ranks of the working poor, a growing category of millions of Americans who play by the rules of the   2 working world and still can't make ends meet. After tapping friends and family, maxing out their credit cards and sufficiently swallowing their pride, at least 23 million Americans stood in food lines last year—many of them the working poor, according to America's Second Harvest, the Chicago-based hunger relief organization. The surge in food demand is fueled by several forces—job losses, expired unemployment benefits, soaring health-care and housing costs, and the inability of many people to find jobs that match the income and benefits of the jobs they lost.

The Center on Budget and Policy Priorities, a Washington think tank,   3 reported recently that 43 million people are living in low-income working families with children. Other government data show the number of people living below the official poverty line grew by more than 3.5 million from 2000 to 2002, to 34.6 million. And the U.S. Department of Agriculture reported that the number of Americans who don't know where their next meal will come from—categorized as "food insecure"—jumped from 31 million to 35 million between 1999 and 2002. "The reach of the economic slowdown has really pulled in a lot of folks who never expected to be poor," said Stacy Dean, director of food stamp policy for the Center on Budget and Policy Priorities. "What you see now is families turning to private relief for what often is a very small amount of help."

"This is not just a function of unemployment. A larger percentage of   4 Americans are working poor, and the numbers have been growing for nine years," said Robert Forney, CEO of America's Second Harvest. "This could be the low-water mark for the economy, but for a whole lot of Americans—40 million of them—the option of [earning] a living wage and benefits? Forget it."

EXPLODING DEMAND

Food pantry operators across the nation—urban, suburban and rural—tell   5 similar stories of exploding food demand from families, senior citizens, and the fastest-growing segment: the working poor. In southern Ohio, where President Lyndon Johnson declared war on poverty 40 years ago, cars will line roadsides for a half-mile or more waiting for the boxed monthly buffet of dry milk, rice, cereal, canned fruit and vegetables, instant mashed potatoes and, on good days, canned meat and chicken. "We're quickly seeing that communities that thought they were immune are now affected, whether urban or suburban," said Lisa Hamler-Podolski, executive director of the Ohio Association of Second Harvest Foodbanks. Rev. Walt Goble, who runs the Care United Methodist Outreach in McArthur, Ohio, a small and long-ago thriving village about 60 miles south of Columbus, said, "We're here from 11:30 to 4:00, or until we run out of food. Usually we run out."

Theresa and Rocky Ware have reluctantly joined the lines at   6
food banks. Last year, in the sparsely populated, nine-county region of
southeastern Ohio, 9.1 million pounds of food were handed out—that's up
from 3.9 million pounds in 2000. In the past three years, the number of
households served by food banks has more than tripled, according to
Second Harvest of Southeast Ohio.

Although the national economy shows fitful statistical signs of   7
recovery, the data do not take into account that declining numbers of
employers offer health insurance and many new jobs pay the minimum
wage, $5.15 an hour.

- Danny Palmer, who lives in the Ohio River village of Cheshire, lost his
  $20-an-hour welding job and now works at Wal-Mart for $5.95 an hour.
  Insurance coverage he got as part of a severance package from his former
  employer runs out next month. He has no health coverage with Wal-Mart.
- Melissa Barringer holds three part-time jobs to augment the income she
  and her husband, Brian, a laborer, earn to support themselves and their
  three teenage children. Last year, their combined income was $18,000.
  "We can't keep up," Melissa Barringer said as her children ate at a soup
  kitchen in Coolville, Ohio.
- Oscar Sanchez shows up every Thursday for bags of canned and dry goods
  at the Catholic Charities' Latin American Youth Center in Chicago's Pilsen
  neighborhood. Sanchez, 52, is a self-employed painter who lost his construction job three years ago. His hourly wage is $7. He has no health insurance.

People seeking food assistance on the rise
Average monthly food stamp users; scale in millions

Note: Fiscal years, beginning in Sept.
Source: U.S. Department of Agriculture, Food and Nutrition Service
Source: Chicago Tribune Company.

- And in the St. Louis suburb of Ferguson, Mary Williams works as a temp and drives her 1983 Mercury Marquis to jobs that pay $7 to $8 an hour. The work is not steady. Neither she nor her son has health insurance.

All of them tell different stories but have one thing in common: They have jobs and are regulars at food pantries.

WHAT THE NUMBERS MISS

The plight of people like the Wares is not reflected in monthly unemployment figures. These Americans fly uneasily beneath the radar of the government's officially recognized economic distress status, the federal poverty line of $12,490 for a couple and $18,850 for a family of four. "The official economic numbers often lag behind the real story," said Gregory Acs, a senior research associate at the Urban Institute, a Washington-based research organization. 8

"Poverty numbers usually tell only part of the story. You can be technically not poor, but you still skip bills and go once or twice a week to the food pantry," Acs said, noting that upward adjustments in poverty levels do not account for all the financial pressures facing families. For example, the share of Americans under age 65 with employer-sponsored health insurance dropped from 70 percent in 1999 to 68 percent in 2002, according to the Urban Institute. Among low-income workers, the percentage dropped from 40 percent to 35 percent. 9

Some of those who are struggling visit Felipe Ayala, who has been running Chicago's Latin American Youth Center for 32 years. "We used to run out of food at the end of the month. Now we can run out at the end of the first week," Ayala said. The increasing demand comes from people who are either out of work or, in the case of Oscar Sanchez, don't earn enough to provide a living for themselves. "It has gotten worse," Ayala said. "All the jobs are in the food industry or else they are in the suburbs. The lines here are always increasing." 10

Sanchez, who is divorced, said he goes every other Thursday to the basement of the old school. People begin to file in at 9 A.M. and move from one metal folding chair to another before they can pick up white plastic food bags on which "Thank You" is printed in red letters. They wait patiently for their turn to get the food bags. "This is what keeps me going," said Sanchez, who has used the pantry for two years. As the weather warms up, Sanchez said, he is hopeful that there will be more work and steady work. He does not expect, however, to break his pattern of regularly visiting the pantry on 17th Street. 11

Nor is Mary Williams particularly hopeful. With three years of college 12
behind her, the 42-year-old former factory worker has not had health insurance since last summer. Williams makes about $400 a month and regularly
visits a Salvation Army food pantry in St. Louis. Williams's battered car is
starting to break down, and sometimes she has to drive up to an hour, one
way, to get to work. "Most of the time it's a struggle," said Williams, a single parent. "And things aren't looking any better."

The pressure on working families has increased in the past few years 13
as many states have cut back Medicaid coverage in the face of their own
budget troubles. Two recent reports show that as many as 1.6 million low-
income people have lost publicly funded health coverage because of state
budget cuts. In response, they cobble together an existence by skipping
meals, borrowing from friends, moving in with family and cutting prescrip-
tion pills in half or bypassing dosages altogether. Some ignore bills, which is
one reason Ohio, for instance, a state hit hard by the recession, has the
highest rate of loan foreclosures in the nation, according to the Mortgage
Bankers Association.

Many are trapped in a bureaucratic vise: They make too much money 14
to qualify for Medicaid, the government's low-income health insurance program, yet too little to buy health coverage. Because they can't afford the
property taxes, the Wares have turned their home over to their adult children, who pay the tax bill. Medical bills from Rocky's treatments for emphy-
sema are mounting. "I get bills and I say to hell with it. They can come and
throw me in jail," Theresa Ware said as she loaded food into the back seat
of her truck.

RESPONDING TO READING

How accurate were your estimates of the poverty line and minimum wage? Did
any of your ideas change from reading the facts and examples in the essay?

CONSIDERING CONTENT

1. Who are the working poor? What is the main point that Jones's article
   makes about them?
2. Give a few reasons for an "exploding food demand" at food banks in this
   country. Can you think of reasons that are not covered in the article?
3. Why does the researcher Gregory Acs say that "poverty numbers usually
   tell only part of the story" (para. 9)? What is the rest of the story?
4. How are health insurance and home ownership related to the topic of
   the working poor?

5. This article was published in 2004. Has the situation of the working poor changed since its publication? If you don't know, how could you find out?

6. Paragraph 3 mentions "private relief." What is that? What other kinds of relief for the poor exist?

CONSIDERING METHOD

1. What is Jones's attitude toward the working poor? How do you know? Choose a sentence and suggest how it would be rephrased by someone with the opposite attitude.

2. From many possible examples, the author chose four to present in paragraph 7. Why do you think he chose these four? What similarities and differences do you see among these four people?

3. The main topic of the article is put into words in paragraph 2. What is the purpose of paragraph 1?

4. Notice the lavish use of descriptive statistics in the article. Did you attempt to understand the numbers? Why or why not? Were they persuasive to you?

5. Did you spend any time looking at the graph from the USDA? Look at it again. What does it show? What conclusions can you draw from it? Take a survey among your classmates about who and who did not inspect this graph when reading the article. What conclusions can you draw from your survey?

6. If this article appeared in your local newspaper, would you read it? Why or why not? The actual article is twice as long as the part we reprint here. Would you read the whole thing if it were in front of you? Why or why not?

7. Jones uses two subheadings to break up the text and guide the reader's focus. Find two more places where subheadings would be suitable, and write them. Your instructor may have you work with two or three classmates.

COMBINING STRATEGIES

"The Working Poor" offers many examples of people who are working yet poor, the problems they encounter, and the solutions they find. The essay also discusses many of the causes and effects of the people's economic situation. List some of the causes and some of the effects mentioned in the article. List some other causes and effects that are not discussed in the article.

WRITING STEP BY STEP: FINANCIAL TROUBLES

A. Brainstorm with classmates about some way to get in trouble financially other than having a low-paying job. Some possibilities are using credit cards too much, buying a house that is too expensive, taking on expenses for others (like family members), having a high-priced hobby, making bad investments, gambling, leasing a vehicle with large payments, and sending children to costly schools.

B. Think of someone you know who has one of the problems you brainstormed. Freewrite for five minutes about the person and the problem. Choose three or four good examples of practices that have put the person into financial trouble.

C. Reread Jones's first paragraph. Write a paragraph to open your essay in which you present a verbal picture that illustrates the person and problem you will be writing about.

D. Develop a description of each example, devoting one or two paragraphs to each one. Be sure to use exact details. Use numbers like prices and percentages if possible.

E. Close with a look at the future. You can choose to suggest how the person might change in the future, or you can close more negatively and tell what will happen if the present course continues. (This second type of closing is what you see in the Jones essay.)

OTHER WRITING IDEAS

1. COLLABORATIVE WRITING. The Writing Step by Step essay focused on one person with a financial problem. Working with several other students, draft an article for your school newspaper that discusses one type of financial problem that college students might have. Provide several different examples, as Jones did in "The Working Poor." Solicit examples from other classmates and friends.

2. Instead of focusing on money difficulties, write an essay of example or illustration about another life problem that many people face.

3. USING THE INTERNET. Find information on one of the institutions mentioned in the Jones article: for instance, Second Harvest, the Center on Budget and Policy Priorities, the Urban Institute, Medicaid, the Mortgage Bankers Association, or the U. S. Department of Agriculture. Write an essay using examples to explain what the institution does or focus on an interesting part of what it does.

4. WRITING ABOUT READING. Write an essay explaining *either* that Jones's article changed your view about the working poor *or* that Jones's article had little influence on your thinking.

GAINING WORD POWER

One elderly citizen referred to himself as "temporarily embarrassed" when he was broke. Brainstorm with classmates about some other euphemisms (mild terms substituted for harsh ones) for *poverty* and *poor*.

EDITING SKILLS: USING COMMAS IN SERIES

Notice where the commas are placed in the following examples containing items in series.

> The surge in food demand is fueled by several forces—job losses, expired unemployment benefits, soaring health-care and housing costs, and the inability of many people to find jobs that match the income and benefits of the jobs they lost.
>
> In southern Ohio, where President Lyndon Johnson declared war on poverty 40 years ago, cars will line roadsides for a half-mile or more waiting for the boxed monthly buffet of dry milk, rice, cereal, canned fruit and vegetables, instant mashed potatoes and, on good days, canned meat and chicken.
>
> In response, they cobble together an existence by skipping meals, borrowing from friends, moving in with family and cutting prescription pills in half or bypassing dosages altogether.

The commas are necessary to let you know when one item ends and another begins. Try making sense of those words without the commas to see what an uphill task reading would be without commas:

> The surge in food demand is fueled by several forces—job losses expired unemployment benefits soaring health-care and housing costs and the inability of many people to find jobs that match the income and benefits of the jobs they lost.

You can see that you have to read twice to figure out which groups of words go together. You might first read "job losses expired" and "unemployment benefits soaring," quite the opposite of the intended meaning.

Look at this sentence, which includes a series:

> After tapping friends and family, maxing out their credit cards and sufficiently swallowing their pride, at least 23 million Americans stood in food lines last year.

Jones doesn't use a comma before the *and* connecting the last item in a series (which is "sufficiently swallowing their pride"). This comma is optional in standard English usage. We like the comma before the conjunction *and*, ourselves. We think it makes the sentence easier to read on the first try. However, you will see educated writers like Jones leaving it out.

EXERCISE

Write a sentence describing a scene you know well or specially observe for this exercise. It could be your own room or a scene from nature or an event on the street. Try to string the descriptive details in a series using a model from Jones's article:

> Cars will line roadsides for a half-mile or more waiting for the boxed monthly buffet of dry milk, rice, cereal, canned fruit and vegetables, instant mashed potatoes and, on good days, canned meat and chicken.

🌐 WEB SITE

www.economytrack.org
The Economic Policy Institute's "Economy Track" provides data and downloadable graphs on jobs, unemployment, and economic activity in the United States.

STUDENT ESSAY USING EXAMPLES

Look Around First

Nick Boyer

As a freshman at Illinois State University, Nick Boyer received an English composition assignment to write an essay of example. He found an amusing topic in his own everyday life.

Have you ever noticed that when people think that no one is around, they do some of the strangest things? What makes the scene interesting (and funny) is that when people realize they are being watched, they try to make it seem as though they are not acting ridiculous.

One experience you can surely relate to is stopping at a red light and noticing the clean-cut businessman in the next car lip-synching to the "easy listening" tunes on the radio. He starts out slowly, but by the time the light turns green, his head is bobbing and his body is swaying like someone trying out for "American Idol." What makes me laugh is that after realizing he's been caught in this act he pretends to inspect his sixty-dollar hairstyle in the rearview mirror, while glancing nervously at me out of the corner of his eye.

"Fire engine! Fire engine! Say it! Fire engine!" I could hear my father yelling in the other room, and I wondered if he was going wild over a passing vehicle or trying to teach the dog to talk. When I peeked around the corner, I sighed in relief to see that he was yelling at an episode of "Family Feud" on television. I watched as he kicked his feet, screamed, and pointed furiously at the innocent contestant who could not hear him. Moments passed before he heard me laughing from behind while he went through his antics. He spun around with an embarrassed look on his face, then turned quickly away, and muttered "how stupid," "show's no good," "just turning the station." He finally sank slowly into his chair like a turtle going into his shell. It made me want to put a mirror between him and the television to show him the real definition of "silly."

Just the other day, as I was making my way to my room at the end of the hall, I heard music accompanied by a continuous thud coming from my sister's room. Curious about what the noise could be, I knocked but didn't get an answer. So I slowly opened the door, and to my amazement I found my sister dancing around the room like a performer on MTV. She was bouncing and hopping and swinging her arms. As she went into a spin, she stopped halfway, froze, and glared at me. Quickly she began trying to reach the center of her back as if she had a terrible itch that she needed

desperately to scratch. She blurted a few mumble words, but I interrupted
her to say, "Nice song, huh?"

  As you can see, people can do some pretty strange things, and the 5
highlight always comes when they're caught. So when you're doing something nutty and you think no one is watching, don't be too surprised when
you look around to find someone laughing at you.

CONSIDERING CONTENT AND METHOD

1. How important is the title? Is it too simple and direct? Would you suggest a more intriguing title?
2. What general claim is the author defending and developing in this essay?
3. How many examples does the author use to support his claim? Are they
   effective? How could they be improved?
4. Can you supply examples from your own experience that would work
   in this essay?
5. What do you think of the ending? How well does it sum up the whole
   essay? Could it be concluded in a different way?

Strategies for Clarifying Meaning: *Definition* and *Explanation*

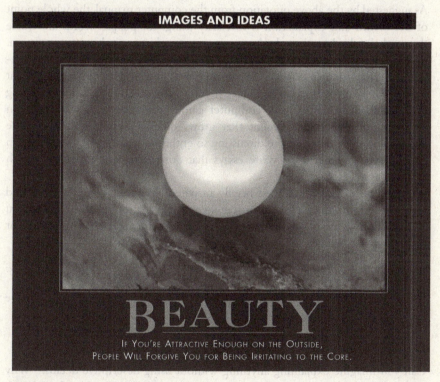

IMAGES AND IDEAS

BEAUTY

IF YOU'RE ATTRACTIVE ENOUGH ON THE OUTSIDE, PEOPLE WILL FORGIVE YOU FOR BEING IRRITATING TO THE CORE.

Source: Despair, Inc.

For Discussion and Writing

What makes this poster funny? How does it contradict most of the clichéd or wise sayings you hear about beauty?

This poster is from a series called Demotivators. Explain the title of the series. Make up your own Demotivator poster, redefining an abstraction like love, honesty, perseverance, courage, hope, or independence. Write a paragraph explaining the caption and what kind of picture you would use.

109

"PowerTalk gives you a single mailbox icon for all incoming and outgoing mail—including fax, voice, electronic mail, and documents. Communication from online services and electronic mail from various sources are routed to your desktop mailbox when you install mail gateways supplied by the vendor," the manual for our new computer operating system cheerfully brags. Sounds great, but we have only the vaguest idea what PowerTalk *is*! How many of the terms in those two sentences would *you* need to have defined or explained? Moreover, how many terms would need definition and explanation for a reader in the 1970s?

THE POINT OF DEFINITION AND EXPLANATION

As suggested by the above quotation from the computer manual, the whole point of **definition** and explanation is to clarify things for people. Words are worse than unhelpful when they don't convey meaning but instead create confusion.

The special vocabulary of any group needs explanation when used to communicate with people outside that group. Some groups develop languages that are incredibly mysterious to outsiders. If you've ever been the outsider listening to a bunch of bridge players, computer gamers, or aerobic class addicts, you know the feeling of bafflement that grows quickly into boredom because you have no idea what they're discussing so enthusiastically. The same thing can happen when you read or write essays that don't define or explain as much material as necessary.

Some words can be defined briefly in parentheses, but complex ideas and terms need more than a phrase or sentence of explanation. In this chapter, you will read whole essays whose main purpose is to define and explain difficult or controversial concepts.

THE PRINCIPLES OF DEFINITION AND EXPLANATION

Definitions and explanations make use of a few basic techniques that can be found in almost all writing.

Descriptive Details

Can you imagine explaining anything without using descriptive details? "Why are you afraid you'll become a slave to your new silk shirt?" a friend might ask you. To explain, you would naturally give the details of caring for it: You must wash it in cold water by hand; then, instead of wringing it, you should wrap it in a clean towel to blot excess water; then it needs to hang dry on a padded hanger away from sun or electric light; when dry, it will be crinkled and must be ironed with a very cool iron; finally, on the day of wearing, it should be steamed while you shower and lightly re-ironed. In other words, you think you will be a servant to it.

Examples

Concepts are frequently defined or explained through examples. The classic Type A personality can be defined through examples of behavior: If Jake is Type A, he is extremely impatient in a long grocery line, he cannot find the time to go to a film starring his favorite actor, and he considers getting a promotion at work a life-or-death issue. He is likely to slam doors and throw books when angry.

In an essay in this chapter, Isaac Asimov uses himself and his garage mechanic as examples to show how subjective people's definitions of intelligence are.

Narration

Aesop's fables, which you probably remember from childhood, make use of narrative, or story, to explain a basic truth about humans. A "sour grapes" attitude is explained by the story of the fox who sees a bunch of delicious-looking grapes but can't reach them; the fox, therefore, comforts itself by deciding that they were probably sour anyway. A writer might define an abstract quality, such as heroism or courage, by telling a story with a hero who acts out the virtue.

In his essay in this chapter, Dennis Baron uses brief narratives to illustrate the "clash of civilizations" that happens when people don't define key terms and basic concepts in the same way.

Comparison

Sometimes we define a word by emphasizing its likeness to something else. For example, we explain what a **fable** is by saying it's a kind of story. Writers use imaginative comparison to clarify meaning, too: "A true friend is a port in a storm" and "A true friend is as comfortable as an old shoe."

A comparison may be used for surprising effect. When the phrase "inner child" first became popular, it struck us as a remarkably apt description of the juvenile traits that lurk within every adult: fun-loving, self-centered, impulsive, dependent. These parts of our selves are easily comparable to children, and the phrase captures the idea well.

Contrast

Sometimes the best way to define something is to contrast it with something different. This technique can be quite simple: *Dearth* is the opposite of *plenty*. Or the definition can consist of a comparison spiked with a contrast. As our friend heard her 5-year-old explain to her 4-year-old, "Death is like going to Oklahoma, only longer."

In some cases, contrast is needed to correct a common misconception about a term. *Schizophrenia*, contrary to popular belief, does not involve having more than one personality. And being *educated*, according to Asimov's garage mechanic, doesn't mean being "smart."

THE PITFALLS OF DEFINITION AND EXPLANATION

When you write a definition or explanation, you risk making certain characteristic mistakes.

Missing Your Audience

Would you explain what a control key is to a computer whiz? We hope not. But if you were writing directions for a beginning word processing course, you'd be foolish *not* to define what a control key is. Analyzing your intended **audience** is important in all writing. If you misjudge what your audience needs to have defined or explained, you will either insult or confuse them.

Going in Circles

Some definitions are called circular because they don't go anywhere. They restate rather than explain. "A *smooth operator* is a person who functions without roughness," for example, tells you nothing. The second part of that definition only rewords the first part. The definition must lead somewhere, like this: "A *smooth operator* is a person who takes advantage of others by using charm and persuasion."

Abstraction

The previous circular definition also demonstrates the flaw of abstraction. It has no **concrete words** to hang onto. A high-flown sentence like "Our ideal leader is the hope of the future" provides no helpful terms about qualities we can actually identify.

Leaving Information Out

To say merely that a fable is a story doesn't get across the whole idea; it conveys only part of it: A fable has special features, like talking animals and a moral lesson. Incompleteness is a pitfall especially of short definitions, such as "Love is never having to say you're sorry." In this chapter, the essay "Mommy, What Does 'Nigger' Mean?" shows that a sentence like "*Nigger* is a degrading label for an African American" is not a full definition.

Of course, an explanation is incomplete when your reader needs to ask for clarification. Sometimes it's hard to see the holes in what you have written yourself because you already know what you're trying to say. You need to enlist a good peer editor to point out whether you have omitted important information.

WHAT TO LOOK FOR IN DEFINITIONS AND EXPLANATIONS

Here are some guidelines to follow as you study the selections in this chapter.

1. *Focus on which term or concept is being defined or explained.* This focus will help you evaluate the essay's effectiveness.
2. *Identify the ways in which the writer develops the idea,* especially through the use of details, narration, example, comparison, and contrast.
3. *Figure out who the intended audience is.* Then think about how the essay would be different if written for a different audience. What definitions and explanations would be added or deleted?
4. *Ask yourself whether the definition or explanation is complete.* If it is not complete, does the writer tell you why?

PREPARING TO READ

What word could be used to label you? Consider even labels that you do not think accurate. Might someone call you a jock? a nerd? an egghead? a bimbo? a tramp? a hero? a male chauvinist? a rabid feminist? a spoiled brat? a bully? a heartbreaker?

••

"Mommy, What Does 'Nigger' Mean?"

••

GLORIA NAYLOR

Gloria Naylor came from a rural, working-class southern background and did not enter college until she was twenty-five, after working as a missionary and a telephone operator. Naylor graduated from Brooklyn College in 1981, and in 1983 she won the American Book Award for best first novel for The Women of Brewster Place. *In this excerpt from an article first published in the* New York Times *on February 20, 1986, Naylor discusses the ways a word's meaning changes according to the context in which it is used.*

TERMS TO RECOGNIZE

necrophiliac *(para. 1)*	someone sexually attracted to corpses
verified *(para. 1)*	proven true
gravitated *(para. 2)*	moved toward
mecca *(para. 2)*	a place regarded as the center of interest or activity
inflections *(para. 3)*	tones of voice
trifling *(para. 8)*	shallow, unimportant
connotation *(para. 9)*	the idea suggested by a word or phrase, in addition to its surface meaning
stratum *(para. 12)*	level
internalization *(para. 12)*	making other people's attitudes a part of your own way of thinking

I remember the first time I heard the word "nigger." In my third-grade   1
class, our math tests were being passed down the rows, and as I handed the papers to a little boy in back of me, I remarked that once again he had received a much lower mark than I did. He snatched his test from me and spit out that word. Had he called me a nymphomaniac or a necrophiliac,

I couldn't have been more puzzled. I didn't know what a nigger was, but I knew that whatever it meant, it was something he shouldn't have called me. This was verified when I raised my hand, and in a loud voice repeated what he had said and watched the teacher scold him for using a "bad" word. I was later to go home and ask the inevitable question that every black parent must face—"Mommy, what does 'nigger' mean?"

And what exactly did it mean? Thinking back, I realize that this 2 could not have been the first time the word was used in my presence. I was part of a large extended family that had migrated from the rural South after World War II and formed a close-knit network that gravitated around my maternal grandparents. Their ground-floor apartment in one of the buildings they owned in Harlem was a weekend mecca for my immediate family, along with countless aunts, uncles, and cousins who brought along assorted friends. It was a bustling and open house with assorted neighbors and tenants popping in and out to exchange bits of gossip, pick up an old quarrel, or referee the ongoing checkers game in which my grandmother cheated shamelessly. They were all there to let down their hair and put up their feet after a week of labor in the factories, laundries, and shipyards of New York.

Amid the clamor, which could reach deafening proportions—two or 3 three conversations going on simultaneously, punctuated by the sound of a baby's crying somewhere in the back rooms or out on the street—there was still a rigid set of rules about what was said and how. Older children were sent out of the living room when it was time to get into the juicy details about "you-know-who" up on the third floor who had gone and gotten herself "p-r-e-g-n-a-n-t!" But my parents, knowing that I could spell well beyond my years, always demanded that I follow the others out to play. Beyond sexual misconduct and death, everything else was considered harmless for our young ears. And so among the anecdotes of the triumphs and disappointments in the various workings of their lives, the word "nigger" was used in my presence, but it was set within contexts and inflections that caused it to register in my mind as something else.

In the singular, the word was always applied to a man who had 4 distinguished himself in some situation that brought their approval for his strength, intelligence, or drive:

"Did Johnny really do that?" 5

"I'm telling you, that nigger pulled in $6,000 of overtime last year. 6 Said he got enough for a down payment on a house."

When used with a possessive adjective by a woman—"my nigger"—it 7 became a term of endearment for husband or boyfriend. But it could be more than just a term applied to a man. In their mouths it became the pure essence of manhood—a disembodied force that channeled their past history of struggle and present survival against the odds into a victorious statement of being: "Yeah, that old foreman found out quick enough—you don't mess with a nigger."

In the plural, it became a description of some group within the com- 8
munity that had overstepped the bounds of decency as my family defined it. Parents who neglected their children, a drunken couple who fought in public, people who simply refused to look for work, those with excessively dirty mouths or unkempt households were all "trifling niggers." This particular circle could forgive hard times, unemployment, the occasional bout of depression—they had gone through all of that themselves—but the unforgivable sin was lack of self-respect.

A woman could never be a "nigger" in the singular, with its connota- 9
tion of confirming worth. The noun "girl" was its closest equivalent in that sense, but only when used in direct address and regardless of the gender doing the addressing. "Girl" was a token of respect for a woman. The one-syllable word was drawn out to sound like three in recognition of the extra ounce of wit, nerve, or daring that the woman had shown in the situation under discussion.

"G-i-r-l, stop. You mean you said that to his face?" 10

But if the word was used in a third-person reference or shortened so 11
that it almost snapped out of the mouth, it always involved some element of communal disapproval. And age became an important factor in these exchanges. It was only between individuals of the same generation, or from an older person to a younger (but never the other way around), that "girl" would be considered a compliment.

I don't agree with the argument that use of the word "nigger" at this 12
social stratum of the black community was an internalization of racism. The dynamics were the exact opposite: the people in my grandmother's living room took a word that whites used to signify worthlessness or degradation and rendered it impotent. Gathering there together, they transformed "nigger" to signify the varied and complex human beings they knew themselves to be. If the word was to disappear totally from the mouths of even the most liberal of white society, no one in that room was naïve enough to believe it would disappear from white minds. Meeting the word head-on, they proved it had absolutely nothing to do with the way they were determined to live their lives.

So there must have been dozens of times that the word "nigger" was 13
spoken in front of me before I reached the third grade. But I didn't "hear" it until it was said by a small pair of lips that had already learned it could be a

way to humiliate me. That was the word I went home and asked my mother about. And since she knew that I had to grow up in America, she took me in her lap and explained.

RESPONDING TO READING

Do you agree that Naylor's relatives used the word *nigger* in a nonracist or counterracist way? Use your own reactions to the word to explain your answer.

CONSIDERING CONTENT

1. What are Naylor's background and social class? How do you know? Why are they significant to the main point of the essay?
2. Why was the child puzzled when the boy called her *nigger*, even though she had heard the word before?
3. List the definitions of the word *nigger* that were used in the author's grandparents' apartment.
4. Reread paragraph 12. How did the African American community's uses of *nigger* make it not racist, according to Naylor?
5. What does the last sentence suggest about the author's mother? What does it suggest about America?

CONSIDERING METHOD

1. What kind of a little third-grader was Gloria Naylor? Why do you think she presents her childhood self as no angel? What effect does this early presentation of self have on the reader?
2. Reread the description of the author's grandparents' apartment. List at least seven words or phrases that appeal to your senses.
3. How is paragraph 12 different from the rest of the essay? How does the appearance of the page prepare you for this difference?
4. The central part of the essay includes many direct quotations. Why do you think Naylor used people's exact words so often?
5. Does Naylor envision her audience as primarily black or primarily white or mixed? Explain.

WRITING STEP BY STEP: MULTIPLE MEANINGS

Following Gloria Naylor's essay as an example, write a paper discussing a term that has various—even contradictory—meanings, depending on context: who says it, when it is used, and whether it is applied to men or women, young or old, individual or group, for example. Like Naylor, you might think of a term, such as *wife, macho, liberal, success, feminist, jock,* or *marriage,* that holds more meaning than you once thought.

A. Before you start your essay, brainstorm and jot down the various ways you have heard your term used. Ask friends and classmates for help if you need it. Remember that your readers probably have their own definitions of the term.

B. See whether your definitions fall into groups. For example, can you separate the negative meanings from the positive ones? Or do different meanings belong to different social, racial, or ethnic groups? Try at least to decide on a reasonable order in which to present your definitions. For example, the most widely used meanings might come first, with rarer and rarer meanings following it until the last one is the rarest.

C. Begin your essay with a brief story, as Naylor does.

D. Launch into the body of your essay by looking back into your past. Write about how you used to think of the term, perhaps as a child.

E. Develop each meaning of the term with an explanation and examples of direct quotations using it. Keep looking at how Naylor develops her meanings.

F. Close the body of your essay with a speculation about why the term has such a variety of meanings. Look at Naylor's paragraph 12 for ideas about how to present your thoughts.

G. Use the last paragraph to reflect on the anecdote you used in the opening of your essay. This is how Naylor concludes her piece. Your discussion of the term has, by now, added a new dimension to the anecdote.

OTHER WRITING IDEAS

1. What is the first memory you have of someone saying something purposely to hurt you? Or a memory of your saying something purposely to hurt someone else? Write an essay about your own and others' response to the harsh words.

2. COLLABORATIVE WRITING. Think of a phrase or word that seems to be plain but is actually used to mean many different things; for example, "Just a minute," "Well," "I'm ready," and "I'll call you," are more slippery than they seem. A group of students in your class can have some fun discussing such sayings and developing ideas for a single report or individual essays.

3. USING THE INTERNET. Do a search using the phrase "language and racism." Locate one or two articles that concern the words used to describe race, and write an essay about the complexities of labeling racial groups.

4. WRITING ABOUT READING. Can you explain Naylor's views about the word *nigger*? Write a summary of her main ideas to help you clarify your understanding. Directions for writing a summary are given at the end of Chapter 1, pp. 13–14.

GAINING WORD POWER

The following words appear in Gloria Naylor's essay. They have an ending, -tion, in common. This ending occurs frequently in our language, making nouns out of verbs: for example, the noun *conversation* comes from the verb *converse*, which means "to talk." Use your dictionary to find the verb behind each of the nouns in the following list, and give a brief definition of the verb. Begin each brief definition with the word *to*. The first one is done.

	Verb	**Definition**
connotation	connote	to imply or suggest
degradation		
description		
generation		
inflection		
internalization		
recognition		
situation		

Now see how it works the other way around. Here is a list of verbs that are used in Naylor's essay. Find the -tion noun that comes from each verb (some are obvious, but for others in the list you will need the dictionary). Be sure to copy the spelling of the noun exactly: Sometimes the first part of the word will change. Then write a brief definition of the noun you have written. We did the first one for you.

	Noun	**Definition**
apply	application	a form to be filled out
consider		
determine		
explain		
gravitate		
humiliate		
migrate		
punctuate		
realize		
receive		
repeat		
transform		
verify		

EDITING SKILLS: HYPHENS

Consider the use of the hyphen—the short dash—in these phrases from Gloria Naylor's essay:

third-grade class   one-syllable word

close-knit network   third-person reference

ground-floor apartment

The hyphenated adjectives, which modify the nouns that come after them, are called *temporary compounds*. They are compound because they consist of two words; they are temporary because the two words usually exist separately. They are hyphenated because they make up a unit that seems more like one adjective than two. Sometimes you need to hyphenate in order to make your meaning clear. Think about these examples:

an Italian art specialist   an Italian-art specialist

a small auto dealer   a small-auto dealer

comic book approach   a comic-book approach

In the second list, the hyphen shows which words go together—the specialist is not Italian, the dealer is not small, and the approach is not comic.

Sometimes, it is difficult to decide whether to hyphenate two words that frequently occur together (back-seat driver), whether to run them together as a compound word (backseat driver), or whether to leave them separate (back seat driver). There is not wide agreement even among professional writers about some of these blends. You will see "Thank you" and "Thank-you" about equally often. Your dictionary should be your guide to making the decision.

EXERCISE

Look up the following combinations to see whether words are hyphenated, compound, or separate. Write out the form your dictionary endorses.

back seat driver   open and shut case

happily married couple   least restrictive environment

girl friend problems   partway finished

back door business deals   part time worker

child like expression   better fitting word

an easy pick up   half baked plan

Look back on the essay you have just written. Did you use any compound words that needed hyphens? Did you leave out any hyphens? Check a dictionary or with your instructor before making any corrections.

WEB SITES

http://voices.cla.umn.edu/artistpages/naylorGloria.php
VG/Voices from the Gaps—a site maintained by the University of Minnesota—provides a biography and other information on Gloria Naylor.
www.salon.com/books/int/2007/04/25/asim/
Author and journalist Jabari Asim discusses the history and politics of the term "nigger" in this interview about his book *The N Word: Who Can Say It, Who Shouldn't, and Why* (2007).

PREPARING TO READ

If you took an intelligence test and scored low, how would you feel? What might you say that the test failed to measure about you?

....

What Is Intelligence, Anyway?

....

ISAAC ASIMOV

Isaac Asimov (1923–1992) was an American, born in Russia, who wrote more than 200 books, including children's stories, popular science, science fiction, fantasy, and scholarly science. With so many intellectual accomplishments, he was well qualified to wonder just what intelligence is—and is not.

TERMS TO RECOGNIZE

KP (*para. 1*)	kitchen patrol (working in the kitchen)
complacent (*para. 2*)	self-satisfied
bents (*para. 2*)	interests, tendencies
oracles (*para. 3*)	divine communications
devised (*para. 4*)	made up
foist (*para. 4*)	impose
arbiter (*para. 4*)	judge
indulgently (*para. 6*)	as if doing a favor
raucously (*para. 6*)	loudly, in a disorderly way
smugly (*para. 6*)	in a self-satisfied way

What is intelligence, anyway? When I was in the Army, I received a kind of aptitude test that all soldiers took and, against a normal of 100, scored 160. No one at the base had ever seen a figure like that, and for two hours they made a big fuss over me. (It didn't mean anything. The next day I was still a buck private with KP as my highest duty.) 1

All my life I've been registering scores like that, so that I have the complacent feeling that I'm highly intelligent, and I expect other people to think so, too. Actually, though, don't such scores simply mean that I am very good at answering the type of academic questions that are considered worthy of answers by the people who make up the intelligence tests—people with intellectual bents similar to mine? 2

For instance, I had an auto repairman once, who, on these intelligence tests, could not possibly have scored more than 80, by my estimate. I always took it for granted that I was far more intelligent than he was. Yet, when anything went wrong with my car, I hastened to him with it, watched him anxiously as he explored its vitals, and listened to his pronouncements as though they were divine oracles—and he always fixed my car.

Well then, suppose my auto repairman devised questions for an intelligence test. Or suppose a carpenter did, or a farmer, or, indeed, almost anyone but an academician. By every one of those tests, I'd prove myself a moron. And I'd *be* a moron, too. In a world where I could not use my academic training and my verbal talents but had to do something intricate or hard, working with my hands, I would do poorly. My intelligence, then, is not absolute but is a function of the society I live in and of the fact that a small subsection of that society has managed to foist itself on the rest as an arbiter of such matters.

Consider my auto repairman, again. He had a habit of telling me jokes whenever he saw me. One time he raised his head from under the automobile hood to say, "Doc, a deaf-and-dumb guy went into a hardware store to ask for some nails. He put two fingers together on the counter and made hammering motions with the other hand. The clerk brought him a hammer. He shook his head and pointed to the two fingers he was hammering. The clerk brought him nails. He picked out the sizes he wanted, and left. Well, doc, the next guy who came in was a blind man. He wanted scissors. How do you suppose he asked for them?"

Indulgently, I lifted my right hand and made scissoring motions with my first two fingers. Whereupon my auto repairman laughed raucously and said, "Why, you dumb jerk, he used his *voice* and asked for them." Then he said, smugly, "I've been trying that on all my customers today." "Did you catch many?" I asked. "Quite a few," he said, "but I knew for sure I'd catch *you*." "Why is that?" I asked. "Because you're so goddamned educated, doc, I *knew* you couldn't be very smart."

And I have an uneasy feeling he had something there.

RESPONDING TO READING

Do you think that people who are academically intelligent are often poor at nonacademic things? Why or why not?

CONSIDERING CONTENT

1. Why do you think that Asimov's high intelligence score "didn't mean anything" in the army?
2. What is the basic conflict discussed in this essay?
3. Why was the repairman sure he would catch "Doc" Asimov with the joke? Was the repairman stereotyping college professors?
4. What might be on an intelligence test written by auto mechanics? carpenters? farmers? parents of preschoolers? portrait painters? What point is Asimov making with this type of suggestion?
5. Which "small subsection" (para. 4) of society has set itself up as the definers of intelligence?
6. What do you think about Asimov's "uneasy feeling"? Do you think the mechanic "had something there"? Or do you think the nature of the joke would fool most people, intelligent or not?

CONSIDERING METHOD

1. Asimov's essay contains two anecdotes (look up the word **anecdote** if you have not already done so). How do the anecdotes help you understand the conflict the writer is discussing?
2. In a fitting reflection of the content of the essay, Asimov uses both highly academic words (*oracles*, *bents*, *arbiter*) and common, informal words. Point out some of the informal words.
3. Count the number of words in each of the six sentences that make up paragraph 4. Notice the variety in sentence length. This variation is a factor that makes writing lively instead of plodding. When you think your own writing sounds plodding, check to see whether you have a good range of sentence lengths. If they are too much alike, try to combine some of the shorter sentences into longer ones or divide long ones into shorter ones.
4. The last paragraph consists of only one sentence. What difference do you see between placing it in this position and simply adding it as a closing sentence to the preceding paragraph?
5. How do you think academics would respond to this essay? Was Asimov writing to them?

COMBINING STRATEGIES

In this seven-paragraph essay exploring a definition, how many paragraphs are devoted to developing an example?

WRITING STEP BY STEP: DEFINING AN ABSTRACTION

Write an essay that investigates the meaning of an **abstract** term—an idea that cannot be directly observed, such as intelligence. You can use some of Asimov's techniques. We also suggest some other methods for developing an extended definition. Use any combination of techniques to develop your definition. To get your thinking started, consider these abstractions:

common sense	humility	educated
optimism	professionalism	cool
courage	resourcefulness	simplicity
generosity	street smart	beauty
laziness	foolish	stubbornness

Choose your own term, but be sure your choice is an abstraction (not something **concrete,** such as *submarine, pizza,* or *tennis*).

A. Begin with the question "What is _____, anyway?"

B. If you have an anecdote that will serve as an extended investigation of the term, include the story, as Asimov did.

C. Use examples of people you know who demonstrate the abstraction you are defining. Show how they behave or think, with specific details.

D. Use description. For example, an abstract feeling may have a counterpart in a certain type of landscape or weather that you could describe, such as "fluffy white clouds" to suggest peace and contentment or "loud thunder and hard-driving rain" to indicate anger.

E. Point out differences. A good definition will make clear the difference between the word you are explaining and other words with similar meanings. You might tell how feeling peaceful is different from feeling happy or calm.

F. Provide a contrast. We often explain words by clarifying what they are *not*. For example, you could point out that laziness does not merely include lying around doing nothing, which could be depression instead.

G. In your closing, let the reader know to what extent the abstraction is important in your own life.

OTHER WRITING IDEAS

1. Write an essay similar to Asimov's on questioning the usual definition of a term. Challenge the term's usefulness or its usual meaning or everyday misuse.

2. USING THE INTERNET. Make up a word for a concept or item that doesn't have a name, as far as you know. These new words, called *sniglets*, are sometimes collected in humorous books. Here are some examples:

BEAVO (n.): a pencil with teeth marks all over it.

FICTATE (v.): to inform a television or screen character of impending danger under the assumption that he or she can hear you.

OPUP (v.): to push one's glasses back up on the nose.

You may need to make up a related group of words and explain how you came up with them in order to write a whole essay. For example, you could make up several sniglets that describe your pet's behaviors. Find a Web site to spark your imagination.

3. COLLABORATIVE WRITING. Instead of presenting a unified definition of a concept, try to write an essay presenting all the different, even contradictory, meanings a certain term could have. For example, if you asked a group of people to explain what *sex appeal* means to them, you would probably get some widely varying answers. Work with a group of classmates to come up with meanings and to draft a group definition.

4. WRITING ABOUT READING. What's your response to Asimov's opening question: "What is intelligence, anyway?" Write an essay in which you define what intelligence means to you, both in yourself and in the people you know. Use the various methods of developing a definition that are discussed in the introduction to this chapter.

GAINING WORD POWER

Complete these sentences in a reasonable way, showing that you understand the vocabulary words included.

1. Troy indulgently promised to take Rachel _____ _____.

2. Because he had a mechanical bent, Mark specialized in _____ _____.

3. _____, the crowd cheered raucously.

4. Dr. Morse foisted his ideas on us when he _____ _____.

5. By setting himself up as the arbiter of good taste in clothes, Sheldon _____.

EDITING SKILLS: USING THE RIGHT TENSE

One of the trickiest skills we learn as we grow up is using the correct tense for verbs. If you have ever learned a foreign language, you are fully aware of the complications of verb tense. In your native language, as you speak, you almost always choose the right tense, but in writing you can get in a snarl.

Asimov's essay shows a combination of tenses. For things that occur in the present or are true in the present, he uses plain old present tense: "I *have* the complacent feeling that I'*m* highly intelligent, and I *expect* other people to think so, too" (para. 2, italics added). For the story about the mechanic, which happened in the past, Asimov uses past tense: "Indulgently, I *lifted* my right hand and *made* scissoring motions with my first two fingers" (para. 6).

In telling stories, speakers and writers sometimes get confused as they go along, and they switch from past to present and back within the same anecdote. But in academic writing you usually stick to the past tense for events that took place in the past. If you're writing about what happened in a film or literary work, however, you can summarize plot in the present tense.

EXERCISE

The following paragraph mixes present and past tenses. Rewrite the paragraph, and put all the verbs into the present tense:

> *Spenser: For Hire* is based on the detective novels of Robert Parker and is several steps above the average television crime series. It is well acted and well worth watching. Robert Ulrich proved that he is an excellent actor in the part of the tough, well-read private investigator Spenser. He is believable when he fought the bad guys, and he was believable when he quotes Shakespeare. But when the script called for him to be cute and kittenish with his girlfriend, Susan, he is not believable. A cute Spenser was simply embarrassing. In the books, Spenser and Susan tease and traded playful insults, but they are not kittenish. The TV show needed to fix that part of their relationship.

Now look at the verb tenses in the essay you wrote in response to the Asimov article. Which tenses did you use? Are they consistent and logical? Check over your writing, and make any needed corrections in the verb tenses.

🌐 WEB SITE

www.thomasarmstrong.com/multiple_intelligences.htm
Describes alternate ways of thinking about intelligence.

PREPARING TO READ

Were you ever embarrassed because you misunderstood or misinterpreted what someone said or wrote? What caused the misunderstanding or misinterpretation? Who was at fault?

. . . .

The Noun Game: A Simple Grammar Lesson Leads to a Clash of Civilizations

. . . .

DENNIS BARON

Dennis Baron is a professor of English and linguistics at the University of Illinois at Urbana-Champaign. He has written extensively about the history and the present state of the English language and has appeared on CNN, NPR, the CBC, and other television and radio stations to discuss language standards and English usage. His most recent book, A Better Pencil: Readers, Writers, and the Digital Revolution, *explores the influence of computers and the Internet on the practices of reading and writing.*

TERMS TO RECOGNIZE

undeniable *(para. 1)*	unquestionably true or real, beyond dispute
drudgery *(para. 2)*	exhausting, boring, unpleasant work
metaphysical *(para. 2)*	concerned with the nature of truth, life, reality
mortified *(para. 6)*	offended, embarrassed, ashamed
animates *(para. 8)*	living beings or entities
permeable *(para. 10)*	porous, allowing something to pass through
indeterminacy *(para. 10)*	uncertainty, the condition of not knowing an exact or definite answer

Everybody knows that a noun is the name of a person, place, or thing. It's one of those undeniable facts of daily life, a fact we seldom question until we meet up with a case that doesn't quite fit the way we're used to viewing things. That's exactly what happened to a student in Ohio when his English teacher decided to play the noun game.

To the teacher, the noun game seemed a fun way to take the drudgery out of grammar. To the student it forced a metaphysical crisis. To me it

1

2

shows what happens when cultures clash and children get lost in the tyranny of school. That's a lot to get from a grammar game.

Anyway, here's how you play. Every student gets a set of cards with nouns written on them. At the front of the classroom are three buckets, labeled "person," "place," and "thing." The students take turns sorting their cards into the appropriate buckets. "Book" goes in the thing bucket. "City" goes in the place bucket. "Gandhi" goes in the person bucket. 3

Ganesh had a card with "horse" on it. Ganesh isn't his real name, by the way. It's actually my cousin's name, so I'm going to use it here. You might guess from his name that Ganesh is South Asian. In India, where he had been in school before coming to Ohio, Ganesh was taught that a noun named a person, place, thing, or *animal*. If he played the noun game in India he'd have four buckets and there would be no problem deciding what to do with "horse." But in Ohio Ganesh had only three buckets, and it wasn't clear to him which one he should put "horse" in. 4

In India, Ganesh's religion taught him that all forms of life are contin- 5 uous, interrelated parts of the universal plan. So when he surveyed the three buckets it never occurred to him that a horse, a living creature, could be a thing. He knew that horses weren't people, but they had more in common with people than with places or things. Forced to choose, Ganesh put the horse card in the person bucket.

Blapp! Wrong! You lose. The teacher shook her head, and Ganesh sat 6 down, mortified, with a C for his efforts. This was a game where you got a grade, and a C for a child from a South Asian family of overachievers is a disgrace. So his parents went to talk to the teacher.

It so happens that I've been in a similar situation. We spent a year in 7 France some time back, and my oldest daughter did sixth grade in a French school. The teacher asked her, "How many continents are there?" and she replied, as she had been taught in the good old U.S. of A., "seven." Blaap! Wrong! It turns out that in France there are only five. So old dad goes to talk to the teacher about this. I may not be able to remember the seven dwarfs, but I rattled off Europe, Asia, Africa, Australia, Antarctica, North America, and South America. The teacher calmly walked me over to the map of the world. Couldn't I see that Antarctica was an uninhabited island? And couldn't I see that North and South America were connected? Any fool could see as much. At that point I decided not to press the observation that Europe and Asia were also connected. Some things are not worth fighting for when you're fighting your child's teacher.

Anyway, let's get back to nouns. School grammar texts typically 8 divide nouns into person, place, or thing. More advanced grammars separate nouns into animates and inanimates, or abstracts and concretes, and they further complicate matters by including phrases, clauses, and entire sentences that aren't actually nouns but function like them. None of this lends itself to buckets, and none of these systems specifically mentions animals. In English, though, animals can clearly be things: "The dog is hungry. Feed it."

However, animals can also be persons: "Babar became king of the elephants when the old king ate a poisoned mushroom and died." They can even be ideas, like the Cheshire cat in "Alice," or the Loch Ness monster: they're not real, so they must be ideas. I guess an animal can't very well be a place, but I'm sure some reader will attack me for placism, arguing yes, it can.   9

But that's not the point, is it? The point is that lots of nouns don't fit   10
neatly into noun buckets. What is East? Is it a place or an idea? Can it exist without West? Or North and South? Calling nouns persons, places, things, ideas, or even animals, is a way to help students recognize nouns when they stumble upon them. It is not meant to limit the imagination or categorize every possible noun the mind can come up with. Anyone looking at all closely at language must see that its categories are suggestive, permeable, inconclusive. As linguists like to say, all grammars leak. Some teachers find this indeterminacy uncomfortable.

Is the point of the noun game to see whether students recognize pos-   11
sible nouns as nouns, or whether their view of the universe agrees with the teacher's? Is education fitting things into buckets, or wondering why the categories don't fit the facts? Does education consist of grading you on how well you can play a game?

So what do I advise Ganesh's parents to do? Forget it, that's what.   12
Ganesh has done more thinking about the nature of language than his teacher has. His performance in the noun game won't keep him out of Harvard, or Ohio State. The teacher isn't going to change. The grade is not important. It's the thought, not the noun, that counts.

RESPONDING TO READING

What do you think of the teacher's "noun game"? Do you think Ganesh deserved a C?

CONSIDERING CONTENT

1. What is the traditional definition of a noun? How does the author expand and revise that traditional meaning?
2. Do you understand why Ganesh put "horse" in the person bucket? Where would you have put it?
3. How much do you actually learn about Ganesh's cultural background?

4. What is the author's opinion of Ganesh's teacher? Cite sentences and details that reveal Baron's feelings about the teacher.

5. Paragraph 11 is made up of three questions. How would you answer those questions? How do you think Baron would answer them?

6. Is this article primarily about cultural differences, or is it about educational practices and values?

CONSIDERING METHOD

1. In which paragraphs does the author use narrative—that is, where does he relate the story of what Ganesh did and what happened to him?

2. Why doesn't Baron use Ganesh's real name?

3. What's the point of the anecdote about the author's daughter in France? Do you think it's needed?

4. Why does the author use the exclamations "Blapp! Wrong!"? What is the tone of these words?

5. Do you understand the references to Babar, the Cheshire cat, and the Loch Ness monster? If not, look them up. Why does Baron include them?

6. The word *placism* (para. 9) seems to be a term that Baron invented, based on an analogy with racism, sexism, ageism, and so forth. Can you figure out what it means? Why does Baron include it?

7. Why does the author use so many questions? Does he expect his readers to answer them? Does he answer them? What purposes do they serve? (See Chapter 10, under Editing Skills, pp. 328–329.)

WRITING STEP BY STEP: EXPLAINING A CULTURAL PRACTICE

In his essay, Dennis Baron focuses on how people define a word according to their cultural background. Consider other practices that vary from culture to culture—whether culture is defined by ethnic or racial background, geography (urban or rural, Southeast or Northwest), religion, education, or socioeconomic level. Think of how you have been surprised or puzzled by some practice outside of your own little world. For example, you may have visited a friend's family who have very different meal habits than your family does, or you might be shocked by how your second cousins on the farm think about animals, or you may find yourself going along with a pal to religious services that strike you as bizarre. Your Step by Step essay will use details, examples, narration, and comparison-and-contrast to explain one of your experiences with cultural variation.

A. Set up the situation in the first paragraph by stating what you thought "everyone knows," or what you thought "everyone does" (a generalization you later found wrong). Baron does this in paragraph 1 of his essay.

B. Explain how you came upon the situation that revealed the cultural difference to you. Use a narrative as Baron does in paragraphs 3-5. What was unexpected about the experience? Why? For example, "I watched aghast as my tender-hearted cousins happily chowed down on the pig they had raised themselves!"

C. Explain how you reacted to the situation. Did you express your surprise or keep it inside? If you expressed it, how did other people respond? For instance, "My farm cousins giggled at my reluctance to fork a piece of Wilbur onto my plate."

D. Write a paragraph about another similar situation you've experienced (see Baron's paragraph 10). "I had noticed that my cousins didn't even have names for the dozen barn cats."

E. Explain the source of the difference you perceived in the situation, through comparing the two cultures that were at odds, as Baron does in paragraph 10.

F. Close by using rhetorical questions to explore a deeper meaning of the cultural difference or to explain your opinion about how the difference should be approached. Baron uses such rhetorical questions in paragraphs 11 and 12.

OTHER WRITING IDEAS

1. What is the difference between a "nerd" and a "geek"? Write an essay in which you define each of these terms and explain the distinctions between them. (Substitute another pair of closely related descriptive terms if you can think of ones you'd prefer to write about.) In addition to consulting reference books, ask a variety of people what they think the difference is between the terms. For help in setting up an essay that compares and contrasts, consult the introduction to Chapter 7, pp. 184–187.

2. COLLABORATIVE WRITING. With a group of three or four classmates, brainstorm a list of words or expressions that you think need defining because they are misleading, unclear, or too indirect. Think about words used in TV commercials, personal ads, real estate descriptions, fast-food restaurants, or menu language. Then, individually or as a group, define the word accurately. As you explain the accurate meaning, explain why the contrived expression was chosen. If the word or name caught on with the public, such as "lite" (for "low-calorie" or "simplified"), "share" (for "tell" or "discuss"), "issue" (for "problem"), or "senior citizen" (for "old person"), speculate about why it became so popular. As a group or as an individual, write an essay about a word like this (or a related group

of such words), explaining the accurate or original definitions and why they came to be used in divergent ways.

3. USING THE INTERNET. At **http://crede.berkeley.edu**, you will find the site for the Center for Research on Education, Diversity, and Excellence. This organization explores how schools can work best in our multiethnic society. Click on "Five Standards" and you will see how CREDE defines effective pedagogy. Write an essay, based on these definitions, about how your own schooling has succeeded and failed in effectiveness.

4. WRITING ABOUT READING. In his conclusion Baron says, "The grade is not important. It's the thought, not the noun, that counts." What do you think he means? Do you agree with him? Have you (or someone close to you) ever gotten a grade that was not as important as what you learned? Use an example or examples from your own experience, if you can, in answering these questions.

GAINING WORD POWER

Dennis Baron uses the words *grade* and *grading* in his article. Both words come from the Latin root meaning "step." See if you can fill in the blanks to complete the following words that also contain this root. Use a dictionary to help you if you get stuck.

G R A D _ _ _ _   a degree of inclination; rate of assent or descent; a slope or ramp (noun)

G R A D _ _ _ _   to complete all the steps of a course and receive a diploma or degree (verb)

G R A D _ _ _ _ _   advancing or moving in small degrees; step-by-step (adverb)

_ _ _ _ _ G R A D _   moving or tending backward; reverting to an earlier or inferior condition (adjective)

Now put the words in the following sentences:

1. The ball player, with constant practice, _____ gained enough confidence and skill to get into the starting lineup.
2. Seniors plan to _____ in early May once they have satisfied the necessary course requirements.
3. Even though the steep _____ of the icy road had been sanded and plowed, cars inched forward.
4. Ken had a _____ sinus infection that refused to respond to antibiotics.

EDITING SKILLS: USING NOUN CLAUSES

In his article Dennis Baron writes about "clauses" that "aren't actually nouns but function like them." Clauses are groups of words that contain a subject and a verb, but the ones that function as nouns are called *dependent* clauses because they are parts of larger sentences. Baron uses a number of these dependent noun clauses in his writing. In fact, the first sentence in the article contains one such clause (we've underlined it for you):

Everybody knows <u>that a noun is the name of a person, place, or thing</u>.

Here's another example from paragraph 4:

You might guess from his name <u>that Ganesh is South Asian</u>.

You can tell when a dependent clause is functioning as a noun by making up another sentence in which you substitute a noun or pronoun for the clause:

Everybody knows <u>the definition of a noun</u>.
You might guess <u>Ganesh's nationality</u> from his name.

The word *that* makes these clauses dependent. In fact, *that* can turn any declarative statement into a noun clause:

A virus causes stomach ulcers. → Medical researchers have determined that a virus causes stomach ulcers.

The Raiders returned to Oakland. → That the Raiders returned to Oakland angered LA football fans.

EXERCISE

Each of the first three sentences in paragraph 5 of "The Noun Game" contains a noun clause. Identify these sentences, copy them, and underline the clauses. Do the same for the two sentences with noun clauses in paragraph 10. Now write sentences of your own imitating those five sentences from Baron's article. If you have time, compare your original sentences with those of some classmates.

WEB SITE

http://illinois.edu/db/view/25
Read other postings by Dennis Baron on his blog, "The Web of Language," which he calls "the go-to site for language in the news."

PREPARING TO READ

Make a list of the subgroups you belong to within the diverse American population. Consider your geographical roots, your language, hobbies, interests, major, and job choice, for example. Are there prejudices against any of the subgroups you belong to? Is the language or jargon shared by the group part of that prejudice?

Viva Spanglish!

Lilly Gonzalez

Lilly Gonzalez is a young writer who graduated from the Medill School of Journalism at Northwestern University in Evanston, Illinois. While in school, Gonzalez was president of Alianza, Northwestern's largest Hispanic/Latino organization. She was the author of a popular column in the Daily Northwestern, *where she once caused a controversy when she defined the term "booty call" and defended carefree sex.*

TERMS TO RECOGNIZE

phonetics (para. 1)   the sounds of speech and their combination to create meaning
inevitable (para. 4)   impossible to avoid
sellout (para. 4)   a person who has betrayed a cause or principle
implicit (para. 6)   understood without direct expression
embrace (para. 6)   to take up eagerly

It was 1985 and I was in a pre-kindergarten class at Palmer Elementary in the small South Texas town of Pharr. My teacher, Mrs. Herrera, thought I didn't know any English, and I had no plans to let her know I did (thanks to my eldest sister, who had made sure I knew English before I entered school). All the other kids in my class spoke only Spanish; I didn't want to be the conceited one who spoke in English. Then one day Mrs. Herrera stumped me with a question I couldn't answer in Spanish. I was forced to say it in English—and just like that, my secret was out. When my Spanish-speaking mother wanted to know why I had refused to speak English in school, I was stumped again. The Spanish word for "embarrassed" (*avergonzada*) wouldn't come to me, so I tried a translation based on

phonetics and told her I had been too *embarazada*. I thought she'd understand my little Spanglish invention, but she just burst out laughing. I, her
four-year-old daughter, had just told her I was too pregnant to speak English.

And that was my first experience with Spanglish, a hybrid of English   2
and Spanish used by U.S. Latinos who live between two coexisting worlds
(Mexican Americans, for example). It wouldn't be the last time Spanglish
backfired on me. In fact, every time I'm surrounded by native Spanish
speakers, I pray that my Spanglish doesn't intrude into the conversation.
But it usually does, and the Spanish pros either smile at me with a pitying
look that says I've lost touch with my heritage or glare critically at me as if
I've just raped their language.

Strangers usually give me the pity smile. At Mexican restaurants, if my   3
server is Latino and my Spanish sounds less than perfect, I'm rewarded with
it. God forbid I should ask for *el menú de lonche* (Spanglish for "lunch menu")
instead of the proper *menú de almuerzo*. I encountered the pity smile when I
met my boyfriend's mother for the first time. She speaks flawless Spanish,
so naturally I was terrified. Around my third Spanish sentence, my Spanglish
popped out. "*Nunca hay donde parquear* (There's never anywhere to park)," I
said, wincing as soon as I had said that last word. *Parquear* is Spanglish for
the Spanish *estacionar*. She gave me the pity smile.

Those who know me better give me the critical glare. I hate the criti-   4
cal glare. Every time my family heads to Mexico to visit relatives, I dread the
inevitable. I'll be talking with my cousins and my Spanglish will trickle into
my otherwise fluent Spanish. They'll call me *pocha*, which means "sellout."
In my Spanish literature classes at Northwestern University, near Chicago,
there's added pressure to speak perfect Spanish. Professors jeer when I
speak up in class and Spanglish flows out of my mouth.

Don't they understand that Spanglish is my native tongue? I grew up   5
on the Texas-Mexico border with both Spanish and English, and my Spanglish is the product of that. I spoke Spanish with my parents, Spanglish with
my siblings and friends, and English with everyone else. My thoughts are in
Spanglish.

I left Texas to go to Northwestern in 1998, but every time I hear Span-   6
glish, I feel I'm home again. There's no better icebreaker than discovering
that you and a stranger both speak it. It carries an implicit understanding
of each other's background (immigrant parents, bilingual environment) and
plight (trying to make it in a country where Latinos are still a minority).
Suddenly, you're amigos, and you're dancing effortlessly between the two
languages. At Latino nightclubs, Spanglish wins me friends in the ladies'
room. Wherever the employees are Spanglish-speaking Latinos, it gets me

perks. And at Northwestern, it has given me my best friends. I was in a dorm hallway my freshman year when I heard them speaking Spanglish, and I impulsively poked my head in their room and joined their conversation. They didn't mind—Spanglish speakers embrace other Spanglish speakers. It's an unwritten law.

And that's why I refuse to give it up, despite the pity smile and the   7
critical glare. I've had a lifetime love affair with Spanglish, *embarazada* or not.

RESPONDING TO READING

What is your usual reaction when you hear foreign languages used in your community? Do you think that this reading will change the way you react to hearing other people around you speaking a language you don't know? Why or why not?

CONSIDERING CONTENT

1. Why were both Spanish and English spoken in Mrs. Herrera's prekindergarten?
2. Where in the essay is the direct definition of Spanglish? What is the definition? How are Spanglish words formed?
3. Why would the writer's cousins call her a sellout for using Spanglish?
4. Gonzalez writes, "My thoughts are in Spanglish." Why is it important what language your thoughts are in? If you have acquired a second language, have you ever found yourself thinking in it? What did it mean, if you did?
5. What do speakers of Spanglish have in common other than a shared vocabulary?

CONSIDERING METHOD

1. What does the title mean? How do you know? Why is it a good title for the essay?
2. What would the essay lose if it began without the opening anecdote?
3. Gonzalez explains three different reactions to her Spanglish. What method does she use to develop these explanations?
4. How would you describe Gonzalez's style—that is, the individuality of her expression? Point out some words and phrases that manifest her style. If you particularly like or dislike this style, explain why.
5. How did the writer help non-Spanish speakers understand the Spanish words in the essay?
6. Reread the opening and closing of the essay. How are they unified?

7. What are the two negative reactions Gonzalez notes in Spanish speakers when she uses Spanglish? What is the difference between these two reactions? What is the positive reaction she finds?

WRITING STEP BY STEP: SUBGROUP IDENTITY

In Preparing to Read, you listed the subgroups to which you belong. In this essay, you will write about one of these subgroups, how people in it are identifiable, and how people react to the subgroup. Choose a subgroup whose members can identify each other fairly easily: for example, fans of a certain kind of music, marathon runners, video game addicts, oil company wives, children of public school teachers, and film buffs.

A. Begin with an anecdote, as Gonzalez did. Use a story that introduces the subgroup in some naturally occurring setting. This should be one or two paragraphs long.

B. Next, provide a direct definition of the subgroup in one paragraph. Explain what the people in it have in common.

C. Think of two or three different reactions that others have when they realize you are a member of this subgroup. If you can, think of both negative and positive reactions, as Gonzalez did. Consider how people within the group and those outside it might react. Then explain each one of these reactions in a paragraph of its own.

D. Close with your ideas about whether your affiliation with this subgroup will be "a lifetime love affair."

E. If possible, unify your closing with your opening through repetition of words or through direct reference to the anecdote you began with.

F. Give your essay a title that comes from the slang, jargon, dress, knowledge base, or behavior of the subgroup.

OTHER WRITING IDEAS

1. Gonzalez writes about how her Spanglish sometimes embarrasses or unnerves her. Write an essay about a habit, behavior, or trait you have that sometimes embarrasses you. Explain why.

2. COLLABORATIVE WRITING. Get together with three or four other students who have seen the film *Spanglish* (or rent it for this writing project). Discuss ideas the movie brings up about assimilation and about retaining native culture. As a group or individually, write an essay explaining two or three issues facing people as they integrate into a new culture.

3. USING THE INTERNET. Do Spanish-speaking children who attend bilingual preschools and elementary schools in the United States become fluent English speakers and readers? Use the Internet to find the results of research studies on this question. Explain your findings in an editorial for your city's newspaper.

4. WRITING ABOUT READING. Gonzalez says that Spanish speakers have both negative and positive reactions when she uses Spanglish. Write an essay in which you identify those reactions and explain, as best you can, why people have them.

GAINING WORD POWER

English is probably the biggest borrower of words from other countries, with over 120 different languages recorded as sources of today's vocabulary. New terms from other countries are called *loan words* or *borrowings*, although they quickly become integrated into the rest of our speech as legitimate English words. What reference books could you use to find the foreign origins of the following words? Write down the word and its origin.

assassin	barbecue
bazaar	chipmunk
jaguar	saga
slogan	tattoo
tea	voodoo

EDITING SKILLS: USING COORDINATION

Experienced writers vary their sentence types and lengths to make their writing more interesting. Writing that contains sentences all of the same type and length is boring to read, regardless of whether the reader understands why. Even Ernest Hemingway, who was noted for his lean, simple sentences, often put two or more together to make longer ones, as Gonzalez does in the following examples:

My teacher, Mrs. Herrera, thought I didn't know any English, and I had no plans to let her know I did.

The Spanish word for "embarrassed" (*avergonzada*) wouldn't come to me, so I tried a translation based on phonetics.

I thought she'd understand my little Spanglish invention, but she just burst out laughing.

The examples are called *compound* sentences because they are made up from two complete sentences. These are the sentences that are put together:

My teacher, Mrs. Herrera, thought I didn't know any English. I had no plans to let her know I did.

The Spanish word for "embarrassed" (*avergonzada*) wouldn't come to me.
I tried a translation based on phonetics.

I thought she'd understand my little Spanglish invention.
She just burst out laughing.

To make short sentences into one longer sentence, you splice them together with coordinating conjunctions. There are only seven of them: *and, but, for, or, nor, yet, so.* Put a comma after each short sentence you are combining, but put a period at the very end. If you are dissatisfied with your writing because it sounds choppy, this method will help you achieve longer sentences.

EXERCISE

Using a comma and a suitable coordinating conjunction, combine the following pairs of sentences into compound sentences.

1. Many people take four or more years of Spanish in school.
   They still can't carry on an ordinary conversation in Spanish.
2. School courses often emphasize the grammar of a language.
   Teachers grade students on how correctly they read and write.
3. Reading and writing are important skills.
   They are not necessary to everyday chat.
4. A conversation-only class aims to help people speak Spanish in real-life situations.
   This skill is crucial to mastery of the language.
5. Only practicing out loud can improve conversational skills.
   Students in a conversation class are required to speak in Spanish, no matter how awkwardly.

WEB SITE

www.pbs.org/speak/seatosea/americanvarieties/spanglish/book
This PBS interview with Ilan Stavans, the author of *Spanglish: The Making of a New American Language* (2003), includes links to additional resources on Spanglish.

STUDENT ESSAY USING DEFINITION AND EXPLANATION

Nothing to Be Scared Of

Kerri Mauger

Before entering Eastern Illinois University, Kerri Mauger attended high school in the south suburbs of Chicago. She wrote this essay for her first-year composition class. Kerri later transferred to a college near her hometown, where she planned to major in special education.

Early on the day of my eleventh birthday, my sister and I were down-   1
stairs watching TV. My mom came down and told us she wanted to talk to
us in my room. We followed her upstairs, where she told us to lie on the
floor. She said that there was a man outside with a gun and we had to hide
so he would not come and get us. I was really scared and confused, and we
stayed in my room for two hours in almost complete silence. When my
father got home, he called the hospital, and I saw my mother taken away by
force. My birthday party was canceled, and I was crushed.

For most of my life, I remember my mother being in and out of hospi-   2
tals. No one was sure what was wrong with her, and it took many years to
put a label on her condition. My mother was finally diagnosed with schizophrenia. It also took me a long time to understand my mother's illness. My
dad was very secretive about her. I think he wanted to protect my sister and
me, but in the long run ignorance hurt us even more.

Schizophrenia is a disabling brain disorder that affects about one   3
percent of Americans. It strikes men and women equally and occurs at similar rates in all cultures and races. At times the symptoms don't appear connected to a severe mental illness, and people with schizophrenia look merely
withdrawn and depressed. That's how our mother often seemed to us, especially at first—as if she no longer enjoyed her family or her life.

But schizophrenics usually decline over time, displaying more serious,   4
more obvious symptoms. These include hallucinations, delusions, and problems with speech and movement. Schizophrenics have a hard time distin-
guishing between what is real and what is imagined. They also have trouble
managing emotions, thinking clearly, and dealing with other people. They
cannot always tell what other people's words and actions mean, so they
often respond strangely and inappropriately.

People who have never encountered someone with schizophrenia may   5
feel uneasy and even frightened by the bizarre and socially unacceptable
behavior. My mother may sit and listen to the voices she hears all day

long, ignoring everything else. She explains that they are communicating with her through telepathy. She replies to these voices and denies that there is anything wrong with her. Some schizophrenics shout angrily at people on the street, believing that they have been insulted or threatened when they have not.

There is no cure for schizophrenia. Medication may help some people   6
with the symptoms, but no drug has helped my mother yet. Psychotherapy can also assist schizophrenics in controlling their thoughts and behavior, and many people with the disorder are able to lead rewarding and meaningful lives.

Along with drugs and therapy, family understanding can help. The   7
person suffering from schizophrenia needs sympathy, compassion, and respect. It is best to stay calm and nonjudgmental. Getting excited or starting to argue with the person can worsen an episode. Schizophrenia is not the person's moral fault or rational choice. It is sometimes easier to laugh at something we fear and do not understand. But ignorance about something like schizophrenia can be hurtful. I love my mother dearly and after many years of being afraid and uninformed, I can finally say I am not scared of her at all. She still is not a "normal" mother, but I know the facts and can deal with whatever comes my way.

CONSIDERING CONTENT AND METHOD

1. Why does the author begin with the incident about her birthday party?
2. Did you follow the explanation of *schizophrenia*? Do you understand the term better now that you've read this essay? Are there any questions about the disease that the author does not answer?
3. How effective are the personal examples and observations that the author includes in paragraphs 2, 3, 5, and 7?
4. How does the conclusion echo the beginning?
5. What is the point of this essay? How is that point clarified in the closing?

CHAPTER 6

Strategies for Sorting Ideas:
Classification and *Division*

IMAGES AND IDEAS

Food Guide Pyramid
A Guide to Daily Food Choices

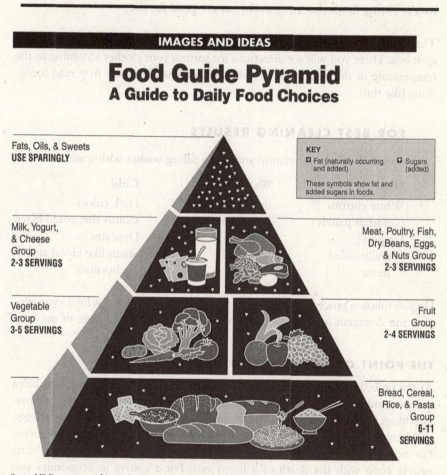

Fats, Oils, & Sweets
USE SPARINGLY

KEY
▼ Fat (naturally occurring and added)   ▼ Sugars (added)

These symbols show fat and added sugars in foods.

Milk, Yogurt, & Cheese Group
2-3 SERVINGS

Meat, Poultry, Fish, Dry Beans, Eggs, & Nuts Group
2-3 SERVINGS

Vegetable Group
3-5 SERVINGS

Fruit Group
2-4 SERVINGS

Bread, Cereal, Rice, & Pasta Group
6-11 SERVINGS

Source: US Department of Agriculture/U.S. Department of Health and Human Services

For Discussion and Writing

What is the point of this method of classifying foods? How many categories are there, and why are they arranged in a pyramid?

In a paragraph or two, classify the foods you eat and those you avoid. Put them in categories and label them; include specific foods in each category. Can you arrange them in a pyramid? If you want, you might make a humorous classification, such as foods you would eat all day long, foods you eat because they're cheap, foods that taste awful but are good for you.

The next time you get ready to do your laundry, look on the back of the detergent box. There you will see directions for sorting your clothes according to the temperature of the water that you should use. The directions may read something like this:

FOR BEST CLEANING RESULTS

Sort and select temperature and begin filling washer with water.

Hot	**Warm**	**Cold**
White cottons	Bright colors	Dark colors
Colorfast pastels	Permanent press	Colors that could bleed
Diapers	Knits	Delicates
Heavily soiled items		Stains like blood and chocolate

Do you follow a procedure like this when you do your laundry? Why do you suppose the detergent makers put directions such as these on the back of the box?

THE POINT OF CLASSIFICATION AND DIVISION

As the preceding laundry example shows, separating and arranging things helps us to accomplish tasks more efficiently and more effectively. This process of "sorting things out" also helps us to clarify our thinking and understand our feelings.

Many writing tasks lend themselves to grouping information into categories. For example, you might write a paper for psychology class on the various ways people cope with the death of a loved one. For a course in economics you might write about the three basic types of unemployment (*frictional*, *structural*, and *cyclical*). This approach—called **classification** and **division**—enables you to present a body of information in an orderly way.

Dividing and classifying also forces you to think clearly about your topic. By breaking a subject down into its distinct parts, or categories, you can look at it more closely and decide what you want to say about each part. For example, if you are writing an essay on effective teaching styles, you might begin by dividing the teachers you have had into the "good" ones and the "bad" ones. Then you could break those broad categories down further into more precise ones: teachers who held your interest, teachers who knew their subjects, teachers who made you do busy work, and so forth. As you develop each category, you have to think about the qualities that impressed you, and this thought process leads you to a better understanding of the topic you are writing about. You may end up writing only about the good teachers, but dividing and classifying the examples will help you to organize your thinking.

THE PRINCIPLES OF CLASSIFICATION AND DIVISION

Most things can be classified or divided in more than one way, depending on the reason for grouping the items. In the laundry example, for instance, you are told to sort the clothes according to the temperature of the water. Putting bright colors with knits doesn't make any sense if you don't know the reason—or basis—for the category: *items to be washed in cold water.* When you divide and classify a topic, be sure to have a sound basis for formulating your categories. The following suggestions will help you develop a useful system of classification.

Give a Purpose to Your Classification

Merely putting facts or ideas into different groups isn't necessarily meaningful. Consider these sentences that classify for no apparent reason:

1. There are five kinds of friends in most of our lives.
2. People deal with their spare money in four basic ways.

How could you give a **purpose** to these ideas? You would have to add a *reason* or declare a *point* for the categories. Here are some revisions that give purpose to these two classifications:

1. a. There are five kinds of friends in most of our lives, and each kind is important in its own way.
   b. Most of us have five kinds of friends, and each one drives us crazy in a special way.

2. a. People deal with their spare money in four ways that reflect their overall attitudes toward life.
   b. People deal with their spare money in four ways, only one of which is truly constructive.

Establish a Clear Basis for Your Classification

If you are going to classify items or ideas, you have to decide which organizing principle you want to use to form your groups. For example, if you are classifying friends, you could group them according to how close you are to them, as Judith Viorst does in her essay in this chapter. Or you could group them according to other principles: how long you have known them, what you have in common with them, or how much time you spend with the people in each group. The important thing is to choose a workable principle and stick with it.

Make Your Groups Parallel and Equal

In a classification essay, you usually announce the groups or classes in the introduction: several ways to handle criticism, four kinds of friends, three types of stress, three levels of intelligence, and so forth. You then devote one section to each group of your classification. A section can be one paragraph or several, but the sections for the major categories should be about equal in length. In a classification essay about friendship, for instance, if you cover "childhood pals" in 150 words, then you should use approximately the same number of words for each of the other kinds of friends.

Experienced writers also present each section in a similar way. For example, in this chapter psychologist David Elkind classifies the three basic types of stress that young people experience. He labels each one with a letter, describes it, and gives examples. He follows the same order—label, description, examples—in covering each type. He also mentions the same two conditions when explaining each type: whether it's foreseeable and whether it's avoidable. This parallel development helps the reader to recognize the similarities and identify the distinctions among the types.

THE PITFALLS OF CLASSIFICATION AND DIVISION

The following advice will help you to avoid some of the problems that writers sometimes encounter in developing an essay of classification.

1. *Know the difference between useful and useless ways of classifying.* Sorting your clothes by brand name probably won't help you get the best cleaning results when doing the laundry. And dividing teachers into those who wear glasses and those who don't is not a very useful way to organize a paper on effective teaching styles. But classifying teachers into those who lecture, those who use a question-discussion format, and those who run small-group workshops might be significant, mainly because such groupings would allow you to discuss the teachers' philosophies, their attitudes toward students, and their effectiveness in the classroom.

2. *Be sure your classification covers everything you claim it covers.* If, for instance, you know some teachers who sometimes lecture and sometimes use small groups, you can't pretend these people don't exist just to make your classification tidy. At least mention exceptions, even if you don't give them as much space as the major categories.

3. *Don't let the basis of division shift.* If you can see a problem with the following classification system, you already understand this warning:

TYPES OF TEACHERS

a. Teachers who lecture
b. Teachers who lead discussions
c. Teachers who have a sense of humor
d. Teachers who run workshops
e. Teachers who never hold office hours

Notice that three types of teachers (a, b, and d) are grouped according to the way they run their classes, but two types (c and e) are defined by some other standard. You can see the confusion these shifting groups cause: Can teachers who lecture have a sense of humor? Don't those who use workshops also hold office hours?

4. *Be sure your groups are parallel or equal in rank.* The following classification illustrates a problem in rank:

KINDS OF POPULAR MUSIC

a. Easy listening
b. Country and western
c. Rock 'n' roll
d. K'naan

Although K'naan does represent a type of popular music distinct from easy listening, country, and rock, the category is not parallel with the others—it is far too small. It should be "rap" or "hip hop," with K'naan used as an example.

5. *Avoid stereotypes.* When you write about types of behavior or put people into groups, you run the risk of oversimplifying the material. The best way to avoid this problem is to use plenty of specific examples. You can also point out exceptions and describe variations; such honesty shows that you have been thinking carefully about the topic.

WHAT TO LOOK FOR IN A CLASSIFICATION

As you read the essays in this chapter, pay attention to these points:

1. *Figure out what the author is classifying.* Then identify the basis for making up the groups and the purpose of the classification.
2. *Look for the specific groups or classes* into which the author has sorted the material. Jot down a brief list of the major categories just to see if you can keep track of them.
3. *Ask yourself if the groups are clearly defined.* Do they shift? Do they cover what they claim to cover? Are they parallel?
4. *Be alert for stereotypes.* How does the author handle exceptions and variations?
5. *Identify the audience.* How do you know who the intended readers are?

PREPARING TO READ

List five or ten of the people you call "friends." Are they all friends to an equal degree? Do you have a flexible meaning for the word *friend*?

··

Friends, Good Friends— and Such Good Friends

··

JUDITH VIORST

A popular humorist who writes essays and light verse for many well-known magazines, Judith Viorst was born in Newark, New Jersey, in 1931 and attended Rutgers University. She has written numerous children's books, including the enduring favorite Alexander and the Terrible, Horrible, No Good, Very Bad Day *(1972), as well as several books for adults, including* Imperfect Control *(1998) and* Suddenly 60: And Other Shocks of Late-Life *(2000). The following selection appeared in her regular column in* Redbook *magazine in 1977.*

TERMS TO RECOGNIZE

ardor (*para. 1*)	enthusiasm, intensity
nonchalant (*para. 2*)	indifferent, offhand
Tuesday-doubles (*para. 7*)	tennis played by four people, in pairs, on Tuesdays
sibling rivalry (*para. 11*)	competition among children for parental favor
dormant (*para. 13*)	sleeping, inactive
revived (*para. 13*)	brought back to life
calibrated (*para. 21*)	adjusted, determined

Women are friends, I once would have said, when they totally love   1
and support and trust each other, and bare to each other the secrets of
their souls, and run—no questions asked—to help each other, and tell harsh
truths to each other (no, you can't wear that dress unless you lose ten
pounds first) when harsh truths must be told. Women are friends, I once
would have said, when they share the same affection for Ingmar Bergman,
plus train rides, cats, warm rain, charades, Camus, and hate with equal
ardor Newark and Brussels sprouts and Lawrence Welk and camping.

In other words, I once would have said that a friend is a friend all the way, but now I believe that's a narrow point of view. For the friendships I have and the friendships I see are conducted at many levels of intensity, serve many different functions, meet different needs and range from those as all-the-way as the friendship of the soul sisters mentioned above to that of the most nonchalant and casual playmates. 2

Consider these varieties of friendship: 3

1. Convenience friends. These are the women with whom, if our paths weren't crossing all the time, we'd have no particular reason to be friends: a next-door neighbor, a woman in our car pool, the mother of one of our children's closest friends or maybe some mommy with whom we serve juice and cookies each week at the Glenwood Co-op Nursery. 4

Convenience friends are convenient indeed. They'll lend us their cups and silverware for a party. They'll drive our kids to soccer when we're sick. They'll take us to pick up our car when we need a lift to the garage. They'll even take our cats when we go on vacation. As we will for them. But we don't, with convenience friends, ever come too close or tell too much; we maintain our public face and emotional distance. "Which means," says Elaine, "that I'll talk about being overweight but not about being depressed. Which means I'll admit being mad but not blind with rage. Which means that I might say that we're pinched this month but never that I'm worried sick over money." But which doesn't mean that there isn't sufficient value to be found in these friendships of mutual aid, in convenience friends. 5

2. Special-interest friends. These friendships aren't intimate, and they needn't involve kids or silverware or cats. Their value lies in some interest jointly shared. And so we may have an office friend or a yoga friend or a tennis friend or a friend from the Women's Democratic Club. 6

"I've got one woman friend," says Joyce, "who likes, as I do, to take psychology courses. Which makes it nice for me—and nice for her. It's fun to go with someone you know and it's fun to discuss what you've learned, driving back from the classes." And for the most part, she says, that's all they discuss. "I'd say that what we're doing is *doing* together, not *being* together," Suzanne says of her Tuesday-doubles friends. "It's mainly a tennis relationship, but we play together well. And I guess we all need to have a couple of playmates." I agree. 7

My playmate is a shopping friend, a woman of marvelous taste, a woman who knows exactly *where* to buy *what*, and furthermore is a woman who always knows beyond a doubt what one ought to be buying. I don't have the time to keep up with what's new in eyeshadow, hemlines and shoes and whether the smock look is in or finished already. But since (oh, shame!) I care a lot about eyeshadow, hemlines and shoes, and since 8

I don't *want* to wear smocks if the smock look is finished, I'm very glad to have a shopping friend.

3. Historical friends. We all have a friend who knew us when . . . maybe   9
way back in Miss Meltzer's second grade, when our family lived in that three-
room flat in Brooklyn, when our dad was out of work for seven months, when
our brother Allie got in that fight where they had to call the police, when our
sister married the endodontist from Yonkers, and when, the morning after we
lost our virginity, she was the first, the only, friend we told.

The years have gone by and we've gone separate ways and we've little   10
in common now, but we're still an intimate part of each other's past. And
so whenever we go to Detroit we always go to visit this friend of our girlhood. Who knows how we looked before our teeth were straightened. Who
knows how we talked before our voice got unBrooklyned. Who knows what
we ate before we learned about artichokes. And who, by her presence, puts
us in touch with an earlier part of ourself, a part of ourself it's important
never to lose.

"What this friend means to me and what I mean to her," says Grace,   11
"is having a sister without sibling rivalry. We know the texture of each
other's lives. She remembers my grandmother's cabbage soup. I remember
the way her uncle played the piano. There's simply no other friend who
remembers those things."

4. Crossroads friends. Like historical friends, our crossroads friends   12
are important for *what was*—for the friendship we shared at a crucial,
now past, time of life. A time, perhaps, when we roomed in college
together; or worked as eager young singles in the Big City together; or
went together, as my friend Elizabeth and I did, through pregnancy, birth
and that scary first year of new motherhood. Crossroads friends forge
powerful links, links strong enough to endure with not much more contact
than once-a-year letters at Christmas. And out of respect for those
crossroads years, for those dramas and dreams we once shared, we
will always be friends.

5. Cross-generational friends. Historical friends and crossroads   13
friends seem to maintain a special kind of intimacy—dormant but always
ready to be revived—and though we may rarely meet, whenever we do connect, it's personal and intense. Another kind of intimacy exists in the friendships that form across generations in what one woman calls her
daughter-mother and her mother-daughter relationships. Evelyn's friend is
her mother's age—"but I share so much more than I ever could with my
mother"—a woman she talks to of music, of books, and of life. "What I get
from her is the benefit of her experience. What she gets—and enjoys—from
me is a youthful perspective. It's a pleasure for both of us."

I have in my own life a precious friend, a woman of 65 who has lived   14
very hard, who is wise, who listens well; who has been where I am and can
help me understand it; and who represents not only an ultimate ideal
mother to me but also the person I'd like to be when I grow up.

In our daughter role we tend to do more than our share of self-   15
revelation; in our mother role we tend to receive what's revealed. It's
another kind of pleasure—playing a wise mother to a questing younger
person. It's another very lovely kind of friendship.

6. Part-of-a-couple friends. Some of the women we call our friends   16
we never see alone—we see them as part of a couple at couples' parties. And
though we share interests in many things and respect each other's views, we
aren't moved to deepen the relationship. Whatever the reason, a lack of
time or—and this is more likely—a lack of chemistry, our friendship remains
in the context of a group. But the fact that our feeling on seeing each other
is always, "I'm *so* glad she's here" and the fact that we spend half the
evening talking together says that this too, in its way, counts as a friendship.

(Other part-of-a-couple friends are the friends that came with the   17
marriage, and some of these are friends we could live without. But sometimes, alas, she married our husband's best friend; and sometimes, alas, she
is our husband's best friend. And so we find ourself dealing with her, some-
what against our will, in a spirit of what I'll call *reluctant* friendship.)

7. Men who are friends. I wanted to write just of women friends, but   18
the women I've talked to won't let me—they say I must mention man-woman
friendships too. For these friendships can be just as close and as dear as
those that we form with women. Listen to Lucy's description of one such
friendship: "We've found we have things to talk about that are different from
what he talks about with my husband and different from what I talk about
with his wife. So sometimes we call on the phone or meet for lunch. There
are similar intellectual interests—we always pass on to each other the books
that we love—but there's also something tender and caring too."

In a couple of crises, Lucy says, "he offered himself, for talking and   19
for helping. And when someone died in his family he wanted me there. The
sexual, flirty part of our friendship is very small, but *some*—just enough to
make it fun and different." She thinks—and I agree—that the sexual part,
though small, is always *some*, is always there when a man and a woman are
friends.

It's only in the past few years that I've made friends with men, in the   20
sense of a friendship that's *mine*, not just part of two couples. And achieving
with them the ease and the trust I've found with women friends has value
indeed. Under the dryer at home last week, putting on mascara and rouge,

I comfortably sat and talked with a fellow named Peter. Peter, I finally decided, could handle the shock of me minus mascara under the dryer. Because we care for each other. Because we're friends.

8. There are medium friends, and pretty good friends, and very good   21
friends indeed, and these friendships are defined by their level of intimacy.
And what we'll reveal at each of these levels of intimacy is calibrated with
care. We might tell a medium friend, for example, that yesterday we had a
fight with our husband. And we might tell a pretty good friend that this
fight with our husband made us so mad that we slept on the couch. And we
might tell a very good friend that the reason we got so mad in that fight
that we slept on the couch had something to do with that girl who works in
his office. But it's only to our very best friends that we're willing to tell all,
to tell what's going on with that girl in his office.

The best of friends, I still believe, totally love and support and trust   22
each other, and bare to each other the secrets of their souls, and run—no
questions asked—to help each other, and tell harsh truths to each other
when they must be told. But we needn't agree about everything (only 12-
year-old girl friends agree about *everything*) to tolerate each other's point of
view. To accept without judgment. To give and to take without ever keeping
score. And to *be* there, as I am for them and as they are for me, to comfort
our sorrows, to celebrate our joys.

RESPONDING TO READING

How many different kinds of friends do you have? How would you categorize
the friends you listed in Preparing to Read? Would Viorst's categories work for
you? Would you have to create any new ones?

CONSIDERING CONTENT

1. What ideas is Viorst giving up, according to the beginning of the essay?
   Why does she begin with what she no longer believes?
2. Make a list of the different kinds of friends discussed in the essay. Which
   kind is the exception from the others?
3. What kind of person is the author of this essay? What kind of life does
   she lead? Look at paragraphs 4, 5, and 11 for evidence. How might the
   writer's life situation limit her audience? Did you feel included?
4. What are the functions friends perform, according to the essay? Are
   there underlying similarities among most of the types?
5. Why do you think the women Viorst interviewed insisted that she discuss man-woman friendships?

CONSIDERING METHOD

1. How do you know when Viorst is beginning a section about a new type of friend? What other method might she use to signal such a shift?
2. What is the relationship between the opening of the essay and the closing?
3. What do the direct quotations do for the essay? Are they from famous people? Think of at least two reasons why they are included.
4. In paragraph 7, you can see the repetition of similar sentence openings. What words are repeated? Find another example of repetition of phrases or structures. What purpose does this repetition serve?

COMBINING STRATEGIES

Look at the ways Judith Viorst develops her explanations for each type of friend. She uses narration, definition, example, comparison and contrast, and cause-and-effect reasoning. Identify instances of at least three of these methods.

WRITING STEP BY STEP: ROMANTIC RELATIONSHIPS

Using Viorst's essay for inspiration, write an essay that classifies several different types of romantic relationships.

A. Brainstorm, with help from friends or classmates if you want it, for ideas about the various couples and kinds of romance you see around you. Jot down everything mentioned, even if it sounds silly or overlapping—you can sort it out later.

B. Choose three to six types to discuss in your essay. When the types seem closely related, you might combine several different ones from your brainstorming notes to make up one type.

C. Make up a label for each type, as Viorst does in "Friends, Good Friends—and Such Good Friends."

D. Develop a section explaining each type. Use examples of people who show each type of romantic attachment if you can—either people you know personally or public figures most of your readers will be able to identify. Interview your friends, as Viorst did, and use direct quotations from your interviews.

E. Be sure to show how the types are similar and different from each other by using comparisons and contrasts as you go along. Look at paragraphs 13 and 21 of Viorst's essay for samples of how to do this.

F. Use signals to show when you are shifting from one type to the next. You could use numbers and/or labels. Or you could use transitional words, like "The second type or style of romance is. . . . "

G. Write an introduction that discusses a misperception (of your own or of others) about romantic relationships. See Viorst's introduction for a model.

H. Close your essay with a statement that draws all the kinds of romance together, telling what they have in common. Alternatively, you may want to close, as Viorst does, by commenting on what you wrote in the introduction.

OTHER WRITING IDEAS

1. There are probably as many kinds of people you dislike as people you like. Write an essay categorizing the types that drive you crazy.

2. COLLABORATIVE WRITING. Judith Viorst wrote another essay in which she classifies the lies we tell. For example, she discusses lies that spare others' feelings, lies that save our own pride, and so on. Get together with a group of classmates to think of your own categories and examples of lies and liars. Have each person in the group list as many types and illustrations as he or she can; compare and discuss your lists. Then write your own essay on this topic.

3. USING THE INTERNET. Classify the variations of a single emotion: anxiety, nervousness, anger, pleasure, embarrassment, confidence, excitement, or pride, for example. Use the search term "emotional literacy" to find Web sites that might help you explore the topic. Remember to acknowledge your sources in your essay.

4. WRITING ABOUT READING. Viorst says that "the sexual part, though small, is always *some*, is always there when a man and a woman are friends." Do you agree? What do you think about friends of the other sex? Are cross-sex friendships different in quality from same-sex friendships? Would you try to restrict your sweetheart in his or her opposite-sex friendships?

GAINING WORD POWER

The following partial sentences include slightly different forms of the preceding Terms to Recognize. Complete each sentence in a reasonable way that shows you understand the word used. Use your dictionary to be sure you grasp the meaning.

1. Elena is an ardent hockey fan, but _____.

   _____

2. Stanley did not understand the fine calibrations of politeness: He often

   _____.

3. After _____, Jean's social life went into a period of dormancy.

4. The writer's nonchalance about spelling was clear when _____.

   _____.

EDITING SKILLS: USING PRONOUNS CONSISTENTLY

When Judith Viorst writes about her own experiences and ideas, she uses the pronouns *I* or *we* to identify herself:

> The friendships *I* have and the friendships *I* see are conducted at many levels of intensity.

> *We* all have a friend who knew *us* when. . . .

When she writes as someone addressing an audience directly, she uses the pronoun *you*:

> [N]o, *you* can't wear that dress unless *you* lose ten pounds first.

And when she writes about a person or persons, she identifies them first and then uses *he, she*, or *they* to refer to them:

> Convenience friends are convenient indeed. *They*'ll lend us *their* cups and silverware for a party.

> Evelyn's friend is *her* mother's age, . . . a woman *she* talks to of music, of books, and of life.

As you see, pronouns refer to three different "persons." Each person expresses a different point of view:

person	singular	plural
First person (the person writing):	I, me, my, mine	we, us, our, ours
Second person (the person written to):	you, your, yours	you, your, yours
Third person (the person written about):	he, him, his, she her, hers, it, its	they, them, their, theirs

Writers often shift from one person to another, especially between first and third, as Judith Viorst does in her essay. But these shifts must be clear and logical. An unnecessary shift can distract or confuse a reader:

> Shift: If a student wants to succeed in graduate school, you have to know the rules of the game.

The sentence is about *a student*, so it's in third person; *you* is a second person pronoun.

> No shift: If a student wants to succeed in graduate school, he or she has to know the rules of the game.

No shift: If students want to succeed in graduate school, they have to know
    the rules of the game.

EXERCISE

Rewrite the following paragraph, making the point of view consistently *third
person* (people/they). You may have to change some verbs to fit with the pronouns you changed.

Most people are interested in music, either as a spectator or as performers.
You can enjoy music by watching MTV or attending concerts. We can also
enjoy playing CDs and listening to music on the radio. Other people want to
make their own music. If we are really serious about playing an instrument or
singing, we can take lessons and join a band or choir. You might prefer, however, to play for your own enjoyment or to entertain your friends and family
at parties. A person has many chances to express his love of music.

☙ WEB SITE

www.bookpage.com/0711bp/judith_viorst.html.
This site offers an interview with Judith Viorst about her popular children's
books.

PREPARING TO READ

Are you an ex-smoker or do you know someone who is? How would you describe the attitudes of former smokers toward their past behavior and toward those who continue to smoke?

••

Confessions of an Ex-Smoker

••

F R A N K L I N   E .   Z I M R I N G

Former smoker Frank Zimring is the William G. Simon Professor of Law and Wolfen Distinguished Scholar at the University of California at Berkeley, where he specializes in criminal justice and family law. Professor Zimring has also done professional consulting on public policy issues, such as drugs and smoking. For example, he currently serves as the principal investigator for the Center on Culture, Immigration, and Youth Violence Prevention. His most recent book, The Great American Crime Decline: Studies in Crime and Public Policy, *was published in 2006. The following, a more personal essay, first appeared in* Newsweek.

TERMS TO RECOGNIZE

watershed (*para. 1*)	critical turning point
cessation (*para. 1*)	stopping, ending
zealot (*para. 1*)	person with intense drive, fanatic
degenerates (*para. 2*)	social misfits
recidivist (*para.3*)	repeater, backslider
anecdotal (*para. 4*)	casual observation
vitriolic (*para. 4*)	harsh, blistering
unmitigated (*para. 6*)	undiminished, absolute
proselytizing (*para. 7*)	attempting to convince, convert
predestination (*para. 7*)	foreordained
excoriate (*para. 10*)	harshly criticize

Americans can be divided into three groups—smokers, nonsmokers, and that expanding pack of us who have quit. Those who have never smoked don't know what they're missing, but former smokers, ex-smokers, reformed smokers can never forget. We are veterans of a personal war, linked by that watershed experience of ceasing to smoke and by the temptation to have just

1

one more cigarette. For almost all of us ex-smokers, smoking continues to play an important part in our lives. And now that it is being restricted in restaurants around the country and will be banned in almost all indoor public places in New York State, it is vital that everyone understand the different emotional states cessation of smoking can cause. I have observed four of them; and in the interest of science I have classified them as those of the zealot, the evangelist, the elect, and the serene. Each day, each category gains new recruits.

Not all antitobacco zealots are former smokers, but a substantial number of fire-and-brimstone opponents do come from the ranks of the reformed. Zealots believe that those who continue to smoke are degenerates who deserve scorn not pity and the penalties that will deter offensive behavior in public as well. Relations between these people and those who continue to smoke are strained.

One explanation for the zealot's fervor in seeking to outlaw tobacco consumption is his own tenuous hold on abstaining from smoking. But I think part of the emotional force arises from sheer envy as he watches and identifies with each lung-filling puff. By making smoking in public a crime, the zealot seeks reassurance that he will not revert to bad habits; give him strong social penalties, and he won't become a recidivist.

No systematic survey has been done yet, but anecdotal evidence suggests that a disproportionate number of doctors who have quit smoking can be found among the fanatics. Just as the most enthusiastic revolutionary tends to make the most enthusiastic counterrevolutionary, many of today's vitriolic zealots include those who had been deeply committed to tobacco habits.

By contrast, the antismoking evangelist does not condemn smokers. Unlike the zealot, he regards smoking as an easily curable condition, as a social disease, and not a sin. The evangelist spends an enormous amount of time seeking and preaching to the unconverted. He argues that kicking the habit is not *that* difficult. After all, *he* did it; moreover, as he describes it, the benefits of quitting are beyond measure and the disadvantages are nil.

The hallmark of the evangelist is his insistence that he never misses tobacco. Though he is less hostile to smokers than the zealot, he is resented more. Friends and loved ones who have been the targets of his preachments frequently greet the resumption of smoking by the evangelist as an occasion for unmitigated glee.

Among former smokers, the distinctions between the evangelist and the elect are much the same as the differences between proselytizing and nonproselytizing religious sects. While the evangelists preach the ease and desirability of abstinence, the elect do not attempt to convert their friends. They think that virtue is its own reward and subscribe to the Puritan theory of predestination. Since they have proved themselves capable of abstaining from tobacco, they are therefore different from friends and relatives who continue to smoke. They feel superior, secure that their salvation was fore-ordained. These ex-smokers rarely give personal testimony on their conversion. They rarely speak about their tobacco habits, while evangelists talk about little else. Of course, active smokers find such blue-nosed behavior far less offensive than that of the evangelist or the zealot, yet they resent the elect simply because they are smug. Their air of self-satisfaction rarely escapes the notice of those lighting up. For active smokers, life with a member of the ex-smoking elect is less stormy than with a zealot or evangelist, but it is subtly oppressive nonetheless.

I have labeled my final category of former smokers the serene. This   8
classification is meant to encourage those who find the other psychic styles of ex-smokers disagreeable. Serenity is quieter than zealotry and evangelism, and those who qualify are not as self-righteous as the elect. The serene ex-smoker accepts himself and also accepts those around him who continue to smoke. This kind of serenity does not come easily nor does it seem to be an immediate option for those who have stopped. Rather it is a goal, an end stage in a process of development during which some former smokers progress through one or more of the less-than-positive psychological points en route. For former smokers, serenity is thus a positive possibility that exists at the end of the rainbow. But all former smokers cannot reach that promised land.

What is it that permits some former smokers to become serene? I   9
think the key is self-acceptance and gratitude. The fully mature former smoker knows he has the soul of an addict and is grateful for the knowledge. He doesn't regret that he quit smoking, nor any of his previous adventures with tobacco. As a former smoker, he is grateful for the experience and memory of craving a cigarette.

Serenity comes from accepting the lessons of one's life. And ex-   10
smokers who have reached this point in their world view have much to be grateful for. They have learned about the potential and limits of change. In becoming the right kind of former smoker, they developed a healthy sense of self. This former smoker, for one, believes that it is better to crave (one hopes only occasionally) and not to smoke than never to have craved at all. And by accepting that fact, the reformed smoker does not need to excoriate, envy, or disassociate himself from those who continue to smoke.

RESPONDING TO READING

Would you add any types of ex-smokers to Zimring's list? What names would you give to each type?

CONSIDERING CONTENT

1. Reread the introduction. What does it reveal about Zimring's attitude toward smoking in general and former smokers more specifically? Find several words, phrases, or sentences that support your answer.
2. Name the four categories of ex-smokers and briefly define the behavior and goal of each group. Do you recognize these groups among the people you know?
3. Return to each category and closely examine what Zimring believes are the motives behind each group's behavior.
4. What is Zimring's attitude toward each group of ex-smokers? Find specific sentences or phrases that support your answer. You might begin by discussing the term he has selected for each category.
5. What is Zimring's purpose for writing this essay? Does he succeed?

CONSIDERING METHOD

1. Review the way Zimring orders the types of ex-smokers and explain the effects of his choosing this sequence.
2. Reread Zimring's second sentence. Why does he say "former smokers, ex-smokers, reformed smokers" when these three groups are essentially the same?
3. In addition to his selection of key terms (*zealot* and *evangelist*, for example), Zimring uses a number of other religious comparisons or concepts to convey his attitudes and ideas. Find several examples and analyze Zimring's motives for this approach to his topic. Paragraph 7 might be a good place to begin.
4. Zimring uses other analogies and comparisons, as well. In the introduction, for example, where he wishes to communicate the intense challenges smokers face when they quit, he likens former smokers to "veterans of a personal war." Locate three more comparisons and describe Zimring's purpose for choosing each.
5. In paragraph 10, Zimring says, "This former smoker, for one, believes that it is better to crave (one hopes only occasionally) and not to smoke than never to have craved at all." What common phrase is Zimring echoing here and why might he have chosen to do this?

WRITING STEP BY STEP: MORE THAN ONE WAY TO SOLVE A PROBLEM

When faced with a challenge or a problem, we can respond in one of several ways, so we often find ourselves brainstorming to discover solutions and then considering the strengths and weaknesses of each approach. We ponder, for example, the problem of how to make housemates or family members share cleaning duties, the challenge of how to make scarce money go further, or the problem of how to break unwelcome news to someone. Choose a problem that could be solved in one of several ways and write an essay using Zimring's approach to quitting smoking as a model of classification.

A. Identify three or four solutions to the problem. On a piece of scratch paper or on your computer screen, brainstorm for a few minutes, jotting down ideas about each solution. If you need help, ask your classmates for ideas about your topic.

B. Decide on a reasonable order to present your solutions—from weakest to strongest (or vice versa), from your first hunch to your last solution, from the worst solution to the best, or along any range that seems reasonable.

C. Choose an attitude to take toward the topic, one that suits your purpose and your audience. This will determine the tone of your writing. In choosing an attitude, you might also consider the severity of the problem—a serious discussion of approaches to bad hair days could provide a humorous mismatch, for example. Franklin Zimring, in a similar way, chose a light tone to discuss a serious topic. However, a match between the topic and the tone is the usual expectation, and you should feel free to align them if you want: a humorous tone for a light topic, and a serious tone for a weighty topic.

D. Begin the essay with an introduction to the problem and the types of solutions you will suggest. As Zimring does, try to reveal your tone in the way you outline the problem and frame the solutions.

E. Write a one- or two-paragraph discussion of your first solution. Begin with a description of the approach.

F. Give the strength of the solution and provide an example of how it is (or would be) used.

G. Follow the strengths by discussing the weaknesses of the approach along with an example of its failings. You can use the same example for both strengths and weaknesses, or if you prefer, you can use different examples to show positive and negative elements.

H. Follow steps, E F, and G for the next two or three approaches you identified in the brainstorming stage.

I. In your closing paragraph, you might follow Zimring's model and write about why one response is better than all the others. On the other hand, you might explain why no solution is perfect.

OTHER WRITING IDEAS

1. Choose either a school setting or a workplace you know well and write about the different approaches people take toward their work. Consider using specific people you know or have read about as examples of the approaches. Be sure to give enough examples and details for your reader to get a clear picture.

2. COLLABORATIVE WRITING. Working with a group of classmates, think of a quality that many people have but that they use in different ways— for example, power, beauty, charm, intelligence, or wealth. Develop an essay that explains three or four approaches to possessing this quality. Choose only one quality and explain three or four displays of it: "Some people use their power for good causes, some for control over others, and some to amass even more power." Consider evaluating each approach or explaining why people differ along these lines.

3. USING THE INTERNET. Identify another bad habit, such as gambling, that large numbers of people are forced to give up. Research the approaches offered on the Internet for ending the habit, and classify these into three or four categories of solutions. Write an essay based on your conclusion.

4. WRITING ABOUT READING. The author offers four types of ex-smokers. Write an essay about types of smokers. What makes them different from one another? Different motives or habits? Different ways of handling attitudes toward them?

GAINING WORD POWER

Zimring uses four key terms in his essay: zealot, evangelist, the elect, and the serene. Use a thesaurus to identify at least two **synonyms** for each of these words (*fanatic* for *zealot*, for example). Review "Confessions of an Ex-Smoker" and find one sample sentence for each of the key terms. Now rewrite those sentences using the synonyms. Write briefly about the effects of these changes on the tone of the sentences.

EDITING SKILLS: AVOIDING SEXIST LANGUAGE

In paragraph 3, Franklin Zimring writes, "One explanation for the *zealot's* fervor in seeking to outlaw tobacco consumption is *his* own tenuous hold on abstaining from smoking" (our italics). When this article first appeared in 1987, it was generally more acceptable to use masculine pronouns to refer to virtually all living beings as if they were male. These days, however, you need to avoid using masculine pronouns to refer to people of both sexes. If Zimring wrote an article for *Newsweek* today, he probably would not write, "The hallmark of the *evangelist* is *his* insistence that *he* never misses tobacco" (para. 6). More likely he would cast that sentence in the plural this way: "The hallmark of *evangelists* is *their* insistence that *they* never miss tobacco." Both sexes are included in all plural pronouns. People don't think either male or female when they read *we, us, our, you, your, they, them, their, ourselves, yourselves, themselves*. So, if you simply write in the plural, the problem disappears.

Occasionally you can revise a sentence to eliminate the pronoun, like this:

(sexist) A tennis player must practice daily to stay at the top of *his* form.
(revised) A tennis player must practice daily to stay in top form.

Or if you find yourself once in a while needing to write a singular sentence for some good reason, it's quite all right to use both male and female pronouns, like this:

Everyone on board must wear a lifejacket for *his or her* own safety.

Just don't do it this way too often, or your writing will get annoyingly cluttered.

EXERCISE

1. Because your readers may be bothered by **sexist language**, you should write in the plural most of the time. For practice, find and revise other examples of sexist language in Zimring's essay.
2. Now go back over the essay you just wrote and check the personal pronouns. Did you use any (such as *he, his, him* or *she, her, hers*) that unfairly or inaccurately exclude the other sex? Make any necessary changes—such as using *she or her* or rewriting in the plural to allow *they, their,* or *them*.

WEB SITE

www.lungusa.org/stop-smoking
Visit the American Lung Association's site for further information on the benefits and challenges of quitting smoking.

PREPARING TO READ

How can you tell when someone has good self-esteem? How do people with good self-esteem handle life's problems?

∙∙

Types of Stress for Young People

∙∙

DAVID ELKIND

David Elkind is a psychologist who specializes in child development and has written influential books on the subject. In this reading from his book All Grown Up and No Place to Go *(1988), he describes three kinds of situations that we all face but that are especially stressful for teenagers.*

TERMS TO RECOGNIZE

expenditure (*para. 3*)	cost
potential (*para. 4, 12*)	possible
foreseeable (*para. 4*)	seen ahead of time
transient (*para. 7*)	temporary, passing away with time
jeopardize (*para. 7*)	threaten
incorporates (*para. 10*)	combines
inevitable (*para. 12*)	certain to happen
introverted (*para. 14*)	withdrawn, not sociable
extroverted (*para. 14*)	outgoing
bouts (*para. 15*)	short periods

Most situations that produce psychological stress involve some sort   1
of conflict between self and society. So long as we satisfy a social demand at the expense of a personal need, or vice versa, the social or personal demand for action is a psychological stress. If, for example, we stay home from work because of a personal problem, we create a new demand (for an explanation, for made-up time) at our place of work. On the other hand, if we devote too much time to the demands of work, we create new demands on the part of family. If we don't manage our energy budgets well, we create more stress than is necessary.

The major task of psychological stress management is to find ways   2
to balance and coordinate the demands that come from within with those that come from without. This is where a healthy sense of self and identity

comes in. An integrated sense of identity . . . means bringing together into a working whole a set of attitudes, values, and habits that can serve both self and society. The attainment of such a sense of identity is accompanied by a feeling of self-esteem, of liking and respecting oneself and being liked and respected by others.

More than anything else, the attainment of a healthy sense of identity   3
and a feeling of self-esteem gives young people a perspective, a way of look-ing at themselves and others, which enables them to manage the majority of stress situations. Young people with high self-esteem look at situations from a single perspective that includes both themselves and others. They look at situations from the standpoint of what it means to their self-respect and to the respect others have for them. This integrated perspective enables them to manage the major types of stress efficiently and with a minimum expenditure of energy and personal distress.

The Three Stress Situations

There are three major types of stress situations that all of us encounter. One   4
of these occurs when the potential stress is both foreseeable and avoidable. This is a *Type A* stress situation. If we are thinking about going on a roller coaster or seeing a horror movie, the stress is both foreseeable and avoidable. We may choose to expose ourselves to the stress if we find such controlled danger situations exciting or stimulating. Likewise if we know that a particular neighborhood or park is dangerous at night, the danger is both foreseeable and avoidable, and we do avoid it, unless we are looking for trouble.

The situation becomes more complicated when the foreseeable and   5
avoidable danger is one for which there is much social approval and sup-port, even though it entails much personal risk. Becoming a soldier in times of war is an example of this more complicated Type A danger. The young person who enlists wins social approval at the risk of personal harm. On the other hand, the young person who refuses to become a soldier protects himself or herself from danger at the cost of social disapproval.

Teenagers are often caught in this more difficult type of situation. If   6
the peer group uses alcohol or drugs, for example, there is considerable pressure on the young person to participate. But such participation often puts teenagers at risk with parents and teachers, and also with respect to themselves. They may not like the image of themselves as drinkers or drug abusers. It is at this point that a sense of identity and a positive feeling of self-esteem stand the teenager in good stead.

A young person with a healthy sense of identity will weigh the danger   7
to his or her hard-won feeling of self-esteem against the feelings associated

with the loss of peer approval. When the teenager looks at the situation from this perspective, the choice is easy to make. By weighing the laboriously arrived-at feeling of self-esteem against the momentary approval of a transient peer group, the teenager with an integrated sense of self is able to avoid potentially stressful situations. It should be said, too, that the young person's ability to foresee and avoid is both an intellectual and an emotional achievement. The teenager must be able to foresee events . . . but also to place sufficient value upon his or her self-esteem and self-respect to avoid situations that would jeopardize these feelings.

A second type of stress situation involves those demands which are **8** neither foreseeable nor avoidable. These are *Type B* stress situations. Accidents are of this type, as when a youngster is hit by a baseball while watching a game, or when a teenager who happens to be at a place in school when a fight breaks out gets hurt even though he was not involved. The sudden, unexpected death of a loved one is another example of a stress that is both unforeseeable and unavoidable. Divorce of parents is unthinkable for many teenagers and therefore also unforeseeable and unavoidable.

Type B stress situations make the greatest demands upon young peo- **9** ple. . . . With this type of stress teenagers have to deal with the attitudes of their friends and teachers at the same time that they are struggling with their own feelings. Such stress situations put demands upon young people both from within and from without. A youngster who has been handicapped by an accident, like the teenager who has to deal with divorce, has to adjust to new ways of relating to others as well as new ways of thinking about himself or herself.

Again, the young person with a strong sense of identity and a feeling **10** of self-esteem has the best chance of managing these stress situations as well as they can be managed. In the case of divorce, for example, the teenager who incorporates other people's perspectives with his or her own is able to deal with the situation better than other teenagers who lack this perspective. For example, one young man, who went on to win honors at an Ivy League school, told his father when he and the mother divorced, "You are entitled to live your own life and to find happiness too."

This integrated perspective also helps young people deal with the **11** death of a loved one. If it was an elderly grandparent who had been suffering great pain, the young person can see that from the perspective of the grandparent, dying may have been preferable to living a life of agony with no hope of recovery. As one teenager told me with regard to his grandfather who had just died, "He was in such pain, he was so doped up he couldn't really recognize me. I loved him so much I just couldn't stand to see him that way." By enabling the young person to see death from the perspective of others, including that of the person who is dying, the young person is able to mourn the loss but also to get on with life.

The third type of stress situation is one in which the potential stress is   12
foreseeable but not avoidable. This is a *Type C* stress situation. A teenager who has stayed out later than he or she was supposed to foresees an unavoidable storm at home. Likewise, exams are foreseeable but unavoidable stress situations. Being required to spend time with relatives one does not like is another stress situation that the teenager can foresee but not avoid. These are but a few examples of situations the teenager might wish to avoid but must learn to accept as inevitable.

To young people who have attained a solid sense of self and identity,   13
foreseeable and unavoidable stress situations are manageable, again, because of self-esteem and the integrated perspective. They look at the situation from the perspective of themselves as well as that of the other people involved and try to prepare accordingly. They may decide, as one young man of my acquaintance did, that "with my folks, honesty is the best policy. I get into less trouble if I tell the truth than if I make up stories." In the case of visiting relatives they do not like, integrated teenagers see it from the perspective of what it means to others, such as their parents. And with respect to stress situations like exams, because they want to maintain their self-esteem, they prepare for the exam so that they will make a good showing for themselves as well as for others.

It is important to say, too, that integrated teenagers come in any and all   14
personality types. Some are introverted and shy, others are extroverted and fun-loving. Some are preoccupied with intellectual concerns, others primarily with matters of the heart. Despite this diversity, they all share the prime characteristics of the integrated teenager: a set of attitudes, values, and habits that enable the young person to serve self and society, and a strong sense of self-esteem.

To be sure, life is complex and varied. Even the most integrated teen-   15
ager, of whatever personality type, may occasionally be so overwhelmed by stress that he or she loses the integrated perspective and suffers bouts of low self-esteem. We need to remember that teenagers are new at the game of stress management and have just acquired the skills they need for this purpose. Nonetheless, the general principle holds true. The more integrated the teenager is with respect to self and identity, the better prepared he or she is to manage the basic stress situations.

RESPONDING TO READING

Identify a source of stress in your own life and see whether you can classify it as Type A, Type B, or Type C. Write in your journal about the stress and whether self-esteem contributes to how you handle it.

CONSIDERING CONTENT

1. According to Elkind, what overall conflict causes most situations of stress?
2. Which type of stress does Elkind think is most difficult for teens? Why is this type the worst?
3. Elkind concentrates on how a teenager with good self-esteem would deal with stressful situations. How would a teen with low self-esteem deal with some of these situations?
4. What is an "integrated perspective" (paras. 3, 11, 13, and 15)? Give an example. Can you think of a synonym for the term?
5. In paragraph 7, Elkind writes, the "young person's ability to foresee and avoid is both an intellectual and an emotional achievement." Explain this statement.

CONSIDERING METHOD

1. How many times does Elkind repeat his main point? Why might a writer repeat the main point several times?
2. Divide the fifteen paragraphs into five main sections. What label could you put on each section?
3. How does Elkind let you know what to expect when you are reading his essay?
4. How do you know when a new paragraph takes up a new type of stress situation?
5. How does Elkind clarify what each type of stress situation is like?
6. Is Elkind writing *to* teenagers or *about* them? How do you know?

WRITING STEP BY STEP: TYPES OF SOCIAL PRESSURE

Using Elkind's classification of types of stress as a model, write an essay in which you investigate types of social pressure in your world. Think about the influences that cause you to think and behave the way you do. Consider which influences you resist and which you accept.

A. Identify two to four types of social pressure you see at work in your environment.
B. Think of some general strength that people could develop that would help them deal with these types of social pressure. Discuss what you mean by this strength in the introduction to the essay.
C. Write a paragraph briefly presenting the types of social pressure you intend to discuss.
D. Explain each type of social pressure in its own section of the paper. Use examples and details to clarify what you mean.
E. For each type, include an explanation of how the basic strength you discussed early in the essay would apply to this type of social pressure.

F. Put in some kind of transitional material or signal when you switch from one type to another. See the editing section at the end of this selection for help.

G. Point out some circumstances in which the basic strength might fail to help a person deal with social pressure.

H. In your closing (one or two sentences), reaffirm the general principle you have developed.

OTHER WRITING IDEAS

1. Classify and explain the types of stress that distinguish a certain period of life other than the teenage years. For example, think about the first year of college, marriage, parenthood, or retirement.

2. USING THE INTERNET. Write an article for incoming freshmen alerting them to the types of stress typically experienced by college students. Offer your readers ideas and resources for handling these pressures. You can find information at Web sites dealing with stress management and reduction, such as **http://stress.about.com/mbody.htm**

3. COLLABORATIVE WRITING. Consider the types of stresses that seem to be assigned by sex. What are the types of stress usually felt most by women? What types of stress are felt most by men? Get together in a mixed-sex group to brainstorm for ideas. Write on either sex but not both.

4. WRITING ABOUT READING. Summarize Elkind's three types of pressure. Give examples of each type from your own life or your friends' lives. Explain what role self-esteem plays in handling these instances of stress.

GAINING WORD POWER

Elkind's essay on stress uses several words and their opposites, their **antonyms**, such as *extroverted* and *introverted*, *inevitable* and *avoidable*, *foreseeable* and *unforeseeable*. Use your dictionary or a dictionary of **synonyms** and antonyms to find the opposites of the following words from the reading. Be sure to choose opposites that are the same part of speech; in the three preceding examples, all the words can be used as adjectives. You may need to use two or three words instead of one. Your dictionary will help you determine parts of speech.

transient	jeopardize
expenditure	potential
incorporate	

EDITING SKILLS: TRANSITIONS

Good writers use **transitions**—words and phrases that help connect ideas—to show how one sentence is related, logically, to the sentence before it. Look at these examples from the Elkind essay.

> On the other hand, the young person who refuses to become a soldier protects himself or herself from danger at the cost of social disapproval. [On the other hand is a transitional phrase indicating that a contrast is about to be made.]

> It should be said, too, that the young person's ability to foresee and avoid is both an intellectual and an emotional achievement. [The word too indicates that this sentence adds material consistent with the sentence before it.]

> Again, the young person with a strong sense of identity and a feeling of self-esteem has the best chance of managing these stress situations as well as they can be managed. [The word again lets you know that this sentence repeats something said earlier.]

Notice that the transitional words are separated from the main sentence with commas.

EXERCISE

Find at least two other sentences in the Elkind essay that include transitional words and copy them exactly.

Now check your own essay to see whether you can provide more transitional "glue" to hold your thoughts together. Transitions can show several types of movement:

Addition: also, too, moreover, next, furthermore, again
Exemplification: for example, that is, for instance
Emphasis: especially, in fact, primarily, most importantly
Contrast: but, on the other hand, nevertheless, however
Comparison: likewise, similarly, also, too
Qualification: admittedly, of course, granted that
Causation: so, consequently, therefore, as a result
Conclusion: finally, in conclusion, in short, at last

Add at least one transitional word or phrase to your own essay.

WEB SITE

www.cio.com/article/29797
An article by David Elkind about the effects of technology on children.

PREPARING TO READ

Have you ever seen *The George Lopez Show* on television? How about *Greetings from Tucson*, *The Brothers Garcia*, *An American Family*, or *Taina*? If so, what do you think of these shows? If not, why do you suppose you haven't seen them?

••

The Latino Show

••

JULEYKA LANTIGUA

A journalist, writer, editor, teacher, lecturer, and translator, Juleyka Lantigua earned a B.A. in Spanish Literature and Government from Skidmore College and an M.A. in journalism from Boston University. She has taken a variety of roles in magazine and book publishing, including the managing editorship of Urban Latino *from 2000 to 2002. She is also a faculty mentor for Radio Ondas, National Public Radio's training program for young Latino journalists. She says she most relishes being a nationally syndicated columnist with* The Progressive *magazine's Media Project. The following article appeared in* The Progressive *in February 2003.*

TERMS TO RECOGNIZE

virtual (*para. 6*)	existing in effect only, not recognized or acknowledged
patriarch (*para. 7*)	male leader of a family, clan, or tribe
formulaic (*para. 12*)	based on an established model or approach
caliber (*para. 13*)	a level of excellence or importance, quality
amalgamation (*para. 14*)	mixture of various elements
ethnic (*paras. 14, 18*)	relating to people who share common and distinctive racial, national, and cultural heritage
generic (*para. 15*)	standing for a whole group, general, common
discernible (*para. 17*)	able to be seen or recognized, observable
suffice (*para. 18*)	meet the needs, be enough

   Lately, Latinos are everywhere on television. We're behind the anchor   1
desk of the local news. We appear on prime time shows as guests or supporting cast members. Some of us have even landed lead roles on network

sitcoms and dramas. And more of us are behind the cameras, at the writing desks, and in production meetings.

We're more visible not because TV executives value us as viewers but   2
because they want to mine our purchasing power. Without offering an actual definition of this group, Nielsen Media Research estimates that there are almost nine million "Hispanic American TV households," a number that has grown by 19 percent in the last five years.

When we talk about the Latino television audience, we're talking   3
about one of two broad groups of viewers: (a) those whose ancestors are from Latin America, Spain, the Spanish-speaking Caribbean, Mexico, or native Mexicans in the Southwest and West Coast territories that were gobbled up by the United States; and (b) those who themselves arrived from one of these countries in the last two decades (like me). This second group probably comprises the 4.5 million Latino households Nielsen qualifies as Spanish-dominant, meaning that only or mostly Spanish is spoken at home.

What networks and advertisers don't realize yet is that those in group   4
"a" differ considerably from those in group "b." Latinos whose families have been here for generations, like millions of Mexican Americans, make up a type of mainstream Latino America, rooted in their heritage but living according to contemporary U.S. culture. Comedian and sitcom star George Lopez put it succinctly: "I'm just an American guy who happens to be of Mexican descent." Lopez, whose show was the most-watched program in its time slot with twelve million viewers through October 30, echoes the sentiment of millions of Latinos whose identities are American first, of Latino descent second. Many in this category are English-dominant or monolingual, having grown up in households where everyone spoke English.

Those in group "b" tend to have a split focus between their new lives   5
in the States and their former or ongoing lives back in their home countries. They are also still experiencing the challenges of becoming fully integrated into American society. Group "b" has not attained the consumer power of group "a."

One obvious result is that the leading Spanish networks, Univision and   6
Telemundo, have a tight hold on Spanish-dominant viewers. Another is the virtual Mexican Americanization of sitcoms, dramas, and commercials on the English networks. And no wonder: Mexican Americans and recently arrived Mexicans constitute a majority of the U.S. Latino population, 58.5 percent, or 20.6 million, according to the Census.

The proof is in the programming. Flipping channels during prime   7
time might go something like this: First, there's *The George Lopez Show* (ABC), a comedy about a Mexican American airplane parts factory manager in

Los Angeles. He is married to a Cuban American, and they have two children. Then, you get to *Greetings from Tucson* (WB), a comedy about a Mexican American married to an Irish American—a household navigating three cultures. On PBS, you can find *An American Family*, a drama about a Mexican American patriarch trying to hold his family together. And finally, *The Brothers Garcia* (Nickelodeon's number-one live-action series), a sitcom about a Mexican American family trying to survive the pitfalls of raising their three kids through childhood and adolescence.

Admittedly, I have enjoyed watching some of these shows, and the writing can be inspired, funny, and original. But I have not connected with *any* enough to bring me back week after week.   8

What's missing from the shows I mentioned is a sense of belonging here *and* somewhere else, having a place to yearn for *and* memories that propel you toward your new life. That sort of immigrant motif could fuel a dramatic series about a different kind of Latino experience in the United States. But a show based on the immigrant experience may never happen, since Latinos are so determined to prove that we belong here as much as the next American.   9

George Lopez told hispaniconline.com, "They wanted to make me an immigrant of some sort. I'd rather get out of the business completely if that's what I have to do." I don't think Lopez, or any other Latino who feels like him, has an obligation to play up his immigrant heritage. He is simply demanding that he be placed in the rightful category of American of Latino descent. I respect that, but this category is not the same as Latino immigrant living in America. That's a political distinction Latino leaders are afraid to make, but it's real. And it ought to be reflected on TV.   10

Here's an idea: Create a Latino version of *Friends* where each of the amigos represents one of the larger groups of Latinos. The casting call for the twenty- and thirty-something roles might read something like this: Seeking a fifth-generation professional Chicana from L.A. who struggles to be independent from, and loyal to, her protective family; a Colombian college student activist who immigrated here as a teen and wants the U.S. to stop funding his country's civil war; an artistic Nuyorican from the Bronx (à la Jennifer Lopez) who dreams of making it big while staying true to her roots; a ninth-generation Tejana technology wiz navigating the social mores of dating outside her culture; and a Dominican law student from Washington Heights who immigrated with her parents as an infant and dreams of returning to become her country's first woman president.   11

This approach may be formulaic, but it addresses two key concepts that programmers and advertisers have not fully grasped.   12

First, the Latino audience, much like the general audience, is broken   13
into age segments; no single show will do. There are the kids who watch *The Brothers Garcia* and *Taina*, Nickelodeon's quirky sitcom about a Puerto Rican high school student who dreams of becoming an entertainer. Their middle-age parents might cozy up to *The George Lopez Show* and *American Family*. And increasingly, there are the twenty-five-to-forty-year-olds who have the lion's share of the spending. We are the folks who wrote letters to Showtime when they threatened to cancel *Resurrection Boulevard*. We're the ones who get hooked on shows like *Frasier, Seinfeld*, and *Friends*. And that is the caliber of show we expect from Latino programs.

Second, we need a show to counter "the generically Latino" charac-   14
ter. Defined by an absolute lack of ethnic identity, these supporting characters have brief exchanges with the white or black lead cast members, rarely finding themselves the protagonists of an episode or even of a storyline. *That '70s Show* is the biggest offender in this category. Barely out of his teens, the generically Latino, heavily accented, and over-the-top post-pubescent character "Fez" is a slimy amalgamation of every woman's nightmarish Latin lover. He orbits around the white cast and waits to deliver, or be the recipient of, a punch line.

On shows like *Law & Order* and *The Practice*, the generic Latino is   15
usually a male criminal of varying ages and degrees of guilt or his helpless mother/sister/wife/ girlfriend who is shocked by the news of his arrest and who stands by his side no matter what. To the producers' credit, these characters don't always have accents, but they are still instantly recognizable by their surnames.

There are exceptions to the forgettable generic Latino. Esai Morales's   16
character on *NYPD Blue* does have storylines written for him, and he often appears in meaningful scenes. Or take nurse Carla Espinosa on the surprise hit *Scrubs*. Played by Judy Reyes, nurse Espinosa has worked for everything she's ever accomplished. She has a preoccupation with her family—namely, her needy mother. And she's in a committed relationship for which she has also worked very hard. Nurse Espinosa is the sole accent-free Latina I tune in to every week, even when it's a rerun. Of all the characters on all the shows, she is most like me and my Latina friends.

The other end of the spectrum has the character of Lucia Rojas-Klein   17
on *Good Morning, Miami*, a sitcom about the team that produces a morning TV show. The drama queen Cuban American co-host who wears daringly unprofessional outfits to work and whose occasional line is barely discernible because of her belabored accent is exactly the kind of walking stereotype non-Latinos learn to love on fluffy television programs. Another show,

CSI: Miami, has no clearly identifiable Latino characters despite being set in one of the most Latino cities in the United States.

For the record, I don't believe Latino actors should be limited to   18
Latino roles. Benjamin Bratt's portrayal of Detective Curtis on *Law & Order* and countless other performers have proven that over and over. But I am saying that Latino characters and programs need to be more developed so that a mere Spanish surname does not suffice to fill the ethnic quota.

RESPONDING TO READING

Before reading this essay, had you thought about whether Latinos are fairly and adequately represented on TV? Did Lantigua convince you that they are not? Can you think of other examples of shows or characters? Do you think you would be interested in watching any of the shows she describes (if you don't already)?

CONSIDERING CONTENT

1. What major division does Lantigua find in the Latino television audience (para. 3)? How do the two groups differ from each other?
2. Why are the English networks dominated by Mexican American shows? What is missing from these shows, in the author's opinion?
3. Lantigua says that "a show based on the immigrant experience may never happen" (para. 9). Why not?
4. What is wrong with "the generically Latino" character (para. 14)?
5. Why does the author like nurse Espinosa on *Scrubs?* Why does she not like the character played by Lucia Roja-Klein on *Good Morning, Miami?*

CONSIDERING METHOD

1. What evidence is there that Lantigua is writing to Latino readers? What other **audiences** does she also hope to reach?
2. The author first divides the Latino audience in paragraph 3. What further division does she make later in the article? What is the point of this second division?
3. How many examples does the author use in her classification? What purpose do they serve?
4. Find three uses of statistics in the article. What points do they make?
5. What is the purpose of describing a Latino version of *Friends* (para. 11)? Is it an effective technique?

WRITING STEP BY STEP: TV PORTRAYALS

Write an essay that classifies the way that a specific group of people are presented on TV. You can choose an ethnic or racial group, as Juleyka Lantigua does, or you can look at a different classification: children, athletes, married couples, doctors, gay people, police, teachers, and so forth. You might want to narrow your topic by focusing on a particular type of show—for example, how parents are portrayed in situation comedies, or how politicians are presented in dramatic shows.

A. Begin by making a list of titles, characters, and other details for the group you have chosen. Ask friends and classmates to help you brainstorm examples; consult *TV Guide* or some other publications about television to gather specific material.

B. Divide the examples into at least three categories that illustrate the way TV shows draw on popular images and **stereotypes**.

C. Reread Lantigua's opening paragraphs. Write an opening for your own essay in which you explain a misconception or distinction that television producers and writers don't seem to recognize. Explain why they are wrong. Or write an opening that gives your overall evaluation of the way your target group is portrayed.

D. Introduce your categories by identifying the basis for your division and classification. Then name and briefly summarize your categories.

E. Choose an especially useful example to explain each category. In each case, examine the image or stereotype in some detail. You will probably need to explain your examples; your readers may not immediately see the distinctions you are making and may not be familiar with the shows.

F. Write a closing that refers to the points you made in your introduction (step C). Like Lantigua, you might suggest what changes could be made in the way this group is presented.

OTHER WRITING IDEAS

1. In the student essay at the end of this chapter, Ben Hardy divides the way he uses recipes into three approaches. Think of something you do in three or four different ways and explain why and how: for example, dressing in the morning, driving your car, talking to a person at a party, doing home repairs, or doing your homework. Using Ben Hardy's paragraph structure as a model, write an essay explaining your three or four approaches to an activity.

2. COLLABORATIVE WRITING. Get together with a group of classmates to discuss how each of you views your roots. Then write an essay that classifies people according to their attitudes toward their own backgrounds—ethnic, religious, cultural, racial, or class roots. For example, in what ways do people who come from a particular economic class relate to their past? What stances do people raised in a specific faith take toward religion in later life?

3. USING THE INTERNET. Visit several Web sites aimed at a specific ethnic group, such as the Latino Issues Forum (**www.lif.org/**) and Hispanic

Online (**www.hispaniconline.com/**), or the Asian American Net (**www.asianamerican.net**) and Asia-Nation: The Landscape of Asian America (**www.asian-nation.org**). Using a classification and division approach, write a report on the topics that seem to be important to this group.

4. WRITING ABOUT READING. Throughout her article, the author uses the word *Latino* to refer to the people under discussion. What does that term mean? How does it differ, if it does, from *Hispanic* (para. 2)? Lantigua also uses the words *Chicana, Colombian, Nuyorican, Dominican,* and *Tejana.* Write an essay about the use of ethnic language in "The Latino Show." Define the terms and explain why the author uses them as she does.

GAINING WORD POWER

In paragraph 4, Lantigua uses the word *monolingual*, which is formed by adding a familiar **prefix** to the word *lingual.* The prefix *mono-* means one, single, or alone; and *lingual* refers to languages. So *monolingual* means "speaking or using only one language." We use this prefix often, as in *monotone* (one tone of voice), *monopoly* (a commercial activity controlled by one company), and *monosyllable* (a word with just one syllable). Can you think of other terms that use this prefix? See if you can figure out the meaning of the following words: monologue, monochromatic, monogamy, monogram, monomania, monorail, monotheism. Then use a dictionary to check your definitions.

EDITING SKILLS: USING APOSTROPHES

Using apostrophes makes most writers at least a bit nervous. To get a grip on this slippery punctuation mark, think about these basic rules:

1. Use an apostrophe to indicate that two words have been pushed together to form a contraction. Put the apostrophe where you leave the letters out.

   would not = wouldn't   is not = isn't
   you are = you're   he is = he's
   they will = they'll   we have = we've

2. Use an apostrophe plus *s* with singular nouns to show possession.

   the heat of the sun = the sun's heat

   the rent for one year = one year's rent

   the wig belonging to Judy = Judy's wig

   cards from UNICEF = UNICEF's cards

3. Use an apostrophe after the *s* with plurals to make them possessive.

   papers from three students = three students' papers

   alibis of four criminals = four criminals' alibis

If the plural does not already end in *s*, add an *s* after the apostrophe.

games for children = children's games

poetry by men = men's poetry

For more information about apostrophes, see Chapter 7, pages 201–202.

EXERCISE

In the Lantigua essay, there are 17 separate words that use apostrophes. Copy the 17 words exactly. Don't count repeats. Next to each one, write whether the apostrophe makes the word a contraction or a possessive. What does the apostrophe in the title *That '70s Show* indicate?

Now return to your classification essay, and make sure that you have used apostrophes correctly.

🌐 WEB SITE

www.laprensa-sandiego.org/archieve/april09-04/study.htm
Report of a study entitled "Looking for Latino Regulars on Prime-Time Television: The Fall 2003 Season," conducted by UCLA's Chicano Studies Research Center.

STUDENT ESSAY USING CLASSIFICATION AND DIVISION

Three Ways to Use a Recipe

Ben Hardy

Ben Hardy, from Syracuse, New York, started kitchen work at 16 as a busboy in a steak house. Over the next few years, he moved up to prep boy and line cook, and then entered a program in food science at the local community college. He aspires to become a chef specializing in French-Asian fusion cuisine.

I like to eat. Not just food in general, but high quality, expertly prepared and presented food. Spoiled by years of fine dining experiences, I am disappointed by most restaurants, so I've turned to preparing food myself. This way, I am solely responsible for what winds up on my plate. However, there is no one handy to blame, no place to send back that dried-out fish or watery sauce. I learned this the hard way, drawn in by luscious food photos and the accompanying "Fast! Easy!" recipes in magazines. These lists of ingredients and instructions, and the disappointment or pleasure that follows, have led me to approach recipes from three different perspectives.   1

Recipe as gospel. Most people, especially those new to the cooking art, take this approach. Sounds simple enough. Clean, chop, measure, bake, and untold delights await you. Wrong. Very few recipes, if followed to the letter, end up with something edible or even recognizable. The exceptions are those that come from test kitchens. The hearty souls in kitchens like *Cooks Illustrated*'s take several hundred pounds of beef and several days of trial-and-error to arrive at *the* recipe for pot roast. There's an obvious advantage to having someone else ruin your first 20 pot roasts. Recipes from test kitchens are often accompanied by detailed explanations of what went wrong with some versions, or why the roasts of your youth were so chewy and tasteless. Test kitchen recipes are like gold nuggets to the culinary prospector, and should be followed almost to the letter. Recipes from other sources require more thought.   2

Recipe as guideline. This is my approach to recipes that I get from the Internet, foodie magazines, and well-meaning friends. When I read most of these recipes I always see something that causes a double-take. Do they really want me to send up smoke signals by putting butter in a skillet on High? Do they really expect those green beans to be something more than olive-colored pulp after 10 minutes of boiling? Do they really think that putting a small clove of garlic in a gallon of bean soup is anything other than a symbolic gesture? Occasionally, a recipe will intentionally call for something unexpected, and if so, the writers say so. But usually they're   3 simply trying to tell you to melt some butter, cook some green beans, or put some flavor into that soup. The guideline approach to recipes means having to figure out the writer's goal for the finished product. It takes some cooking know-how, but it's important to understand *why* recipes ask for certain ingredients or methods, rather than focus on *how* they want you to do things.

Recipe as inspiration. I easily read 100 recipes for every one I actually   4
attempt. That sounds like a great deal of work for small payoff, but there is a purpose to all that time spent browsing. I'm looking for ideas. I have no intention of trying out that two-week Peking duck with orange coriander glaze. But, it never occurred to me to pair a citrus fruit with coriander seeds. That might come in handy some day. A simple recipe for braised cabbage (cabbage, butter, chicken stock, salt) might make a straightforward side dish. But, what if I stirred in some cooked linguine and chunks of corned beef at the end? It'd be an interesting take on traditional corned beef and cabbage. Besides interesting ingredient ideas, some recipes contain an inspired technique. A preparation for chicken stew might have you bake the chicken *before* browning it in a skillet. Forget the rest of the recipe: this sounds like a good way to cook a chicken breast as an entrée. I never baked (rather than boiled) a fresh beet before I saw the method called for in a cold beet salad recipe. Now I always bake beets for superior flavor, regardless of the final preparation.

Recipes are like family. They can instruct and inspire as well as infuri-   5
ate us. Sometimes it's tempting to skip the yearly reunion or holiday gathering and order take-out instead. But you might miss hearing how your Aunt Sally poached a peach in red wine and rosemary—right after she mentioned you seem to be putting on a little weight.

CONSIDERING CONTENT AND METHOD

1. Why do you think the writer chose the topic of using recipes? Why is it a good topic for him? Think about some limited, special skill you have pursued in your spare time or your studies, or both.
2. How many examples does Ben Hardy use for each approach he explains? Is there any general point where an added example would have been useful to you as a reader? Do you think a non–cook could understand the essay?
3. How would you describe the style of the student essay (formal, general, informal, colloquial)? Explain what words or phrases help you identify the style.
4. What comparison does Hardy make in the closing paragraph? Does this comparison make sense to you? Why or why not? What else could approaching recipes be compared to for an interesting closing?

CHAPTER 7

Strategies for Examining Two Subjects: *Comparison* and *Contrast*

IMAGES AND IDEAS

For Discussion and Writing

Examine closely the two men portrayed in this famous advertisement for Apple computers. How are they different? In what ways are they similar?

Write a brief paper in which you compare and contrast the values and lifestyles suggested by the two figures in the ad. Consider age, body type, clothes, hairstyle, stance, facial expression, and so forth. What point is the designer of the ad making about the differences between the two people?

Every day we use **comparison-and-contrast** thinking to make decisions in our personal lives. Should I wear the pink shirt or the teal? Should I take my lunch to work or eat out? Will it be Taco Bell or McDonald's? Should I write a check or use my credit card? Often the factors influencing an everyday decision are weighed so quickly in our minds that we may not be aware of having examined both sides. But when faced with a major decision, we think longer and may even make a list of pros and cons: "Reasons for Getting a New Car" on the left side of the sheet; "Reasons for Keeping Old Blue" on the right side. Intelligent decision making helps keep our lives from lapsing into chaos. Comparing and contrasting serve as useful tools in the struggle.

THE POINT OF COMPARISON AND CONTRAST

Technically, we *compare* things that are similar and *contrast* things that are different. But in order to contrast things, we have to compare them. And a comparison will often point out the differences of items being compared. You can see how fuzzy the distinction gets, so don't worry about it.

Using Comparisons to Explain

Using comparisons is a dandy writing strategy for explaining something your readers don't know much about by comparing it to something they do know about. For instance, geologists like to explain the levels in the earth's crust by comparing them to the layers in an onion. Or if you want to explain something complicated, like the way our eyes work, you could compare the human eye to a camera, which is simpler and more easily understood.

Using Comparisons to Persuade

Comparisons can be an effective technique in persuasive writing to help clarify and convince. People who believe that illegal drugs should be decriminalized often compare the current drug-related gang warfare to the alcohol-related crime wave during Prohibition in the 1930s. When alcohol was made legal again, the gangsters were out of business and the violence subsided. The same thing would happen today, the argument goes, if drugs were legalized. Such a comparison, called an **analogy,** can be quite convincing if you can think of one that is sensible and clearly parallel.

Using Contrast to Decide

You can set up a contrast to help clarify differences—if, for instance, you are faced with a choice between products or people or pets or proposals (or whatever). You might want to make this investigation for your own benefit or to convince someone else that one thing is preferable to another. Say, your boss asks you to find out which photocopying machine would be the best buy for the office. Because the machines are all fairly similar, your report would focus on the differences in order to determine which one would give the best results for the least money. Or if you are trying to determine whether to borrow money or get a part-time job to help pay next year's tuition, you should consider carefully the advantages and disadvantages of each choice.

THE PRINCIPLES OF COMPARISON AND CONTRAST

Since the purpose of comparing and contrasting is to show similarities or differences, good organization is crucial to success. There are two standard ways of composing this kind of writing: the **block-by-block** *pattern* and **the point-by-point pattern.** These patterns can, of course, be expanded to include consideration of more than two elements.

Using the Block-by-Block Plan

Particularly useful for responding to comparison-or-contrast essay examination topics is this simple method of organization:

1. State your purpose.
2. Present key features of the first part of your comparison.
3. Make a transition.
4. Present corresponding features of the second part of your comparison.
5. Draw your conclusions.

This simple plan serves perfectly for showing how something has changed or developed: your earliest views about AIDS compared with the way you think now; Madonna's first album compared with her latest one; Picasso's early work compared with his later paintings; hairstyles ten years ago compared with hairstyles today. You will see how effectively this plan works when you read the first two essays in this chapter.

Similarities and Differences

A variation on the block-by-block plan is to cluster the points of comparison and contrast according to similarities and differences. Consider, for instance, the proverbial apples and oranges comparison. An advertising executive for the apple industry might organize a fact sheet promoting apples by first clustering the similarities between apples and oranges (their nutritional value and availability, for example) and then emphasizing their differences (more varied uses for apples and their lower cost). The purpose, to sell apples, is best served by posing the comparison but emphasizing the favorable contrasts.

Using the Point-by-Point Plan

When you have time to carefully organize your ideas, you may want to present the material in a way that highlights individual differences. In other words, you choose the points of comparison that best illustrate the similarities or differences and then organize the material to contrast those features.

Each major section of the comparison covers one point in terms of both (or all) the things being compared or contrasted. For example, a nutritionist might organize the fact sheet on apples and oranges by drawing conclusions one section at a time about the relative nutritional value, availability, and use, covering both apples and oranges under each of these points. For consistency, either apples or oranges would be discussed first in each section, like this:

APPLES VERSUS ORANGES

1. Relative cost
   a. Orange prices remain fairly constant throughout the year.
   b. Apples are least expensive during the fall harvest season.

2. Nutritional value
   a. Oranges contain lots of vitamins A and C and have 62 calories.
   b. Apples offer fiber and have 81 calories.

3. Availability
   a. Oranges are generally available year round.
   b. Apples are best during the fall.

4. Use
   a. Oranges can be used as snacks, salads, main dishes, and desserts.
   b. Apples can be used as snacks, salads, main dishes, and desserts.

You could use exactly the same material in writing a block-style essay as you would with this point-by-point pattern. The differences lie in the way you arrange your material.

THE PITFALLS OF COMPARISON AND CONTRAST

If you are using a block pattern, be sure to follow the same order in making your comparison. If you are writing about the differences between waterbeds and airbeds, you could start by explaining the main features of the waterbed—something like this:

1. Fill it with a hose
2. Adjusting for comfort tricky
3. Needs a heater
4. Heavy when full of water
5. Reasonable in cost

Then, after switching to your discussion of airbeds, take up the same features in the same order:

1. Inflate it with a button
2. Adjusting for comfort easy
3. No need for a heater
4. Light when full of air
5. Expensive to buy

Keep the same order in your point-by-point organization, too. After grouping all of the preceding information under headings something like these:

1. Comfort
2. Convenience
3. Cost

Be careful to discuss first waterbeds, then airbeds; waterbeds, then airbeds; waterbeds, then airbeds—in presenting the material in each category. As you read Sakamoto's "Conversational Ballgames," notice that she gives parallel details when explaining English and Japanese conversations.

Avoid Using Too Many Transitional Words

True, comparison-and-contrast writing involves making lots of **transitions,** but you won't necessarily need to signal each one with a transitional word. In the block pattern, you will need an obvious transition to let your readers know that you're going to shift to the second item or idea. You'll write a sentence such as, "Airbeds, *on the other hand*, are an excellent buy for several reasons" or "*On the contrary*, waterbeds can sometimes prove troublesome to maintain."

But when you follow the point-by-point pattern, you will probably not want to signal every shift back and forth with a transitional term. (Did you notice that the term *but* in the previous sentence provided a transition between paragraphs?) With the point-by-point method of organization, you will be making contrasts under each point. If you try to signal each one, your prose may get clunky. Once you have established the shifts back and forth, let your readers be guided by the pattern—and make sure you stick to it.

Avoid Repetition in Concluding

In a brief comparison or contrast essay, you need not summarize all your points at the end. Your readers can remember what you've said. Instead, draw a meaningful conclusion about the material. Maybe you'll want to assert that two apparently different religions are basically the same. Or you might stress that the differences are so crucial that conflict will always exist. If you are comparing products, come out in favor of one over the other—or else declare that neither amounts to a hill of beans—or perhaps invite your readers to judge for themselves. Just be sure to make a point of some sort at the end.

WHAT TO LOOK FOR IN COMPARISON AND CONTRAST

As you study the essays in this chapter, pay particular attention to the organization and the *continuity* (what makes it flow).

1. Look for a pattern (or maybe a combination of patterns) that each writer uses in presenting the material. Decide whether you think the method of organization is effective or whether there might be a better way.

2. Underline the transitional terms (such as *on the other hand, but, still, yet, on the contrary, nevertheless, however, contrary to, conversely, consequently, then, in other words, therefore, hence, thus, granted that, after all*). Notice what sort of meaningful links are provided between paragraphs when no purely transitional terms appear.

3. Look at the introductions and conclusions to see what strategies are used to set up the comparison or contrast at the beginning and to reinforce the writer's point at the end.

PREPARING TO READ

What is a breakdown in communication? Have you ever had such a breakdown? Describe it and consider why it happened. For instance, was it the fault of the personalities involved, of different expectations, of a poorly understood topic, or of a generation gap?

••

Conversational Ballgames

••

Nᴀɴᴄʏ Mᴀsᴛᴇʀsᴏɴ Sᴀᴋᴀᴍᴏᴛᴏ

Nancy Masterson Sakamoto was born in Los Angeles and lived in Japan from 1972 to 1981, where she developed her ideas about how the two cultures can understand and appreciate each other. Her marriage to a Japanese man, Satoru Sakamoto, and her teaching in Japanese schools and in Honolulu, Hawaii, have given her personal insight into cultural differences. Her book Polite Fiction: Why Japanese and Americans Seem Rude to Each Other *(1982) argues that the two cultures have conflicting codes to guide social encounters: In the United States, the fundamental social fiction is "You and I are equal," while in Japan, the fundamental social fiction is "I am in awe of you."*

After I was married and had lived in Japan for a while, my Japanese gradually improved to the point where I could take part in simple conversations with my husband, his friends, and family. And I began to notice that often, when I joined in, the others would look startled, and the conversation would come to a halt. After this happened several times, it became clear to me that I was doing something wrong. But for a long time, I didn't know what it was. 1

Finally, after listening carefully to many Japanese conversations, I discovered what my problem was. Even though I was speaking Japanese, I was handling the conversation in a Western way. 2

Japanese-style conversations develop quite differently from western-style conversations. And the difference isn't only in the languages. I realized that just as I kept trying to hold western-style conversations even when I was speaking Japanese, so were my English students trying to hold Japanese-style conversations even when they were speaking English. We were unconsciously playing entirely different conversational ballgames. 3

A western-style conversation between two people is like a game of tennis. If I introduce a topic, a conversational ball, I expect you to hit it 4 back. If you agree with me, I don't expect you simply to agree and do nothing more. I expect you to add something—a reason for agreeing, another example, or a remark to carry the idea further. But I don't expect you always to agree. I am just as happy if you question me, or challenge me, or completely disagree with me. Whether you agree or disagree, your response will return the ball to me.

And then it is my turn again. I don't serve a new ball from my original 5 starting line. I hit your ball back again from where it has bounced. I carry your idea further, or answer your questions or objections, or challenge or question you. And so the ball goes back and forth.

If there are more than two people in the conversation, then it is like 6 doubles in tennis, or like volleyball. There's no waiting in line. Whoever is nearest and quickest hits the ball, and if you step back, someone else will hit it. No one stops the game to give you a turn. You're responsible for taking your own turn and no one person has the ball for very long.

A Japanese-style conversation, however, is not at all like tennis or 7 volleyball; it's like bowling. You wait for your turn, and you always know your place in line. It depends on such things as whether you are older or younger, a close friend or a relative stranger to the previous speaker, in a senior or junior position, and so on.

The first thing is to wait for your turn, patiently and politely. When 8 your moment comes, you step up to the starting line with your bowling ball, and carefully bowl it. Everyone else stands back, making sounds of polite encouragement. Everyone waits until your ball has reached the end of the lane, and watches to see if it knocks down all the pins, or only some of them, or none of them. Then there is a pause, while everyone registers your score.

Then, after everyone is sure that you are done, the next person in line 9 steps up to the same starting line, with a different ball. He doesn't return your ball. There is no back and forth at all. And there is always a suitable pause between turns. There is no rush, no impatience.

No wonder everyone looked startled when I took part in Japanese 10 conversations. I paid no attention to whose turn it was, and kept snatching the ball halfway down the alley and throwing it back at the bowler. Of course the conversation fell apart: I was playing the wrong game.

This explains why it can be so difficult to get a western-style discus- 11 sion going with Japanese students of English. Whenever I serve a volleyball, everyone just stands back and watches it fall. No one hits it back. Everyone waits until I call on someone to take a turn. And when that person speaks, he doesn't hit my ball back. He serves a new ball. Again, everyone just watches it fall. So I call on someone else. This person does not refer to what the previous speaker has said. He also serves a new ball. Everyone begins again from the same starting line, and all the balls run parallel. There is never any back and forth.

   Now that you know about the difference in the conversational ball-   12
games, you may think that all your troubles are over. But if you have been trained all your life to play one game, it is no simple matter to switch to another, even if you know the rules. Tennis, after all, is different from bowling.

RESPONDING TO READING

Does knowing the rules of communication help you communicate? Think of an example. Or, as Sakamoto says, is knowing the rules only part of learning to communicate well?

CONSIDERING CONTENT

1. How did the writer end up having conversations in Japanese?
2. Summarize your understanding of the difference between Japanese and Western-style conversations. For instance, if you had two transcripts of conversations, how could you tell the Western from the Japanese?
3. How much does a reader have to know about tennis and bowling to understand the essay? Is playing tennis or bowling necessary? Why or why not?
4. Why does the cultural difference described in the essay cause a problem in the writer's English class?
5. Does Sakamoto place a higher value on one conversational style over the other? Explain why you answered *yes* or *no*.

CONSIDERING METHOD

1. Reread paragraphs 4 through 9. Are the details arranged in a block-by-block plan or a point-by-point plan? Imagine the essay developed by the other plan. Why do you think Sakamoto chose the plan she used?
2. List the features that are developed for both the bowling and the tennis comparisons.
3. Sakamoto's conclusion brings the two sports together to make a final point: "But if you have been trained all your life to play one game, it is no simple matter to switch to another, even if you know the rules." Summarize this idea in different words. Why doesn't the author develop the idea further with examples and details?

4. Look at the parallel structure of a sentence in paragraph 3: "I realized that just as I kept trying to hold western-style conversations even when I was speaking Japanese, so were my English students trying to hold Japanese-style conversations even when they were speaking English." The parallelism of the phrasing makes the parallelism in the content easy to follow. Write a sentence on any topic, following the model by filling in the blanks with any number of words: "I realized that just as I kept trying to _____ even when _____ , so were [or was] _____ trying to _____ even when _____."

WRITING STEP BY STEP: EXTENDED COMPARISONS

Sakamoto contrasts two conversation styles by explaining them in terms of two sports, bowling and tennis. In your Step by Step essay, you will contrast two people's personal styles by comparing them to two sports (as Sakamoto does), two games (bridge and poker, for example), or two animals (puppy and snake, for example). First, you need to identify two people you know (or know a lot about) who have markedly different ways of living, thinking, communicating, or all three. The term *personal style* is shorthand for a wide range of someone's habits, mannerisms, thoughts, preferences, and behaviors. Then, you need to think about what sports, games, or animals can serve as good comparisons for the personal styles of the two people. Would one of these people be more like a Frisbee game and the other like a round of golf? Would one be like Word Search and the other one like the *New York Times* crossword? To stimulate your imagination, get together with some classmates to brainstorm lists of games, sports, and animals and their usual characteristics with classmates, if time permits.

A. In your first paragraph, explain (1) how you know both people and (2) when you began to see fundamental differences between them. (This might take two paragraphs if you need space to develop both points.)

B. In your second or third paragraph, introduce the imaginative comparison you intend to use in your essay. Notice how Sakamoto leads up to her sentence, "We were unconsciously playing entirely different conversational ballgames" (para. 3), to introduce her ballgame comparison between Japanese and Western conversations.

C. In the next three paragraphs, develop the comparison between Person A and Sport A (or Game A, or Animal A), as Sakamoto does in paragraphs 4 through 6 for Western conversations and tennis. Each paragraph should develop one aspect of the comparison. For example, if Person A is like a puppy, you might have one paragraph on how friendly she is, one paragraph on how lively she is, and one paragraph on how exasperating she can be.

D. In the next three paragraphs, develop the comparison between Person B and Sport B (or Game B, or Animal B), as Sakamoto does in paragraphs 7 through 9 for Japanese conversations and bowling. As you did in the section on Person A, develop one aspect of the comparison in each paragraph of this section of the essay.

E. In your last paragraph, briefly state how the contrast operates in your own life. For example, does understanding both people help you communicate with them? Does it make you prefer one over the other? Does the contrast between them pose problems for you?

OTHER WRITING IDEAS

1. USING THE INTERNET. Business people operating in foreign countries need advice about social customs abroad. At **www.overseasdigest.com/ odarticles/converse.htm,** you can read six general tips for international conversations. Observe several conversations in your own group of friends, classmates, or family. Write an essay explaining four to six general rules for an outsider who wishes to join conversations in your group.

2. COLLABORATIVE WRITING. People of different ages sometimes see things differently. Write about an attitude (toward work, religion, education, sports, television, the law, technology, or something else) that you think is different for people who are older or younger than you. Consult with your peers as well as people from the other generation to find out what their understanding of this difference is. Incorporate any useful ideas into your essay.

3. WRITING ABOUT READING. In paragraph 2, Sakamoto identifies that she was having trouble "handling the conversation." What does this mean? Write an essay giving two or three examples in which you or someone else handled a conversation poorly. What rules were being violated? Be sure to contrast each example with how it would've been handled well, or at least adequately.

4. Write an essay that compares texting with emailing, or Facebook with My Space (or some other social networking site). Try using the Similarities and Differences approach (see p. 184).

GAINING WORD POWER

Did you think that we forgot to start with a Terms to Recognize list? Review the essay and see whether you can decide why there are no Terms to Recognize. Using a dictionary or thesaurus, use a fancier, more formal, or less familiar term for each of the following terms from the essay:

take part in (*para. 1*)

joined in (*para. 1*)

come to a halt (*para. 1*)

carry the idea further (*para. 4*)

depends on such things (*para. 7*)

no rush (*para. 9*)

In what writing situation would you decide to use terms like the ones you listed rather than ones that Sakamoto used?

EDITING SKILLS: COMMAS AFTER DEPENDENT ELEMENTS

Copy these sentences from the reading exactly. As you write, look for a pattern they all follow.

Even though I was speaking Japanese, I was handling the conversation in a Western way.

If you agree with me, I don't expect you simply to agree and do nothing more.

Whenever I serve a volleyball, everyone just stands back and watches it fall.

Each of these sentences has two parts. Notice that the second part, after the comma, can stand alone as a sentence; it's called an **independent clause.** If you read the first part alone, it does not sound complete. The first part is called a **dependent clause** for this reason. When you write a sentence in which the *independent* part comes after a *dependent* part, you need to put in a comma to separate the two.

EXERCISE

Put commas in the following sentences:

While planning is important do not overschedule your time.

Since the best courses fill up early plan at least a term or two in advance.

If you cannot write well you will be at a disadvantage.

Now fill in the blanks to make complete sentences below:

Although studying is the major task of college life, _____

_____.

Because grades are important to some employers, _____

_____.

_____, Henry

went to the basketball game.

Next, write three sentences that follow this dependent-comma-independent pattern.

Finally, check your essay to be sure that you have included the commas in sentences like these.

WEB SITE

www.cesl.arizona.edu/custom.html

The Center for English as a Second Language (CESL) at the University of Arizona offers a comprehensive program to prepare ESL students from other countries for academic, professional, and social success in the United States. At the Web site above, you will find CESL's tip sheet on "Getting Along in the USA: Some Customs and Culture Tips." What are your reactions to seeing your own culture from a potential outsider's point of view? Or, if you have been an outsider to U. S. culture, do you agree with the tip sheet's assertions? The tip sheet gives you plenty of material to discuss and write about concerning U. S. conventions of behavior.

PREPARING TO READ

Are you the kind of person who gets fidgety if the socks aren't tidily arranged by color in your drawer? Or are you a casual type who seldom manages to get the socks from the laundry basket into the drawer? Have you tried to change, or do you not feel any need to?

••

Neat People vs. Sloppy People

••

Suzanne Britt

Suzanne Britt is a freelance journalist who teaches English at Meredith College in Raleigh, North Carolina. She has written for the New York Times, *the* Baltimore Sun, *and* Newsday. *In her collection of witty essays* Skinny People Are Dull and Crunchy Like Carrots *(1982), Britt clearly favors fat folks. In the following essay, which comes from her book* Show and Tell *(1983), she sides solidly with slobs, demonstrating that taking an unusual stand—even a not very reasonable stand—can be an effective strategy for humorous writing.*

TERMS TO RECOGNIZE

vs. (*title*)	abbreviation of *versus*, meaning in contrast with or against
rectitude (*para. 2*)	uprightness, correctness
metier (*para. 3*)	a person's area of strength or expertise
excavation (*para. 5*)	digging out, uncovering and removing
meticulously (*para. 5*)	giving great attention to details
scrupulously (*para. 5*)	carefully doing the right thing
cavalier (*para. 6*)	free and easy
vicious (*para. 9*)	hateful, spiteful
salvaging (*para. 9*)	saving from destruction, rescuing
swath (*para. 12*)	a long strip
organic (*para. 12*)	having to do with living things

I've finally figured out the difference between neat people and sloppy   1
people. The distinction is, as always, moral. Neat people are lazier and
meaner than sloppy people.

Sloppy people, you see, are not really sloppy. Their sloppiness is   2
merely the unfortunate consequence of their extreme moral rectitude.

Sloppy people carry in their mind's eye a heavenly vision, a precise plan, that is so stupendous, so perfect, it can't be achieved in this world or the next.

Sloppy people live in Never-Never-Land. Someday is their metier. 3
Someday they are planning to alphabetize all their books and set up home catalogues. Someday they will go through their wardrobes and mark certain items for tentative mending and certain items for passing on to relatives of similar shape and size. Someday sloppy people will make family scrapbooks into which they will put newspaper clippings, postcards, locks of hair, and the dried corsage from their senior prom. Someday they will file everything on the surface of their desks, including the cash receipts from coffee purchases at the snack shop. Someday they will sit down and read all the back issues of *The New Yorker*.

For all these noble reasons and more, sloppy people never get neat. 4
They aim too high and wide. They save everything, planning someday to file, order, and straighten out the world. But while these ambitious plans take clearer and clearer shape in their heads, the books spill from the shelves onto the floor, the clothes pile up in the hamper and closet, the family mementos accumulate in every drawer, the surface of the desk is buried under mounds of paper, and the unread magazines threaten to reach the ceiling.

Sloppy people can't bear to part with anything. They give loving 5
attention to every detail. When sloppy people say they're going to tackle the surface of the desk, they really mean it. Not a paper will go unturned; not a rubber band will go unboxed. Four hours or two weeks into the excavation, the desk looks exactly the same, primarily because the sloppy person is meticulously creating new piles of papers with new headings and scrupulously stopping to read all the old book catalogues before he throws them away. A neat person would just bulldoze the desk.

Neat people are bums and clods at heart. They have cavalier attitudes 6
toward possessions, including family heirlooms. Everything is just another dust-catcher to them. If anything collects dust, it's got to go and that's that. Neat people will toy with the idea of throwing the children out of the house just to cut down the clutter.

Neat people don't care about process. They like results. What they 7
want to do is get the whole thing over with so they can sit down and watch the rasslin' on TV. Neat people operate on two unvarying principles: Never handle any item twice, and throw everything away.

The only thing messy in a neat person's house is the trash can. The 8
minute something comes to a neat person's hand, he will look at it, try to decide if it has immediate use and, finding none, throw it in the trash.

Neat people are especially vicious with mail. They never go through 9
their mail unless they are standing directly over a trash can. If the trash can
is beside the mailbox, even better. All ads, catalogues, pleas for charitable
contributions, church bulletins, and money-saving coupons go straight into
the trash can without being opened. All letters from home, postcards from
Europe, bills and paychecks are opened, immediately responded to, then
dropped in the trash can. Neat people keep their receipts only for tax purposes. That's it. No sentimental salvaging of birthday cards or the last letter
a dying relative ever wrote. Into the trash it goes.

Neat people place neatness above everything, even economics. They 10
are incredibly wasteful. Neat people throw away several toys every time they
walk through the den. I knew a neat person once who threw away a perfectly good dish drainer because it had mold on it. The drainer was too
much trouble to wash. And neat people sell their furniture when they move.
They will sell a La-Z-Boy recliner while you are reclining in it.

Neat people are no good to borrow from. Neat people buy everything 11
in expensive little single portions. They get their flour and sugar in two-
pound bags. They wouldn't consider clipping a coupon, saving a leftover,
reusing plastic non-dairy whipped cream containers, or rinsing off tin foil
and draping it over the unmoldy dish drainer. You can never borrow a neat
person's newspaper to see what's playing at the movies. Neat people have
the paper all wadded up and in the trash by 7:05 A.M.

Neat people cut a clean swath through the organic as well as the 12
inorganic world. People, animals, and things are all one to them. They are
so insensitive. After they've finished with the pantry, the medicine cabinet,
and the attic, they will throw out the red geranium (too many leaves), sell
the dog (too many fleas), and send the children off to boarding school
(too many scuff marks on the hardwood floors).

RESPONDING TO READING

Do you think that Britt is right in preferring sloppy people? In your journal,
make a list of some advantages of being neat; then make a list of some disadvantages of being sloppy.

CONSIDERING CONTENT

1. In the first paragraph, what is the moral difference that Britt finds
   between neat and sloppy people? Is this the difference you would give?
   Is she serious about this moral difference? How can you tell?
2. Does the essay have a thesis statement? If so, where does it appear?

3. What is "Never-Never Land," mentioned at the beginning of paragraph 3? Do you know where the term comes from?
4. What kinds of things does Britt say messy people are always planning to do? Point out her exact details.
5. What faults does she find with neat people? Again, point out details from every paragraph.
6. Is she being fair? If not, can you explain why not?

CONSIDERING METHOD

1. How does Britt let you know in her opening paragraphs that she isn't entirely serious?
2. Which pattern of organization does she use in presenting her contrast?
3. Can you find a transitional sentence that leads smoothly into the second part of the contrast?
4. Point out several words that Britt uses for humorous exaggeration. Point out several humorous examples.
5. You probably noticed that this essay has no conclusion. Would it be more effective if it had one, do you think? Try writing a brief concluding sentence and see whether it adds or detracts.

COMBINING STRATEGIES

Britt employs a number of writing strategies in developing her essay. Her organization is a block-by-block comparison/contrast, and the entire piece involves definition—neat people and sloppy people. She also employs lots of examples, illustrations, explanations, and descriptions. Although the writing is humorous, its tongue-in-cheek purpose is persuasion. Reexamine the essay and identify an example of each of these strategies.

WRITING STEP BY STEP: CONTRASTING TYPES OF PEOPLE

Get together with a few friends or classmates to discuss various kinds of people who can be classified into types the way Britt does with neat versus sloppy (such as *plump vs. thin, fun-loving vs. serious, perky vs. droopy,* or *exercise nuts vs. couch potatoes*). In this brainstorming session, jot down any details that might be useful to include in an essay comparing the two types you choose. You can make your contrast either humorous or serious. If you decide to be humorous, you will probably also decide to defend the less positive group—praising fat folks instead of thin people, for instance. Or you may decide to make fun of both sides by contrasting two negative types, such as *eggheads vs. airheads.*

A. Begin with a two- or three-sentence introduction letting your readers know that you'll be contrasting two types of people and favoring one group (as Britt puts it, "Neat people are lazier and meaner than sloppy people").

B. Organize your contrast in a block pattern, first discussing the important characteristics of one type, then the same or similar characteristics of the other type.

C. Be sure to include plenty of examples that will show your readers the behavior you're explaining. Take another look at Britt's essay, and notice the kinds of details she uses—how many of them and how specific: not just *a corsage* but *the dried corsage from their senior prom*, not just *a recliner* but a *La-Z-Boy recliner*, not just *the geranium* but *the red geranium*.

D. In the body of your essay, begin every paragraph (as Britt does) with the name of your type—*plump people*, for instance. Vary this system of deliberate repetition once or twice by adding a transition, like the one Britt adds at the start of her fourth paragraph: "*For all these noble reasons and more*, sloppy people never get neat." (Leave out the *noble* part unless you're being funny.) Consider transitions like these:

Besides all these features, plump people . . .
In addition to these troubles, plump people . . .
Furthermore, plump people . . .
As a matter of fact, plump people . . .

E. When you finish discussing your first type, include a transitional sentence. Britt shifts smoothly from praising sloppy people to criticizing neat ones with this sentence: "A neat person would just bulldoze the desk" (end of para. 5).

   If you can't come up with a similar sentence that supplies a bridge from one type to the next, it's just fine to begin the second half of the contrast with a transitional term like one of these:

Thin people, *on the other hand*, . . .
Contrary to popular belief, thin people . . .
Thin people, *however*, . . .
By contrast, thin people . . .

F. If you can think of some insight concerning your contrast, offer it as a conclusion. But don't simply tack on something obvious. That's worse than no conclusion at all. Be sure to end your last paragraph with an impressive sentence—either a short, forceful one or a nicely balanced one, like Britt's. Work on that final sentence. Make it one that leaves your readers feeling satisfied.

OTHER WRITING IDEAS

1. Using a block-by-block pattern, contrast two types of players in a sport or game such as basketball, tennis, poker, chess, or a video game. In your conclusion explain what you think causes the differences between the two types.

2. USING THE INTERNET. Britt humorously presents neat people as being overly particular, but excessively neat people sometimes can have serious problems. Visit the Web site of the Obsessive Compulsive Foundation (**www.ocfoundation.org/**) and read about this psychological disorder. Write an essay contrasting an obsessively neat person with someone who is just normally neat. You could use Adrian Monk, the obsessively neat detective on the popular TV series *Monk*, as a prime example; if you're not a *Monk* watcher, substitute someone you know who exhibits obsessive/compulsive traits. You might also compare the obsessive form of another trait—such as punctuality, caution, or perfectionism—with its normal form.

3. COLLABORATIVE WRITING. Get together with friends or classmates, and discuss major life changes that you and they have experienced. Talk about what your lives were like before and after the changes occurred. Consider situations such as life before marriage and life after; life in your folks' home and life in the dorm or your own apartment; life at your previous job and life at your new one. Then write an essay about one of your life changes, telling first what your life was like before, then how things were after. Focus on one factor of your experience that changed greatly, like the amount of freedom or the amount of responsibility you had.

4. WRITING ABOUT READING. Starting with the lists you made in responding to Britt's essay, write one of your own organized like hers (but probably with a more serious tone) showing how neatness makes life easier and sloppiness leads to problems. Include plenty of details and examples to show the advantages of being tidy and the folly of being perpetually scattered.

GAINING WORD POWER

In her last paragraph Britt writes of the "*organic* as well as the *inorganic* world." You know from the Terms to Recognize that *organic* means "having to do with living things." So what does the same word mean when you add the **prefix** *in*-? That prefix commonly means "no," "not," or "without." Thus, in her sentence *inorganic* means "not organic"—having to do with things that are *not* living.

This prefix is quite common, partly because it has several different meanings. Besides making a word negative, *in*- often means "in," "into," "within," or "toward," as in a baseball *infield*, an *inboard* motor, or to *instill* values.

Knowing these meanings of this prefix can help you make sense of new words. For each of the following terms, write out the meaning of the prefix *in-*, followed by the meaning of the **root** word, as in this example using *indefinite*:

in- = not   *definite* = certain, precise, clear

Get help from your dictionary if you need it.

inhale	inhuman	insomnia
injustice	inland	inability
inroad	invisible	indigestion
indirect	inlay	insane

EDITING SKILLS: USING APOSTROPHES

Apostrophes probably cause more problems than other marks of punctuation. Even experienced writers feel shaky about using them. If you study the following rules about using apostrophes, you should be able to use them more confidently.

1. *Use an apostrophe to indicate that a noun is possessive.* Possessive nouns usually indicate ownership, as in *Miguel's hat* or *the lawyer's briefcase*. But sometimes the ownership is only loosely suggested, as in *the rope's length* or *a week's wages*. If you are not sure whether a noun is possessive, try turning it into an *of* phrase: *the length of the rope, the wages of a week*.
   a. If the noun does not end in *s*, add *'s*.
      Rita climbed into the driver's seat.
      The women's lounge is being redecorated.
   b. If the noun is singular and ends in *s*, add *'s*.
      The boss's car is still in the parking lot.
      Have you met Lois's sister?
   c. If the noun is plural and ends in *s*, add only an apostrophe.
      The workers' lockers have been moved.
      A good doctor always listens to patients' complaints.

2. *Use an apostrophe with contractions.* Contractions are two-word combinations formed by omitting certain letters. The apostrophe goes where the letters are left out, not where the two words are joined.

does not = doesn't	he is or he has = he's
would not = wouldn't	let us = let's
you are = you're	I am = I'm

3. *Do not use an apostrophe to form the plural of a noun.* The letter *s* gets pressed into service in a number of ways; its most common use is to

show that a noun is plural (more than one of whatever the noun names). No apostrophe is needed with a simple plural:

> Two *members* of the starting team are suspended for the next three *games* for repeated curfew *violations*.

EXERCISE

1. Examine this sentence from paragraph 11 in Suzanne Britt's essay: "You can never borrow a neat person's newspaper to see what's playing at the movies." Two words in this sentence end in 's; one is possessive and one is a contraction. Do you see the difference? Explain how you can tell.
2. Find two other possessive nouns in Britt's essay, and explain what they mean by turning each into an *of* phrase.
3. Find two other contractions that end in 's in Britt's essay. What do these contractions stand for?
4. Find six other contractions in Britt's essay, and explain their meaning.
5. Find several examples of plural nouns that end in *s* (without an apostrophe).

Now go back over the essay you have just written, and check your use of apostrophes. Have you left an apostrophe out of a possessive? Have you put an unneeded apostrophe in a plural noun? Have you misplaced any apostrophes in contractions?

For more information about apostrophes, see Chapter 6, pages 178–179.

✦ WEB SITE

http://owl.english.purdue.edu/owl/resource/621/01
You can print out the Online Writing Lab's handout on using apostrophes and consult it when writing and editing your papers.

PREPARING TO READ

Have you ever noticed that girls and boys play differently? Think about preschool, playground, and athletic activities. Why do you think those differences occur?

••

A Whole New Ballgame

••

BRENDAN O'SHAUGHNESSY

A former teacher and coach at St. Ignatius College Prep in Chicago, Brendan O'Shaughnessy now lives with his family in Indianapolis, where he writes for The Times of Northwest Indiana *as the paper's state bureau chief. He has also written freelance for the* Chicago Tribune, *which is where the article reprinted below appeared on December 1, 2002.*

TERMS TO RECOGNIZE

baiting (*para. 2*)	teasing, needling
insinuation (*para. 2*)	an implied meaning or reference
incredulous (*para. 4*)	unbelieving, doubting, skeptical
gaffe (*para. 4*)	a social blunder or mistake
demeanor (*para. 10*)	outward behavior
intimidated (*para. 11*)	made timid or fearful

1   The first day of freshman basketball tryouts, I learned that coaching girls is different. I was demonstrating the correct way to set a cross screen. I positioned my legs shoulder-width apart and crossed my hands—fists clenched—over my groin to protect myself from the injury that all men fear. I paused, confused, understanding from the girls' bewildered looks that something was wrong. The other coach, a 15-year veteran of coaching girls, recognized my rookie mistake and bailed me out. He raised his arms and covered his chest, and I knew that I had entered alien territory.

2   I had coached boys basketball for six years before circumstances in the athletic department forced me to switch to "the other side." I looked forward to the challenge in the same way that I had anticipated the move from teaching at an all-boys' school to a coed institution five years before. At the very least, I figured, I would be more likely to get cookies at

Christmas and a gift at the awards banquet. Baiting a feminist friend, I told her that I was excited about the change because I could be more relaxed, less intense, and besides, I wouldn't get any technicals. I just assumed girls didn't take their basketball as seriously as boys. The insinuation hit its mark. She scolded me, saying that girls were just as eager to win and play well as boys. She also suggested I read Madeleine Blais's *In These Girls, Hope Is a Muscle*, a book about a girls team's basketball season.

From the book and from my teaching experience, I began the season   3
with certain expectations about coaching girls. I would need to be more encouraging, less critical. Most boys need a little tearing down before they can be rebuilt on a more solid fundamentals base. Boys want to be Allen Iverson and inherently assume they know more than their old-school coach, who watched "Hoosiers" one too many times. Girls, whose experience of playground games and watching the all-stars is often limited, do not start with as many bad habits. I expected they would be more coachable. They wouldn't need their inflated athletic egos broken down, but rather built from the ground up.

Smugly thinking I was prepared, I got a rude awakening with my   4
screen-setting gaffe that first day. Imagine my incredulous stare when a girl trying out, in an attempt to explain why she had thrown up and had to sit out of wind sprints, told me she hadn't run since gym class—the year before. I was also surprised—and relieved—that we did not have to cut, since only 20 girls stuck out the trials for the two teams. With boys, two or three times as many students usually came out for the teams as could be taken.

I immediately noted differences in the early practices. Girls' attention   5
to directions was far superior to the boys, most of whom found it physically impossible not to be distracted by any movement anywhere in the gym. Whereas the boys generally either went deadpan or shot me the evil "how dare you" death stare when I corrected their play, the girls often sincerely apologized for any mistake. My stereotypically gawky center, when told not to leave her feet on defense, said, "I know. I'm sorry. I'm terrible." Embarrassed, I tripped out a halting reassurance. I tried to build up her confidence by calling her "the rebound machine," but she just thought I was goofy.

Strangest of all, they actually wanted to talk to me and the other   6
coach, something teenage boys found equivalent to having their nose hairs, if they had any, individually plucked out in front of an audience of teenage girls. The girls came running up before practice to tell us about their classes, about who said what at lunch, about who had spilled perfume on her uniform. Uncomfortable after years of boys slinking away into corners, I usually responded, "Stretch out."

Before the first game, I realized that some of their silliness was simply   7
due to their age, not their sex. In the pregame huddle, the other coach said
we needed to play hard or go home with a big L. One of the girls asked if
everyone would have to take the "L" home instead of the bus if we lost.
During the game, one player attempted to high-five a referee after making a
shot. But it was more than their tender age. While I was giving a post-game
speech, one player interrupted and said, "Those are the coolest sweatpants.
They zip all the way down." When my grandfather died, the whole team
signed a condolence card with individual attempts to comfort me. Another
time, returning from a late game, when the bus broke down on the highway
in 15-degree weather, one player cut the tension with, "Coach, want a
chocolate-chip cookie? I made them."

I began to observe that the team split into two groups: the hard, ag-   8
gressive players and the softer, nice players. One side had girls who would
steal a ball from their teammates in order to shoot. The other side had girls
who apologized to their defenders if they scored. Some would crash the
boards and clear out space with vicious elbows, and others would avoid any
chance of injury or even breaking a sweat. The aggressive group rolled their
eyes at the limp-wristed run of one girl they called "the dancer" or "Basketball Barbie." The timid girls rolled their eyes and called our best shooter a
"ball hog."

After six wins and a growing gulf between the cliques, we experienced   9
our first loss. Actually, we got blown out by 35 points. We could barely get the
ball down the court. A coach learns all he needs to know about his team by
how they react to a loss. My team began to motivate each other in practice.
They started to pull for each other. Best of all, the gap between the groups of
player types began to slowly close. In time, we were a single unit again.

And I was swept up in the intensity of their effort. I don't know   10
exactly when it began, but it was cemented when I was called for a technical
foul in a Christmas tournament game. Whereas boys' freshman coaches
tend to be overly passionate, like myself, sporting buzz cuts and angry
demeanors, girls' coaches usually were more welcoming. One informed us
that her name was Poppy, offered our team bagels and Gatorade, and said,
"We're all about fun here." It was all I could do to refrain from saying,
"We're all about kicking your butt."

Fast forward to the conference championship game, where we faced   11
the same team that had blown us out by 35 earlier in the season. Since
then, this powerhouse had won every game, none by fewer than 20 points.
Not intimidated this time, our girls played them even for a quarter. When
the opponent went on a second-quarter run, I impolitely objected to an
over-the-back foul and was hit with another technical. Shocked, I realized

that I had been given more technicals in a single season of coaching girls than I ever had as a boys' coach. My feminist friend would be proud. The team responded. The collective jaw of the bench dropped to the hardwood when "Basketball Barbie" hit a shot, slapped the floor and yelled, "C'mon, girls, let's play some defense." I couldn't have been more pleased if it had been my own daughter.

No, it didn't lead to a win, but we never gave up either, clawing to a   12
nine-point loss and the bittersweet distinction of holding that team to their narrowest margin of victory all season. Even in defeat, the girls had come a long way in their separate challenges. Some had overcome a natural timidity by learning to play aggressively, and others had learned to trust their team. My lesson? New depths to the same game I've always loved.

RESPONDING TO READING

Have you watched both girls and boys play basketball? Did you observe any differences between the teams in the way they played? Do you think, as O'Shaughnessy does, that the girls are just as dedicated to winning as the boys?

CONSIDERING CONTENT

1. What are the rewards O'Shaughnessy anticipates or initially expects as a result of switching from coaching boys to coaching girls?
2. In paragraph 2, what are *technicals*? Why did he think he wouldn't get any technicals coaching girls?
3. What expectations did he have about how he would need to coach girls differently than boys? What differences does he actually find?
4. In paragraphs 4, 5, and 6, he says that in early practices he notes differences between the girls' and boys' behavior. What are some of those differences?
5. The girls refer to one of their teammates with a "limp-wristed run" as "Basketball Barbie." What sort of player do you envision from that name?
6. How does being called for a technical foul let the coach know his team is now "a unit" and "cemented"? Why would his feminist friend be proud that he received more technicals coaching girls than boys?

CONSIDERING METHOD

1. How does O'Shaughnessy capture your interest in his opening paragraph?
2. His essay is organized using a point-by-point contrast. Why do you think he chose this pattern rather than using the simple block-by-block method?

3. What other patterns of development can you identify in the essay?
4. Why do you think he mentions his feminist friend near the beginning and again near the end?
5. What does his use of basketball jargon (*cross screen, wind sprints, blown out, over-the-back foul*) tell you about his intended audience?
6. What is the author's thesis? Is it stated or implied?

WRITING STEP BY STEP: THEN AND NOW

Think of a situation, place, object, or person *then* and *now*. Choose something that has changed a lot: wedding receptions years ago and today, your desk before and after cleaning, your sluggish first computer and your smart new computer, your childhood tennis shoes and your new athletic shoes, your granny then and now.

Write a comparison focusing mainly on the *now*, but mentioning the *then* occasionally to show the contrast. If you can get your friends to help, brainstorm with them to think of good points you can use in drawing the comparison. You need qualities that fit both *then* and *now*, but think of a lot more details about the *now*.

A. Begin by giving the subject of your comparison in a sentence or two. Don't state it directly but imply it: "I had no idea that wedding receptions were not always elaborate productions until my mom told me about her wedding thirty years ago," or "I was slow to appreciate the benefits of my new computer because it took so much effort to learn to use it. My old computer was easy by comparison."

B. As you discuss the *now*, remind your readers, whenever you take up a new point, how it was *then*. Use transitional words when you need them: *by comparison, on the other hand, on the contrary, but, still, after all, like, nevertheless, contrary to, however, granted that.*

C. In your last paragraph, tell how you feel about the change. Would you rather have the *then* instead of the *now*—or do you find the *now* a great improvement?

D. If you're stuck for an ending, try concluding with a question and then answering it: "If I had known then how much easier my computer would make writing, would I have complained so loudly? Maybe not," or "If I could go back to planning a reception that cost less than $10,000, would I? You bet I would!"

OTHER WRITING IDEAS

1. Think of two possible views on one of these aspects of life: the value of work, the role of family, or the importance of sports. Write a paper contrasting two people who represent the two views.

2. COLLABORATIVE WRITING. In a small group discuss gender stereotypes—the way society expects women and men to behave. From the notes you take, choose three or four categories—such as manner of speaking, walking, dressing, and showing emotion; or typical careers, leisure activities, and taste in movies. Organize your essay using the point-by-point method, first doing the women's role, then the men's (or the reverse, but be consistent from section to section). At the end, draw a conclusion about how society treats people who do not conform to these roles and expectations.

3. USING THE INTERNET. Visit the Gender Equity in Sports site at **http: bailiwick.lib.uiowa.edu/ge/GEREDESIGN.html,** click on the "About Title IX" link, and read the material. Then, with this information in mind, speculate in writing about the role Title IX may have played in bringing about the changes that O'Shaughnessy observed.

4. WRITING ABOUT READING. Consider how our society's expectations for girls are reflected in O'Shaughnessy's article. Does it also reveal society's expectations for boys? Discuss the ways in which the author shows how gender roles in organized sports have changed and whether you see these changes as positive or negative.

GAINING WORD POWER

Decide whether the italicized words in the following list are used correctly. Then, write *yes* or *no* beside each sentence. After you finish, look back at the Terms to Recognize definitions to check your work.

_____1. Billy Bob's *demeanor* made him appear lazy and disinterested.

_____2. Secretly he studied hard and made *incredulous* improvement.

_____3. Then a jealous classmate *intimidated* that he had cheated.

_____4. I thought that such an *insinuation* was outrageous and spiteful.

_____5. So, I bought him a double latte *gaffe* as a reward for his success.

EDITING SKILLS: CHOOSING *ITS* OR *IT'S*

Look at this sentence from O'Shaughnessy's article:

The insinuation hit its mark.

Why does he use *its* and not *it's* in that sentence?

Now look at the uses of *it's* and *its* in the following sentences:

It's been a hard day's night.

It's raining on my parade.

> This knife has lost *its* edge.
>
> That horse just won *its* last race.

Notice that in the first two sentences, the words *it has* or *it is* can be substituted for *it's*. Not so in the next two sentences. Those two uses of *its*—without the apostrophe—are possessive, as in "Each piece has *its* own place in the puzzle."

You can use the substitution test to see whether you have used the right form. If you have written *it's*, you should be able to read the sentence with *it is* or *it has* instead. That substitution won't work with the possessive *its*, which carries a sense of ownership or belonging.

> The plan failed because of *its* flaws.
>
> I like that sitcom in spite of *its* dysfunctional characters.

Many writers are tempted to put an apostrophe in the possessive *its* because so many other possessives require apostrophes: the *plan's* flaws, the *sitcom's* characters. No wonder it's confusing. Try putting the possessive *its* on a mental list with the other possessives—*his, hers, ours, theirs*—which also have no apostrophes. This mental grouping may help you choose the correct form.

EXERCISE

Fill in the blanks in the following sentences with *its* or *it's*. Be prepared to explain your choices.

1. Your proposal has much in _____ favor, but _____ unlikely that the committee will vote for it.
2. _____ an old car, but _____ paint job is new.
3. The dog bit _____ own tail; _____ not an exceptionally smart dog.
4. _____ important that a company give _____ employees job security.
5. _____ a whole new ballgame.

WEB SITE

www.womenssportsfoundation.org/Issues-And-Research.aspx
This page from the Women's Sports Foundation highlights current isues in gender equity and suggests topics for action.

PREPARING TO READ

Before looking at the following essay, consider whether you think children are born smart or whether they get smart by studying hard in school. Jot down your thoughts in your journal.

The Trouble with Talent: Are We Born Smart or Do We Get Smart?

K ATHY S EAL

A California-based freelance journalist, Kathy Seal frequently writes about children and education in such popular magazines as Parents *and* Family Circle. *In the essay we reprint here, first published in* Lear's *magazine in July 1993, she examines an attitude that may help to explain why math scores of American children have fallen far behind those of children in Japan.*

TERMS TO RECOGNIZE

rote (*para. 4*)	routine, mechanical repetition
efficacy (*para. 12*)	ability to bring about an effect
rampant (*para. 12*)	widespread, out of control
per se (*para. 16*)	in and of itself
mammoth (*para. 19*)	huge
conviction (*para. 19*)	firmly held belief

Jim Stigler was in an awkward position. Fascinated by the fact that Asian students routinely do better than American kids at elementary math, the UCLA psychologist wanted to test whether persistence might be the key factor. So he designed and administered an experiment in which he gave the same insolvable math problem to separate small groups of Japanese and American children.

Sure enough, most American kids attacked the problem, struggled briefly—then gave up. The Japanese kids, however, worked on and on and on. Eventually, Stigler stopped the experiment when it began to feel inhumane: If the Japanese kids were uninterrupted, they seemed willing to plow on indefinitely.

"The Japanese kids assumed that if they kept working, they'd eventu- 3
ally get it," Stigler recalls. "The Americans thought 'Either you get it or you
don't.'"

Stigler's work, detailed in his 1992 book *The Learning Gap*, shatters 4
our stereotypical notion that Asian education relies on rote and drill. In
fact, Japanese and Chinese elementary schoolteachers believe that their
chief task is to stimulate thinking. They tell their students that anyone who
thinks long enough about a problem can move toward its solution.

Stigler concludes that the Asian belief in hard work as the key to suc- 5
cess is one reason why Asians outperform us academically. Americans are
persuaded that success in school requires inborn talent. "If you believe that
achievement is mostly caused by ability," Stigler says, "at some fundamental
level you don't believe in education. You believe education is sorting kids,
and that kids in some categories can't learn. The Japanese believe *everybody*
can master the curriculum if you give them the time."

Stigler and his coauthor, Harold W. Stevenson of the University of 6
Michigan, are among a growing number of educational psychologists who
argue that the American fixation on innate ability causes us to waste the
potential of many of our children. He says that this national focus on the
importance of natural talent is producing kids who give up easily and artful
dodgers who would rather look smart than actually learn something.

Cross-cultural achievement tests show how wide the gap is: In a series 7
of studies spanning a ten-year period, Stigler and Stevenson compared
math-test scores at more than 75 elementary schools in Sendai, Japan;
T'aipei, Taiwan; Beijing, China; Minneapolis; and Chicago. In each study,
the scores of fifth graders in the best-performing American school were
lower than the scores of their counterparts in the worst-performing Asian
school. In other studies, Stigler and Stevenson found significant gaps in
reading tests as well.

Respect for hard work pervades Asian culture. Many folk tales make 8
the point that diligence can achieve any goal—for example, the poet Li Po's
story of the woman who grinds a piece of iron into a needle, and Mao Tse-
tung's recounting of an old man who removes a mountain with just a hoe.
The accent on academic effort in Asian countries demonstrates how expectations for children are both higher and more democratic there than in
America. "If learning is gradual and proceeds step by step," says Stigler,
"anyone can gain knowledge."

To illustrate this emphasis, Stigler videotaped a Japanese teacher at 9
work. The first image on screen is that of a young woman standing in front
of a class of fifth graders. She bows quickly. "Today," she says, "we will be
studying triangles." The teacher reminds the children that they already know

how to find the area of a rectangle. Then she distributes a quantity of large paper triangles—some equilateral, others right or isosceles—and asks the class to think about "the best way to find the area of a triangle." For the next 14 1/2 minutes, 44 children cut, paste, fold, draw, and talk to each other. Eventually nine kids come to the blackboard and take turns explaining how they have arranged the triangles into shapes for which they can find the areas. Finally, the teacher helps the children to see that all nine solutions boil down to the same formula: $a = (b \times h) \div 2$ (the area equals the product of the base multiplied by the height, divided by two).

Stigler says that the snaillike pace of the lesson—52 minutes from start to finish—allows the brighter students enough time to understand the concept in depth, as they think through nine different ways to find the areas of the three kinds of triangles. Meanwhile, slower students—even learning-disabled students—benefit from hearing one concept explained in many different ways. Thus children of varied abilities have the same learning opportunity; and the result is that a large number of Japanese children advance relatively far in math. 10

Americans, on the other hand, group children by ability throughout their school careers. Assigning students to curricular tracks according to ability is common, but it happens even in schools where formal tracking is not practiced. 11

So kids always know who the teacher thinks is "very smart, sorta smart, and kinda dumb," says social psychologist Jeff Howard, president of the Efficacy Institute, a nonprofit consulting firm in Lexington, Massachusetts, that specializes in education issues. "The idea of genetic intellectual inferiority is rampant in [American] society, especially as applied to African-American kids." 12

A consequence is that many kids face lower expectations and a watered-down curriculum. "A student who is bright is expected just to 'get it,'" Stigler says. "Duller kids are assumed to lack the necessary ability for ever learning certain material." 13

Our national mania for positive self-esteem too often leads us to puff up kids' confidence, and we may forget to tell them that genius is 98 percent perspiration. In fact, our reverence for innate intelligence has gone so far that many Americans believe people who work hard in school must lack ability. "Our idealization of a gifted person is someone so smart they don't have to try," says Sandra Graham of UCLA's Graduate School of Education. 14

Columbia University psychologist Carol Dweck has conducted a fascinating series of studies over the past decade documenting the dangers of believing that geniuses are born rather than made. In one study, Dweck and 15

UCLA researcher Valanne Henderson asked 229 seventh graders whether people are "born smart" or "get smart" by working hard. Then they compared the students' sixth and seventh grade achievement scores. The scores of kids with the get-smart beliefs stayed high or improved, and those of the kids subscribing to the born-smart assumption stayed low or declined. Surprisingly, even kids who believed in working hard but who had low confidence in their abilities did very well. And the kids whose scores dropped the most were the born-smart believers with high confidence.

Dweck's conclusion: "If we want our kids to succeed, we should empha-   16
size effort and steer away from praising or blaming intelligence per se."

Psychologist Ellen Leggett, a former student of Dweck's at Harvard,   17
has found that bright girls are more likely than boys to believe that people are born smart. That finding could help to explain why many American girls stop taking high school math and science before boys do.

Seeing intelligence as an inborn trait also turns children into quitters,   18
says Dweck. "Kids who believe you're born smart or not are always worried about their intelligence, so they're afraid to take risks," Dweck explains. "But kids who think you can get smart aren't threatened by a difficult task or by failures, and find it kind of exciting to figure out what went wrong and to keep at it." Or, in Jeff Howard's words, "If I know I'm too stupid to learn, why should I bang my head against the wall trying to learn?"

Getting Americans to give up their worship of natural ability and to   19
replace it with the Asian belief in effort seems a mammoth undertaking. But Dweck maintains that it's possible to train kids to believe in hard work. The key to bringing kids around, says Dweck, is for the adults close to them to talk and act upon a conviction that effort is what counts.

The Efficacy Institute is working on exactly that. The institute's work   20
is based on theories that Howard developed as a doctoral candidate at Harvard, as he investigated why black students weren't performing in school as well as whites and Asians. Using the slogan "Think you can; work hard; get smart," the institute conducts a seminar for teachers that weans them from the born-smart belief system.

"We tell teachers to talk to kids with the presumption that they can   21
all get As in their tests," explains project specialist Kim Taylor. Most kids respond immediately to their teachers' changed expectations, Howard says. As proof, he cites achievement-test scores of 137 third grade students from six Detroit public schools who were enrolled in the Efficacy Institute program during 1989 and 1990. The students' scores rose 2.4 grade levels (from 2.8 to 5.2) in one year, compared with a control group of peers whose scores only went up by less than half a grade level.

Institute trainers now work in approximately 55 school districts, from   22
Baltimore to St. Louis to Sacramento. In five cities, they're working to train
every teacher and administrator in the school district.

While current efforts for change are modest, no less a force than the   23
Clinton administration is weaving this new thinking into its education
agenda. During a talk this past spring to the California Teachers Association, U.S. Secretary of Education Richard Riley pledged to work on setting
national standards in education. "These standards," he says, "must be for
all of our young people, regardless of their economic background. We must
convince people that children aren't born smart. They get smart."

RESPONDING TO READING

Did reading the essay change your mind about kids being born smart or getting
smart through hard work? In your journal explain how you think Americans'
attitudes on the subject could be changed, especially if the government or the
National Education Association decided to spend money on the effort.

CONSIDERING CONTENT

1. According to researchers, what happened when groups of American
   kids and groups of Japanese kids were given insolvable math problems
   to work on?
2. How do most Americans think Asian students are taught? According to
   researchers quoted by Seal, is this impression true?
3. How did the Japanese instructor teach about triangles in the example
   given in paragraph 9? What are the advantages of this method of
   teaching?
4. What is the typical American attitude about learning—that kids are
   born smart or that they get smart by working hard? What is the Japanese attitude?
5. Do you know what Seal means by "our national mania for positive self-
   esteem" (para. 14)? What problems do researchers think it causes?
6. How is the Efficacy Institute trying to change the American attitude
   and instead "train kids to believe in hard work" (para. 19)?

CONSIDERING METHOD

1. How does Seal's opening sentence help get you interested in her
   material?
2. Find two specific examples that help readers understand why the Japanese kids beat the American kids on achievement tests. How helpful are
   these examples?

3. What other method of providing evidence and explaining ideas does the author use in the second part of her article about Americans' attitudes?
4. Seal employs the block organization for her contrast. Find the sentence in which she makes the transition from explaining how Japanese kids learn to considering how American kids learn. What transitional term does she use?
5. The essay has a brief concluding section following the contrast of the two educational systems. What is the purpose of these final paragraphs (19–22)?
6. The essay concludes with a direct quotation (para. 23). What makes this ending effective?

WRITING STEP BY STEP: TWO POINTS OF VIEW

Think of an issue on which you and your parents—or you and your spouse—strongly disagree. With your parents, for instance, you might differ in your attitudes toward premarital sex; or they might disapprove of your taste in music, clothing, or hairstyles. With your spouse, you might disagree about household chores, childcare, financial matters, or vacation plans. Choose an issue that you feel confident you are right about, but be sure that you are also quite familiar with the evidence for the opposing point of view.

A. Begin your essay by presenting the problem, as Kathy Seal does in her introduction when she states "the fact that Asian students routinely do better than American kids at elementary math" (para. 1). You can start by admitting that you have this heated disagreement in your immediate family about whatever it is.
B. Next explain how other members of your family view this matter, just as Seal explains how Japanese schoolchildren are taught math (paras. 2–10). Try to include brief specific examples as Seal does in paragraphs 8 and 9. And be fair. Give as much space to presenting this opposing view as you will give to your own viewpoint in the second part of the essay.
C. Write a transitional sentence similar to the one that Seal uses at the start of paragraph 11: "Americans, on the other hand, group children by ability throughout their school careers."
D. Now, present your side of the issue. Offer plenty of specific examples. The evidence that Seal uses in analyzing the attitudes of Americans about how children learn are mainly quotations from researchers, but these quotations are full of specifics—problems, beliefs, research studies, testing results.
E. If possible, include a final section similar to Seal's paragraphs 19–22 in which she tells what the Efficacy Institute is doing to encourage

American kids to work harder in school. Try to think of a way of resolving the problem you described in your essay. It's possible that focusing on the opposing viewpoint (as you did in the first part of your essay) may reveal a middle ground. Look for a compromise. If you find a solution that stops short of involving the law and justice system, present it here.

F. If you can think of no way of resolving the problem, conclude by admitting that you and your family will simply have to agree to disagree. But consider the final quotation in Seal's essay. Modeling the deliberate repetition of a word, try to end with two forceful sentences similar to these: "We must convince people that children aren't born smart. They get smart" (para. 23).

OTHER WRITING IDEAS

1. Using a block pattern of organization, write a comparison for your classmates of two sports. Focus your attention on which one is more complicated to play or more fun to watch, and use your comparison to explain why you think so.

2. USING THE INTERNET. Write an essay, using your own experience as well as those of people you know, to contrast the pros and cons of family vacations. Use an Internet search engine to visit the sites of typical vacation destinations (the Grand Canyon, Las Vegas, Disneyland, and so forth) to gather additional ideas. In your brainstorming, consider the preferences of both the parents and the children, but write from the viewpoint of one or the other.

3. COLLABORATIVE WRITING. Seal thinks Americans should "give up their worship of natural ability" and "replace it with the Asian belief in effort." She quotes psychologist Carol Dweck's assertion "that it's possible to train kids to believe in hard work" (para. 19). Do you believe that hard work is what's required in learning? Get together with a group of classmates and discuss whether this is an entirely useful idea. What advantages did Seal include in her essay? What additional advantages or distinct disadvantages were generated in your brainstorming session? Write an essay contrasting the two viewpoints and conclude by recommending one side or the other.

4. WRITING ABOUT READING. Seal provides an interesting illustration of the way a Japanese teacher presents a concept in math instruction (para. 9). Write an essay contrasting that technique with the way you were taught some concept (like in math, grammar, or spelling) in grade school or high school. Conclude by stating which method you think is better and why.

GAINING WORD POWER

In paragraph 10, Kathy Seal uses the interesting word *snaillike* to describe the slow pace of the Japanese teacher's math instruction. The term *-like* is a **combining form** meaning "resembling or characteristic of." By adding *-like* to other words (many of them names for animals), you can produce useful new descriptive terms. You could write, for instance, of a child's shell-like ear, and your readers would be able to picture the delicate curve of the ear. Notice that you hyphenate *shell-like*, when there are three *l*s together, but not *snaillike*, when there are only two.

1. Add *-like* to the end of each word listed below.

    war   child   bird   barn   ostrich
    bell   lady   cat   flower   cow

2. Then write a definition that includes the characteristic conveyed by that new word: *slow as a snail, curved like a shell*.

3. Finally, write a sentence for each new word that makes use of the descriptive characteristic: The *snaillike* traffic on the freeway resulted from an accident.

EDITING SKILLS: USING DASHES

The dash is a handy mark of punctuation that will give **emphasis** to whatever follows it—as long as you don't use it too often. Notice how the dash works in this sentence from Seal's essay:

> Sure enough, most American kids attacked the problem, struggled briefly— and then gave up.

Seal could have used a comma after *briefly*, but she chose the dash because readers pay more attention to what follows a dash than to what follows a comma. Using the dash is unusual, unexpected—thus emphatic.

You can also use a pair of dashes to set off a few words in the middle of a sentence if you want to emphasize them, as Seal does here:

> Meanwhile, slower students—even learning-disabled students—benefit from hearing one concept explained in many different ways.

Commas would be quite correct there but dashes give emphasis to the words set off.

There's another handy use for the dash—to avoid comma clutter. Look at this sentence from Seal's essay:

> Then she distributes a quantity of large paper triangles—some equilateral, others right or isosceles—and asks the class to think about "the best way to find the area of a triangle."

Again, commas would be correct before and after that phrase, but when the group of words set off contains one or more commas, putting dashes around it makes the whole sentence easier to read.

Finally, you can use a dash instead of a colon to introduce an example, as Seal does here:

> Many folk tales make the point that diligence can achieve any goal—for example, the poet Li Po's story of . . . and Mao Tse-tung's recounting of. . . .

When typing, use two hyphens to form a dash (—), but if you are writing on a word processor, you may find that it has a separate key for the dash. In either case, do not put a space before or after the dash. And remember not to use dashes too often, or they will lose their good effect.

EXERCISE

Put in a dash or replace a comma with a dash whenever you think it would improve the sentence.

1. My friend Yolanda said she just turned twenty-nine for the third time.
2. It's time I started saving for a Florida vacation, for a cruise to the Bahamas, for a new Lexus, for my retirement.
3. All kinds of spices, even pepper, garlic, and onion, give Eddie indigestion.
4. Madonna's costume, what there was of it, shocked even broad-minded me.
5. Marvin had only one chance and a slim one at that.

Now examine the sentences in the essay you just wrote. Can you improve any of them by inserting dashes? Try to revise at least two of your sentences using dashes.

🌐 WEB SITE

www.efficacy.org

To find further information about ways in which "virtually all children can get smart," visit this Web site for the Efficacy Institute.

STUDENT ESSAY USING COMPARISON AND CONTRAST

Watching from All Sides

Lynn Cooper

When her children had reached school age, Lynn Cooper returned to Illinois State University to finish her degree in speech and theater education. She acted in several plays in high school and in community theater, experiences that led her to choose her major and to write this essay.

New styles of plays and productions in contemporary theater have 1 forced designers and architects to experiment with the orientation of the audience to the stage. One of the most prominent examples of these designs is the arena stage. Also called theater in the round, this kind of staging can be quite intimate because it puts the audience in raised seats on all sides with the players performing in the round space in the middle. In contrast, the traditional theater is usually larger and seats the whole audience in front of the acting area, looking into a boxlike set through a frame or *proscenium arch*. Any theatergoer can easily see the differences between these two arrangements. The necessary differences in scenic design, lighting design, and acting techniques may not be as apparent, but they are crucial to the performance and its reception.

For the scenic designer, arena staging offers challenges not present in 2 a proscenium set. In order to keep the view clear all around, the setting in which the action takes place must be indicated without the aid of the large, high vertical scenic backdrops that are employed on the traditional stage. These often represent a relevant background like a starry sky, an apartment's back wall, or a cityscape. Without the usual *flats* or artificial walls to paint and decorate, designers for a show done in the round must find other ways to convey the nature and mood of the setting. The designer for an arena production focuses instead on smaller details, such as set furniture and handheld props, which the closer audience will be able to see much more clearly. But because the audience is seated all around, these set pieces must look presentable from all views. A kitchen counter on a traditional stage can have an unfinished back, but a kitchen counter in the round has to be realistic from all sides. This requirement means more construction and finishing time for arena sets.

Lighting must also be designed differently for these two types of pre- 3 sentation. In an arena stage, lighting should look more natural because it can and must be focused on the stage from all directions. But since the play must also be seen from all sides, lighting problems are in some ways compounded. For example, in a proscenium setting, the lighting designer need not worry about lights shining in the spectators' eyes, a common problem when staging in the round. Arena lighting must also strictly define the playing area in a pool of light, whereas the proscenium playing space is usually established by the flats and backdrops. Also, actors in the arena must be adequately lit from all four sides, unlike actors in a proscenium frame who usually don't need to be lit from the back and sides.

The actors, too, must alter their techniques to suit the circumstances.   4
The most conspicuous difference is that acting on a proscenium stage requires a less natural style of movement. For one thing, actors have to direct their performances downstage—that is, toward the audience out in front of them—and avoid facing upstage or turning too much to the sides. Also, in order to be seen and heard by the people in the balcony and the back rows, actors on a proscenium stage need to project their voices and exaggerate their facial expressions and gestures. By contrast, the actors in theater in the round are always facing away from some audience members, so the artificial need to display all actions toward one direction disappears, but the necessity of being expressive from the back emerges. Moreover, this more realistic movement, combined with the comparative intimacy of theater in the round, demands more truth and subtlety in all elements of the performance. This style also requires greater attention from the actors, most of whom find concentration easier in the familiar proscenium theater, where the audience is farther away. Nevertheless, in spite of, or perhaps because of, these greater demands on their skills, some actors enjoy doing arena plays even more than acting on regular stages.

Clearly, the differences between proscenium and arena staging are   5
important in producing plays. The modern theater in the round is one in a long progression of possible methods of theatrical presentation, each of which has created new production problems as well as dramatic advantages. These variations in staging alter the audience's relationship to both the play and its performance and can change how the theatergoer responds to and understands the production.

CONSIDERING CONTENT AND METHOD

1. What purpose and audience did Lynn have in mind when writing this essay? How does the last sentence of the essay help to answer this question?

2. Do a quick outline of the major points in this essay. Which method of comparison and contrast has Lynn used to achieve her purpose? The same material could also be presented in this way:
   I. Introduction
   II. The proscenium arch presentation of a play
      A. Scenic design
      B. Lighting design
      C. Acting techniques
   III. The arena presentation of a play
      A. Scenic design
      B. Lighting design
      C. Acting techniques
   IV. Conclusion
   Assume that Lynn considered this other plan for her development. Imagine what the essay would be like. Why might she choose the arrangement she finally used?
3. Are the transitional phrases in this essay helpful and well placed? Identify several examples and explain their value to the essay.
4. Has Lynn used adequate illustration to support and clarify her points about each type of staging? Which examples work best?
5. Are the theater terms in the essay adequately defined? Explain.

Strategies for Explaining How Things Work:
Process and *Directions*

IMAGES AND IDEAS

© 1993 John McPherson/Dist. by Universal Press Syndicate

"Here you go, right on page 13 of the manual: 'Never stop walking while the treadmill is on.'"

Source: CLOSE TO HOME © 2002 John McPherson. Reprinted With Permission of UNIVERSAL PRESS SYNDICATE. All Rights Reserved.

For Discussion and Writing

Cartoons are often funny because we recognize ourselves, or people we know, acting in slightly exaggerated ways in familiar situations. Do you know people like the two characters in this cartoon? Have you found yourself in a similar situation? Write a brief response to John McPherson's cartoon. Focus on what makes it humorous and what pointers it might provide for writing and reading actual instructions.

Listen to our rural relatives explaining how to get to the family reunion: "Just follow the hard road down to where the Snivelys' cow barn used to stand before the fire; then turn off on the gravel track and go a piece until you get to the top of the second big rise after the creek. Look for Rabbithash's old pickup." All eighty-six aunts, uncles, and cousins find these directions perfectly clear, but anyone from farther away than Clay City is going to have some difficulty getting there before the potato salad goes funny.

THE POINT OF WRITING ABOUT PROCESS AND DIRECTIONS

When you want to include second-cousins-once-removed and even complete strangers in your audience, you will try to write out directions that don't rely on so much in-group information (such as where the Snivelys' barn *used* to be). Communicating directions so that almost anyone can understand them is a difficult task, as you know if you have ever tried to do it. Explaining a process is quite similar: After you've performed a certain task over and over, it's hard to explain to someone else exactly how it's done. Do you remember how hard it was to shift the manual transmission while turning the corner when you first learned to drive? Could you easily explain it to a 16-year-old? And when a child asks, "Where does the rain come from?" wouldn't most people rather come up with a cute story than really grapple with the workings of nature?

But sometimes, frequently on the job, you must come up with an orderly, step-by-step explanation of how something is done or how it works. The explanation may be just part of a larger report or essay; for example, proposing a solution to the company's mail problems must include an account of how the current mail system works. This chapter includes models of several types of **process writing.**

THE PRINCIPLES OF PROCESS AND DIRECTIONS

The basic organizing principle behind process and direction writing involves time. You are usually concerned with a series of events, and these events may not float through your mind in the same order they should appear in your written work. Your readers will be frustrated and confused by flashbacks or detours to supply information that you should have covered earlier. Therefore, the scratch outline takes on great importance in this type of writing effort. A blank piece of unlined paper or a new document in your word processing program will help you to get started. On this page, you will list the steps or stages of the process as you first think of them—only be sure to space the items widely apart. In the spaces you can add points you forgot the first time through: These can be major steps ("Collect the dog shampoo and old towels before you attempt to collect the dog"), substeps ("Pile up more old towels than you think you will possibly need"), or warnings ("Don't speak to your pet in a tone of panicky sweetness; he'll know you're up to something"). Once you consider your notes complete, read through them while visualizing the process to pinpoint anything you have forgotten.

"How to Wash Your Dog" doesn't represent the only angle you can take on process writing, although it is a useful one. In "Shopping Can Be a Challenge," Carol Fleischman uses an extended example to outline the strategies and pitfalls of being a shopper who also happens to be blind. Michael Leddy's directions on "How to E-mail a Professor" combine recommendations and examples about what to write with warnings about what not to write. Emily Nelson's "Making Fake Flakes" reveals a trick of movie-making magic by tracing the prop department's creation of potato-flake "snow" in a variety of settings. In your future writing projects, all these techniques for explaining a process and giving directions will be useful.

THE PITFALLS OF PROCESS AND DIRECTIONS

The problems you encounter in process writing usually have their roots in understanding your audience. For instance, several years ago when we first joined the Internet, we were assured that the printed directions we received were quite complete. They began, "Once you are connected to the CCSO Terminal, follow these steps to log on." Once we were *what*? To *what*? Obviously, the directions were written for people much more "connected" than we are. You have no doubt had similar experiences; hundreds of cartoons around Christmas time portray frantic parents trying to follow "easy" assembly instructions for their children's toys.

Reviewing Your Process

When you revise your process writing, think about the people who will be reading it. Ask yourself these questions:

1. Have I chosen the best starting point? Think about how much your audience already knows before you decide where to begin describing the process. Don't assume your readers have background knowledge that they may not have. And remember that your audience may need to be persuaded to learn what you wish to teach.

2. Have I provided enough definitions of terms? See Chapter 5 for help in writing definitions and deciding when they are needed.

3. Have I been specific enough in the details? "Dig a trench" is more specific than "Dig a hole," but how deep should the trench be? How wide? How long?

Addressing Your Audience

Another decision you will need to face in your process writing concerns not only who your audience is but also how you intend to speak to them. In this book, we address you, our readers, as "you." This straightforward, informal voice is desirable in much writing. Sometimes, you can keep the informality yet leave the "you" out, using **imperative** sentences (or commands) such as "Gather the towels before catching the dog," or "Dig a trench two feet wide." You may also choose to describe a **third person** performing or observing the process: "The experienced video game player works quickly," or "The first feature a palm reader examines is the life iine, running from between the thumb and first finger in a curve down to the wrist." However you decide to deal with addressing your audience, you should be careful not to mix these approaches accidentally.

WHAT TO LOOK FOR IN PROCESS AND DIRECTIONS

The readings in this chapter differ greatly in their treatment of topics, even though they have process and directions in common. As you read, consider these questions:

1. What are the differences among the introductions? Can you account for these differences by looking at the purpose of each author?

2. How does each author signal where a new step, stage, or part begins?

3. How does each author address the readers? Is this way of addressing readers suitable?

4. Are there any points at which you would like further details or explanation? Where, what, and why?

5. What strategies other than process and directions appear within these readings—for example, narration, description, or comparison and contrast?

PREPARING TO READ

How do you respond when you encounter people with disabilities? Have you had any specific experiences that led to significant or even slight changes in your attitudes or behaviors in these situations?

••

Shopping Can Be a Challenge

••

CAROL FLEISCHMAN

Carol Fleischman, who lives in Niagara Falls, New York, is a regular contributor to the Buffalo News. *Her articles cover a wide range of everyday events, from yard sales to wedding showers, but her recurring theme is life as a blind person, especially the joys and challenges of working with assistance dogs. "Shopping Can Be a Challenge" first appeared in 1998 and won the International Association of Assistance Dog Partners "Best Article of the Year Award."*

TERMS TO RECOGNIZE

ritual (*para. 1*)	set form or order of events
beeline (*para. 2*)	straight path, direct route
booming (*para. 5*)	deep, resonant sound
in earshot (*para. 6*)	within hearing distance
chastised (*para. 14*)	strongly criticized, scolded
preoccupied (*para. 23*)	busy, distracted
reminiscent (*para. 24*)	similar to, reminding one of
foiled (*para 24*)	prevented, stopped

Have you ever tried to buy a dress when you can't see? I have, because I'm blind. At one time, I would shop with friends. This ritual ended after the time I happily brought home a dress a friend had helped me choose, and my husband, Don, offered a surprising observation: "The fit is great, but do you like all those huge fish?" The dress went back. Now I rely on Don and my guide dog, Misty, as my shopping partners.   1

We enter the store and make a beeline for the dress department. Don usually sees two or three salespeople scatter. The aisles empty as if a bomber had come on the scene. Then I realize I'm holding the "live wire." But I'm not judgmental—once I, too, was uneasy around large dogs. Although Misty is better behaved than most children, I know a 65-pound German shepherd is imposing.   2

On one recent shopping trip, a brave saleswoman finally approached 3
us. "Can I help you?" she said to my husband.

"Yes, I'm looking for a dress," I replied. (After all, I'm the one who 4
will be wearing it.) "Maybe something in red or white."

"RED OR WHITE," she said, speaking very slowly and loudly even 5
though my hearing is fine. I managed not to fall as Misty jumped back on
my feet, frightened by the woman's booming voice.

Don was distracted too. I heard him rustling through hangers on a 6
nearby rack. I called his name softly to get his attention, and another man
answered my call. Bad luck. What were the chances of two Dons being in
earshot?

"This is great!" Don said, holding up a treasure. I swept my hand 7
over the dress to examine it. It had a neckline that plunged to the hemline.
"Hmmm," I said. I walk three miles daily with Misty and stay current with
fashion, but I'm positive this costume would look best on one of the Spice
Girls. Finally, I chose three dresses to try on.

Another shopper distracted Misty, even though the harness sign 8
reads: "Please do not pet. I'm working." She said, "Your dog reminds me
of my Max, who I recently put to sleep," so I was sympathetic. We discussed
her loss for 15 minutes. Some therapists don't spend that much time with
grieving clients.

Don was back. He told me the route to travel to the dressing room. 9
I commanded Misty: right, left, right, and straight ahead. We wove our way
past several small voices.

"Mom, why is that dog in the store?" 10

"Mom, is that a dog or a wolf?" 11

And my personal favorite: "But that lady's eyes are open." 12

I trust parents to explain: "The lady is giving her guide dog com- 13
mands. Her dog is a helping dog. They're partners." I questioned whether
this positive message had been communicated, though, when I heard an
adult say: "Oh, there's one of those blind dogs."

Other people, though well-intentioned, can interfere with my 14
effective use of Misty. Guide dogs are highly trained and very dependable
but occasionally make potentially dangerous mistakes. On my way
through the aisles, Misty bumped me into a pointed rack, requiring my
quick action. I used a firm tone to correct her, and she dived to the
ground like a dying actress. Witnessing this performance, another
shopper chastised me for being cruel. I was shocked. Misty's pride was
hurt, but I needed to point out the error in order to avoid future
mistakes. If I did not discipline her, what would prevent Misty from
walking me off the curb into traffic?

Composing myself, I was delighted by the saleswoman's suggestion: 15
"Can I take you to your dressing room?" I was less delighted when she
grabbed me and pushed me ahead while Misty trailed us on a leash. I wriggled
out of the woman's hold. Gently pushing her ahead, I lightly held her elbow in
sighted-guide technique (called so because the person who sees goes first).

"This is better. Please put my hand on the door knob. I'll take it from   16
here," I said.

In the room, Misty plopped down and sighed with boredom. I sighed   17
with relief that she was still with me. On one shopping trip, I was so preoccupied with trying on clothes that Misty sneaked out beneath the dressing room's
doors. I heard her tags jingling as she left but was half-dressed and couldn't
retrieve her. Fortunately, Don was outside the door and snagged her leash.

I modeled the dresses for Don and, feeling numb, bought all three.   18
As we left the store, Misty's magnetism, reminiscent of the Pied Piper's,
attracted a toddler who draped himself over her. She remained calm, as he
tried to ride her. The boy's fun was soon foiled by his frantic mother. When
we returned to our car, I gave Misty a treat and lots of praise. A good day's
work deserves a good day's pay for both of us.

"Shop till you drop" or "retail therapy" could never be my motto.   19
To me, "charge" means going into battle.

RESPONDING TO READING

Does shopping ever feel like a battle to you? Do any of your reasons for feeling
that way overlap with Fleischman's? Can you come up with other imaginative
comparisons for the shopping experience?

CONSIDERING CONTENT

1. Why did Fleischman stop shopping with her friends? What makes her
   husband and dog better shopping partners?
2. List the mistakes made by the people Fleischman encounters as she
   shops. Now make a list of proper etiquette for interacting with a person
   who is blind.
3. What reasons does Fleishman offer for sighted people's troublesome
   behaviors? Can you provide other reasons?
4. Why does Fleishman say she is "feeling numb" in paragraph 18? What
   other emotions does she experience during this shopping trip?

CONSIDERING METHOD

1. Identify the stages of Fleischman's typical shopping trip. Why does she
   choose not to use a more direct, step-by-step format for her process essay?
2. Describe Fleischman's tone. Does it change over the course of the essay?

3. How does Fleischman offer proof in paragraph 7 that she stays "current with fashion"?
4. In the second paragraph, Fleischman writes, "The aisles empty as if a bomber had come on the scene." Find other examples of words and phrases that continue this battle comparison.

COMBINING STRATEGIES

Fleischman uses an extended example, narration, and description to provide a clear understanding of her shopping process and to achieve a persuasive purpose. What are the advantages of her approach? What other strategies might be used with this topic if one were writing for a different audience, such as trainers of assistance dogs?

WRITING STEP BY STEP: A PERSONAL APPROACH TO SHOPPING

You probably have your own shopping style. Write an essay called "Shopping Can Be _____," filling in the blank with the word that best captures your feelings about this everyday activity. You will be following the form of "Shopping Can Be a Challenge."

A. Start by asking a question that will catch most readers' interests.
B. Develop your introduction with an illustration of a past shopping experience that shaped your current technique or attitude.
C. Use an extended example of a typical shopping expedition to organize your essay. Be sure to provide concrete support—names, dialogue, description of people and places.
D. Select one of the comparisons you came up with in your Responding to Reading response and use it to help convey your tone and purpose throughout the essay. For example, you might compare shopping to a treasure hunt, which would suggest an entertaining, exciting experience. Also revise your phrasing—nouns, adjectives, adverbs, and verbs—to further communicate your attitude. For example, if your image as a shopper is "The Great Hunter," here is a revision you might make:

First draft: The hunt was almost over, but I managed to buy some discount socks at the last minute.
Revision: The hunt was almost over, but I managed to snare some small game (discount socks) at the last minute.

OTHER WRITING IDEAS

1. Choose an activity that you do and explain to your readers how they would benefit from doing it too.

2. COLLABORATIVE WRITING. Meet with your classmates to discuss other challenges that people with disabilities experience in their everyday activities. Talk about a range of disabilities and then construct a list of problems commonly encountered by people with these different types of disabilities. Consider things like conducting a conversation or performing simple actions. Write an essay based on the results of your group brainstorming and personal experiences.

3. USING THE INTERNET. Interacting with the blind is also an issue in the workplace. Visit Internet sites offering advice on this topic, then write a process essay on meeting and interacting with the blind in a work environment.

4. WRITING ABOUT READING. Write a summary of Fleischman's article. Follow the directions on pp. 13–14.

GAINING WORD POWER

In paragraph 8, Fleischman writes about a dog that was "*recently* put to sleep." In paragraph 3, we read the phrase "one *recent* shopping trip." Both words share the meaning of new or not long ago. *Recent* is an adjective, describing the noun *trip*. *Recently* is the adverb form of the same word; adverbs describe words other than nouns, in this case the verb *put*. Most adverbs are made by adding –*ly* to adjectives; for example, *happily* comes from *happy* (para. 1), *usually* comes from *usual* (para. 2), and *finally* comes from *final* (para. 3).

This reading includes ten other adverbs that end in –*ly*. Find at least five of them. Then write their adjective form, checking with the dictionary for spelling if necessary. Then express the shared meaning between the two forms, again using the dictionary. Here's an example to get you started:

> Adverb: slowly
> Adjective: slow
> Shared meaning: at a low speed, not moving quickly

EDITING SKILLS: USING PARENTHESES

When you want to include an idea that is interesting but not crucial to your discussion, put it in parentheses. Here's an example from Fleischman's third and fourth paragraphs:

> On one recent shopping trip, a brave saleswoman finally approached us. "Can I help you?" she said to my husband.
>
> "Yes, I'm looking for a dress," I replied. (After all, I'm the one who will be wearing it.)

The interaction is captured in the dialogue (speech or conversation recorded in writing), but in the final parenthetical sentence, Fleischman comments on the dialogue, and the parentheses tell the reader that the remark is reinforcement for the implied (but unspoken) point she is making. This example shows the use of parentheses to highlight a mocking tone.

Parentheses are also used in these ways:

1. To enclose brief definitions within a sentence (like the examples in the previous paragraph):

   I tightly held her elbow in a sight-guide technique (called so because the person who sees goes first).

   Writers use transitions to improve *continuity* (the flow of their ideas).

   Notice that the period goes after the parenthesis at the end unless the whole statement begins and ends within the parentheses.

2. To enclose examples and brief explanations (like the one in item 1 and this one you are presently reading).

3. To enclose dates within a sentence:

   John Stuart Mill (1806–1873) favored women's equality with men.

EXERCISE

Find five examples of parentheses in this chapter and explain which of the uses discussed applies to each example.

Then look at the essay you just completed. Is there any material that should be enclosed in parentheses? Consider adding a definition, a date, a comment, or a brief explanation with parentheses that would add to the reader's understanding of your ideas.

WEB SITE
www.support-dogs.org.uk/contents.php
The Web site Support Dogs Online offers advice on a variety of uses for assistance dogs, from alerting people with epilepsy about an upcoming seizure to performing everyday tasks, such as turning on lights and opening doors.

PREPARING TO READ

Who is your favorite e-mail or text message correspondent? Why do you like the messages from this person? To whom do you write e-mails or texts, and why? Do you keep any e-mails to read or refer to later, or do you let them all go into the trash?

••

How to E-mail a Professor

••

MICHAEL LEDDY

An English professor at Eastern Illinois University in Charleston, Michael Leddy posted the following advice on his blog in 2005 and found it unexpectedly popular: It still gets roughly a hundred hits a day, and many more at the start of semesters. Leddy earned his PhD at Boston College. His interests include modern and postmodern American poetry and fiction.

TERMS TO RECOGNIZE

cryptic (*para. 2*)	puzzling
salacious (*para. 2*)	sexy
rote (*para. 4*)	standard, memorized
stilted (*para. 4*)	phony-sounding, stiff and unnatural

I've read enough e-mails to know that many college students could   1
benefit from some guidelines for writing an e-mail to a professor. Here they are:

   Write from your college or university e-mail account. That immediately   2
lets your professor see that your e-mail is legitimate and not spam. The cryptic or cutesy or salacious personal e-mail address that might be okay when you send an e-mail to a friend is not appropriate when you're writing to a professor.

   Include the course number in your subject line. "Question about   3
3009 assignment" is clear and sounds genuine, while "a question" looks like spam. "Question about English assignment" or "question about assignment," without identifying the class you're in, may leave your professor with the chore of figuring that out. For someone teaching large lecture classes, that might mean reading through hundreds of names on rosters. But even for a professor with smaller classes, it's a drag to get an e-mail that merely says "I'm in your English class and need the assignment." All your English

professor's classes are English classes; she or he still needs to know which one is yours. Consider, in light of this advice, the following examples:

An e-mail from "qtpie2005" with the subject line "question."

An e-mail from a university account with the subject line "question about English 2011 essay."

Which one looks legitimate? Which one looks like spam?

Think about what you're saying. Most students are not accustomed   4
to writing to their professors. Here are some ways to do it well:

a. **Choose an appropriate greeting.** "Hi/Hello Professor [Blank]" is always appropriate. Substitute "Dear" and you've ended up writing a letter; leave out "Hi" and your tone is too brusque.

b. **Avoid rote apologies for missing class.** Most professors are tired of hearing those standard apologies and acts of contrition. If you missed class because of some especially serious or sad circumstances, it might be better to mention that in person than in an e-mail.

c. **Ask politely.** "Could you e-mail me the page numbers for the next reading? Thanks!" is a lot better than "I need the assignment."

d. **Proofread what you've written.** You want your e-mail to show you in the best possible light.

e. **Sign with your full name, course number, and meeting time.**

Maggie Simpson
English 3703, MWF 10:00

Signing is an obvious courtesy, and it eliminates the need for stilted self-identification ("I am a student in your such-and-such class").

One don't, and one last do: 5

Don't send unexpected attachments. It's bad form. Attaching an essay with a request that your professor look it over is very bad form. Arrange to meet your professor during office hours or by appointment instead. It's especially bad form to send an e-mail that says "I won't be in class today," with a paper or some other coursework attached. Think about it: Your professor is supposed to print out your essay because you're not coming to class?

When you get a reply, say thanks. Just hit Reply and say "Thanks," or a little bit more if that's appropriate. The old subject line (which will now have a "Re:" in front) will make the context clear. I don't think that you need to include a greeting with a short reply, at least not if you refer to your professor in your reply. And you don't need to identify yourself by course number and meeting time again.

Many e-mail messages end up never reaching their intended   6
recipients, for reasons of human and technological error, so it's always appropriate to acknowledge that someone's message got through. It's also

plain courtesy to say thanks. (Your professor will remember it too.) When you reply, you should delete almost everything of your professor's reply (quoting everything is rarely appropriate in e-mail). Leave just enough to make the original context clear.

So what would a good e-mail to a professor look like?   7

> Hi Professor Leddy,
> I'm working on my essay on William Carlos Williams and I'm not sure what to make of the last stanza of "Spring and All." I'm stuck trying to figure out what "It" is. Do you have a suggestion? Thanks!
> Maggie Simpson
> Eng 3703, MWF 10:00

And a subsequent note of thanks: 8

> >"It" is most likely spring, or life itself. But have you
> > looked up "quicken"? That'll probably make
> > "It" much clearer.
> It sure did. Thanks for your help, Professor.
> Maggie Simpson

RESPONDING TO READING

Why do you think this blog found instant popularity on the Internet? What other inside-information blogs by professors would college students find valuable?

CONSIDERING CONTENT

1. Did you learn anything new from reading Leddy's blog? What advice do you already follow? What advice will you follow in the future?
2. Do you disagree with any of the points Leddy makes? Explain your objection and show an alternative to Leddy's way.
3. What kind of content should not appear in a student-to-professor e-mail, according to Leddy? Why not?
4. Do you have any more questions about e-mailing professors, not answered by Leddy's blog? What are they? Write an e-mail to your instructor asking your question.

CONSIDERING METHOD

1. Leddy's advice consists of several *dos* and *don'ts*. How many *dos* are there? How many *don'ts*?
2. What order does the author use in presenting his *dos* and *don'ts*?
3. What is Leddy's basic strategy for developing each of his points?

4. Who is Leddy's audience? Where does he identify this audience? Where else can you tell that he has a good sense of whom he's writing for? What background knowledge about this audience does the writer have?

WRITING STEP BY STEP: MESSAGE MISTAKES

Leddy focuses on advice about messages between two specific groups of people, students and professors. In your Step by Step essay, write about message mistakes that could happen between almost any e-mail or text users. First, think about any e-mail (or text message) mistakes you have made yourself. Survey your friends to see what errors they have made in this communication medium. Make a written list as you think and discuss the subject and take notes on examples your friends tell you about. Then you may decide to focus upon a certain type of e-mail mistake or maybe two related types, because you probably can't cover everything in a class paper.

A. Begin your essay with a sentence about why people may be interested in the error (or errors) you will discuss. For instance, is it particularly common (as in student mistakes in e-mailing professors), especially embarrassing (accidentally sending an e-mail to the wrong people), or socially destructive (failed attempts at humor or irony)?

B. Each section of your essay should begin with a basic *do* or *don't* rule, as Leddy's does. Make a list of these. You may have only two or three of these, or up to ten if each one covers a narrower range of material—this is what you see in Leddy's blog. Make sure that each section will help the reader avoid the type of mistake(s) you are discussing.

C. For each rule, add explanatory development as Leddy does. Consider explaining the *why* behind the rule, as he does after telling you to identify your course number, in paragraph 3: "All your English professor's classes are English classes; she or he still needs to know which one is yours."

D. For each rule, add one or two examples. Use a bad example of the error under discussion, a good example that would correct the problem, or both. See Leddy's paragraph 4, where he gives a good and then a bad example of politeness in requesting an assignment.

E. Let a friend or classmate read your essay and make suggestions. Your writing may make someone else think of a highly relevant detail or example that you have overlooked.

F. Leddy closes his essay with a desirable sequence of messages between a student and professor. Consider closing your essay with an especially good or bad example of the type of email you are discussing.

G. If you like what you've written, post it on your blog, a message board, or a class e-mail blast.

OTHER WRITING IDEAS

1. Leddy tells college students how to e-mail professors. Write an essay about how to e-mail, text message, or write to some other specific audience: for example, your older relatives, your boyfriend or girlfriend, your students, your unwanted admirer, your high school classmates.

2. USING THE INTERNET. Read Garrison Keillor's classic essay on How to Write a Personal Letter at **www.docstoc.com/docs/4684178/ How-To-Write-A-Letter-Garrison-Keillor-wrote-this.** Write an essay about the role of the personal letter today. Is it completely obsolete? Why or why not? How could the practice of writing personal letters be revived? Why might our society want to revive it?

3. COLLABORATIVE WRITING. Get together with several classmates and discuss other forms of communication for which you could give advice about being polite and effective. You might discuss, for example, telephone conversations, complaints to businesses, recommendation letters, sympathy notes, answering machine messages, job application letters, love letters, a Dear John letter, orders in a restaurant, requests for help in a foreign country. When you've gathered a sufficient number of points about a particular kind of communication, write a blog posting similar to Leddy's. You can write individually or as a group, depending on your instructor's directions.

GAINING WORD POWER

Whenever you write, you choose a *level of formality*: in order from most casual to most proper, *colloquial* for your pals, *informal* for peers and acquaintances, *general* for an unknown or mixed audience, and *formal* for superiors and dignitaries. You need to be able to choose words that are appropriate for your chosen level of formality. For example, Leddy writes in paragraph 3, "it's a drag," knowing that his audience of college students will feel comfortable with the slang. If he were writing more formally, he might say, "it is burdensome," getting rid of the contraction and using a non-slang descriptor. He would also change the rest of his essay to match the new formal level. Write at least one more formal rewording that might substitute for each of the informal expressions below (all are from the Leddy blog). A thesaurus or dictionary may help you.

1. cutesy
2. looks like spam
3. Think about what you're saying.
4. Most professors are tired of
5. in the best possible light
6. It's bad form.
7. end up

EDITING SKILLS: USING COLONS BEFORE LISTS

In paragraph 3, Leddy writes, "Consider, in light of this advice, the following examples:" and follows with an indented pair of examples. In paragraph 4, he writes, "Here are some ways to do it well:" and follows with an indented and boldfaced list of rules. Notice that each of the introductory elements is a complete sentence and ends with a colon.

When you highlight a list, example, or set of examples by indenting each one, using boldfaced type to label the items, or marking each one with a design like a black dot (or bullet), you usually introduce the list right before the first item, like this:

- Here is an example:
- There are five methods to scare away pigeons:
- Follow these tips to stick to your diet:

The colon tells the reader that the example, methods, or tips will come next.

In most cases, prose composition requires that the introductory material is a complete sentence, not a fragment. Do not, therefore, use a colon before a series introduced by a verb or a preposition.

> *Colon:* You will need the following items for this class: a laptop computer, a spiral notebook, a pen, and a calculator.
>
> *No Colon:* For this class you will need a laptop computer, a spiral notebook, a pen, and a calculator.
>
> *No Colon:* You will also be graded on attendance, participation, and listening skills.

In Chapter 10, under Editing Skills, you will learn another common use for the colon.

EXERCISE

Find two more instances of a sentence and a colon introducing a list or example in Leddy's blog. Then find two instances of this use of colon in the essay "Friends, Good Friends—and Such Good Friends" by Judith Viorst (Chapter 6). Find one instance where Leddy violates the complete-sentence rule for introductory material with a colon. Can you speculate on why this fragmentary introduction is acceptable?

🌐 WEB SITE

www.ehow.com

This site contains advice on how to do just about everything, from scaring pigeons off your balcony to deciding whether someone likes you romantically. Both amateurs and experts share their techniques. Not only can you learn useful methods at ehow.com, but you can see how other people handle process writing. This helpful Web site also includes over 150,000 how-to videos.

PREPARING TO READ

How important are special effects to your enjoyment of movies and TV? When you watch TV sitcoms and dramas, do you notice when something seems wrong or fake or out of place?

● ●

Making Fake Flakes

● ●

EMILY NELSON

Emily Nelson is a staff reporter for the Wall Street Journal. *Her reports are often feature articles drawn from recent business and entertainment news. "Making Fake Flakes" first appeared in the* Journal *in June 2003.*

TERMS TO RECOGNIZE

riddled (*para. 1*)	punctured with numerous holes
props (*para. 2*)	articles or objects used by actors
sloshing (*para. 2*)	splashing, floundering
formula (*para. 3*)	a set model or prescription
alien (*para. 4*)	outsider, a being from outer space
lavish (*para. 4*)	abundant, extravagant, grand
acrylic (*para. 5*)	synthetic plastic
dubbing (*para. 6*)	inserting, substituting for the original
mussed (*para. 8*)	made messy, disordered
pulverizes (*para. 11*)	crushes, breaks into pieces

1   A special-effects whiz in Hollywood, Howard Jensen can create fireball explosions and make cars look riddled with bullets. But his current job—to create falling snow for TV shows such as *Boston Public*—is one of the hardest, he says. So he turned to potato flakes.

2   Turn on the TV, and that gentle, romantic snow falling is, quite likely, the same stuff sold at the supermarket for making mashed potatoes. Props crews can easily load the potato flakes into rolling drums on cranes that sprinkle down flakes. Industrial fans, called "Ritters" in the industry after their inventor, keep the flakes aloft. From afar, the effect looks just like idealized snow. Up close, however, potato flakes look like . . . potato flakes. They don't melt when they land on a person or on the ground. And they have a way of turning into potatoes. The cast of *ER* once found itself sloshing through mashed potatoes when it rained during filming.

Snow, it turns out, is a big production worry for TV studios these   3
days. For years, much of TV was set indoors in the same style that made
Archie Bunker's living room so familiar in *All in the Family.* Today, viewers
raised on big-budget movies expect greater realism and seasonal, outdoor
shots in TV productions, a formula that's worked well for NBC's *Law and
Order.* Many sitcoms, including *Malcom in the Middle,* regularly use outside
scenes. Moreover, networks are asking shows to change seasons with the
calendar, which gives viewers a sense they're watching in real time.

But while TV studios can create talking animals and alien neighbors,   4
snow can be trickier. Unlike rain, snow doesn't make any noise. For a good
thunderstorm, technicians simply mix in lightning and raindrop sounds on a
soundtrack. Even a frosty puff of breath is hard to reproduce without
expensive digital manipulation. And unlike lavish movies that travel to wintry locales and use elaborate post-production digital effects, budgets in
television are often tight. Production schedules are so short that most dramatic shows must crank out an episode every eight days, leaving little
money or time to add in special effects.

Depending on a script's demands—blizzard or flurries?—TV crews mix   5
in a variety of materials. Besides potato flakes, firefighters' foam, acrylic
flakes, soap and starch products, slivers of plastic (which can sting actors in
high winds), polyester blankets (best for roofs and backdrops), and real ice
are popular.

Snow scenes on TV call for unusual shortcuts. Characters on a   6
sitcom standing in the snow, for example, rarely talk. That's because the
snow-blowing machine makes a racket—usually replaced with background
music alone, to save the expense of dubbing in dialogue. When the plot on
Dawson's Creek called for the cast to go on a ski trip, the outdoor shots were
close-ups, allowing the crew to cover just a small area with fake snow—in
this case a white foam used by fire departments.

"We've attempted many ways, and I can't say any of them look too   7
convincing," says Paul Stupin, the show's executive producer, who says
small TV screens are more forgiving than movie screens. *Dawson's Creek,* set
in Massachusetts, also takes meteorological license, filming in North Carolina where it rarely snows. On *Friends* recently, the cast admired a snowfall
by looking out the window—a cheap shorthand that requires attaching a
tumbler above the window frame, which sprinkles white plastic flakes. Producers hoped viewers didn't notice that in the same scene, Chandler walks
in without so much as a flake on his coat.

Jonathan Prince, executive producer and writer for NBC drama   8
American Dreams, wanted snow so badly for a recent shoot that he changed
the plot of an episode to afford it. For a romantic but fake snowfall on star

Meg Pryor's first kiss, Mr. Prince had Meg and her family arrive late to church, thereby avoiding the need to hire congregation extras. In search of the perfect setting for a snowball fight, Mr. Prince ordered in truckloads of crushed ice. On the day before filming, as the cast played with the ice on the Los Angeles lot, Mr. Prince watched, in horror, as hair and make-up got mussed and, even worse, it looked like they were throwing white rocks.

"Real snowballs don't explode in powdery fluff the way we wish they 9 do," Mr. Prince says regretfully. "They only do that on television." So the props crew brought in potato flakes. "We were throwing mashed potatoes at each other," he says. "There are no runny noses. It's perfect TV."

Sometimes TV shows in colder climates manage to write snow out 10 of the script to avoid finding or making it, as when writers for *Everwood,* a new TV drama set in Colorado, added an unusually warm breeze that the town celebrates with a festival in one episode. They reversed the weather in two other episodes, writing in a blizzard that keeps everyone housebound and keeps the cameras inside. A show where the cast never gets outside is called "a bottle episode."

Another problem with real ice is that it's expensive. Potato flakes 11 cost about $90 per 50-pound box; last year, a winter episode of *Ally McBeal* required five boxes. North Hollywood Ice Co., charges $130 per ton of ice, usually with a 10-ton minimum, plus tax and $35 an hour each for five operators. Sold in large blocks, the ice is fed through a noisy snow blower that chips it, pulverizes it, and blows it out airborne through a hose. This is good for laying snow on the ground but not falling snow. Crushed ice does-n't float—it falls with a thud or melts. Potato flakes or plastic versions fall more realistically. "We still haven't figured out a way to get it lofting down and pretty," says Fred Rymond, manager at North Hollywood, which hauled 30 tons of ice, in blocks weighing 300 to 400 pounds each, to a set for a recent blizzard on *Boston Public.*

Idahoan Foods sells its potato flakes in major supermarket chains 12 such as Albertson's and Safeway, but it also ships the same stuff in 800-pound shipments to special-effects companies, says Ruth Shriver, a sales coordinator at the Lewisville, Idaho, potato processor. When Ms. Shriver spotted snow falling while watching *The West Wing* recently, she said, "Is that potato flakes? It could be my stuff."

RESPONDING TO READING

Will having learned how artificial snow is made change your experience of watching TV? Will it take away from the romantic mood the director is often aiming for in outdoor winter scenes, for example?

CONSIDERING CONTENT

1. What are the most common materials used to create fake snow on TV?
2. Why do TV characters who are simply standing in snow stay silent? What other pitfalls do the special effects people run into when using artificial snow and how do they solve each problem?
3. What do time and cost have to do with the decisions TV studios make about their use of special effects?
4. What's a "Ritter"? What other production terms are introduced and defined in the essay?

CONSIDERING METHOD

1. Why does Nelson begin her introduction with images of "fireball explosions" and cars "riddled with bullets"?
2. How many different snow-making techniques are described in the essay? Can you identify a plan for how Nelson ordered her examples?
3. Find examples of Nelson's use of humor in "Making Fake Flakes." Why did she choose this tone for a process essay?
4. Why does Nelson use so many different TV shows to illustrate her points? Would a single extended example work?
5. Why does Nelson include the brief account of Ruth Shriver's experience at the end of the essay?

WRITING STEP BY STEP: BEHIND THE SCENES OF A PROCESS

Choose a topic and a process similar to the ones in "Making Fake Flakes." Your topic should be something everyone is familiar with, like snow on TV; however, the details of the process itself should offer readers a few surprises or new insights, like how difficult it is to create that snow using potato flakes and ice. You might, for example, reveal some behind-the-scenes secret about a job you have performed (dipping perfect soft-serve ice cream cones, frying perfect fries, quieting uncontrollable children) or a hobby you have perfected (staying upright while windsurfing, keeping up your stamina on a cross-country bike race, sewing a designer knock-off at half the price).

A. Direct your writing to a general audience. Assume that the majority of your readers would not be familiar with the details of the process, that most of them, for example, have never worked at a fast-food restaurant or sewn their own clothes.
B. Begin by calling your readers' attention to the difference between what they think they know about your process and the point you wish to make about it. Nelson, for example, wishes to counter the idea that complex special effects are more difficult to achieve than simple ones.

C. Because your purpose is to inform, not instruct, organize your essay as Nelson does, providing the what, when, how, and why of your process by providing several successful examples and a few failed ones.

D. Develop your essay with specific details and colorful, concrete language to keep your reader's interest and attention. Nelson, for example, describes cars "riddled with bullets," and amuses her readers with images of the cast of *ER* "sloshing through mashed potatoes when it rained during filming."

E. If possible, conclude your essay with an amusing incident or reference, as Nelson does.

OTHER WRITING IDEAS

1. Write an essay in which you use process to explain a problem and then suggest a solution. For example, show how being overweight is a problem and then offer guidelines for losing weight. Other topics are smoking, excessive alcohol consumption, lack of work experience, poor study habits, and chronic lateness.

2. COLLABORATIVE WRITING. Identify and explain the stages of an emotional process, such as falling in love (or falling out of love). Work with a group of your classmates to come up with emotional processes and ideas about the different stages before you write your individual essay.

3. USING THE INTERNET. Look on the Internet, using a search engine such as Google or Yahoo, to find a complicated set of instructions, like those for programming a cell phone. Study them until you figure them out. Then write a new set of instructions that a beginner would find easy to follow.

4. WRITING ABOUT READING. "Making Fake Flakes" is about creating illusions, making what's not real seem real. Have you ever tried to create an illusion to make people believe in something that wasn't true? For example, did you ever convince your parents you were ready to take on adult responsibilities, when, in fact, you weren't quite sure yourself that you were ready? Select such an experience and explain how you achieved your goal of creating an illusion.

GAINING WORD POWER

romantic   seasonal   frosty

wintry   dramatic   powdery

The preceding words are all used as *adjectives* in the reading. That is, they describe or modify other words (nouns) to make their meaning more specific and vivid. Look back through the reading to find the adjective-plus-noun combinations. We have done the first example for you.

(2) romantic ____snow____   (4) wintry _____

(3) seasonal _____   (4) dramatic _____

(4) frosty _____   (9) powdery _____

The adjective *romantic* obviously comes from the noun *romance*. Using your dictionary, find the nouns that are related to these other four adjectives:

industrial (2)	noun:_____
expensive (4)	noun:_____
digital (4)	noun:_____
meteorological (7)	noun:_____

Now list one other related word, its meaning, and its part of speech for the four adjectives. Use your dictionary for help. For example, *expensive* is related to the verb *expend*, which means "to lay out." Both have to do with spending. Choose one set of three related words and try using them in three sentences of your own.

EDITING SKILLS: PUNCTUATING QUOTATIONS

Quotations from experts and from your reading will often enhance your writing. However, most people find the punctuation of quotations tricky. This exercise will help you put the periods, commas, and quotations marks in the right places. (For advice on using single quotation marks inside regular double quotations marks, see pages 57–59.)

EXERCISE

Copy the following passages *exactly*:

"We've attempted many ways," says Paul Stupin, the show's executive producer, "and I can't say any of them look too convincing."

"Real snowballs don't explode in powdery fluff the way we wish they do," Mr. Prince says regretfully. "They only do that on television." So the props crew brought in potato flakes. "We were throwing mashed potatoes at each other," he says. "There are no runny noses. It's perfect TV."

When Ms. Shriver spotted snow falling while watching "The West Wing" recently, she said, "Is that potato flakes? It could be my stuff."

Notice that you can put the tag line (the part that tells who is being quoted) before the quotation, after the quotation, or in the middle of the quotation. Exchange your copies with a classmate and check each other's writing for exact, accurate placement of all the punctuation. Then look at your process essay to make sure you have punctuated quotations correctly.

☙ WEB SITE

http://entertainment.howstuffworks.com/question171.htm
At this HowStuffWorks.Com site, the complex real-time and digital processes for creating the *Stars Wars* light sabers are concisely and clearly explained. Links on the site take you to explanations of other special effects techniques, as well.

PREPARING TO READ

Think of the last time you needed more than words to understand something—perhaps directions for putting together a toy or furniture or barbecue. Why did you need pictures as well as words? Can pictures ever make processes more confusing rather than less? Why do you think this might be?

••

Change Agent: How Baker Pulled Off the "Werewolf" Metamorphosis

••

STEVE DALY

Steve Daly is a staff writer for Entertainment Weekly. *For the special 2007 Oscar guide, he wrote this account of how Rick Baker made a human actor into a werewolf onscreen. Baker won the first Academy Award for makeup in 1982, for his work on* American Werewolf, *and he is now known as a film prosthetics genius. Daly's description benefits from a combination of written words and photographs. Without the photos, it would be difficult for the reader to understand the amazing process described in the words.*

Writer-director John Landis told Rick Baker the big metamorphosis scene in *American Werewolf* "should be painful." So it was, on screen and on set. Star David Naughton endured more than a week's filming encased in fur-covered latex pieces glued to his body. "We tortured him," says Baker. For full-figure shots designed to sell the idea of the wolf's expanded torso (complete with pronounced rib cage and extremely narrow hips), the crew cut a hole in a raised floor (top photo), laid a breast piece over Naughton, then ran metal rods up through two separate animatronic legs, puppeteering them from below to complete the illusion that it was all one were-man. Separate fake hands and feet were rigged for other close-ups to expand via cables and pistons, and a dummy "change-o-head," which involved 10 months' work to get a single shot lasting a few seconds, showed the werewolf's snout growing. Says Baker, "We never had time to test a lot of the transformation stages. We did the makeup on the day, and shot it."

The man-into-wolf scene took place in bright lighting. Says Baker, "I kept worrying, can't we turn the light down a little?"

Source: © 1981 Bob Willoughby / MPTV.net

FOR DISCUSSION AND WRITING

Many processes are best explained with a combination of words and graphics. For instance, directions for cooking and sports techniques often depend on graphics for clarity. Looking around at home, at your workplace, and at school, make a list of examples where written text and graphics are combined to explain a process or give directions. Choose one example and explain what the graphics contribute beyond the words.

OTHER WRITING IDEAS

1. Write some basic instructions for using a machine, such as a microwave oven, a photocopier, a cell phone, a washing machine. Write for readers who don't know how to work the machine. Include one or more graphics (such as a diagram or chart) to help explain how the process works.
2. What exactly is the "goth look"? What steps do you think the people in the photo on the next page took to create the appearance they wanted?

Source: J. Sackermann/Das Fotoarchiv.\Photolibrary/Peter Arnold, Inc.

3. Using a diagram or drawing, explain some sports activity that you know well, such as how to hit a forehand in tennis, how to throw a curve ball or a spiral pass, how to bowl a strike, how to execute a swan dive.

WEB SITE

www.themakeupgallery

The Makeup Gallery features nearly 5,000 images of actresses in character and prosthetic makeup from literally hundreds of movies and TV shows. The transformations from actress into character are illustrated with before and after shots and, wherever possible, with behind-the-scenes shots of the makeup process. Who do you think visits this site and why?

STUDENT ESSAY USING PROCESS AND DIRECTIONS

A Graceful Stride

Ann Moroney

Ann Moroney wrote this essay in her first-semester English class at Eastern Illinois University. She attended a large high school in the western suburbs of Chicago and came to Eastern Illinois to major in journalism and information sciences.

A common misconception about hurdle races is that the runner "jumps" over the hurdle. This observation is completely false. A hurdle runner does just that—runs. The hurdler takes long steps, or strides, over the hurdle and sprints on to the next one. As simple as this process may sound, running hurdles is complicated. For one thing, the hurdle itself is thirty-three inches high, which comes to about the hip. "Stepping" over something this high is really quite difficult, as I found out my freshman year in high school. I also had to master a number of other skills to run hurdles efficiently.

The first problem to tackle when it comes to running hurdles is the fear. At every one of my races, I sat in my blocks looking at the line of hurdles in front of me with fear in my heart. No matter how good I became or how long I'd been running, I always felt *fear*: fear that I'd trip over the hurdle and fall on the track, fear that I'd knock the hurdle over in front of everybody, and fear that I'd actually get over the first hurdle with no problem and become a hurdler for four years. Throughout my experience, I found only one way to get over the fear: stop thinking and start running.

The main thing to concentrate on is form. Form is the way the runner carries himself or herself over the hurdles. The better the form is, the faster the run will be. Form includes many elements. The runner must coordinate legs, arms, torso, and eyes into a fluid sprint through ten hurdles on 100 meters of track.

The lead leg, the one to go over the hurdle first, should be slightly bent, but more or less straight in front of the body. The toe should be pointing toward the sky and the heel should line up with the middle of the hurdle. (As my former track coach Ms. Tolefree always said, "Heel to the Gill," referring to the brand name printed directly in the middle of the hurdle.) Just as the body comes over the hurdle, the lead leg should snap down to the ground. The goal is to bring the leg down as close to the back of the hurdle as possible without actually hitting it. The sooner the feet are on the ground, the faster the runner can continue running.

The runner must also concentrate on the trail leg—the one that comes second over the hurdle. The knee should be bent with the leg at the side, the thigh parallel to the hurdle. (Imagine sitting on the ground with one leg bent at the side, mimicking a frog.) As the lead leg snaps down, the trail leg will be following over the hurdle. The hip will rotate so the leg is once again perpendicular to the ground. The knee should snap up to the chest as close as possible, as this will help the runner stretch out the stride. (As Ms. Tolefree was fond of saying, "Your knee is like the scope on a rifle. It directs where your stride will go. If your knee is high, your stride will be long. If it's low, your stride will be short.") After clearing the hurdle, the runner must continue striding through the rest of the hurdles.   5

Another important part of form is arms; they not only keep balance, but they also keep the form tight. The arm opposite the lead leg is the lead arm. It should be reaching out in front of the body toward the toe of the lead leg. The other arm, the one opposite the trail leg, is the trail arm. It should come back in a biceps-flexing fashion and stay at the side until the body is clear of the hurdle. It's usually a good idea to keep the hands open; a closed fist takes up energy and tenses the muscles in the rest of the body.   6

The final elements of form have to do with small, yet significant, mechanics. Air time is a major factor when running hurdles. The goal is to remain in the air for as little time as possible; the faster the feet return to the track, the faster the runner can continue running. So the body should be as low to the hurdle as possible without hitting it. Also, the torso should lean slightly forward—but not be bent, because taking the time to straighten up will slow the runner down. A slight lean forward will get the runner over the hurdle and on to the next one. The final point involves the eyes. Hurdlers should not look at the hurdle they are about to step over. Looking further down the track instead of directly in front of them keeps runners running.   7

Running hurdles takes time, practice, and commitment. During the split second it takes to clear a hurdle, the runner must take into account a wide variety of movements to run the race successfully. A good, hard practice schedule is the only way to acquire a productive hurdling technique. And developing a graceful stride is not as easy as it looks.   8

CONSIDERING CONTENT AND METHOD

1. Why does the author begin with a misconception? Is that a good way to begin?
2. What information did you find new and interesting? Was there anything you didn't understand? Did this essay increase your appreciation of hurdling?
3. Were you surprised that this essay was written by a female student? Why or why not?
4. Where does the author include personal comments? Do these comments add or detract from the explanations?
5. What do you think of the comments from the coach, Ms. Tolefree? Why are they included?

CHAPTER 9

Strategies for Analyzing Why Things Happen:
Cause and Effect

U.S. Suicide Rates Among Persons 10–24 Years, by Race/Ethnicity and Sex, 2000–2006

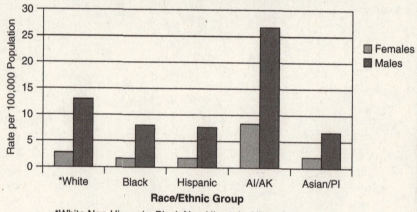

*White Non-Hispanic, Black Non-Hispanic, Hispanic, American Indian/Alaskan Native, Asian/Pacific Islander

For Discussion and Writing

The illustration above is a clustered bar graph—the suicide rate for each racial or ethnic group is represented in a cluster, and each cluster has a bar for female suicides and a bar for male suicides. Examine the data displayed in the graph. What information stands out? Can you speculate on why there is such a wide difference in suicide rates among young people from different racial or ethnic groups? What about the gender difference? Do you think that social and political changes in the United States might alter the patterns you see in this chart? For example, what changes might lower the high rate of suicide among native populations? How and why?

Human beings are naturally curious. We all want to know why. Why does the car keep stalling? Why are some people better at math than others? Why does a leaf change color? Why did Donald Trump and his latest girlfriend break up? This common human impulse to understand why things happen provides a powerful motive for reading and writing.

THE POINT OF CAUSE-AND-EFFECT WRITING

We study causes and their effects in order to understand events and solve problems. If we can find out why the car keeps stalling, we can fix it. If we can figure out why some people are good at math, maybe we can help those who aren't. If we know why a leaf changes color, we'll have a greater appreciation for nature and its processes. If we know why Trump and his girlfriend split, we might get on *Oprah*. A lot of the writing done in college courses requires cause-and-effect thinking; students are frequently asked to explain things like the origins of the Russian Revolution, the roots of prejudice, the causes of volcanic eruptions, the effects of hunger on learning, the reasons for Hamlet's delay. The good news about this kind of writing is that it feeds off the natural curiosity of both reader and writer. Inquiring minds want to know why, and you get to tell them.

When you develop an essay by analyzing causes, you are explaining to your readers *why* something happened. If you go on to explore the effects, you are analyzing *what* happened—the consequences. For example, if your topic is divorce and you write "Why Teenage Marriages Fail," that's primarily a cause paper. But if you write "What Divorce Does to Young Children," that's primarily an effect paper. You will probably stick to one **purpose** in a single essay, but you might take up both causes and effects if you have the time and the assignment allows you to.

THE PRINCIPLES OF CAUSE-AND-EFFECT WRITING

Analyzing cause-effect relationships is one of the primary methods of reasoning. It requires careful thinking and planning.

Types of Causes and Effects

When you think about causes and effects, you need to realize that they can be *immediate* or *remote*. The immediate causes are usually the obvious ones; they occur just before a result appears. An immediate cause for breaking up with your boyfriend might be that he didn't call you last night to tell you he'd be two hours late. But you also know there are deeper, more important reasons for the breakup, for example, his habit of forgetting to call and his general lack of concern for your feelings. These are the remote causes, the ones further removed from the effect they produce. They are also called *underlying causes* because they are often more difficult to see.

Effects can also be immediate or remote. The immediate effect of failing to get gas is that your car stops running. But the remote effects can stretch out for quite a while: You block traffic and cause an accident; you're late for class and miss an important lecture; you do poorly on the next exam and get a lower grade in the class; your car insurance goes up because of the accident; you have to change majors because you don't have the required grade point average to be admitted into advanced courses. Remote effects are also called *long-term effects*.

Patterns of Cause and Effect

1. If you want to focus on causes, begin by describing a condition or problem or result (such as breaking up with your boyfriend), and then fully explain the causes or reasons (for the breakup). With this approach, you may be able to use **chronological order** (according to time) if you can trace the causes from the earliest to the most recent. More likely, though, your organization will fall into some **logical order** that reflects the relative importance of the causes: from the least significant to the most critical or from personal reasons to more general ones.

2. If you want to focus on effects, start with some condition or event and explain the consequences. For example, you might begin by describing the breakup with your girlfriend and then go on to show how it affected you. Again, you can present the effects chronologically: At first you were depressed; then you began to spend more time with your friends; you also had more to time to study, so your grades improved; finally, you began to date again and found a much better girlfriend. Or you can arrange the effects according to importance: from a fairly obvious result to the most subtle, from effects on yourself to effects on other people.

3. Since causes and effects are closely related, you might find that tracing a chain or sequence of events, including both causes and effects, is the best way to approach your topic. In a causal chain the first cause produces an effect, which becomes the cause of the next effect, and so on. In the example about running out of gas, there were two chains. First, running out gas caused a blocked intersection, which led to an accident, which resulted (some time later) in higher insurance costs. Also, running out of gas caused you to be late for class and miss an important lecture, which contributed to a lower grade, which affected your grade point average, which prevented you from getting into the advanced program, which caused you to change majors. If you decide to describe a chain of causes and effects, be sure to outline it carefully.

THE PITFALLS OF CAUSE-AND-EFFECT WRITING

An explanation of causes and effects won't be successful if your readers find your thinking fuzzy or flawed. Here are some ways to avoid the most common faults of cause-effect reasoning:

1. Don't mix causes and effects. When talking informally about why things happen, you may shuttle back and forth between causes and their effects. But in writing, you need to follow a clear pattern: focus on causes, focus on effects, or describe an orderly chain of causes and effects.

2. Don't settle for obvious causes and immediate effects. Your explanations will be much more convincing if you look for underlying causes and long-term effects. As Jade Snow Wong shows in her essay in this chapter, her date with a fellow student provided an opportunity to stand up to her parents, but it was not the cause of her rebellion. The "real" causes ran much deeper. It is, of course, possible to go too far back in searching for causes. You'll need to exercise some judgment in deciding which reasons are still valid and relevant.

3. Don't oversimplify. Most conditions and events are complex, involving multiple causes and numerous effects. In a short essay, you may have to concentrate on the primary reasons, but be sure to let your readers know that's what you are doing.

4. Don't omit any key links in a chain of causes and effects. You don't have to spell out every single step in a sequence of events, but be certain that your readers will be able to follow and make all the right connections themselves.

5. Don't worry about absolute proof. In explaining causes and effects, you can't always prove conclusively why something happened. But offer as much evidence as you can to help the reader see the connections that you see. You always need to support your causes and effects with specific details—examples drawn from personal experience, statistics, and statements by experts. You may want to conduct interviews and collect your own information or visit the library to find material on your topic.

WHAT TO LOOK FOR IN CAUSE-AND-EFFECT WRITING

As you read the selections in this chapter, ask yourself these questions:

1. Does the writer focus on causes or effects, or does the essay consider both? Make a list of the causes and the effects as you read.
2. Look for the point, or purpose, of the author's explanation of causes and effects.
3. Decide what kind of causes or effects the author presents—immediate, remote, or both. Does the writer follow a chain of causal relationships?

4. Does the author have a particular audience in mind? How can you tell?

5. What is the tone of the essay? Does the author sound serious, humorous, angry, irritated, sad, regretful, or something else? How does that tone relate to the author's purpose and audience?

6. Notice what writing strategies the author uses to develop the explanations. Take note of examples, descriptions, narratives, comparisons, definitions, and so on.

PREPARING TO READ

Do you enjoy horror movies? Why do you like to watch them? How do you react when you view them? If you don't enjoy horror movies, can you explain why they do not appeal to you?

•••

Why We Crave Horror Movies

•••

STEPHEN KING

You know Stephen King as the master of terror, the author of a string of best-selling horror novels. And you have probably seen some of the movies made from his novels: Carrie, Misery, Christine, Pet Sematary, *and* Firestarter *(among others). In the following essay, King offers an entertaining explanation of why people like being scared out of their wits.*

TERMS TO RECOGNIZE

grimaces (*para. 1*)	twisted facial expressions
hysterical (*para. 1*)	emotionally uncontrolled
province (*para. 3*)	proper area or sphere
depleted (*para. 3*)	used up, drained, worn out
innately (*para. 4*)	naturally, essentially
reactionary (*para. 4*)	wanting to return to an earlier time
menaced (*para. 6*)	threatened, endangered
voyeur (*para. 6*)	a peeping Tom, someone who enjoys watching something private or forbidden
penchant (*para. 7*)	a strong fondness or inclination
psychic (*para. 7*)	mental, psychological
status quo (*para. 9*)	existing condition or state of affairs
sanctions (*para. 10*)	expressions of disapproval, punishments
anarchistic (*para. 11*)	disorderly, ignoring the rules
morbidity (*para. 12*)	an interest in gruesome and horrible things
subterranean (*para. 12*)	underground

I think we're all mentally ill; those of us outside the asylums only hide   1
it a little better—and maybe not all that much better, after all. We've all
known people who talk to themselves, people who sometimes squinch their
faces into horrible grimaces when they believe no one is watching, people

who have some hysterical fear—of snakes, the dark, the tight place, the long drop . . . and, of course, those final worms and grubs that are waiting so patiently underground.

When we pay our four or five bucks and seat ourselves at tenth-row 2 center in a theater showing a horror movie, we are daring the nightmare.

Why? Some of the reasons are simple and obvious. To show that 3 we can, that we are not afraid, that we can ride this roller coaster. Which is not to say that a really good horror movie may not surprise a scream out of us at some point, the way we may scream when the roller coaster twists through a complete 360 or plows through a lake at the bottom of the drop. And horror movies, like roller coasters, have always been the special province of the young; by the time one turns 40 or 50, one's appetite for double twists or 360-degree loops may be considerably depleted.

We also go to re-establish our feelings of essential normality; the 4 horror movie is innately conservative, even reactionary. Freda Jackson as the horrible melting woman in *Die, Monster, Die!* confirms for us that no matter how far we may be removed from the beauty of a Robert Redford or a Diana Ross, we are still light-years from true ugliness.

And we go to have fun. 5

Ah, but this is where the ground starts to slope away, isn't it? 6 Because this is a very peculiar sort of fun, indeed. The fun comes from seeing others menaced—sometimes killed. One critic has suggested that if pro football has become the voyeur's version of combat, then the horror film has become the modern version of the public lynching.

It is true that the mythic, "fairy-tale" horror film intends to take away 7 the shades of gray. . . . It urges us to put away our more civilized and adult penchant for analysis and to become children again, seeing things in pure blacks and whites. It may be that horror movies provide psychic relief on this level because this invitation to lapse into simplicity, irrationality and even outright madness is extended so rarely. We are told we may allow our emotions a free rein . . . or no rein at all.

If we are all insane, then sanity becomes a matter of degree. If your 8 insanity leads you to carve up women like Jack the Ripper or the Cleveland Torso Murderer, we clap you away in the funny farm (but neither of those two amateur-night surgeons was ever caught, heh-heh-heh); if, on the other hand, your insanity leads you only to talk to yourself when you're under stress or to pick your nose on your morning bus, then you are left alone to go about your business . . . though it is doubtful that you will ever be invited to the best parties.

The potential lyncher is in almost all of us (excluding saints, past 9 and present; but then, most saints have been crazy in their own ways), and every now and then, he has to be let loose to scream and roll around in the grass. Our emotions and our fears form their own body, and we recognize that it demands its own exercise to maintain proper muscle tone. Certain of these emotional muscles are accepted—even exalted—in civilized society; they are, of course, the emotions that tend to maintain the status quo of civilization itself. Love, friendship, loyalty, kindness—these are all the emotions that we applaud, emotions that have been immortalized in the couplets of Hallmark cards and in the verses (I don't dare call it poetry) of Leonard Nimoy.

When we exhibit these emotions, society showers us with positive   10
reinforcement; we learn this even before we get out of diapers. When, as children, we hug our rotten little puke of a sister and give her a kiss, all the aunts and uncles smile and twit and cry, "Isn't he the sweetest little thing?" Such coveted treats as chocolate-covered graham crackers often follow. But if we deliberately slam the rotten little puke of a sister's fingers in the door, sanctions follow—angry remonstrance from parents, aunts and uncles; instead of a chocolate-covered graham cracker, a spanking.

But anticivilization emotions don't go away, and they demand   11
periodic exercise. We have such "sick" jokes as, "What's the difference between a truckload of bowling balls and a truckload of dead babies?" (You can't unload a truckload of bowling balls with a pitchfork . . . a joke, by the way, that I heard originally from a ten-year-old.) Such a joke may surprise a laugh or a grin out of us even as we recoil, a possibility that confirms the thesis: If we share a brotherhood of man, then we also share an insanity of man. None of which is intended as a defense of either the sick joke or insanity but merely as an explanation of why the best horror films, like the best fairy tales, manage to be reactionary, anarchistic, and revolutionary all at the same time.

The mythic horror movie, like the sick joke, has a dirty job to   12
do. It deliberately appeals to all that is worst in us. It is morbidity unchained, our most base instincts let free, our nastiest fantasies realized . . . and it all happens, fittingly enough, in the dark. For those reasons, good liberals often shy away from horror films. For myself, I like to see the most aggressive of them—*Dawn of the Dead*, for instance—as lifting a trap door in the civilized forebrain and throwing a basket of raw meat to the hungry alligators swimming around in that subterranean river beneath.

Why bother? Because it keeps them from getting out, man. It keeps   13
them down there and me up here. It was Lennon and McCartney who said that all you need is love, and I would agree with that.

As long as you keep the gators fed.   14

RESPONDING TO READING

Do you agree with King that we are all mentally ill and that our "anticivilization emotions don't go away"? Respond to these ideas in your journal.

CONSIDERING CONTENT

1. What does King mean when he says that we are all mentally ill? What is the nature of the "insanity" that we share?
2. What are the obvious reasons for enjoying horror movies? What are some of the not-so-obvious reasons?
3. King refers to our "anticivilization emotions" that occasionally need exercise. What are these emotions? Why do they need to be exercised?
4. Do you think Stephen King is biased in his defense of horror movies? Do you think you would respond differently to this essay if it were written by someone you had never heard of?

CONSIDERING METHOD

1. King begins with a startling statement about insanity. What is the effect and point of this opening?
2. How does he maintain the insanity theme throughout the essay? Do you think this is an effective strategy?
3. At what point in the essay does King reveal that he will be dealing with causes?
4. Does King deal with immediate causes or long-term causes or both? In what order does he arrange the causes he discusses?
5. Identify comments or passages that you think are humorous. What does the humor contribute to this essay?
6. What is the function of the two one-sentence paragraphs (paras. 5 and 14)?

COMBINING STRATEGIES

King uses several *comparisons* to explain and support his defense of horror movies. What points does King make by comparing horror movies to the following?

a. riding a roller coaster

b. public lynching

c. mythic fairy tales

d. sick jokes.

Do you think these are good comparisons?

WRITING STEP BY STEP: ENTERTAINMENT CRAVINGS

Think of another form of entertainment that people seem to crave, and write an essay explaining why. You might write about soap operas, MTV, video games, action movies, reality TV, sports programs, jogging (or other exercise activities), bodybuilding, shopping, online chat rooms, or the like.

A. Begin with a startling statement, as Stephen King does.
B. Give background about the subject by explaining your opening statement.
C. Discuss the obvious or immediate causes first. Identify at least three reasons and explain them.
D. Then examine the long-term or underlying causes. Show how these causes produce the craving that you are writing about.
E. Be sure to name specific programs or games.
F. Use figurative language and analogies to help explain the causes. Even include a little humor the way King does, if you want to.
G. Write a conclusion in which you comment on the behavior you have analyzed. Make your comment an outgrowth of your discussion of underlying causes.

OTHER WRITING IDEAS

1. Write an essay about the effects of watching too much TV. Use your own observations and experiences to support your conclusions.
2. COLLABORATIVE WRITING. Working with a group of classmates, interview a variety of people to find out why they like a certain type of entertainment (TV hospital shows, arcade games, stock car races, line dancing, rock concerts, ballet, situation comedies, or the like). Ask them to give you specific reasons. Then write a group report explaining why this form of entertainment is popular. Use several direct quotations from the interviews to support your explanations.
3. USING THE INTERNET. Find out what researchers say about the effects of television violence on children. Be sure to locate sites that offer more than one point of view. Then write an essay for parents, informing them of these effects and suggesting what they can do to counter them. See the Appendix on "Writing with Sources" for details about how to give proper credit to your sources.
4. WRITING ABOUT READING. Check out King's ideas about the cravings for horror movies by watching one and analyzing your reactions to it. Did the movie "re-establish [your] feelings of essential normality"? In what ways did it provide "psychic relief" or satisfy your "anticivilization emotions"? How did you feel before watching the movie? How did you feel afterwards?

GAINING WORD POWER

What does it mean to do "a complete 360"? (King uses the expression in para. 3.) You may know that 360 refers to the number of degrees in a circle and that the phrase means to go all the way around to where you started, to travel in a complete circle. One way of expressing the opposite idea is to say you did "an about-face," which is a military command for pivoting around to face in the opposite direction.

Both of these phrases—"a complete 360" and "an about-face"—are figurative expressions; they're supposed to put a picture in our minds by referring to an object (like a circle) or an action (like a military maneuver). **Figurative language** requires interpretation; we have to figure out the references and imagine the picture that the writer wants to put in our minds. Here are some more figurative phrases that Stephen King uses in his essay. Explain what they mean and tell what you see in your mind's eye. If you're not sure of what King means, ask other people for their interpretations.

1. "those final worms and grubs that are waiting so patiently underground"
2. "tenth-row center"
3. "shades of gray"
4. "clap you away in the funny farm"
5. "the couplets of Hallmark cards"
6. "before we get out of diapers"
7. "lifting a trap door in the civilized forebrain and throwing a basket of raw meat to the hungry alligators swimming around in that subterranean river beneath"

EDITING SKILLS: CHECKING PRONOUN REFERENCE

Whenever you use pronouns (words such as *he, she, it, his, her, their,* etc., that stand in for nouns), you must be sure that each has a clear antecedent (the noun that the pronoun stands for). If the antecedents aren't clear, your readers can get lost. Look at this sentence from Stephen King's essay:

We've all known people *who* talk to *themselves*, people *who* sometimes squinch *their* faces into horrible grimaces when *they* believe no one is watching. . . .

The pronouns *themselves, who, their,* and *they* all clearly refer to the antecedent *people.*

Several pronouns are especially troublesome when they appear without specific antecedents: *this, which,* and *these.* King uses these words eleven times. Sometimes he places them right before the nouns they refer to—"this roller coaster," "this level," "this invitation," "these emotions"—so there is no misunderstanding about what they mean. But in other instances, he uses *this*, *these*, and *which* as free-standing pronouns. Find these other uses (in paras. 3, 6, 9, 10, and 11), and see if you can name the thing or idea to which these pronouns refer. Do you think King has used these pronouns clearly?

EXERCISE

The following sentences are vague because they contain pronouns without clear antecedents. Rewrite each sentence to make it clear.

Example: Clyde made Gary do his homework.

Revisions: Gary did his homework because Clyde made him.

Gary did Clyde's homework because Clyde made him.

1. Hampton aced the history test because he made it so easy.
2. Carlo is working on the railroad in Tennessee, which depresses him.
3. Kesha dropped out of school after they took away fall break.
4. Our cat chased the ground squirrel until he got tired.
5. Although Juan's mother is a chemist, Juan hates it.
6. Rosa tried to support herself by painting and acting. This was a mistake.
7. Mel blamed his failure on his choice of occupation, which was unfortunate.
8. Washington wore a sombrero and sequined gloves to the prom. This was a big hit.

Now look at the essay you have just written. Pay particular attention to your use of pronouns. Make sure each has a clear antecedent.

🌐 WEB SITE

www.stephenking.com

Find out more about Stephen King's views on horror stories and other aspects of writing at the official online resource for news and information about King and his works.

PREPARING TO READ

Did your parents ever forbid you to do something that you went ahead and did anyway? What happened? How did you feel about it later?

• •

Fifth Chinese Daughter

• •

JADE SNOW WONG

Jade Snow Wong grew up in San Francisco, the daughter of immigrant parents who brought with them from China an ancient and rigid set of family traditions. The following excerpt from Wong's autobiography, Fifth Chinese Daughter, *recounts the inevitable conflict between traditional parents and a young woman who is beginning to discover a different world beyond her home and neighborhood.*

TERMS TO RECOGNIZE

oblige (*para. 2*)	accommodate, please
adamant (*para. 3*)	unyielding, inflexible
edict (*para. 3*)	command, rule
incurred (*para. 4*)	acquired, taken on
nepotism (*para. 7*)	favoritism shown to relatives
incredulous (*para. 12*)	unwilling to admit or accept what is heard; unbelieving
unfilial (*para. 12*)	disrespectful to parents
revered (*para. 12*)	honored, respected
innuendos (*para. 14*)	sly suggestions, indirect hints
devastated (*para. 15*)	crushed, overwhelmed
perplexed (*para. 16*)	puzzled, confused

By the time I was graduating from high school, my parents had done their best to produce an intelligent, obedient daughter, who would know more than the average Chinatown girl and should do better than average at a conventional job, her earnings brought home in repayment for their years of child support. Then, they hoped, she would marry a nice Chinese boy and make him a good wife, as well as an above-average mother for his children. Chinese custom used to decree that families should "introduce" chosen partners to each other's children. The groom's family should pay handsomely to the bride's family for rearing a well-bred

1

daughter. They should also pay all bills for a glorious wedding banquet for several hundred guests. Their daughter belonged to the groom's family and must henceforth seek permission from all persons in his home before returning to her parents for a visit.

But having been set upon a new path, I did not oblige my parents 2 with the expected conventional ending. At fifteen, I had moved away from home to work for room and board and a salary of twenty dollars per month. Having found that I could subsist independently, I thought it regrettable to terminate my education. Upon graduating from high school at the age of sixteen, I asked my parents to assist me in college expenses. I pleaded with my father, for his years of encouraging me to be above mediocrity in both Chinese and American studies had made me wish for some undefined but brighter future.

My father was briefly adamant. He must conserve his resources for 3 my oldest brother's medical training. Though I desired to continue on an above-average course, his material means were insufficient to support that ambition. He added that if I had the talent, I could provide for my own college education. When he had spoken, no discussion was expected. After this edict, no daughter questioned.

But this matter involved my whole future—it was not simply asking for 4 permission to go to a night church meeting (forbidden also). Though for years I had accepted the authority of the one I honored most, his decision that night embittered me as nothing ever had. My oldest brother had so many privileges, had incurred unusual expenses for luxuries which were taken for granted as his birthright, yet these were part of a system I had accepted. Now I suddenly wondered at my father's interpretation of the Christian code: was it intended to discriminate against a girl after all, or was it simply convenient for my father's economics and cultural prejudice? Did a daughter have any right to expect more than a fate of obedience, according to the old Chinese standard? As long as I could remember, I had been told that a female followed three men during her lifetime: as a girl, her father; as a wife, her husband; as an old woman, her son.

My indignation mounted against that tradition and I decided then 5 that my past could not determine my future. I knew that more education would prepare me for a different expectation than my other female schoolmates, few of whom were to complete a college degree. I, too, had my father's unshakable faith in the justice of God, and I shared his unconcern with popular opinion.

So I decided to enter junior college, now San Francisco's City 6 College, because the fees were lowest. I lived at home and supported myself with an after-school job which required long hours of housework and cooking but paid me twenty dollars per month, of which I saved as much as possible. The thrills derived from reading and learning, in ways ranging from chemistry experiments to English compositions, from considering new ideas of sociology to the logic of Latin, convinced me that I had made a correct choice. I was kept in a state of perpetual mental excitement by new Western subjects and concepts and did not mind long hours of work and study. I also made new friends, which led to another painful incident with my parents, who had heretofore discouraged even girlhood friendships.

The college subject which had the most jolted me was sociology.   7
The instructor fired my mind with his interpretation of family relationships. As he explained to our class, it used to be an economic asset for American farming families to be large, since children were useful to perform agricultural chores. But this situation no longer applied and children should be regarded as individuals with their own rights. Unquestioning obedience should be replaced with parental understanding. So at sixteen, discontented as I was with my parents' apparent indifference to me, those words of my sociology professor gave voice to my sentiments. How old-fashioned was the dead-end attitude of my parents! How ignorant they were of modern thought and progress! The family unit had been China's strength for centuries, but it had also been her weakness, for corruption, nepotism, and greed were all justified in the name of the family's welfare. My new ideas festered; I longed to release them.

One afternoon on a Saturday, which was normally occupied with my   8
housework job, I was unexpectedly released by my employer, who was departing for a country weekend. It was a rare joy to have free time and I wanted to enjoy myself for a change. There had been a Chinese-American boy who shared some classes with me. Sometimes we had found each other walking to the same 8:00 A.M. class. He was not a special boyfriend, but I had enjoyed talking to him and had confided in him some of my problems. Impulsively, I telephoned him. I knew I must be breaking rules, and I felt shy and scared. At the same time, I was excited at this newly found forwardness, with nothing more purposeful than to suggest another walk together.

He understood my awkwardness and shared my anticipation. He   9
asked me to "dress up" for my first movie date. My clothes were limited but I changed to look more graceful in silk stockings and found a bright ribbon for my long black hair. Daddy watched, catching my mood, observing the dashing preparations. He asked me where I was going without his permission and with whom.

I refused to answer him. I thought of my rights! I thought he surely   10
would not try to understand. Thereupon Daddy thundered his displeasure
and forbade my departure.

I found a new courage as I heard my voice announce calmly that I   11
was no longer a child, and if I could work my way through college, I would
choose my own friends. It was my right as a person.

My mother had heard the commotion and joined my father to face   12
me; both appeared shocked and incredulous. Daddy at once demanded the
source of this unfilial, non-Chinese theory. And when I quoted my college
professor, reminding him that he had always felt teachers should be revered,
my father denounced that professor as a foreigner who was disregarding the
superiority of our Chinese culture, with its sound family strength. My father
did not spare me; I was condemned as an ingrate for echoing dishonorable
opinions which should only be temporary whims, yet nonetheless inexcusable.

The scene was not yet over. I completed my proclamation to my   13
father, who had never allowed me to learn how to dance, by adding that I
was attending a movie, unchaperoned, with a boy I met at college.

My startled father was sure that my reputation would be subject to   14
whispered innuendos. I must be bent on disgracing the family name; I
was ruining my future, for surely I would yield to temptation. My mother
underscored him by saying that I hadn't any notion of the problems
endured by parents of a young girl.

I would not give in. I reminded them that they and I were not in   15
China, that I wasn't going out with just anybody but someone I trusted!
Daddy gave a roar that no man could be trusted, but I devastated them in
declaring that I wished the freedom to find my own answers.

Both parents were thoroughly angered, scolded me for being shame-   16
less, and predicted that I would some day tell them I was wrong. But I dimly
perceived that they were conceding defeat and were perplexed at this breakdown of their training. I was too old to beat and too bold to intimidate.

RESPONDING TO READING

Has college affected you in the same way that it affected Jade Snow Wong?
Write in your journal about the effects college has had on you; compare your
reactions to Wong's.

CONSIDERING CONTENT

1. What did you learn about Wong's parents and their traditional beliefs in
   the first paragraph?

2. What caused Wong to rebel against her parents? What situations and experiences contributed to her quest for independence?

3. Why was Wong sure that more education would prepare her for a different future from her classmates? Did it?

4. Why did the sociology course affect Wong so strongly? What did she learn in that course that changed her views and fed her rebellion?

5. What action did Wong take to demonstrate her independence? Why did she choose this particular way of disobeying her parents? Do her actions seem risky and rebellious to you?

6. In what ways was Wong a lot like her father? Which of his beliefs and attitudes actually contributed to his daughter's rebellion?

CONSIDERING METHOD

1. Why is the first paragraph important? How does the information in this paragraph prepare you for Wong's actions?

2. What does Wong accomplish by mentioning her oldest brother? What is she trying to show?

3. What is the function of the questions in paragraph 4? Why does Wong express these ideas in questions instead of in statements? (See pages 328–329 for an explanation of rhetorical questions.)

4. How much time passes in this selection? How does Wong indicate the passage of time? Where does she move back in time? Why does she do so?

5. Paragraph 8 opens with these words: "One afternoon on a Saturday . . ."What do these words signal? What mode of writing begins at this point?

6. Wong doesn't use direct quotations or quoted conversation. How does she report what she said to her parents and what they said to her? What is the effect of this indirect presentation?

7. How would you describe the **tone** of this selection? Does Wong sound angry, sad, upset, calm, confident, relieved, happy, or what?

WRITING STEP BY STEP: BECOMING OUR PARENTS

As we grow older, we sometimes change our minds about our parents. We begin to see things more from their point of view. Think of a piece of advice, a household rule, or a parental opinion that you used to hate but now understand. If you don't want to write about your parents, think of another adult, such as a teacher or a coach, who set down rules or gave advice that you once rejected but now think appropriate. Write an essay in which you explain what caused you to change your mind.

A. Begin with a statement of your general point. You might say something like "I used to think my parents' advice was outdated and pointless, but a lot of it makes sense to me today" or "Now that I'm coaching pee-wee soccer, I follow some of the same rules I used to hate when I was a player."

B. Explain the particular rule, opinion, advice, or guideline you used to resist. Re-create specific incidents and arguments you used to have that illustrate your earlier response.

C. Analyze your change in attitude. Cite specific reasons or causes, and explain them.

D. If there was a key incident or turning point in your thinking, focus on that event and describe it in detail.

E. Conclude by revealing how you feel about this change in thinking. Does it mean that you've grown up or that you've sold out?

OTHER WRITING IDEAS

1. Write an essay about why adolescents leave home. Or write an essay about the effects of their leaving home.

2. COLLABORATIVE WRITING. Explain why some jobs or professions seem to be done mainly by women (like childcare, housework, nursing, elementary school teaching). As you plan your paper, talk to some women who do these jobs or who are preparing to enter one of these professions, and ask their opinions. Also talk to some men, and ask them how they would feel about teaching grade school, being a nurse, cleaning houses, or taking care of children for a living.

3. USING THE INTERNET. Talk to someone who comes from a cultural background different from yours. If you can, spend some time with this person's friends and family. Also locate Internet sites that will give you information about this cultural group. Then, with your classmates as audience, write an essay explaining what you learned about this culture and how it affected your attitudes toward these people.

4. WRITING ABOUT READING. In the last paragraph, Wong writes that she "dimly perceived" that her parents "were conceding defeat and were perplexed at this breakdown of their training" (para. 16). What were they conceding and why were they perplexed? Write an essay that answers these questions. Include personal experiences that might help to explain or support your conclusions.

GAINING WORD POWER

Come up with definitions of your own for the italicized words in the following sentences. Use the clues from the surrounding words and sentences to help you. Then check your definition against a dictionary definition.

1. "Chinese custom used to *decree* that families should 'introduce' chosen partners to each other's children." (para. 1)
2. "Having found that I could *subsist* independently, I thought it regrettable to *terminate* my education." (para. 2)
3. "I pleaded with my father, for his years of encouraging me to be above *mediocrity* in both Chinese and American studies had made me wish for some undefined but brighter future." (para. 2)
4. "My *indignation* mounted against that tradition and I decided then that my past could not determine my future." (para. 5)
5. "I was kept in a state of *perpetual* mental excitement by new Western subjects and concepts and did not mind long hours of work and study." (para. 6)
6. "My new ideas *festered*; I longed to release them." (para. 7)
7. "He was not a special boyfriend, but I had enjoyed talking to him and had *confided* in him some of my problems. *Impulsively*, I telephoned him. I knew I must be breaking rules, and I felt shy and scared." (para. 8)
8. "I was too old to beat and too bold to *intimidate*." (para. 16)

EDITING SKILLS: USING PARALLEL STRUCTURE

Look at these last two sentences from paragraph 3 in Wong's essay:

When he had spoken, no discussion was expected.

After his edict, no daughter questioned.

When you look at the sentences in this format, with one on top of the other, you can see how they match up in size and form. This correspondence is called **parallelism,** or parallel structure. Parallel structure often occurs within a sentence, as the following sentences from Wong's essay show. (The parallel parts are italicized for you.)

As long as I could remember, I had been told that a female followed three men during her lifetime: *as a girl, her father; as a wife, her husband; as an old woman, her son.*

I was *too old to beat* and *too bold to intimidate.*

Writers use parallel structure to catch the reader's attention and, as Wong does, to compare or contrast important points. Parallel structures also add **emphasis** and variety to a sentence or paragraph.

EXERCISE

Copy two of the sentences previously quoted; write two or three sentences of your own that imitate Wong's use of parallel structure. Then examine the following sentences, and write your own sentences that imitate the parallel structures.

1. "This freedom, like all freedoms, has its dangers and its responsibilities."
   —James Baldwin

   Imitation: This new attendance policy, like all school policies, has its supporters and its critics.

2. "We must stop talking about the American dream and start listening to the dreams of Americans."
   —Reubin Askew

   Imitation: We must stop asking silly questions and start questioning silly policies.

Look over your own essay and revise two or three sentences, using parallel structure. Read the new sentences aloud. If they sound clear and effective, keep them in your essay.

🌐 WEB SITE

http://sun3.lib.uci.edu/~dtsang/aas2.htm

This is the Web site for Asian American Studies Resources: an extensive collection of sites for studying Asian cultures, compiled by Daniel Tsang, the Asian American Studies Bibliographer for the library at the University of California at Irvine.

PREPARING TO READ

Do you eat fast food? How much and how often? Do you think it's healthy?

••

Supersize Me

••

GREG CRITSER

Educated at Occidental College and UCLA, Greg Critser lives in Pasadena, California. He is a regular contributor to USA Today, *the* Los Angeles Times, *and* Harper's Magazine. *In 1999, his articles on obesity won a James Beard nomination for best feature writing, and he is frequently interviewed by PBS and other news media on the subject of food politics. The following selection comes from the second chapter of his book* Fat Land: How Americans Became the Fattest People in the World *(2003).*

TERMS TO RECOGNIZE

contentious (*para. 4*)	quarrelsome, heated
truculent (*para. 9*)	fierce, hostile, aggressively self-assertive
entrepreneurism (*para. 10*)	the practice of taking business risks
primal (*para. 10*)	primary, first in importance
maligned (*para. 14*)	criticized, attacked, smeared
table d'hôte (*para. 15*)	a complete meal offered at a fixed price
à la carte (*para. 15*)	a menu or list that prices each item separately
immutable (*para. 21*)	unchangeable, permanent
maw (*para. 23*)	the mouth or jaws of a hungry animal

David Wallerstein, a director of the McDonald's Corporation, hated   1
the fifth deadly sin because it kept people from buying more hamburgers.
Wallerstein had first waged war on the injunction against gluttony as a
young executive in the theater business. At the staid Balaban Theaters chain
in the early 1960s, Wallerstein had realized that the movie business was
really a margin business; it wasn't the sale of low-markup movie tickets that
generated profits but rather the sale of high-markup snacks like popcorn
and Coke. To sell more of such items, he had, by the mid-1960s, tried
about every trick in the conventional retailer's book: two-for-one specials,

combo deals, matinee specials, etc. But at the end of any given day, as he tallied up his receipts, Wallerstein inevitably came up with about the same amount of profit.

Thinking about it one night, he had a realization: People did not want to buy two boxes of popcorn *no matter what.* They didn't want to be seen eating two boxes of popcorn. It looked piggish. So Wallerstein flipped the equation around: Perhaps he could get more people to spend just a little more on popcorn if he made the boxes bigger and increased the price only a little. The popcorn cost a pittance anyway, and he'd already paid for the salt and the seasoning and the counter help and the popping machine. So he put up signs advertising jumbo-size popcorn. The results after the first week were astounding. Not only were individual sales of popcorn increasing; with them rose individual sales of that other high-profit item, Coca-Cola.

Later, at McDonald's in the mid-1970s, Wallerstein faced a similar problem: With consumers watching their pennies, restaurant customers were coming to the Golden Arches less and less frequently. Worse, when they did, they were "cherry-picking," buying only, say, a small Coke and a burger, or, worse, just a burger, which yielded razor-thin profit margins. How could he get people back to buying more fries? His popcorn experience certainly suggested one solution—sell them a jumbo-size bag of the crispy treats.

Yet try as he may, Wallerstein could not convince Ray Kroc, McDonald's founder, to sign on to the idea. As recounted in interviews with his associates and in John F. Love's 1985 book, *McDonald's: Behind the Arches*, the exchange between the two men could be quite contentious on the issue. "If people want more fries," Kroc would say, "they can buy two bags."

"But Ray," Wallerstein would say, "they don't want to eat two bags—they don't want to look like a glutton."

To convince Kroc, Wallerstein decided to do his own survey of customer behavior, and began observing various Chicago-area McDonald's. Sitting in one store after another, sipping his drink and watching hundreds of Chicagoans chomp their way through their little bag of fries, Wallerstein could see: People *wanted* more fries.

"How do you know that?" Kroc asked the next morning when Wallerstein presented his findings.

"Because they're eating the entire bagful, Ray," Wallerstein said. "They even scrape and pinch around at the bottom of the bag for more and eat the salt!"

Kroc gave in. Within months receipts were up, customer counts were   9
up, and franchisees—the often truculent heart and soul of the McDonald's
success—were happier than ever.

Many franchisees wanted to take the concept even further,   10
offering large-size versions of other menu items. At this sudden burst of
entrepreneurism, however, McDonald's mid-level managers hesitated.
Many of them viewed large-sizing as a form of "discounting," with all the
negative connotations such a word evoked. In a business where "whole-
some" and "dependable" were the primary PR watchwords, large-sizing
could become a major image problem. Who knew what the franchisees,
with their primal desires and shortcutting ways, would do next? No, large-
sizing was something to be controlled tightly from Chicago, if it were to
be considered at all.

Yet as McDonald's headquarters would soon find out, large-sizing   11
was a new kind of marketing magic—a magic that could not so easily be
put back into those crinkly little-size bags.

Max Cooper, a Birmingham franchisee, was not unfamiliar with   12
marketing and magic; for most of his adult life he had been paid to conjure
sales from little more than hot air and smoke. Brash, blunt-spoken, and
witty, Cooper had acquired his talents while working as an old-fashioned
public relations agent—the kind, as he liked to say, who "got you into the
newspaper columns instead of trying to keep you out." In the 1950s with
his partner, Al Golin, he had formed what later became Golin Harris, one
of the world's more influential public relations firms. In the mid-1960s, first
as a consultant and later as an executive, he had helped create many of
McDonald's most successful early campaigns. He had been the prime
mover in the launch of Ronald McDonald.

By the 1970s Cooper, tired of "selling for someone else," bought a   13
couple of McDonald's franchises in Birmingham, moved his split-off ad
agency there, and set up shop as an independent businessman. As he began
expanding, he noticed what many other McDonald's operators were noticing: declining customer counts. Sitting around a table and kibitzing with a
few like-minded associates one day in 1975, "we started talking about how
we could build sales—how we could do it and be profitable," Cooper
recalled in a recent interview. "And we realized we could do one of three
things. We could cut costs, but there's a limit to that. We could cut prices,
but that too has its limits. Then we could raise sales profitably—sales, after
all, could be limitless when you think about it. We realized we could do that
by taking the high-profit drink and fry and then packaging it with the low-
profit burger. We realized that if you could get them to buy three items for

what they perceived as less, you could substantially drive up the number of walk-ins. Sales would follow."

But trying to sell that to corporate headquarters was next to impossible. "We were maligned! Oh, were we maligned," he recalls. "A 99-cent anything was heresy to them. They would come and say 'You're just cutting prices! What are we gonna look like to everybody else?'" 14

"No no no," Cooper would shoot back. "You have to think of the analogy to a fine French restaurant. You always pay less for a *table d'hôte* meal than you pay for *à la carte,* don't you?" 15

"Yes, but —" 16

"Well, this is a *table d'hôte,* dammit! You're getting more people to the table spending as much as they would before—and coming more often!" 17

Finally headquarters relented, although by now it hardly mattered. Cooper had by then begun his own rogue campaign. He was selling what the industry would later call "value meals"—the origin of what we now call supersizing. Using local radio, he advertised a "Big Mac and Company," a "Fish, Fry, Drink and Pie," a "4th of July Value Combo." Sales, Cooper says, "went through the roof. Just like I told them they would." 18

Though it is difficult to gauge the exact impact of supersizing upon the appetite of the average consumer, there are clues about it in the now growing field of satiety—the science of understanding human satisfaction. A 2001 study by nutritional researchers at Penn State University, for example, sought to find out whether the presence of larger portions *in themselves* induced people to eat more. Men and women volunteers, all reporting the same level of hunger, were served lunch on four separate occasions. In each session, the size of the main entree was increased, from 500 to 625 to 700 and finally to 1000 grams. After four weeks, the pattern became clear: As portions increased, all participants ate increasingly larger amounts, despite their stable hunger levels. As the scholars wrote: "Subjects consumed approximately 30 percent more energy when served the largest as opposed to the smallest portion." They had documented that satiety is not satiety. Human hunger could be expanded by merely offering more and bigger options. 19

Certainly the best nutritional data suggest so as well. Between 1970 and 1994, the USDA reports, the amount of food available in the American food supply increased 15 percent—from 3300 to 3800 calories or by about 500 calories per person per day. During about the same period (1977–1995), average individual caloric intake increased by almost 200 calories, from 1876 calories a day to 2043 calories a day. One could argue 20

which came first, the appetite or the bigger burger, but the calories—they
were on the plate and in our mouths.

By the end of the century, supersizing—the ultimate expression of   21
the value meal revolution—reigned. As of 1996, some 25 percent of the
$97 billion spent on fast food came from items promoted on the basis of
either larger size or extra portions. A serving of McDonald's french fries
had ballooned from 200 calories (1960) to 320 calories (late 1970s) to
450 calories (mid-1990s) to 540 calories (late 1990s) to the present
610 calories. In fact, everything on the menu had exploded in size. What was
once a 590-calorie McDonald's meal was now . . . 1550 calories. By 1999,
heavy users—people who eat fast food more than twenty times a month—
accounted for $66 billion of the $110 billion spent on fast food. Twenty
times a month is now McDonald's marketing goal for every fast-food eater.
The average Joe or Jane thought nothing of buying Little Caesar's pizza
"by the foot," of supersizing that lunchtime burger or supersupersizing an
afternoon snack. Kids had come to see bigger everything—bigger sodas,
bigger snacks, bigger candy, and even bigger doughnuts—as the norm;
there was no such thing as a fixed, immutable size for anything, because
anything could be made a lot bigger for just a tad more.

There was more to all of this than just eating more. Bigness: The   22
concept seemed to fuel the marketing of just about everything, from cars
(SUVs) to homes (mini-manses) to clothes (super-baggy) and then back
again to food (as in the Del Taco Macho Meal, which weighed four
pounds). The social scientists and the marketing gurus were going crazy
trying to keep up with the trend. "Bigness is addictive because it is about
power," commented Inna Zall, a teen marketing consultant, in a page-one
story in *USA Today*. While few teenage boys can actually finish a 64-ounce
Double Gulp, she added, "it's empowering to hold one in your hand."

The pioneers of supersize had achieved David Wallerstein's dream.   23
They had banished the shame of gluttony and opened the maw of the
American eater wider than even they had ever imagined.

RESPONDING TO READING

After reading this selection, do you think you'll try to change your eating
habits? Why or why not?

CONSIDERING CONTENT

1. What did David Wallerstein figure out about moviegoers and the
   amount of popcorn they bought? What did he do about it?

2. Why did McDonald's managers resist the idea of offering large-size versions of menu items?
3. What scheme did Max Cooper come up with to raise sales at McDonald's?
4. What did the 2001 Penn State study reveal about the effect of portion size on eating behavior?
5. What link between supersizing and caloric intake does Critser make? Does this conclusion seem valid and reasonable?
6. According to Critser, how has the concept of "bigness" spread beyond the fast food market? Do you agree that "Bigness is addictive because it is about power"?

CONSIDERING METHOD

1. What is Critser's point of view? Who are his intended readers, and what message does he want to convey to them?
2. Explain the **analogy** between "value meals" and the menu in a fine French restaurant (paras. 14–18). Does this seem like a valid comparison?
3. Who are the two sources for the first part of the article (paras. 1–18)? Why does Critser rely on these people for the information in this part?
4. Look at the statistics in paragraphs 19, 20, and 21. What point do they support in each paragraph? What are their sources?
5. What effects does the closing paragraph achieve?

WRITING STEP BY STEP: GETTING TO THE ROOT CAUSES

Greg Critser examines the problem of increased obesity in Americans and uncovers a surprising cause: the supersizing of fast foods. In this writing assignment you will have a similar goal.

Think of a problem or condition that you know something about, and look beneath the surface to discover both the *immediate* and the *remote* (or *underlying*) causes. One place to start is on your campus: the lack of a daycare center, a parking crisis, the widespread occurrence of cheating or plagiarism, trouble getting the courses needed to graduate, the ineffectiveness of student government, or the difficulty in obtaining funds for a new student group. You could also write about a family problem, if you think it would interest your readers.

A. Brainstorming is a productive way to discover the best topic for this assignment. Don't stop at the first problem that comes to mind, but remember that you must know the topic well enough to explore it in some depth. Also review past issues of your campus newspaper or chat with classmates, teachers, and friends to identify possibilities.

B. Once you've decided what to write about, make a list of all the causes that you and others have thought of so far, even the ones you don't necessarily see as important or correct.

C. Cluster these causes on your list. Put immediate or easily observable causes in one group, indirect or less easily seen ones in another. Next, cluster around the indirect causes, trying to identify where those causes might originate. Critser's examination led him to supersizing and then to value meals, which led him to the connection between portion size and consumption, and finally to the possible link between increased calories and the growing popularity of fast food.

D. You will need to select the most important causes for the problem to allow you space to explain each one fully. Consider which points are least familiar, even surprising, to your readers and most likely to influence their thinking on the problem. A new perspective can sometimes move those with set ideas to reconsider their views.

E. A scratch outline of your chain of causes will let you know how well prepared you are to begin your draft. If the chain reveals a need for more examples or explanations, return to brainstorming and further conversations with people who know about the problem.

F. Before you begin the draft, review Critser's organization. He takes a chronological approach, starting with the first step in the process of increasing serving sizes. He could have started with the final effects—increased calories and obesity—and worked his way back to the primary causes. Your readers' familiarity with the problem and their attitudes toward it should help you decide where to start and how to organize your points.

G. In your conclusion, consider using Critser's technique of summing up his main message and driving the point home. Or you could try putting the next step in the hands of your readers by suggesting what they can do with the information and insights you have given them.

OTHER WRITING IDEAS

1. Brainstorm a list of causes for some problem you are facing, such as paying your bills, getting all your work done, dealing with a difficult friend or teacher, sticking to your diet. Organize the list into immediate and long-term causes. Write an essay analyzing the causes of your problem and concluding with your solution.

2. COLLABORATIVE WRITING. Conduct an informal survey among your friends and relatives about their favorite junk food: What do they like about it? When do they eat it? How often? Using this information, do some freewriting about why you think people love this kind of food.

Then gather your thoughts, and write an essay about the popularity of junk food.

3. USING THE INTERNET. Some researchers claim that your cell phone can be hazardous to your health. Search for information about the suspected harmful effects of long-term cell phone use. Then write an article for your peers about these effects. See the appendix on "Writing with Sources" for details about using and crediting your sources.

4. WRITING ABOUT READING. In the last five paragraphs of his essay, Critser examines the links between supersizing and increased food consumption in America. Review those paragraphs and write an evaluation of them. What claims does Critser make? How persuasive are his evidence and conclusions?

GAINING WORD POWER

Explain as thoroughly as you can what the following phrases mean in Critser's essay.

1. the fifth deadly sin (para. 1)
2. high-markup snacks (para.1)
3. cost a pittance (para. 2)
4. mid-level managers (para. 10)
5. hot air and smoke (para. 12)
6. the prime mover (para. 12)
7. kibitzing with like-minded associates (para. 13)
8. went through the roof (para. 18)

EDITING SKILLS: ELIMINATING WORDINESS

A good writer would never write only short, simple sentences, but a good clean sentence is better than a wordy, cluttered one. Look at these spare sentences from Critser's article:

It looked piggish.

People wanted more fries.

Kroc gave in.

A less skillful writer might have used a lot more words to say the same thing, like this:

It would make them appear to be gluttonous and piggish to people who might be watching.

The general public desired to consume additional french-fried potatoes.

Finally, after much hemming and hawing, Kroc relented and yielded in the end to Wallerstein's opinion.

There's nothing actually wrong with those sentences except what English teachers call *verbiage* and everybody else calls **wordiness.** Be careful not to say the same thing twice ("gluttonous and piggish," "relented and yielded," and "finally" and "in the end"). And avoid these common expressions:

Wordy	Concise
tall in height	tall
past history	history
blue in color	blue
advance forward	advance
expensive in price	expensive
consensus of opinion	consensus
continue to remain	remain
join together	join
few in number	few
positive benefits	benefits
at this point in time	at this time

EXERCISE

If you have trouble saying things succinctly, practice by streamlining the following wordy sentences. Keep the same meaning but eliminate the extra words. Here's an example:

The masculine-gendered style used online in ListServe communications is, at this point in time, characterized by an adversarial attitude.

(Revised) The male style used in communications on ListServe is adversarial.

1. It is my desire to be called Ishmael.
2. In my opinion there are many diverse elements about this problem that one probably ought to at least think about before arriving at an opinion on the matter.
3. The obnoxious children were seldom corrected or reprimanded because their baffled and adoring parents thought their objectionable behavior was normal and acceptable.
4. There came a time when, based on what I had been reading, I arrived at the feeling that the food we buy at the supermarkets to eat is sometimes, perhaps often, bad for us.

5. By and large, a stitch sewed or basted as soon as a rip is discovered may well save nine times the amount of sewing necessary if the job is put off even for a relatively short time.

Now go through your final draft one more time looking only for verbal clutter. Then, in the words of Mark Twain, "When in doubt, leave it out."

🌐 WEB SITES

www.naturalnews.com/fast_food.html
This site provides articles, features, and online resources covering the health consequences of fast food consumption.

www.fatcalories.com
Find information here about fast foods that can help reduce the risk of obesity, diabetes, high blood pressure, and heart disease.

PREPARING TO READ

Have you ever made a transition from school to work? From high school to college? Did you have any problems with this transition? If so, what caused the difficulties? If not, why not?

•••

Young Workers with Dyslexia, ADD Find Office Less Accommodating Than School

•••

Sue Shellenbarger

In her "Work and Family" column for the Wall Street Journal, *Sue Shellenbarger has explored people's attempts to be competent and satisfied with both work and home life. She also writes about current psychological research on topics like happiness, child-raising, and sex roles. Shellenbarger's columns were collected in a book,* Work Family, *in 1999, and her book on women's midlife crises,* The Breaking Point, *was published in 2006.*

TERMS TO RECOGNIZE

dyslexia (*para. 1, 6*)	severe difficulty in reading and writing
deemed (*para. 3*)	judged, considered to be
entitlement (*para. 4*)	what is deserved automatically
impair (*para. 6*)	damage, make worse
autistic (*para. 6*)	markedly disordered in communication and social skills

John Brennan, who has dyslexia and attention deficit disorder (ADD), was a hard-working student in high school, earning B's and C's with the help of special accommodations, such as extra assistance reading his test questions. But entering the workplace after graduation was a shock. Mr. Brennan says he enrolled in a training program to service luxury cars, but he was criticized for "holding the class back" and dismissed. Then he joined an auto-repair shop that promised him training, but says the shop sidetracked him instead into a dead-end job. Fed up with trying to work for

1

other people, Mr. Brennan says he has enrolled in junior college near his Acton, Mass., home, with plans to start his own business.

Amid rapid growth in diagnoses of learning disabilities and special-education programs to address them, more young adults are entering the workplace with known learning differences and a history of receiving accommodations. But few employers have adapted training or job expectations for workers with learning disabilities. The lack of special accommodations has meant a rude awakening for many young workers, fueling on-the-job tensions and a rising tide of discrimination complaints.   2

While the 1990 Americans With Disabilities Act (ADA) entitles some workers with disabilities to job accommodations such as a quieter work-space, it doesn't require employers to offer the same broad services schools must provide learning-disabled pupils under federal law. Under the ADA, employers aren't required to make accommodations if it would inflict "undue hardship" on the business. Employers don't have to eliminate essential job duties or create new jobs. The law provides no protection if an employee is deemed unqualified, a definition that varies based on the job. "The boss-employee relationship is very different from the teacher-student relationship," says Dale S. Brown, an author and advocate for people with learning disabilities.   3

To be sure, many employers aren't aware of employees' learning disabilities or don't know how to accommodate them. Also, some employees have an undue sense of entitlement. Attorney Patricia H. Latham of Washington, D.C., tells of a client with ADD who kept arriving at work late. "They're angry with me, and I don't think they should be, because that's part of my problem," the woman said and asked Ms. Latham to write her bosses a letter. Ms. Latham refused, telling the woman, "your employer doesn't have to put up with your being late to work." Instead, she suggested making a habit of arriving early, leaving a margin for error.   4

Such tensions are fueling discrimination complaints. Claims to the Equal Employment Opportunity Commission and state and local agencies that cite "learning disability" as one basis for alleged discrimination rose 74% from 1993 to 2003, according to an analysis of EEOC data by Cornell University's Employment and Disability Institute. Also, unemployment among people with learning disabilities remains stubbornly high. A 2006 federal study of 11,000 youth who received special-education services in school shows only 40% are employed a year or two after high-school graduation, compared with 63% of same-age young adults in the general population.   5

While no reliable data on learning disabilities in the work force exist, about 4.4%, or 7.5 million, of adults ages 21 through 64 have lasting   6 mental disabilities of some kind that impair learning, remembering or concentrating, says a Cornell University analysis of Census data. In the past, many learning disabilities such as ADD, dyslexia, mild autistic conditions, memory disorders and other problems went undiagnosed. Workers typically hid their impairments, avoided jobs that exposed them or suffered from misperceptions that they were lazy or stupid. But now that more people are recognizing that they have learning disabilities, says Susanne Bruyere, director of the Employment and Disability Institute at Cornell University, many are "also more confident" in asking for accommodations.

The fact that learning disabilities often can't be seen tends to make employers less sympathetic than they might be to someone with an obvious impairment. "We think it's heroic when a person with one leg climbs a mountain. But when a dyslexic works 70 hours a week to do a 40-hour-a-week job," co-workers think he's inefficient, Ms. Brown says.   7

If a learning disability starts to interfere with your job, Ms. Latham recommends acting promptly. "Don't allow a period of poor performance," she says and advises explaining your disability with confidence, providing documentation and requesting the accommodations you need. Most accommodations, such as providing written instructions, cost employers little or nothing.   8

The best solution is to find a job where a learning disability doesn't hurt your performance—or even enhances it. Jaime Gomez, a Texas customer-service worker, says he hasn't told his current supervisors about his ADD, because "you don't know what kind of reaction you'll get." But his position is such a good fit that it doesn't matter. After several job changes, he found a post that requires only a few hours a day of desk work, with the rest spent traveling to see an ever-changing list of regional customers. He loves the work, he says.   9

RESPONDING TO READING

Review the answers you gave to the Preparing to Read questions for this article. Did any of your transition experiences seem similar to those that learning disabled people have in moving from school to work? How did Shellenbarger's article affect your opinion or understanding of these issues?

CONSIDERING CONTENT

1. Why are more young adults today entering the workplace with a history of receiving special treatment for learning disabilities?
2. What is "an undue sense of entitlement" (para. 4)? Give an example of how a person with learning disabilities might show an undue sense of entitlement.

3. Learning disabilities usually can't be outwardly seen. What effect does this have on how others react to students and workers with learning disabilities?
4. Shellenbarger writes that Jaime Gomez's job is a "good fit" for his condition. What makes it a good fit?
5. What advice does Shellenbarger give to workers with learning disabilities?

CONSIDERING METHOD

1. Look at the first part of the first sentence in each paragraph (after the introduction). Try to point out how this phrase or clause helps the reader see how the ideas are linked to the content of the preceding paragraph.
2. Notice the use of statistics in paragraphs 5 and 6. Did you find these statistics to be good support for the main point of the essay? How deeply did you think about these statistics—for example, can you recall the main point of some of them without looking back at the article?
3. The introduction and conclusion of this article use a similar strategy. What is it? What other strategy could be used for opening and closing this essay?

WRITING STEP BY STEP: THE PERSON-JOB FIT

Vocational psychologists focus on the *P-E fit*—person-environment fit, or the match between a person and his or her work environment. This match is the key to job satisfaction, performance, and stability. Jaime Gomez, the last example in Shellenbarger's article, found a good P-E fit in his customer service work. The job was ideal for a person with attention deficit disorder. In your Step by Step essay, you will be considering a personal characteristic and how it affects work. Focus on one personal quality that is difficult to change and think about how it might be a problem in some work environments. For instance, Shellenbarger tells of John Brennan's failure in two training programs due to his ADD. If possible, interview a boss or hiring staff about what kind of employee they find problematic at their workplace. To get your thinking started, here are some personality qualities that could affect someone's work:

introversion	idealism	naiveté
extroversion	negativity	bluntness
being a night owl	openness	paranoia
sense of humor	curiosity	timidity
independence	perfectionism	rebelliousness
dependence	dreaminess	

Choose one of these, or another enduring characteristic, and write an essay about how it could affect a person's job satisfaction or performance.

A. Begin your essay, as Shellenbarger does, with a paragraph giving an example of a person with the quality you chose and his or her work experiences. You can use yourself, someone you know, a composite of several people, or a made-up person for this example. The goal is to make your reader start thinking about the personal quality and how it operates in a job setting.

B. Write one or two paragraphs about how a job setting might provide a "rude awakening" (para. 2) to people with the personal quality you chose. Explain what it is about certain work, bosses, or activities that would be uncomfortable for such people. If relevant, tell how the rude awakening might come from a contrast between school and work settings, as Shellenbarger does.

C. Discuss how co-workers perceive someone with this quality. Give an example from everyday life on the job to illustrate your point.

D. Write a paragraph about how common or rare the quality is in the population of workers. (You may need to do some research to acquire this information.) If you can't find the official data, estimate how many times you have run across workers with this quality and ask your friends how often they have seen such workers.

E. Write a paragraph giving advice to a person with this quality. Shellenbarger suggests providing employers with information about the characteristic and says that the best solution is finding a job where the quality doesn't hurt you, or even helps you. Decide what the best course of action is for someone with the characteristic you are discussing.

F. Close with a paragraph giving an example of someone who successfully implemented the advice you gave in step E.

OTHER WRITING IDEAS

1. USING THE INTERNET. Look up the content of the 1990 Americans With Disabilities Act. Investigate what effects this law has had in the past 20 years. Write an essay explaining these effects.

2. Why is there rapid growth in the diagnoses of learning disabilities? In an essay focusing on causes, explore two or three separate reasons for the rising number.

3. COLLABORATIVE WRITING. Think about a big transition you have experienced: from school to work, a change of major in college, a move to a different city or country, or a transfer from one school or job to another. Get together with a small group of classmates or friends to make a list of

such changes and exchange personal stories about them. Then write your individual essay focusing on the causes for the transition, the effects of the transition, or the chain of cause and effect that occurred. These patterns are described near the beginning of this chapter under "Patterns of Cause and Effect."

4. WRITING ABOUT READING. What are your feelings about job accommodations for people with learning disabilities? For instance, when is it the employer's responsibility to accommodate the disability, and when is it the employee's responsibility to adapt to a job or leave it? Did Shellenbarger's article make you change your previous attitude? If so, how did it persuade you?

GAINING WORD POWER

Look at this sentence from Sue Shellenbarger's article:

In the past, many learning disabilities such as ADD, dyslexia, mild autistic conditions, memory disorders, and other problems went undiagnosed.

Why did the writer use the spelling *past* instead of the same-sounding *passed*? Words like *past* and *passed*, which are pronounced the same but have different meanings and different spellings, are called **homophones.** There are a lot of these sound-alike words in English, as well as many that sound almost alike, and they cause problems for some writers. You can't just learn how to spell these words; you have to match the spelling with the meaning. And your computer's spell-checker won't help you choose the right one. Keeping a list of the ones that give you trouble will increase your awareness and save you time when you edit.

Each of the following words from Shellenbarger's essay has a common homophone (or near-homophone). Identify the homophone, and then write sentences that show the differences in meaning.

1. then (*para. 1*)
2. are (*para. 2*)
3. quite (*para. 3*)
4. very (*para. 3*)
5. know (*para. 4*)
6. undue (*para. 4*)
7. they're (*para. 4*)
8. your (*para. 4*)
9. cite (*para. 5*)
10. past (*para. 6*)
11. seen (*para. 7*)
12. poor (*para. 8*)
13. need (*para. 8*)
14. hours (*para. 9*)

EDITING SKILLS: USING COMMAS AFTER INTRODUCTORY CLAUSES AND PHRASES

Writers put a comma after a word or group of words that comes in front of the main part of the sentence. That main part is called the **independent clause** because it can stand alone as a sentence. Look at these examples from Shellenbarger's column (italics added):

> *While the 1990 Americans With Disabilities Act entitles some workers with disabilities to job accommodations such as a quieter workspace,* it doesn't require employers to offer the same broad services schools must provide learning-disabled pupils under federal law.

> *If a learning disability starts to interfere with your job,* Ms. Latham recommends acting promptly.

The italicized groups of words that come before the commas are called **dependent elements:** They cannot stand alone as sentences. If someone only said one of these in conversation, you would find yourself waiting for the rest of the statement to finish the thought.

Writers also put commas before and after dependent elements when they come in the middle of an independent sentence. Here are some examples from Shellenbarger's essay (italics added):

> Most accommodations, *such as providing written instructions,* cost employers little or nothing.

> Jaime Gomez, *a Texas customer-service worker,* says he hasn't told his current supervisors about his ADD.

These dependent elements are called **interrupters:** They break up the flow of the sentence, which can be understood as a whole statement without them.

EXERCISE

Copy the following sentences, putting in commas where needed.

1. The rabbit nevertheless does shed fur.
2. Like most people Ralph does not know the name of his congressional representative.
3. Speaking of travel would you like to go to Seattle next week?
4. Jazz some people believe is America's greatest contribution to the arts.
5. The result as we have seen is not a pretty one.
6. That patient said the nurse is acting strangely.

Check the essay you have just written to be sure you have used commas to separate dependent elements from the rest of the sentence.

🌐 WEB SITES

http://online.wsj.com/article/work_and_family.html
You can read a recent "Work and Family" column by Sue Shellenbarger at this site.

http://wfnetwork.bc.edu
The Alfred P. Sloan Work and Family Research Network, from Boston College, is an online source of information about work and family. The site offers teaching resources, information from leading scholars in the field, news about public policy, easy-to-read summary sheets, and work-family topic pages.

STUDENT ESSAY ANALYZING CAUSES

Almost a Winner

Brian L. Carter

Brian Carter was raised in Portland, Oregon. After high school, he worked at casinos in Reno, Nevada, where he became interested in statistics and human folly, leading him to a psychology major. He wrote this essay when he returned to community college.

One of my first jobs, after turning twenty-one, was carrying slot-machine change for customers in a major casino in Reno. I wore a thick canvas apron loaded with about ten pounds of rolled quarters, nickels, and dimes. My simple task was to seek out slot customers in need of coins, and plenty were. On some shifts I never stopped moving. It was a physically demanding job, but mentally it was a snooze. So I amused myself by observing the behavior of the slot players. I decided that most were irrational at best, and insane at worst. What rational person purchases $20 worth of nickels to play a slot machine that has a maximum jackpot of $7.50? Why would someone play a machine and refuse to leave, even to go to the bathroom? Something was going on here. In no other human activity do people act like this. What is it about slot machines that gives them the power to produce such potentially destructive effects? 1

The question was answered when I took a basic psychology class. I learned about B. F. Skinner, a psychologist who conducted experiments on the behavior of animals and humans. In a series of famous experiments, he showed that pigeons could quickly learn to peck a bar to get a pellet of food for each peck. If it took three bar pecks to produce a food pellet, the pigeons would keep pressing even faster. When rewards (like food) come at a constant rate, such as every three or five responses (pecks), this is called a fixed schedule. Skinner then made the reward occur on a variable, random schedule: a food pellet might drop on the 17th peck or the 10th peck, or even twice in a row. This produced even more energetic bar pecking compared to fixed schedules. Skinner also used a random schedule and then stopped dropping food pellets altogether, just to see how long the pigeons would continue to bar peck. He was astonished to see them peck for hours with no reward. Then, when it seemed like the pigeons were going to give up, dropping just one food pellet would cause them to begin bar pecking again, for hours. 2

I realized slot machines operated on much the same principle. Their rewards were certainly random, one could go several plays without winning 3 anything, but an occasional reward would cause the player to keep going long into the night. Now, the behavior of slot players made sense to me. I began to see them as trapped pigeons in one of Skinner's laboratory experiments, conditioned to think they would receive another reward soon if they just kept playing.

But things were to get worse for these slot pigeons. The introduction   4 of the computerized slot machine, which directly controlled the outcome of every spin of the wheels, was about to go beyond the work of Skinner. By law, a slot machine is only required to show, accurately, which combination of wheel symbols pays which amounts—for example, three cherries in a row pays $3, or four Cadillacs in a row pays $500. There is no law that says slot machines must display how likely it is for each winning row of symbols to show up. The odds are the ratio of no-pay tries to payoff tries, and these are heavily in favor of the casino.

Yet, the computer slot-machine companies introduced a scheme that   5 would hook slot players more than ever before. All slot reel combinations either pay off or don't pay off. But the slot manufacturers came up with the idea to include far more "near misses" in their nonpay combinations. In this setup a slot player would see two Cadillacs on the pay line but a third Cadillac just missing the line. Because slot machines display three lines on each try, the tempting third Cadillac would appear just above or just below the actual line, and these near misses would occur more often than they would by chance. The payouts of the machine would be the same mathematically as before. A near miss pays as much as a wide miss—that is, nothing. But this rigged system gave the illusion that the slot player was always getting close to the jackpot. Not only wins, but near-wins also acted as random rewards. Put this little trick on top of the psychological influences already operating on the slot player, and you can see why the casinos should be offering free diapers to slot players.

Luckily for the slot players, the Nevada Gaming Control Board   6 banned this practice. The board ruled that slot machine reels *must* operate at random and cannot be fixed to show a higher than random rate of near misses. This ruling reinstated the status quo and returned slot players to mere pigeons, pumping money into a device that will surely bankrupt them if they play it long enough. The casinos didn't protest the gaming board's ruling. They still have the most powerful means of getting money from their customers: the psychology of reinforcement scheduling.

CONSIDERING CONTENT AND METHOD

1. Does the introduction encourage you to read on? If so, what caught your interest?
2. What is the difference between a fixed and a variable schedule of rewards? Name something in your life that has a fixed schedule of rewards, and something that has a variable schedule. Does the difference make you behave differently in these settings?
3. What causes slots players to keep playing even though they usually lose?
4. What effect did computerization have on the sequencing of slot machine symbols? Why was computerization necessary for this effect?
5. Explain the effect of near misses on slot machine players. Have you noticed any similar effects of near misses in other areas of life?

CHAPTER 10

Strategies for Influencing Others:
Argument and *Persuasion*

IMAGES AND IDEAS

Source: www.advertisingarchive.co.uk

For Discussion and Writing

What point does this poster make? Does it make its point by appealing to your reasoning or to your emotions? Create your own parody of a well-known advertisement. A parody imitates a serious work but exaggerates or adds details that poke fun at the original. Write a paragraph or two explaining what advertisement you are parodying, what changes you plan to make, and what point your parody makes.

You already know when to use persuasion: when you hope to get your readers to agree with you and maybe, as a result, to take some kind of action—like giving you a refund or picketing city hall. And on essay tests and in classroom assignments you are often asked to take a stand or support a conclusion.

All the writing strategies that you studied in previous chapters can be used to persuade your readers or to argue a point. You can use comparison/contrast to demonstrate the superiority of whole wheat over white bread, or cause-effect analysis to convince your readers that rap music reinforces violent attitudes toward women, or definition to show that computer nerds are more interesting than most people think. In this chapter, you will use all the strategies for organizing your thoughts and ideas as you learn how to influence readers' opinions about controversial or unfamiliar issues.

THE POINT OF ARGUMENT AND PERSUASION

Your purpose in this type of writing is to encourage the readers to accept your point of view, solution, plan, or complaint as their own. Traditionally, the word **persuasion** refers to attempts to sway the readers' emotions, while the word **argument** refers to tactics that address the readers' logic. Most convincing writing today mixes the two types of appeal. A personal testimony from a paraplegic accident victim pleading with readers to use their seat belts persuades through emotional identification. A list of statistics concerning injury rates before and after seat belt laws went into effect argues the point through rationality. A combination of the two tactics would probably be quite effective. In everyday language, *persuasion* means influence over the audience, whether emotional or rational.

THE PRINCIPLES OF ARGUMENT AND PERSUASION

Presenting a conventional persuasive essay involves five tasks:

1. State the **issue** your essay will address, and put it in a context: Why is it controversial or problematic? Why do people care about it? Why do people disagree about it?
2. State your main point or thesis. What point of view, solution, or stance do you wish the readers to adopt? This is your **claim.**
3. Provide well-developed **evidence** on your own side of the issue. You can develop your point through facts, statistics, examples, expert testimony, and logical reasoning (cause and effect, analogy), just to name a few strategies. This is the longest part of a conventional argument, and each piece of evidence will probably take a paragraph or more to develop.
4. Respond to opposing viewpoints. This is called the **refutation** section. Especially when arguments against your own are widely known, you need to acknowledge them and counter them, or your essay will have obvious holes in it. You might minimize their importance, demonstrate that they are not logical or factual, or offer alternative ways of thinking about them.

5. Close by reminding your reader of your main point and the strength of your evidence. Many persuasive essays include a call to action, encouraging readers to do something in support of your cause.

Writers often alter this conventional plan, especially tasks 3 and 4. There are several typical arrangements you can use to fit your topic, audience, purpose, and the nature of your evidence.

The Counterargument

You can anticipate what people on the other side of the issue would say and organize your argument as a point-by-point refutation. This approach works well for tackling controversial topics and for clearing up common misconceptions. In this chapter, for example, "The Case for Reality TV" cites various criticisms of reality television and then responds to them.

The Pro and Con Argument

Another way to present an argument is to look at the pros and cons of an issue. These may also be called advantages and disadvantages or strengths and weaknesses. This approach is commonly used when you are trying to make a difficult decision or settle a dispute amicably.

The Problem–Solution Argument

You can use this approach when you want to argue directly for a change in a policy or system. You need to identify the problem, demonstrate that it's relevant or serious, explain why current methods aren't working, propose a solution, and show how it will work. Sometimes you can merely call people's attention to a problem without offering a solution, but most of the time you will want to recommend a course of action to reduce or eliminate the problem. In this chapter, "Hot or Not: Reality TV Can Be Harmful to Women" presents a serious indictment of shows like *Are You Hot?* and concludes by calling for parents to "be assertive and prohibit their daughters from watching" such programs.

THE ELEMENTS OF GOOD ARGUMENT

Claims, evidence, and refutation are the basic building blocks of argument. You must understand them in order to write persuasively and effectively.

Claims

The "engine" that propels any argument is its claim. Claims fall into three categories:

1. *Claims of fact* assert that something is true: "Women currently do not receive equal pay for equal work."

2. *Claims of value* support or deny the worth or merit of something: "Getting a college education is more important than playing sports."
3. *Claims of policy* state that certain conditions, courses of action, or practices should be adopted: "A six-month maternity leave policy ought to be required by law."

For any argument to be effective, it must begin with a claim that's significant, reasonable, and supportable by evidence.

Evidence

Some of the most frequently used kinds of evidence are these:

- *Personal observation or experience*: "I came the closest to achieving a decent fit between income and expenses only when I worked seven days a week." This is the least widely accepted form of evidence because it comes from a narrow band of experience and may not be representative. But it can be very persuasive in communicating the human significance of an issue.
- *Facts*: "Rents usually have to be less than 30 percent of one's income to be considered 'affordable.'" Facts are noncontroversial pieces of information that can be confirmed through observation or by generally accepted sources; they are persuasive to the extent that they relate to the statement they support.
- *Relevant examples*: "One waitress shares a room in a boarding house for $250 a week; another lives with her mother; the night cook pays $170 a week for a one-person trailer; the hostess lives in a van parked behind a shopping center at night." Examples are most persuasive when they are objective and clearly relevant.
- *Testimony*: "Maggie Spade of the Economic Policy Institute explains that the low-income housing crisis exists partly because it is not reflected in the official poverty rate, which is based on the cost of food, not shelter." Testimony should come from sources that the readers will accept as credible; it carries its greatest weight when the meaning of the facts or data is not self-evident and some judgment or interpretation is required to reach a conclusion.
- *Data*: "Almost 60 percent of poor renters, amounting to a total of 4.4 million households, spend more than half of their income on shelter." This is probably the most readily accepted form of evidence because of its apparent objectivity and scope.

To be persuasive, all evidence in support of a claim must meet certain standards:

1. It must be reasonably up to date.
2. It must be sufficient in scope.
3. It must be relevant to the claim.

Thus, you wouldn't use 1997 unemployment data in support of a 2010 policy decision (recentness). Neither would you rely on unemployment data from only one month to formulate a long-term unemployment policy (scope). Nor would you use employment data from Canada to comment on the American unemployment picture, unless your argument involved an overall comparison of the two countries' economies (relevance).

Refutation

Arguments always assume that other points of view are possible; otherwise, there would be no reason to argue. You may feel so strongly about an issue that you want to attack those who disagree with you and ridicule their opinions, but that strategy can backfire, especially if you're trying to influence readers who are undecided. Your case will be strengthened if you treat opposing views with respect and understanding.

This acknowledgment of and response to the opposing views is called *refutation*. There is no best place in an argument to refute the opposition. Sometimes you will want to bring up opposing arguments early and deal with them right away. Another approach is to anticipate objections as you develop your own case point by point. Wherever you decide to include your refutation, your goal is to point out problems with the opponents' reasoning and evidence. You can refute opposing arguments by showing that they are unsound, unfair, or flawed in their logic. Frequently, you will present contrasting evidence to reveal the weakness of your opponents' views and to reinforce your own position.

When an opposing argument is so compelling that it cannot be easily countered, you should concede its strength. This approach will establish that you are knowledgeable and fair-minded. You can sometimes accept the opponents' line of thought up to a certain point—but no further. Or you can show that their strong point addresses only *one* part of a complex problem.

A SAMPLE ANNOTATED ARGUMENT

The following essay about the controversy surrounding the HPV vaccine was written by a student at Eastern Illinois University. The writer makes a claim of policy: that the vaccine should be given to all recommended patients. She then presents the major objections to this policy and refutes the opposing arguments. The marginal notes identify key features and strategies in building an argument.

Misunderstood Medicine

••

Stephanie Pescitelli

Claims of fact | Last year, the Food and Drug Administration (FDA) approved a vaccine that is 100 percent effective in preventing a virus that will infect 6 million people in the United States this year. This virus is responsible for 70 percent of the cases of the second most deadly cancer in women; it is also directly related to six other types of cancer and associated with warty growths on the vocal cords of children. It may seem obvious that this medical

Claim of policy (thesis) | miracle should be given to all recommended patients to prevent the pain and cost of cancer and disease, but several sociological and psychological factors are blocking widespread administration in the United States. Currently, only the state of Texas has a plan to make this vaccine compulsory. Why is there resistance to receiving this vaccine's benefits?

Claim of fact | The virus is the human papillomavirus (HPV). The vaccine is Gardasil, which is administered in three doses and, according to the American Cancer Society (ACS), will prevent infection of four out of 100 sexually transmitted HPV strains. Two of these strains are responsible for 70 percent of all cervical cancer cases, and the other two cause 90 percent of | Evidence (data)

Claim of policy | genital warts. The vaccine is currently available to the public, but its health-preserving potential can be maximized only if immunization is made mandatory for girls ages 11–12, as recommended by the Advisory Committee on Immunization Practices. | Evidence (expert testimony)

First major objection | Gardasil, however, is different from most other vaccines: the virus it prevents is spread through sexual activity. Some parents of preteens argue that administering a vaccine intended to prevent a sexually transmitted disease (STD) will undermine their rights to discuss the sensitive issues of sex with their daughters at a later time. In an article in the *Washington Post*, the associate executive director of the Christian Medical and Dental Associations, Gene Rudd, argues for these parental rights: "There are those who would say, 'We can provide a better, healthier alternative than the vaccine, and that is to teach abstinence.'" Religious and family organizations have also claimed that eliminating fear of contracting this virus will encourage promiscuity in young women. In Texas, as an acknowledgment of these concerns, parents opposed to having their daughters receive the HPV vaccine for personal and religious reasons can opt out and make their children exempt.

Refutation of first objection

However, preserving a loved one's brief innocence is no excuse for failing to protect her from a potentially harmful virus, and possibly even life-threatening cancer. While remaining abstinent is the best way to avoid infection, the American Cancer Society reports that 7% of males and females become sexually active before age 13, 24% of females are active by age 15, 40% by age 16, and 70% by age 18. These statistics, combined with the fact that four out of five sexually active females will contract HPV during their lifetime, make clear why early administration is imperative. Furthermore, the ACS report states that there is no evidence that the vaccine encourages recipients to engage in sexual activity as a result of a lifted fear of STDs.

Evidence (data)

Evidence (expert opinion)

Second major objection

Other people argue that the HPV vaccine should not be required of sixth graders because it was only recently approved, and its long-term safety and efficiency have not been established. Parents of three girls in Texas have sued Governor Perry, claiming that he has overstepped his authority with his mandate. Their attorney, Kenneth Chaiken, is quoted in the *Austin Chronicle*, declaring that "The school-age girls of Texas are not guinea pigs who

Evidence (example)

may be subjected to medical procedures at the apparent whim of Texas' governor."

Refutation of second objection | While it is true that a vaccine intended to prevent one health problem should not introduce another, Gardasil's safety and efficiency *have* been tested and proven, according to the FDA and a panel of twenty-one scientists on a board for the ACS. The only issue in question is whether or not the vaccine will require booster shots down the road, and there is no way to tell how long it will take to determine this possibility. Waiting for the data will unnecessarily expose millions of people to HPV. | Concession

| Evidence (expert testimony)

Conclusion: summary of refutation | The health and well-being of American citizens should not be placed in the hands of those who rely on biased rumors and media hype. Rather, this and all other health policy decisions should be based on medical science and the judgment of health professionals. *The Journal of Family Practice* projects that if the rest of the United States followed Texas's suit, 200,000 cases of HPV infection could be prevented, as well as 3300 cases of cervical cancer. Failure to implement this vaccine will do an injustice to both current and future victims of cervical cancer across this nation. How can we deny our daughters, sisters, mothers, and ourselves the safety from such a fate? | Evidence (expert testimony data)

THE PITFALLS OF ARGUMENT AND PERSUASION

If you follow the preceding suggestions, you should be able to write a convincing essay. But there are some risks to be aware of in this kind of writing.

Taking on Too Much

Narrowing your topic is always a good idea, but it's especially important in argumentation. You won't be able to write a sensible essay on "What's Wrong with the American Economy." Select a more manageable problem, such as unemployment or unbridled greed. Even those problems are probably too broad to cover in a short essay. Always consider moving the issue closer to home. For example, if someone in your family has been unemployed, you are probably equipped to write about the psychological effects of unemployment on the individual. If you have found yourself in terrifying and unnecessary credit card debt, you can probably write persuasively about uncontrolled consumerism. In these cases, you have credibility to discuss the issue. Credibility is an important part of your appeal, and you will notice that each author in this chapter establishes the right to claim knowledge about his or her subject, either explicitly or implicitly.

Mistaking the Audience

The readers you most want to reach with a controversial essay are the ones in the middle—those who are undecided and might be swayed by your ideas. People with extreme opinions on either side are likely to be unmovable. Even with persuadable audiences, you must expect some resistance. Be sure your tone does not bolster this resistance by being insulting or condescending. The voice of sweet reason and a "we're in this together" attitude invite your readers to agree with you.

Logical Fallacies

Flaws in reasoning can undermine your cause and harm your credibility. Be sure that you are not guilty of these common logical fallacies:

1. **Overgeneralization.**   Recently, a national survey found that the number of unmarried women among highly educated people was much larger than among the less educated. Articles on the alarming shortage of men willing to marry educated females abounded, and solutions to the difficulty were proposed. Actually, most of the single, educated females had chosen their unmarried status. The problem was the false generalization that all unmarried women *wanted* husbands and were seeking them. The shortage of marriage-minded men was not proven.

2. **Either-or thinking.** Be sure that you don't present only two alternatives when more exist. For example, some writers in education want us to believe that either we set national standards for mathematical achievement, or our children will continue to fall behind other countries' children in math skills. The fallacy is that national standards are not the only route to high math achievement: smaller classes, better teaching conditions, early intervention policies, and parent involvement are just a few ideas left out of the either-or reasoning. (In fact, the existence of national standards is not correlated with math achievement internationally.)

3. **False analogy.** Analogy is a compelling form of argument, but you must take care that the two cases you compare are really similar. If you argue

that your college should imitate a successful general education program used at another university, you must be sure that the two institutions have similar students, faculty, goals, and organizational structures. Otherwise, adopting a plan that works for someone else could be disastrous. Recently, a U.S. congressman claimed that foreign dignitaries, while in our country, should say the Pledge of Allegiance because, similarly, we show respect at the Olympics when other countries' national anthems are played. The analogy falls apart when you consider what the Pledge of Allegiance actually *says*.

4. **Faulty claims about causation.** Remember that two things that occur closely in time or one after the other are not necessarily causally related. In our cities, ice cream sales and murder rates both increase in the summer; can we say that eating ice cream causes aggression? No, probably it's the heat that encourages both. We say "children who are hugged are more likely to be nice," and "children who are beaten are more likely to be unpleasant." But the causes and effects could be the other way around. Maybe nice children are hugged *because* they're nice, and unpleasant children get beaten *because* they're unpleasant.

WHAT TO LOOK FOR IN ARGUMENT AND PERSUASION

Here are some questions to ask yourself as you study the selections in this chapter.

1. What issue is being addressed? What stance or point of view am I being asked to adopt?
2. What claim or claims does the author make? What kind of claims are they? Are they significant and reasonable?
3. Does the author explain the issue clearly and completely? Are there any holes or gaps in the author's thinking?
4. What evidence does the author use to support the claims? Is this evidence sufficient, relevant, and up to date?
5. Does the writer refute possible objections? How effective is this refutation? Has the author ignored any important objections?
6. Is the conclusion satisfactory? Has the author persuaded me?

DEBATE: DO SAME-SEX COUPLES MAKE GOOD PARENTS?

The growing acceptance of homosexuals in traditional social roles—public office, marriage, adoption, religion, education, military service—remains problematic and unsettling for many Americans. Some politicians and religious leaders are especially concerned about homosexuals having children. They feel that same-sex households lack the appropriate gender role models, endorse unconventional sexuality as a valid option, and expose children to possible ridicule and rejection by their peers.

Yet, despite this opposition, families headed by gay men and lesbians now number in the tens of thousands, according to the Family Equality Council. The majority of homosexual parents are raising children from earlier heterosexual marriages. But for same-sex couples who want their own children, there are more resources than ever: Internet sites that offer information about sperm donors and surrogate mothers; children's books that feature same-sex parents; adoption agencies that accept gay men and lesbians as parents; and networks that provide social support and legal advice. Even some clergy members are indirectly blessing these families by baptizing their children.

The following articles touch on many of the issues in this debate, which is really part of the larger debate on the changing shape and redefinition of the American family.

PREPARING TO READ

Were you or was anyone you know raised by a same-sex couple? If so, how does that family situation affect relationships with peers? If you don't know anyone like this, how do you imagine you would feel if you found out that a friend's parents were homosexual? Do you think that knowledge would alter your feelings for your friend or his or her parents?

••

Two Mommies Is One Too Many

••

James C. Dobson

James Dobson is the founder and chairman of Focus on the Family, a Christian nonprofit organization that describes itself as "dedicated to nurturing and defending families worldwide." A licensed psychologist in California, Dobson has written a number of books that set forth his social and religious views, including Dare to

Discipline *(1982)*, Bringing Up Boys *(2003), and* Marriage Under Fire *(2004). The following article appeared in the December 18, 2006, issue of* Time *magazine.*

TERMS TO RECOGNIZE

social conservatives *(para. 1)*	those who believe in traditional values and institutions, and generally regard change as suspect
implicit *(para. 1)*	suggested, unspoken, understood
phenomenon *(para. 3)*	something that happens or exists in society and nature
emulate *(para. 3)*	copy, do something the way someone else does
intuitively *(para. 5)*	based on a feeling rather than knowledge or facts
purview *(para. 6)*	accepted range or scope of someone's job, role, or activity
legacy *(para. 7)*	result or carryover from a previous time or event

A number of social conservatives, myself included, have recently been   1
asked to respond to the news that Mary Cheney, the Vice President's daughter, is pregnant with a child she intends to raise with her lesbian partner. Implicit in this issue is an effort to get us to criticize the Bush Administration or the Cheney family. But the concern here has nothing to do with politics. It is about what kind of family environment is best for the health and development of children, and, by extension, the nation at large.

With all due respect to Cheney and her partner, Heather Poe, the   2
majority of more than 30 years of social-science evidence indicates that children do best on every measure of well-being when raised by their married mother and father. That is not to say Cheney and Poe will not love their child. But love alone is not enough to guarantee healthy growth and development. The two most loving women in the world cannot provide a daddy for a little boy—any more than the two most loving men can be complete role models for a little girl.

The voices that argue otherwise tell us more about our politically cor-   3
rect culture than they do about what children really need. The fact remains that gender matters—perhaps nowhere more than in regard to child rearing. The unique value of fathers has been explained by Dr. Kyle Pruett of Yale Medical School in his book *Fatherneed: Why Father Care Is as Essential as Mother Care for Your Child*. Pruett says dads are critically important simply because "fathers do not mother." *Psychology Today* explained in 1996 that "father-

hood turns out to be a complex and unique phenomenon with huge consequences for the emotional and intellectual growth of children." A father, as
a male parent, makes unique contributions to the task of parenting that a
mother cannot emulate, and vice versa.

According to educational psychologist Carol Gilligan, mothers tend   4
to stress sympathy, grace, and care to their children, while fathers accent
justice, fairness, and duty. Moms give a child a sense of hopefulness; dads
provide a sense of right and wrong and its consequences. Other researchers
have determined that boys are not born with an understanding of "male-
ness." They have to learn it, ideally from their fathers.

But set aside the scientific findings for a minute. Isn't there some-   5
thing in our hearts that tells us, intuitively, that children need a mother and
a father? Admittedly, that ideal is not always possible. Divorce, death,
abandonment and unwed pregnancy have resulted in an ever-growing
number of single-parent families in this culture. We admire the millions of
men and women who have risen to the challenge of parenting alone and
are meeting their difficult responsibilities with courage and determination.
Still, most of them, if asked, would say that raising children is a two-person
job best accomplished by a mother and father.

In raising these issues, Focus on the Family does not desire to harm   6
or insult women such as Cheney and Poe. Rather, our conviction is that
birth and adoption are the purview of married heterosexual couples.
Traditional marriage is God's design for the family and is rooted in biblical
truth. When that divine plan is implemented, children have the best opportunity to thrive. That's why public policy as it relates to families must be
based not solely on the desires of adults but rather on the needs of children
and what is best for society at large.

This is a lesson we should have learned from no-fault divorce.   7
Because adults wanted to dissolve difficult marriages with fewer strings
attached, reformers made it easier in the late 1960s to dissolve nuclear
families. Though there are exceptions, the legacy of no-fault divorce is
countless shattered lives within three generations, adversely affecting
children's behavior, academic performance, and mental and physical
health. No-fault divorce reflected our selfish determination to do what
was convenient for adults, and it has been, on balance, a disaster.

We should not enter into yet another untested and far-reaching   8
social experiment, this one driven by the desires of same-sex couples to
bear and raise children. The traditional family, supported by more than
5,000 years of human experience, is still the foundation on which the
well-being of future generations depends.

Mom's the Word

••

JEFF PEARLMAN

Jeff Pearlman is a staff correspondent for Newsday, *a daily newspaper that primarily serves Long Island and the New York City borough of Queens. Best known for his work on sports, Pearlman has written two successful books about baseball:* The Bad Guys Won, *an account of the 1986 New York Mets, and* Love Me, Hate Me *(2006), an unauthorized biography of Barry Bonds. The following article appeared in the April 10, 2005, edition of* Newsday.

TERMS TO RECOGNIZE

closer *(para. 3)*	a baseball pitcher brought in late in the game to protect a lead and close out the game
Grapefruit League *(para. 4)*	teams that train and play pre-season exhibition games in Florida
longevity *(para. 10)*	long life, staying power
stigma *(para. 13)*	mark of shame or disapproval
hapless *(para. 18)*	unlucky
frustrated *(paras. 24, 26)*	annoyed, impatient, discouraged
relented *(para. 25)*	gave in
brigade *(para. 37)*	a large group

SARASOTA, Fla.—Within the four walls of the major league club-house, the concept of homosexuality fits about as comfortably as a pair of mittens on a porcupine. For the most part, men who love men and women who love women are not gays or lesbians, but "queers" and "dykes." Trip over a mitt and you're a "faggot." As for ideas of civil unions and gay mar-riage—forget about it. "Baseball is very set in its ways," Cincinnati Reds out-fielder Jacob Cruz said. "Always has been." 1

Within these confines, there is a man who seems to hover above it all. 2
He is a 25-year-old right-handed relief pitcher with the Reds, a quiet Long Island kid with blazing brown eyes and a blazing 95-mph fastball. He is as open as he needs to be, not afraid to tell the truth about his family, but aware that its implications might not sit perfectly with the 40 or so other young men who surrounded him recently in the Reds' spring training club-house. "I'm a blue-state guy in a red-state sport," Joe Valentine said. "But that won't stop me from being proud of who I am."

Who is Joe Valentine? He is a 1997 graduate of Deer Park High 3
School. He is a former All-American at Jefferson Davis Community College
in Alabama. He is a happily married North Babylon resident who wants to
start a family. He is a potential future closer for the Reds.

One more thing. Consider the following dialogue, which took place 4
on a lazy spring training morning between a pitcher fighting to make the
club and a baseball writer wrapping up another run-of-the-mill Grapefruit
League interview.

"Joe, can I give your parents a call?" 5
"Sure." 6
"OK, what are their names?" 7
"Deb and Doreen." 8

That's right: Joe Valentine is the son of two gay women. He tells you 9
this without an iota of emphasis, almost as if he were explaining the
mechanics of a slider or giving directions to the nearest 7-Eleven. There is
no additional explanation, no awkward pause for effect. Nothing. "It's no
different than having a mother and father," he said. "These are the two
women who raised me, and they are wonderful people. It's just not a big
deal to me. Why should it be?"

In an enlightened world, it shouldn't. But major league baseball is 10
to enlightenment what Pauly Shore is to career longevity. It took until 1959
for every team to have at least one black player. There never has been a
female umpire. And in the history of the league, no active player has ever
come out of the closet to express his homosexuality.

"I've got nothing against those people," Washington Nationals relief 11
pitcher T.J. Tucker said recently. "But I don't get why anyone would want to be
like that." Moments after Tucker's comment, a Nationals front office employee
approached a reporter and asked him not to bring the subject of homosexuality into the clubhouse. "Makes the players uncomfortable," the employee said.

Years ago, then-Giants second baseman Jeff Kent was changing out 12
of his uniform when he glanced at the nearby reporters and cracked, "There
are no queers here, are there?" The comment barely raised an eyebrow.

Valentine is aware of the stigma. That is why his family asked that this 13
story not be published until Valentine secured a spot on the major league
roster. "We've almost never been treated badly," said Deb Valentine, Joe's
birth mother. "But we live in the real world, and you don't 100 percent
know how people will react." Here's the startling thing: Thus far in Joe
Valentine's life, few have reacted.

Born in Las Vegas on Christmas Eve 1979, Joe is the biological son of 14
Deb Valentine and a man she prefers not to discuss, a man Joe does not
know. Deb declined to discuss the circumstances of the pregnancy, but
when she delivered Joe at Sunrise Hospital, the person by her side was
Doreen Price, her life partner since they first met in a bowling alley in 1975.

At the time, homosexuality was an unacceptable lifestyle in approxi- 15
mately 99 percent of America. Las Vegas was the 1 percent. "Vegas was
Vegas," Deb said. "Open-minded. Accepting. Embracing. Doreen was my
coach in the hospital, and nobody there raised an eyebrow. Vegas was
10 times more liberal than New York is even today. Being gay just wasn't
a big deal."

The couple operated a hair salon in Las Vegas, and in 1982 moved 16
to North Babylon, where they opened Hair Studio 231, which lasted
four years. When Joe was just 16 months old, Doreen was throwing him
a baseball. At 2, he fielded his first grounder with his nose. "Blood all over,"
Doreen said. "But we wiped it off, and he was back looking for the baseball."

At age 5, Joe signed up for Little League, and by 8 he was one of the 17
best athletes around. His gift was a strong right arm. His Little League
coach for two seasons? Doreen, who had played competitive softball. "Joe
could always throw," she said. "I mean, he had a real powerful arm. And he
kept working and working to get better. I think we knew he was a special
kind of baseball player."

Remarkably—and against all hardball logic—Valentine rarely pitched. 18
He was a catcher whose greatest joy came from nailing a hapless runner
trying to swipe second. Young Joe loved everything about squatting behind
the plate. The power of calling a game. The dirt crumbling between his
fingers. The pop-pop-pop of rawhide meeting leather. The collisions at
home. "I wanted to be in the middle of the action," he said. "Not making
random appearances here and there."

By the time he arrived at Deer Park as a sophomore in 1994 (Joe 19
attended St. Anthony's in Huntington as a freshman), Valentine was one of
the better young ballplayers on Long Island. "He was exceptional," Deer
Park coach Carmine Argenziano said. "Even when we had pitchers who had
poor moves and couldn't hold anyone on, no one would run on Joe. He was
a weapon back there." In fact, Argenziano once said, "He used to throw it
back to our pitchers harder than they threw it to him. It was scary."

Meanwhile, Deb and Doreen attended every Deer Park game. People 20
in the stands assumed Deb was Joe's "mom" and Doreen his "aunt," and
none of the three would argue. "If it eases what people need to believe,"
Doreen said, "so be it."

Joe swears he never has been embarrassed by his family. It is all he   21
has ever known. But the unpredictability of facial expressions that greet
"These are my mothers" is, well, awkward. Making things easier, the two
women never held hands, kissed or hugged at the games. Partially to avoid
controversy, but also because it's not who they are. "We went to watch
baseball," Doreen said. "We're not trying to make statements."

By the end of his senior year, most of his teammates and their   22
parents knew Joe was the product of a gay relationship. Heck, the kids used
to hang out at Joe's house. "One day I heard a teacher talking about Joe,
and that he had two mothers," Argenziano said. "I was shocked, truly
shocked. But you know what? I also didn't care. Those two women did a
helluva job raising one fine man. A helluva job."

College recruiters began showing up during Valentine's senior season   23
in 1997. Not big time schools like Arizona State and Miami, but local colleges willing to overlook his so-so hitting ability.

After batting .370 as a senior and making his second All-County   24
team, Valentine played for the Bayside Yankees, a summer-league team that
has produced more than 20 major league players. During Valentine's first
summer with Bayside, coach Marc Cuseta often was frustrated by his
catcher's refusal to take the mound. "You know how high school kids are,"
Cuseta said. "They wanna be the star, bat third and be in the lineup every
day. Joe was no different."

But when it finally became clear to Valentine that his future as a   25
catcher was limited because of his hitting, he relented. In the summer of
1998, Bayside turned him into its closer, and after several weeks of just
throwing mid-90s fastballs and hoping they sailed over the plate, Valentine
picked up the slider that's now his major-league "out" pitch.

Valentine accepted a scholarship to Dowling College but grew   26
frustrated with the program and left during his first semester. Eventually,
Cuseta called an old pal, Keith Griffin, the baseball coach at Jefferson
Davis CC in Brewton, Ala., and told him about an under-the-radar pitcher
with an infinite upside.

Joe Valentine was moving to the heart of the Bible Belt. With his gay   27
parents. They expected the worst. When Deb and Doreen followed Joe
south and settled into an apartment in nearby Pensacola, Fla., they
envisioned one hostile face after another. This was Alabama, after all,
onetime home of church bombings and tree lynchings. Perhaps if they
played it cool, nobody would notice. But inevitably, someone would get the
picture, that Joe's "aunt" (wink-wink) wasn't his aunt. It didn't take long.

"I remember people finding out and thinking it was something to   28
joke about," Valentine said. "They'd say, 'Oh, so you must be gay, huh?'"

"What?" Valentine would reply.   29

"Well, you must be gay," one person said. "But how come you don't   30
act all foo-fooey? You're not elegant. You're just a regular guy."

"What the hell is 'foo-fooey?'" Valentine says now. "People can be so   31
incredibly narrow-minded. But I'm not someone who starts fights over this
stuff. I'm a patient guy."

Deb and Doreen attended every Jefferson Davis game that season,   32
becoming unofficial team mothers as their son compiled an 8-1 record and
was named to the NJCAA All-Region XXII team. They'd invite Joe's teammates out for lunch and dinner. Sometimes even cook. Gay? Straight? Most
of the players were just happy to be looked after.

"If you're a good boy, I don't care if you're from Mars," Griffin said.   33
"And Joe was as good a boy as I've ever had around. He's hardworking,
he's very competitive, and he's got a big heart. I'll tell you, very few seemed
to care that his parents were gay. They were wonderful people. And Joe—
he's a man's man."

Valentine's decision to attend Jefferson Davis was a good one. In   34
June 1999, he was selected by the Chicago White Sox in the 26th round of
the amateur draft.

Throughout his six-year, four-organization professional baseball   35
career, Joe Valentine rarely has volunteered information about his parents.
Again, it's not that he's embarrassed. But why risk starting trouble? Every
so often, however, when he's comfortable, Valentine lets his guard down.
Three years ago, while playing for the Double-A Birmingham Barons,
Valentine roomed with Gary Majewski, a right-handed pitcher from
Houston. One night they were watching TV, shooting the breeze. "I don't
remember how we got on the subject," said Majewski, now with the
Nationals. "He just sort of told me. I was like, 'Um, OK.' Joe is a cool dude."

And Valentine can play. After bouncing from the White Sox to the   36
Tigers to the White Sox to the A's to the Reds, he made his big league debut
with Cincinnati in 2003. He pitched in 24 games last season, going 2-3 with
four saves and a 5.22 ERA. He initially struggled in spring training this year
but made the Reds out of camp. Valentine pitched the eighth inning of a
6-1 victory over the Mets on Thursday, striking out two, and pitched a
scoreless seventh against Houston last night, retiring Craig Biggio, Jeff
Bagwell, and Morgan Ensberg on grounders.

Deb and Doreen, who are retired and live in North Port, Fla., plan on   37
seeing Joe pitch as often as possible. And when they show up in the family

area after games, surrounded by the brigade of wives and husbands and kids, their son will, as always, proudly greet them with a hug. They are his loved ones. His moms.

"I don't see myself as an activist for gay rights, although I will speak up if I need to," Valentine said. "I think people need to judge others for who they are. Not by any prejudiced ideas or thoughts. I'm a baseball player who was raised by two wonderful, loving mothers. How can anyone criticize that?"   38

RESPONDING TO READINGS

After reading these essays, have your opinions and feelings about same-sex parents changed in any way? Explain.

CONSIDERING CONTENT

1. What objections does James Dobson have to same-sex parenting?
2. Which of Dobson's views are refuted by the story of Joe Valentine's two moms?
3. What does Dobson mean when he refers to "our politically correct culture"? What point is he making with this reference?
4. What does Joe Valentine mean when he says "I'm a blue-state guy in a red-state sport"?
5. Why did Deb and Doreen not hold hands, kiss, or hug at the games they attended? Why does Valentine rarely volunteer information about his parents?
6. Dobson admits that a family that has both a mother and a father is an ideal that "is not always possible," and he says he admires the millions of single parents in the country (para. 5). Why, then, does he object to same-sex households that have two parents?

CONSIDERING METHOD

1. What support does Dobson offer for his claim that "children do best on every measure of well-being when raised by their married mother and father"?
2. What authorities does Dobson cite to bolster his argument? How effective are these citations?
3. What is "no-fault divorce" and what lesson does Dobson claim Americans should have learned from it? What do you think about comparing no-fault divorce to gay parenthood?
4. Why does Pearlman include quotations from Valentine's coaches (paras. 22, 33)? What point is Pearlman trying to make by quoting these opinions?

5. Why did Pearlman use the title "Mom's the Word"? What common expression does it echo? What's the relevance to the article?

6. Pearlman's argument consists of an extensive example. Dobson's argument consists of a series of claims with supporting details. Were these good choices given the authors' goals? Would the reverse strategy work as well for either author?

7. Reread the final paragraph in Dobson's article? How effective was it for you as a reader? Would it be convincing to someone opposing Dobson's overall point of view?

8. Why does Pearlman close with a quotation from Joe Valentine? Is it effective? How do you think Dobson would respond to Valentine's final question?

WRITING STEP BY STEP: TAKING SIDES ON SAME-SEX PARENTING

Write an essay in which you argue either for or against same-sex parenting.

A. Before you start writing, make lists of reasons why you support and why you oppose homosexuals having children. Next to each reason, try to write a brief response or a counterargument. Decide the position you would like to argue.

B. Identify at least three major reasons to support your choice. These reasons will be your claims.

C. Start your essay by stating your position and giving a brief overview of your main claims.

D. Take up each of your claims one by one. Explain each reason in its own separate paragraph and provide evidence to demonstrate the validity of that reason. If you want, you can use quotations from the essays you have just read, but be sure to give credit to the authors you are quoting.

E. Be sure to consider any objections to your claims that readers might have. Consult the notes you made for step A. If you're not sure what these objections would be, ask classmates, friends, family members, or instructors for their ideas. You might also find additional information on Internet sites such as those listed at the end of this chapter. Refute these objections by minimizing their importance, questioning their factuality, providing a contrary example, or offering a different point of view. You can include your refutations as part of the argument for each claim, or you can put them in a separate paragraph.

F. Close by summarizing your main ideas. Consider using a clincher sentence to drive home your major claim, as Dobson and Pearlman do.

OTHER WRITING IDEAS

1. COLLABORATIVE WRITING. Write the paper outlined in the Step by Step assignment, but argue for or against one of the following issues. Feel free to narrow these topics further if you find them too general.

   a. It should (should not) be harder than it is now to get a divorce.

   b. Having a working mother does (does not) harm a child's welfare.

   c. Free speech should (should not) be restricted on the Internet.

   d. Giving clean needles to intravenous drug users is (is not) the best way to decrease the spread of AIDS in America.

   e. Date rape is (is not) a serious problem on college campuses.

   f. The selling of human organs for transplant should (should not) be legalized.

   g. People should (should not) give money to panhandlers.

   h. Over-the-counter drugs should (should not) be regulated more closely.

   If these topics don't appeal to you, choose a controversial issue that you feel strongly about. Before you begin writing, get together with a group of classmates to brainstorm arguments for and against the topic you have chosen. If possible, interview people whose experience might provide firsthand insight into the topic.

2. USING THE INTERNET. Find out about same-sex marriage, civil unions, family partnerships, and gay adoptions in other countries. You can find information at **www.religioustolerance.org/hom_mary.htm**. Write a report that would be suitable for a class in sociology or cultural studies, summarizing your research.

3. WRITING ABOUT READINGS. Analyze the strategy that each author uses to present his ideas about same-sex parents. Which approach do you think is more effective? Be sure to cite specific details in explaining your conclusions. You can use your thoughts about question 6 in Considering Method as a starting point.

GAINING WORD POWER

The prefix *hetero-* means "other, opposite, or different," and the prefix *homo-* means "same." So *heterosexual* means "attracted to people of the opposite sex," and *homosexual* means "attracted to people of the same sex." Do you know other words that use these same prefixes? What is the difference between a heterogeneous society and a homogeneous one? What is a homonym and how is it different from a heteronym? Would you prefer a heterochromatic painting or a homochromatic one? Use a dictionary to help you answer these questions.

EDITING SKILLS: SUBJECT-VERB AGREEMENT

Look at the verbs in the following sentences:

The fact <u>remains</u> that gender <u>matters</u>.

Joe <u>swears</u> he has never been embarrassed by his family.

He <u>tells</u> you this without an iota of emphasis.

Fatherhood <u>turns</u> out to be a complex and unique phenomenon.

The verbs that we have underlined are in the present tense; they express actions that are happening at the present time or that happen all the time. We also use the present tense to state facts or general truths. You will notice that the verbs end in *s*. That's because the subject of each verb is singular (fact, gender, Joe, he, fatherhood). When the subject of a present-tense verb is *he, she,* or *it*—or a noun that could be replaced by *he, she,* or *it*—we put an *s* on the end of the verb.

This ending is an exception. Present-tense verbs with other subjects do not require the *s* ending:

Moms <u>give</u> a child a sense of hopefulness; dads <u>provide</u> a sense of right and wrong and its consequences.

We <u>admire</u> the millions of men and women who have risen to the challenge of parenting alone.

I <u>think</u> people need to judge others for who they are.

Because we don't always put an ending on a present-tense verb, some people forget to add it. That causes an error in subject-verb agreement. And sometimes it is difficult to tell what the subject of a verb really is, as in this sentence:

Gay parenting, like no-fault divorce and single mothers, <u>remains</u> unacceptable in come circles.

The subject of the verb <u>remains</u> is <u>parenting</u>, but the words in between might lead a writer to think that <u>no-fault divorce and single mothers</u> are the subjects—and to mistakenly leave the *s* ending off. Phrases that intervene between the subject and the main verb often mislead writers about what the verb needs to agree with. Now take a look at this example:

Opponents of gay marriage often <u>argue</u> that same-sex households don't provide good role models for children.

Can you figure out why there is no *s* on the verb <u>argue</u>? That's because the subject is <u>opponents</u>, a word that does not mean *he, she,* or *it*. When trying to figure out the subject-verb agreement, you just have to forget about the words that come between <u>opponents</u> and <u>argue</u>.

EXERCISE

In each of the following sentences, underline the subject and then circle the verb that agrees with it. Example:

A <u>verb</u> in the present tense take/(takes) an s ending when its subject is *he, she,* or *it*—or a noun that means *he, she,* or *it.*

1. An anthropologist study/studies buildings, tools, and other artifacts of ancient cultures.
2. Anthropologists always look/looks for signs of social change.
3. A box of fruit arrive/arrives at the house every month.
4. An adult student who has children find/finds little time for partying.
5. Low scores on the Scholastic Aptitude Test discourage/discourages students from applying to some colleges.
6. It give/gives me great pleasure to introduce tonight's speaker.
7. The first baseman, along with most of his teammates, refuse/refuses to sign autographs after the game.
8. Bonsai trees require/requires careful pruning.
9. Many movies of the past year contain/contains scenes of violence.

Now check over the essay you have just written. Look at all the verbs, especially those in the present tense. Did you use the *s* ending on the appropriate verbs? Edit your writing carefully for subject-verb agreement.

☙ WEB SITES

www.focusonthefamily.org
More details about James Dobson's views and writings can be found on the Focus on the Family Web site.

www.colage.org/resources/research.html
The organization Children of Lesbians and Gays Everywhere (COLAGE) presents facts, figures, and research findings on children with gay parents.

DEBATE: HOW REAL IS REALITY TV?

Reality TV, the lineup of unscripted or semi-scripted shows starring nonprofessional actors, has developed strong groups of both supporters and detractors as it has grown over the years since 2000. Fans call it an entertaining, unpredictable change from standard television drama, while foes revile the medium for being silly, insulting to both audiences and participants, and even mentally unhealthy.

The following articles touch on issues relevant to the relationship between reality and television. These are also part of a larger debate about how our popular culture shapes our lives—and vice versa.

PREPARING TO READ

Are you, or is someone you know, a reality-TV addict? Have you ever been surprised by an acquaintance's strong opinions about this form of entertainment? Why do you think people have such intense points of view on the subject? Have you seen people's lives affected by their devotion to certain television programs or formats?

••

Reality Television: Issues and Controversies

•••••••••••••••••••••••••••••••••••••••

Facts on File

Facts on File is a researchers' database that includes "Facts on File Issues and Controversies," an online resource that explores topics in today's politics, business, culture, education, and society. Each topic is presented with key facts, arguments, history, and the current context. The articles are written by Facts on File's expert authors and editors. The database includes over 900 in-depth articles providing pro and con thinking on controversial subjects. Find it at http://factsonfile .infobasepublishing.com.

TERMS TO RECOGNIZE

purport (*para. 1*)	claim
spawned (*para. 2*)	gave birth to
adhering to (*para. 4*)	following

resonant (*para. 4*)   meaningful
voyeurism (*para. 5*)   obsessive observation of sensational events
formulaic (*para. 7*)   following an established pattern
counterparts (*para. 7*)   corresponding persons or things

"Reality television" is a broad term, covering various television pro-   1
grams that purport to be more "true to life" than purely fictional dramas
and situation comedies. The typical reality show features ordinary people
(i.e., non-actors) who are placed in apparently unscripted—and therefore
unpredictable—situations. The unique format of reality television lends it a
spontaneous quality that has attracted huge audiences, and considerable
controversy, around the world.

In the U.S., the popularity of reality television has surged dramatically   2
since 2000, when the landmark show *Survivor* debuted on CBS. *Survivor*,
which pits groups of contestants from different backgrounds against
each other in seemingly hostile wilderness environments, popularized a
competitive format for reality shows and spawned numerous imitators.
Other influential reality shows soon followed, including *American Idol*
(Fox, 2002–present), a hugely popular singing contest, and *The Apprentice*
(NBC, 2004–present), a business-themed competition.

Not all popular reality shows have been based on the competitive   3
format, however. Some have involved filming the everyday lives of regular
people or celebrities, while others have focused on themes such as blind
dating, makeovers, and "hidden camera" pranks. Although the different
types of reality shows might appear distinct from each other on the surface,
they often share common production techniques, and they can attract
acclaim or criticism for very similar reasons.

Advocates of reality television shows argue they are generally more   4
representative of "real life" than scripted television programs, which are
often criticized for adhering to predictable dramatic formulas. In essence,
fans maintain that reality television is more relevant and resonant to them
than fictional television. They also praise competitive reality shows, such as
American Idol and *The Amazing Race* (CBS, 2001–present), for showcasing the
talents of previously "undiscovered" contestants and pushing them to
perform at their best.

Critics of reality television, on the other hand, argue that it often   5
treats its subjects cruelly. For instance, failed *American Idol* contestants are
sometimes subjected to ridicule from the judges that damages their self-
esteem, detractors assert, while competitors on *Survivor* are often placed
in uncomfortable or potentially hazardous situations. Critics have also

attacked other reality shows, such as MTV's *The Real World* (1992–present) and CBS's *Big Brother* (2000–present), for allegedly exposing their subjects to emotional strain and encouraging destructive behaviors such as binge drinking. At their very worst, reality shows exploit their subjects, encourage voyeurism, and amount to a "dumbing down" of television and American culture as a whole, critics assert.

In light of such concerns, a heated debate has arisen over the perceived merits, flaws, and cultural impact of reality television. Television experts, sociologists, and other interested observers have raised a series of key questions on the issue: Does reality television too often exploit its subjects, or does it actually help them to achieve recognition and success? Is it a bold alternative to fictional entertainment, or is it actually less satisfying than scripted drama and comedy? And how "real," exactly, is reality television? Is it genuinely "true to life," or is it more artificial and engineered than it appears to be?

Advocates of reality television describe it as a refreshing change of pace from scripted (and often formulaic) entertainment. They describe the competitive format of many reality shows as energetic and exciting, and credit programs such as *American Idol* with allowing "everyday" people to demonstrate their talents and potentially find fame and success. There is nothing inherently cruel about reality television, supporters assert; reality shows simply reflect the highs and lows of "real" life more honestly than their fictional counterparts. In short, reality shows are stimulating, fun, and inoffensive, advocates say.

Critics of reality television, on the other hand, argue that it exploits "everyday" people who are typically unprepared for being thrust into the media spotlight. Reality show contestants are often mocked and exposed to mental or physical harm, and watching their suffering amounts to voyeurism, detractors contend. They further assert that reality shows are artificially engineered and therefore dishonest in their presentation of "real" events. Ultimately, scripted television programs are more socially relevant and intelligent—and far less manipulative—than reality shows, critics conclude.

The Case for Reality TV: What the Snobs Don't Understand

M ICHAEL H IRSCHORN

Following a successful period as editor of the award-winning entertainment news site Inside.com, Michael Hirschorn became Executive Vice President for Original Programming and Production for the television channel VH1 in 2001. He is also a prolific contributing editor for the magazine Atlantic Monthly. *Hirschorn writes columns giving his point of view on media topics. He has recently written about agents of world chaos, the decline of* Time *and* Newsweek *magazines, and the cult of quirkiness.*

TERMS TO RECOGNIZE

reignite (*para. 1*)	set on fire again
bemoaning (*para. 2*)	complaining about
per (*para. 2*)	according to
barbarians (*para. 2*)	uncivilized people
patronize (*para. 3*)	act superior
template (*para. 4*)	pattern
august (*para. 5*)	respected
visceral (*para. 5*)	gut-level
admixture (*para. 6*)	combination
redacted (*para. 6*)	edited
auteurs (*para. 6*)	stylish filmmakers
kludge (*para. 6*)	mixture
eschewing (*para. 6*)	avoiding
lugubriousness (*para. 6*)	exaggerated gloominess
found matter (*para. 6*)	existing materials

This past January, I had the pleasure of serving as official spear-catcher for a *CBS Evening News* report on the increasing levels of humiliation on *American Idol* and other reality-TV shows, including some on my channel, VH1. The segment featured snippets of our shows *I Love New York* (a dating competition with an urban vibe) and *CelebrityFit Club* (which tracks the efforts of overweight singers and actors to get back in shape, and, by extension, reignite their careers). "VH1, among other things, showcases faded celebrities who are fat," said the CBS correspondent Richard Schlesinger.

In between shots of me fake working at my computer and fake   2
chatting with the amiable Schlesinger while fake strolling down our
corporate-looking hallway, I took my best shot at defending the alleged
horrors of *AI* and *CelebrityFit Club*. But it was clear that CBS News was set on
bemoaning what it saw as yet another outrage against the culture. The
central complaint, per Katie Couric's intro to the report, was that more
people had watched *American Idol* the previous week than watched the State
of the Union address on all the broadcast networks combined. When the
segment ended, Couric signed off with an extravagant eye roll. "We're doing
our part here at CBS News," she seemed to be saying, "but the barbarians
are massing at the gates, people." A line had been drawn in the sand, as if
the news were now akin to an evening at the Met.

Is there an easier position to take in polite society than to patronize   3
reality TV? Even television programmers see the genre as a kind of visual
Hamburger Helper: cheap filler that saves them money they can use elsewhere for more-worthy programming. Reality shows cost anywhere from a
quarter to half as much to produce as scripted shows. The money saved
on *Extreme Makeover: Home Edition*, the logic goes, allows ABC to pay for
additional gruesome medical emergencies and exploding ferries on *Grey's
Anatomy*. NBC's crappy *Fear Factor* pays for the classy *Heroes*.

As befits a form driven largely by speed and cost considerations,   4
reality TV is not often formally daring. Fifteen years after MTV's *The Real
World* set the template for contemporary reality TV by placing seven
strangers in a downtown Manhattan loft, reality television has developed
its own visual shorthand: short doses of documentary footage interspersed
with testimonials (often called OTFs, for "on-the-fly" interviews) in which
the participants describe, ex post facto, what they were thinking during the
action you are watching.

The current boom may be a product of the changing economics of   5
the television business, but reality TV is also the liveliest genre on the set
right now. It has engaged hot-button cultural issues—class, sex, race—that
respectable television, including the august *CBS Evening News*, rarely touches.
And it has addressed a visceral need for a different kind of television at a
time when the Web has made more traditionally produced video seem as
stagey as Molière.

Reality TV may be an awkward admixture of documentary (with its   6
connotations of thousands of hours of footage patiently gathered, re-
dacted by monk-like figures into the purest expression of truth possible in
90 to 120 minutes) and scripted (with its auteurs and Emmys and noble
overtones of craft). But this kludge also happens to have allowed reality

shows to skim the best elements of scripted TV and documentaries while eschewing the problems of each. Reality shows steal the story structure and pacing of scripted television, but leave behind the canned plots and characters. They have the visceral impact of documentary reportage without the self-importance and general lugubriousness. Where documentaries must construct their narratives from found matter, reality TV can place real people in artificial surroundings designed for maximum emotional impact.

The resistance to reality TV ultimately comes down to snobbery, usu- 7
ally of the generational variety. People under 30, in my experience, tend to embrace this programming; they're happy to be entertained, never mind the purity of conception. As an unapologetic producer of reality shows, I'm obviously biased, but I also know that any genre that provokes such howls of protest is doing something interesting. Try the crab.

Danger: Reality TV Can Rot Your Brain

···

OLIVER JAMES

Oliver James, a child psychologist, writes on mental health topics and produces television documentaries in Great Britain. His bestselling book Britain on the Couch: Why We're Unhappier Compared with 1950 Despite Being Richer *was made into a series for Britain's Channel 4. His creative documentaries have included* Prisoner XYY/334422, *an exploration of the psychology of a psychopath in prison, and* Prozac Diary, *in which artists took the drug and reported its effect on their work.*

TERMS TO RECOGNIZE

docusoap (*para. 1*)	combination of documentary and soap opera
plumbed (*para. 2*)	probed
insidious (*para. 2*)	sneaky
wannabe (*para. 2*)	a person who aspires to be
atavistic (*para. 3*)	like a primitive form
McJobs (*para. 4*)	low-level jobs
pinning (*para. 5*)	attaching

aspirant (*para. 5*)	hopeful
unprecedented (*para. 8*)	never seen before
plethora (*para. 8*)	abundance
inauthenticity (*para. 9*)	fakeness

We have endured far too much Reality TV this year, most of it bad, some of it dreadfully so. This weekend, at last, the parade of grotesque characters and public humiliation comes to an end with the closing episode of ITV's *Popstars the Rivals*. Recent viewing figures suggest that the genre has begun to run its course, just as its predecessor the docusoap eventually did. But there may be still greater atrocities in store before we see the back of it: we will soon have the unique pleasure of watching Kelly Osbourne vomiting on *The Osbournes,* and also from America comes word of an RTV show in which contestants volunteer for cosmetic surgery and agonise in humiliating detail about their feelings of unattractiveness.

Our sensitivities have been battered unceasingly by the ever-descending levels of taste plumbed by the producers of these shows. But far more insidious and dangerous is the effect they have on our mental health. I have interviewed some of the wannabe contestants and I am sure that, at least in some cases, participation is damaging. And the problem goes beyond that. Compared with, say, soap operas, RTV is more harmful to viewers as well.

The content of too much RTV is values-rotting and depression-inducing. For a large slice of the population, watching it has largely replaced social life itself. When we are not at work, viewing other people living their lives on TV now constitutes a considerable part of our existence. Does anyone know how much harm this is doing to us? In 2000 I made a brief film on the subject of the emotional impact of RTV on contestants, to be discussed by TV professionals at the Edinburgh Television Festival. On the platform were a number of powerful figures, including the head of BBC One and an atavistic RTV producer who could not conceive of any scenario that she would rule out for RTV coverage. There were "no limits," she said, apart from those (very weak ones) that the regulatory authorities placed upon her.

For my film I interviewed Alan, a 24-year-old who was about to go on a "desert island" RTV programme. Although of average weight for his height, he believed himself to be plump. He also thought he was ugly and unattractive, yet the production team and I felt he was perfectly good look-ing. He had underperformed at university, graduating with a 2:2, and had been drifting without clear career plans, doing McJobs. He was not having as much success with girls as he would like. He hoped that he would be a hit as a contestant, and a career in TV presenting would be accompanied by an unlimited supply of babes.

Alan was mildly depressed, but instead of confronting this he was 5 pinning his hopes on RTV to raise his mood by raising his status. I suspect that his tale is typical (needless to say, none of the broadcasters has done any research into the psychiatric status and motives of aspirant contestants or their outcomes after appearing, so I can only speculate) because, above all, RTV is a young person's game. A quarter of Channel 4's audience is aged 16–34 but they form half the audience of *Big Brother*. Hardly any participants in any RTV shows have been over 30 (the honourable exceptions were both BBC endeavours—*The Stone Age* and *Castaway*).

RTV encourages an "as if" life, a sort of second-hand living, more 6 than any other genre because it blurs the lines between fact and fiction more powerfully than any other. There can be little doubt that it is profoundly damaging.

Like a soap opera in reverse, it involves viewers with the characters for 7 weeks on end and in such a way that you easily forget that these are real people. At the same time, to a frightening extent, the young watching RTV are fantasising that It Could Be Me. People "just like me" are plucked from obscurity and given prominence merely because they happened to be in the right place at the right time. Viewers become so identified with these characters as an extension of themselves that they are far more interested in what happens to the characters than to their own, real, intimates and family.

Of course, not everyone is equally at risk of losing their grip on 8 reality. The risk is much greater for people from unstable and emotionally deprived backgrounds—the majority of us. For the minority, probably no more than a third, whose needs were met in early childhood and who come from stable, reasonably harmonious families, modern life provides unprecedented opportunities for self-expression. But for the majority who did not have such a childhood, the plethora of new choices means a high risk of making bad ones—such as wanting to be part of RTV or feeling inappropriately involved as a viewer.

Above all, RTV offers young people a fake social life, decreasing the 9 likelihood that they will seek a real one. At the same time, because RTV usually entails some kind of beauty contest in which your personality or appearance are being judged, it fosters destructive social comparisons and induces inauthenticity in the process.

Hot or Not: Reality TV Can Be Harmful to Women

••

A NNE B ECKER

Educated at Harvard in both medicine and anthropology, Anne Becker has devoted her career to studying how culture affects eating disorders and body image. She is on the editorial board of the International Journal of Eating Disorders *and was co-editor of the journal* Culture, Medicine, and Psychiatry. *Her book* Body, Self, and Society: The View from Fiji *is an exploration of how modernization, especially television, influenced the body image of teenaged girls in the South Pacific.*

TERMS TO RECOGNIZE

comely (*para. 1*)	nice-looking
scrutinized (*para. 3*)	examined closely
onus (*para. 7*)	blame

Are You Hot?, the ABC reality show in which comely competitors submit to a panel of judges for appearance-rating, might not be so hot for young female viewers, says one eating disorders expert.   1

The more frequently young women watch the show, which seeks to crown the sexiest people in America, the more dissatisfied they are with their appearance and the more likely they are to resort to unhealthy weight control habits, says Randall Flanery, Ph.D., an associate professor of community and family medicine at Saint Louis University in Missouri.   2

"[The show] emphasizes that how you look is more important than who you are or what you do. It really narrows the worth of the individual," Flanery says. "The viewer identifies with the person being scrutinized, but at the same time can participate with the critics and make fun of the person. The net result is the viewer gets reinforced that appearance is the most important thing, and they are not measuring up."   3

Though female adolescents and young women are most prone to developing negative body images from shows like *Are You Hot?*, they are exactly the individuals who tune into such shows and other potentially harmful media, says Flanery, who also runs an eating disorders program. "Those who we're most concerned about are going to watch it more and be   4 most influenced by it," he said. "The more you're primed to look at those factors, the more they affect you."

A study recently published in the *American Journal of Health and Education* showed that women who read health and fitness magazines were significantly more likely to have practiced unhealthy weight control methods than were moderate or infrequent readers, says Steven Thomsen, Ph.D., the study's author and an associate communications professor at Brigham Young University in Provo, Utah. 5

Nearly 80 percent of frequent readers had induced vomiting, 73 percent had taken diet pills and 60 percent had used laxatives. And women who limited their daily caloric intake read health and fitness magazines more frequently than those who did not restrict their diets. 6

Flanery put the onus on young women's parents to be assertive and prohibit their daughters from watching *Are You Hot?* and similar programs. "They can counterbalance that distorted view of what's important and emphasize a healthy alternative message," he said. "You're more than what you look like." 7

Loose Ends

· ·

RITA DOVE

In 1992, Rita Dove became the poet laureate of the United States at age 40, the youngest person ever to be appointed to this post. Dove is known for straightforward poems that reflect her life and the experiences of African Americans. In 1987 she won the Pulitzer Prize for Thomas and Beulah, *a series of poems about the lives of the title characters, from their southern origins through their lives in Akron in the 1960s.*

TERMS TO RECOGNIZE

begrudgingly (*para. 1*)	unwillingly
cajoled (*para. 6*)	wheedled
subterfuges (*para. 6*)	tricks
gloss (*para. 7*)	explanation
spew (*para. 7*)	blurt
estrangement (*para. 8*)	separation
catalyst (*para. 8*)	active ingredient

pyrotechnics (*para. 8*)   fireworks
projected (*para. 9*)   seen on a screen
existential (*para. 9*)   real-life
repartee (*para. 9*)   banter
corollary (*para. 9*)   logical extension
salient (*para. 10*)   relevant

For years the following scene would play daily at our house: Home 1
from school, my daughter would heave her backpack off her shoulder and
let it thud to the hall floor, then dump her jacket on top of the pile. My husband would tell her to pick it up—as he did every day—and hang it in the
closet. Begrudgingly with a snort and a hrrumph, she would comply. The ritual interrogation began:

"Hi, Aviva. How was school?" 2

"Fine." 3

"What did you do today?" 4

"Nothing." 5

And so it went, every day. We cajoled, we pleaded, we threatened with 6
rationed ice cream sandwiches and new healthy vegetable casseroles, we
attempted subterfuges such as: "What was Ms. Boyers wearing today?" or:
"Any new pets in science class?" but her answer remained the same: I dunno.

Asked, however, about that week's episodes of *MathNet,* her favorite 7
series on Public Television's *Square One,* or asked for a quick gloss of a segment of *Lois and Clark* that we happened to miss, and she'd spew out the
details of a complicated story, complete with character development,
gestures, every twist and back-flip of the plot.

Is TV greater than reality? Are we to take as damning evidence the 8
soap opera stars attacked in public by viewers who obstinately believe in
the on-screen villainy of Erica or Jeannie's evil twin? Is an estrangement from
real life the catalyst behind the escalating violence in our schools, where
children imitate the gun-'em-down pyrotechnics of cop-and-robber shows?

Such a conclusion is too easy. Yes, the influence of public media on 9
our perceptions is enormous, but the relationship of projected reality—
i.e., TV—to imagined reality—i.e., an existential moment—is much more
complex. It is not that we confuse TV with reality, but that we prefer it to
reality—the manageable struggle resolved in twenty-six minutes, the witty
repartee within the family circle instead of the grunts and silence common
to most real families; the sharpened conflict and defined despair instead of
vague anxiety and invisible enemies. "Life, my friends, is boring. We must
not say so," wrote John Berryman, and many years and "Dream Songs"

later he leapt from a bridge in Minneapolis. But there is a devastating
corollary to that statement: Life, friends, is ragged. Loose ends are the rule.

What happens when my daughter tells the television's story better   10
than her own is simply this: the TV offers an easier tale to tell. The salient
points are there for the plucking—indeed, they're the only points presented—
and all she has to do is to recall them. Instant Nostalgia! Life, on the other
hand, slithers about and runs down blind alleys and sometimes just fizzles
at the climax. "The world is ugly, / And the people are sad," sings the country bumpkin in Wallace Stevens's "Gubinnal." Who isn't tempted to ignore
the inexorable fact of our insignificance on a dying planet? We all yearn for
our private patch of blue.

RESPONDING TO READINGS

After reading these articles, have you developed your own opinion on "How
Real Is Reality TV?" Have you changed any of your earlier ideas about it? Or
have you decided that the whole controversy is overblown?

CONSIDERING CONTENT

1. Divide a page in two columns. From the five readings in this section,
   compile two lists of key phrases describing the pros and cons of reality
   television. Which column has more compelling content, in your opinion?
   Compare lists with other students' and add relevant items to your own.
2. What was Hirschorn's role on the *CBS Evening News* report? Did he
   think the report was fair? How do you know?
3. Why is it easy to look down on reality TV (as Hirschorn asserts)?
4. Some of the writers suggest that younger people accept and enjoy reality TV more than older people do. Do you think this is true? Why might
   there be a generational split?
5. Ann Becker focuses on one reality TV show and on one type of audience harmed by it. Identify these focuses. Can you generalize Becker's
   argument to apply to more than this one show and audience?
6. Becker closes by urging parents to take control of their daughters' television fare. Do you think this is a good solution to the problem she
   describes? Why or why not? What other solution can you envision?
7. How does Dove explain the charm of scripted television? From what
   she says in "Loose Ends," do you think she would be for or against
   reality television shows?
8. Dove's closing remark may be a reference to the adage, "A tiny patch
   of blue is not heaven." How does this saying relate to the meaning of
   her essay?

CONSIDERING METHOD

1. Go back and reread the first paragraph in each of the five articles in this section. Do you remember which one gripped your attention best upon your first reading? How do the opening tactics differ? Which ones appeal to you?

2. Explain the references and allusions in the essays: an evening at the Met, Hamburger Helper, Molière, McJobs, John Berryman, Wallace Stevens. Why do you think the writers make references to specific names from elsewhere in the culture than television? Which of these references were meaningful to you, and why?

3. Look at the television offerings that are named to contrast with reality TV: *Grey's Anatomy*, *Heroes*, soap operas, the State of the Union address, and *CBS News*. How do these contrasts help you understand the writers' points?

4. Becker's essay can be divided into two types of evidence about the influence of culture on girls' behavior. What are the two types? Which paragraph makes a logical link between the two types? Do you think the link is strong enough to unify the essay? Why or why not?

5. Without reading Oliver James's biographical note, how might you know he is a British author? Point out specific words and phrases that clue you in.

6. Why does Hirschorn repeat the word *fake* in paragraph 2?

7. Point out some differences in tone and purpose between Rita Dove's essay and the others. Explain why the Dove essay displays these differences.

8. Oliver James makes some startlingly broad generalizations: "For a large slice of the population, watching it [RTV] has largely replaced social life itself" (para. 3), "There can be little doubt that it [RTV] is profoundly damaging" (para. 6), "Viewers become so identified with these characters as an extension of themselves that they are far more interested in what happens to the characters than to their own, real, intimates and family" (para. 7), "The risk is much greater for people from unstable and emotionally deprived backgrounds—the majority of us" (para. 8), "RTV offers young people a fake social life, decreasing the likelihood that they will seek a real one" (para. 9). Did you notice these statements when you first read the article? What do you think of them? What makes them valid? What makes them questionable?

WRITING STEP BY STEP: PROS AND CONS OF A REALITY TV SHOW

Regardless of whether you are a fan, choose a specific reality television show to present as a Facts on File writer might. Watch at least one episode (preferably more) and talk to other people who have seen the show. Jot down main ideas from the fans of the show and opposing main ideas from people who hate it. You can look back at the readings in this section and your responses to Considering Content questions to get inspiration about what pros and cons other authors have pointed out. See whether these pros and cons apply to the specific show you will be writing about. Like the writers in this section, you may want to mention some other television fare that compares and contrasts with the show you are reviewing.

A. Introduce your essay by setting the show in the context of reality TV—how does it fit the definition of reality TV? Explain the basic setup of the show and what elements are always included in each episode.

B. In the next paragraph, go into the show's place in history. Is it a new twist on an older reality show? How is it different from other, similar reality shows? How long has it been on the air? What are public reactions to it?

C. Next, explain why the show has advocates. Why do they like it? In this paragraph, concentrate on why they prefer it to traditional television dramas and documentaries.

D. In the next paragraph, show the point of view of the show's critics. Why do they dislike it? Concentrate on why they think traditional television shows are preferable.

E. Alternate with a new paragraph on the show's good points. Focus this time on specific features of this show that make it worthwhile.

F. Now, focus on features that make the show undesirable—exploitive, silly, misleading, dangerous, or whatever. This paragraph should also use specific features, as in step E.

G. Write a concluding sentence that predicts the future of this reality TV show. Be sure to suggest why you think this is the future.

OTHER WRITING IDEAS

1. COLLABORATIVE WRITING. In a small group, exchange your Step by Step essays and read each other's work. Decide on one essay to develop further. The small group should watch the show and gather to discuss how each paragraph could be elaborated with more logical reasoning, evidence, or examples. Consider adding two more paragraphs, a new step G (an additional argument on the pro side) and a step H (an additional argument on the con side). Also consider using print and Internet sources about the show to develop the ideas in the essay with specific facts and figures. Either as a group or individually, write a longer, better Facts on File type review of the show.

2. USING THE INTERNET. Use the World Wide Web to help you find out more about topics briefly mentioned in the essays in this section. For example,

    a. The economic roots of reality TV
    b. Early predecessors of reality TV
    c. Imitation of TV violence, TV plots, or TV situations in real life
    d. Attacks in real life of actors who play bad guys on TV shows

Use the facts you discover to develop an essay exploring the intersection of popular culture and social behavior.

3. WRITING ABOUT READING. Both James and Becker point out certain audience segments who are at risk of being harmed by what they see on television. Do you think that some people may be more easily influenced by TV than others? What are some risk factors that you have noticed? Is there a way to protect certain types of viewers from certain dangers of TV viewing? Write an essay explaining a risk-factor problem and proposing a solution, or explaining the problem and rejecting a proposed solution (for instance, see Becker's advice to parents at the closing of her essay).

GAINING WORD POWER

Make a list of loaded language (highly connotative language) used in the articles in this section. In his very first paragraph, for example, Oliver James uses the powerful words *dreadfully, grotesque, humiliation, atrocities,* and *vomiting.* Michael Hirschorn refers to Katie Couric's *extravagant eye roll* (para. 2) and uses the descriptors *gruesome* and *crappy.* Which of the five authors you read uses the most emotionally charged words and phrases? What effect does this usage have on you as a reader? Select a few examples and rewrite them to achieve a different, perhaps more neutral effect.

EDITING SKILLS: USING QUESTIONS

Notice how the Facts on File article poses questions to sum up a controversy in paragraph 6:

> Does reality television too often exploit its subjects, or does it actually help them to achieve recognition and success? Is it a bold alternative to fictional entertainment, or is it actually less satisfying than scripted drama and comedy? And how "real," exactly, is reality television? Is it genuinely "true to life," or is it more artificial and engineered than it appears to be?

These are **rhetorical questions;** they don't require answers. In fact, authors often intend to answer them for their readers. You can use rhetorical questions for various purposes: to provoke thought, to set a tone, to add emphasis to a point, to assert or deny a claim indirectly, or to establish the direction of a discussion. They will add variety to your writing, but like any special technique, they lose their effect when used too often.

EXERCISE

1. Find rhetorical questions in the pieces by Dove, Hirschorn, and James. Copy them exactly. Speculate on what purpose each rhetorical question serves. Change one or two of them into regular statements and see how they work in their context.
2. Look at one of the essays you have written for this course and find a spot where you could have used a rhetorical question for one of the five purposes. Rewrite the surrounding sentences from your essay, with the new rhetorical question included. Explain why you like the new version better, or why not.

WEB SITES

www.realitytvworld.com
Reality TV World provides coverage of nearly 300 reality television programs. It is the Internet's leading resource for reality television news and information. This site is built for fans and includes gossip, blogs, updates, and stories about the shows and stars.

www.museum.tv/eotvsection.php?entrycode=televisionst
The Museum of Broadcast Communication provides a Web site on television studies, an area of cultural criticism. The site presents a long essay on the subject, a bibliography of written works on television, and key words to use in exploring this subject area. Here you will find intellectual, academic points of view on popular culture and society.

DEBATE: CAN MONEY BUY HAPPINESS?

In 1978 three psychologists interviewed two groups of subjects: winners of the Illinois state lottery and victims of devastating accidents. They asked both groups a battery of questions about their lives, and when they tabulated the results, they found some puzzling results. Of course, the lottery winners rated winning as highly positive, and the accident victims ranked their experience as very negative. But the winners didn't consider themselves to be any happier at the time of the interviews than the accident victims did. In fact, the lottery winners said they took significantly less pleasure in everyday activities than did the accident victims. Furthermore, the accident victims expected to be happier than the lottery winners within a few years.

We all know the legend of King Midas, who sought happiness in gold and, in the end, his pursuit made him miserable. And we often hear sayings like "more money does not make you happy." But if money does not make people happy, what does? Does money matter at all? Where and how do people find happiness? The following articles address these and other questions about the nature and sources of happiness.

PREPARING TO READ

How do you define happiness? Do you think most people are happy? What makes you happy? Do you think you would be happier if you had more money?

••

Whether People Define Themselves as Happy Depends on the Era

••

CYNTHIA CROSSEN

A graduate of Macalester College in St. Paul, Minnesota, Cynthia Crossen has been a reporter and editor at the Wall Street Journal *since 1983. She has covered publishing, financial news, and marketing, and has written the "Dear Book Lover" column for the weekend edition of the* Journal. *She is the author of two books:* Tainted Truth: The Manipulation of Fact in America *(1994) and* The Rich and How They Got That Way *(2000).*

TERMS TO RECOGNIZE

theologians (*para. 2*)	religious scholars
wrangled (*para. 2*)	argued nosily and persistently
innately (*para. 2*)	naturally
vexed (*para. 3*)	annoyed
thwarted (*para. 3*)	prevented from happening, blocked
futile (*para. 6*)	pointless
felicity (*para. 6*)	contentment
predicated on (*para. 7*)	based on, depended on
corollary (*para. 9*)	logical consequence or outcome
aberration (*para. 9*)	a departure from what is normal or desirable

To me, the most interesting statistic from the Pew Research Center's   1
recent poll on happiness wasn't that 84% of the 3,000 Americans interviewed described themselves as being "very" or "pretty" happy. Nor was
it that 15% said they weren't so happy. It was that 1% of the sample—
30 people—couldn't say if they were happy or not.

Maybe those "don't knows" were historians. Because for the past   2
2,500 years, scholars, theologians, and politicians have wrangled over the
definition of happiness and, more specifically, what makes people happy.
Is it sensory pleasure? Satisfied desires? Freedom from sorrow or pain?
Purposeful labor or a life of leisure? Is it luck? Money? Goodness? Or is it
just an accident of biology, some people seemingly born cheerful, others
innately crabby?

Perhaps because the Declaration of Independence staked out the   3
pursuit of happiness as one of three unalienable rights of humans,
Americans seem particularly vexed when their happiness is thwarted.
Indeed, in the 19th century, Americans filed hundreds of lawsuits in federal
and state courts accusing the government and fellow citizens of impeding
their sacred right to happiness, writes Darrin M. McMahon in his new book,
Happiness. But when an unhappy American complained to Benjamin Franklin that his country was not fulfilling its promise to him, Franklin was said
to have replied, "The [Declaration of Independence] only gives you the right
to pursue happiness. You have to catch it yourself."

America's earliest settlers, like their Old World forebears, were suspi-   4
cious of happiness that wasn't associated with morality and Christianity.
"The Puritans regarded virtue as the basis of prosperity, rather than prosperity as the basis of virtue," wrote Reinhold Niebuhr in *The Irony of American*

History. In a sermon to the General Court of the Massachusetts Colony in 1663, John Higginson preached, "When the Lord stirred up the spirits of so many of his people to come over into the wilderness, it was not for worldly wealth or better livelihood. . . . Nor had they any rational grounds to expect such things in such a wilderness."

But by the time Alexis de Tocqueville toured America in 1831, that attitude had begun to change: Happiness had become less about being good, more about feeling good. And with the country's nearly infinite natural resources and new technologies for exploiting them, almost anyone willing to work hard could achieve a comfortable prosperity. If happiness was a full stomach, a roaring fire, and a few trinkets that, as Jean Jacques Rousseau suggested, were desirable mainly because your neighbors desired them, then maybe happiness didn't have to be postponed until you went to heaven.

Americans never stop thinking of the good things they have not got, Tocqueville wrote. No one could work harder to be happy than Americans, until finally, "Death steps in . . . and stops him before he has grown tired of this futile pursuit of that complete felicity which always escapes him."

Indeed, where Old World happiness was predicated on not having to work, especially doing manual labor, in America, work was increasingly considered a source of satisfaction, even pleasure. That was convenient for a capitalist democracy, where ever-increasing consumption stoked the engine of industrial growth. Millions of immigrants who fled the poverty of their native countries during the 19th and early 20th centuries sought in America the kind of happiness that comes from freedom from want. But because people adapt so quickly to higher levels of affluence, many found themselves on what economists call a "hedonic treadmill," working harder to make more money to buy things that make them—but only temporarily—happy.

The word *happy* is derived from an Old Norse word *happ*, meaning chance or luck; the word *hapless*, from the same root, means unfortunate. Until the past two centuries, happiness was considered a gift of God or the gods; people could pursue it, but they couldn't control it, and they certainly couldn't will it. That notion also changed in the 20th century, as attaining happiness became a question of mind over matter. In 1952, Norman Vincent Peale's bestselling book *The Power of Positive Thinking* declared, "You can think your way to success and happiness."

The idea that people can engineer their own happiness with the right combination of material and emotional goods has a corollary: Those who are unhappy have failed. As Mr. McMahon writes, "For a society in which the unhindered pursuit of happiness is treated as a natural, God-given right, the inability to make steady progress along the way will inevitably be seen as an aberration, a suspension of the natural order of things."

So, on second thought, maybe the most interesting statistic in the 10
Pew poll isn't the 30 respondents who didn't know if they were happy or not. It's that 15%—450 people—admitted that despite living in a culture that believes happiness can be bought, willed, and chosen, they haven't fulfilled what some think is a good citizen's duty to be happy.

Income and Happiness

· ·

ED DIENER

Ed Diener is the Joseph Smiley Distinguished Professor of Psychology at the University of Illinois at Urbana-Champaign, where he has been on the faculty for the past 34 years. Diener's research focuses on the psychology of well-being. He has published over 260 articles and books, including Happiness: Unlocking the Mysteries of Psychological Wealth *(2008), written with his son Robert Biswas-Diener. The following column appeared in the* Observer, *a publication of the American Psychological Society.*

TERMS TO RECOGNIZE

replicated (*para. 2*)	verified by similar tests or studies
correlation (*paras. 2, 4, 5*)	a close connection, especially when one condition causes the other
per-capita (*para. 4*)	an average, based on the number of people who live in a particular place
disintegrated (*para. 4*)	fell apart

Martin Seligman and I, as well as many others, have now collected a 1
substantial amount of data on the relation of money and well-being, but these data are often misunderstood. Below I clarify some of the conclusions from this area of study.

The Rich Are on Average Happy

Some people think that our data show that money does not matter 2
for happiness, or even that rich people are unhappy. To the contrary, it is a highly replicated finding that individuals who are well-off financially are on

average happier than poor people. Although the correlation between income and happiness in national samples is small in the United States, it is nevertheless true that the richest people are on average more satisfied with their lives than the poorest group. It also appears, however, that increasing income makes more difference at varying levels of poverty, perhaps because it relates to the meeting of basic needs. As one ascends the income ladder, it produces diminishing returns for happiness.

The relation between income and happiness must also be considered   3
in a cultural context. The Maasai of Africa have virtually no cash income: they have their cattle. But the Maasai can meet most of their basic needs, and they are not exposed to Western media. In contrast, homeless people in California—who often have much greater income than the Maasai—are on average not nearly as happy. They do not possess what others around them have, and it requires much greater income to meet basic needs in their society. Thus, income must be considered in the context of people's needs and desires.

Wealth of Nations

There is a strong correlation between the wealth of nations and the   4
average happiness found in them. Again, the effects are strongest when viewing the poor nations, and there is a leveling off of well-being after nations reach a per-capita income in the $12,000 range. The unhappiest nations, even unhappier than poor nations, are the former Soviet-bloc countries where the political and economic system disintegrated. It appears that instability and the loss of income may be worse than simply having low income.

Causal Direction: From Happiness to Wealth?

It has usually been assumed that the correlation between income and   5
happiness is due to money affecting feelings of well-being. But some of our recent research suggests that at least some of the causal influence goes in the other direction: that cheerful people are likely to make more money than unhappy people. Cheerful people are also more likely to make friends, and as we discovered, quality of well-being may be more influenced by the strength of a person's relationships than by money.

The High Cost of Winning

••

PAM LAMBERT AND ALEX TRENIOWSKI

This article appeared in the March 15, 2004, issue of People Weekly *magazine. The lead reporters, Pam Lambert and Alex Treniowski, used information gathered by contributors from six different locations throughout the United States and England.* People *magazine frequently reports on the fortunes and misfortunes of lottery winners.*

TERMS TO RECOGNIZE

windfall (*paras. 1, 7*)	an unexpected gain or profit
frittered away (*para. 3*)	wasted, squandered
tolerantly (*para. 8*)	without criticizing
lavished (*para. 9*)	gave generously and excessively
parasite (*para. 13*)	freeloader, one who lives off others
ramshackle (*para. 15*)	poorly maintained, falling to pieces
bizarre (*para. 16*)	strange or unusual

Millions of Americans daydream about hitting a megamillion jackpot—and assume all that's left is to live happily ever after. Could happen. Or—as these unlucky lottery winners show—a sudden windfall can also lead to divorce, bankruptcy, and (gulp) even hit men.   1

> **Jay Sommers, 36**
> **Won: $5.8 million**
> **Outcome: Lost it all, delivered pizza**

Oh, to be young, handsome, and suddenly so rich you can outshop Paris Hilton! Jay Sommers was 20 when he won a fifth of a $28.9 million lottery jackpot in Michigan in 1988. With his first annual $290,000 payment he bought not one but five new cars. "I blew all of the check in 2½ months," says Sommers. "What 20-year-old wins that kind of money and is sensible with it?"   2

Oh, to be young, handsome, and suddenly so broke you're delivering pizza! Spending so fast he couldn't pay taxes, Sommers asked a friend who is a businessman to manage his loot. His pal persuaded Sommers to swap his annual checks for a discounted lump-sum payout. One day in the   3 mid-'90s Sommers went to the bank and discovered all his money was gone—frittered away by his friend's bad investments and shady deals. Sommers sued his friend and won the case, but spent much of his $887,000 settlement paying off lawyers and debts. To make ends meet during the case he took the pizza-delivery job. "People recognized me and it was humiliating," says Sommers, 36. "One minute I'm famous and five years later I'm broke. It's been a roller coaster ride."

Single and living near Detroit, Sommers now does construction work and is a racecar driver trying to make it big in NASCAR. "I'm still bitter and I'll be bitter the rest of my life," he says. "I think I'd be further along today if I had never won."

Callie Rogers, 17
Won: $3.5 million
Outcome: Lost fiancé, peace of mind

After supermarket clerk Callie Rogers, then 16, bagged her jackpot last June, "I just sat there crying," the British teen recalls. Over the coming months there would be more tears in store. First, jealousy reared its ugly head. "People I didn't know were saying bad things about me," she says. Then her 25-year-old boyfriend proposed—and told her she'd have to buy her own ring, promising to pay her back. She ended up dumping him. "I knew he was a loser before I got rich," she says now.

These days things are looking brighter for Rogers. She has a new, live-in boyfriend, 24-year-old Nicky Lawson. "He's got his own money," Rogers says. "He bought me my ring."

Andrew "Jack" Whittaker, 56
Won: $314.9 million
Outcome: Embarrassing busts, stolen bucks

As Andrew "Jack" Whittaker should be able to attest, tippling and toting around large stashes of cash don't make for a winning ticket. Since bagging the largest single Powerball jackpot ever on Christmas Day, 2002, a lump-sum windfall of $113.4 million after taxes, the married contractor from Scott Depot, W.Va., has survived a series of misadventures that sound like something from *The Sopranos*. During the past eight months Whittaker, 56, has been drugged at a strip club and robbed of $545,000 (it was recovered); arrested for threatening to have a bar manager and his family killed (he faces a March court date); and charged with drunk driving after state police found him sitting in his Cadillac SUV on the side of the interstate on Jan. 25, allegedly slumped over the wheel with the vehicle running. Said Whittaker, whose blood-alcohol level registered 0.190, twice the legal limit: "I wasn't driving, absolutely wasn't driving."

Many locals seem inclined to view Whittaker's troubles tolerantly,   8
however, especially since he earmarked $14 million to establish a foun-
dation that delivers food, clothing, and scholarships to the state's poor. "I
just keep on doing what I'm doing," Whittaker said after his DUI arrest,
"and tell everyone my personal life is my own business."

Billie Bob Harrell Jr., 50
Won: $31 million
Outcome: Lost his marriage—and his life

Billie Bob Harrell Jr. was just about broke when he played the Texas   9
Lotto Jackpot in June 1997. But then six ping-pong balls landed the right
way and Harrell, 48, was $31 million richer. He quit his job at Home Depot
and with his first $1.24 million check took his family to Hawaii, gave tens
of thousands to his church, lavished cars and houses on friends and family.
He even bought 480 turkeys for the poor. "He played Santa Claus," says his
mother, Agnes. "He seemed to think everything would be all right. But it
never was the same again."

Suddenly strangers were calling demanding donations; Harrell   10
changed his phone number several times. The strain of it all damaged his
marriage, and less than a year after winning Harrell split from his wife.
Reckless spending and lending led him to make a bad deal with a company
that gives lottery winners lump-sum payments in exchange for their annual
checks, and Harrell wound up with much less than what he had won. But
by then, it seemed, all he wanted was to have his family back. One night in
1999, just before he was set to meet his ex-wife for dinner, his oldest son
found him dead of a shotgun wound. "Winning the lottery," Harrell had
earlier told a friend, "was the worst thing that ever happened to me."

Today Harrell's mother does not believe her son took his own life,   11
despite a police report ruling it a suicide. In the bedroom that night police
found a note they believe was meant for his ex-wife. "I didn't want this,"
Harrell wrote. "I just wanted you."

Denise Rossi, 53
Won: $1.3 million
Outcome: Stripped of her winnings

Blindsided—that's how Thomas Rossi felt when Denise, his wife of   12
26 years, hit him with divorce papers in 1997. "I thought we got along good,"
says Rossi, 70, a photographer. "I couldn't understand it. She wanted me to
move out of the house very fast. It wasn't like her to act this way."

Two years later it all made sense. A letter addressed to his ex-wife   13
that mistakenly arrived in his new Los Angeles apartment revealed she had

won a lottery. Rossi learned Denise had scored $1.3 million in the California lottery on Dec. 28, 1996—11 days before she filed for divorce. He took her to court for not disclosing the money, and the judge awarded Rossi the entire haul. According to her lawyer, Denise could have kept half and perhaps all of her loot had she been honest, but the court ruled "her failure to disclose was a fraud," he says. Since then Denise has disappeared (she could not be located for comment), but not before trashing Rossi. "I was very happy to be free of this person that was like a parasite," she told NBC's *Dateline* in 2000. "[Winning the lottery] has brought me really nothing but grief and headache."

Receiving $48,000 after taxes every year, meanwhile, has given Rossi   14 "peace of mind," he says. "If it wasn't for the lotto, Denise and I would probably still be together. Things worked out for the best."

William Post, 64
Won: $16.2 million
Outcome: Brother hired a hit man to kill him, divorce, bankruptcy

Gone are the days when William Post, 64, would find a pair of pants   15 he liked and buy 400 of them. Gone too are the mansion, the farm, the half-dozen cars, and the diamonds. In fact, looking around Post's ramshackle home in Franklin, Pa., you'd never suspect that 16 years ago he won $16.2 million. And yet despite declaring bankruptcy in 1994 and suffering from health problems, including severe asthma, Post maintains, "I'm a very happy man now. Money can't buy peace of mind."

As an overnight multimillionaire, that was certainly something that   16 eluded the one-time circus cook. In 1994 his brother Jeffrey pleaded no contest to hiring a hit man to kill Post and his then wife, Connie, allegedly in order to get his hands on Post's estate. (Jeffrey is serving 20 years probation.) Spooked by the plot, Connie left Post not long after. From there things deteriorated further, in large part because of Post's lavish and sometimes bizarre spending sprees. "As soon as the stores opened he'd want to go and buy stuff," says his daughter Gladys Burrous, 42. "Everything, anything."

Today Post lives on a $558 monthly Social Security disability check   17 and has $43 in the bank. "He probably is happier," says Burrous of her father. "When he won, he really didn't know how to handle it."

RESPONDING TO READINGS

After reading these articles, would you change the definition of happiness that you gave in your Preparing to Read answer? How would you now answer the question, "Can money buy happiness?"

CONSIDERING CONTENT

1. Why did Americans in the 19th century file hundreds of lawsuits against the government and their fellow citizens?

2. What was the Puritans' attitude toward happiness and prosperity? How did this attitude change? What may have caused this change (para. 5)?

3. What kind of happiness was found by immigrants who had fled poverty in their native countries?

4. Explain what a "hedonic treadmill" is. Have you ever experienced or witnessed such a phenomenon?

5. Which statistic from the Pew Research Center poll did Crossen initially find "most interesting"? Which statistic did she find most interesting "on second thought" (para. 10)? Why did she change her mind?

6. What claim does the example of the Maasai of Africa support?

7. According to Ed Diener, which countries are the unhappiest? Why are they unhappier than poor nations?

8. Diener says it's likely that cheerful people make more money than unhappy people. Do you agree? Can you explain why it might be true?

9. Were you surprised by what happened to the lottery winners described in the article from *People* magazine?

10. What general claim do you think "The High Cost of Winning" was trying to argue? Do you think it was successful?

CONSIDERING METHOD

1. In paragraph 2, Cynthia Crossen asks a series of questions. Why does she ask so many questions? What effect does this approach produce?

2. Why does Crossen include the information about the root meaning of the word *happiness*?

3. Crossen quotes from a number of sources. Which ones helped you to understand the points that the author was making?

4. Why did the writers from *People* magazine use headings to present their examples? How effective is this use of headings? Are the examples presented in any particular order?

5. Why doesn't "The High Cost of Winning" have a concluding paragraph? Try writing a conclusion that sums up the main messages of this article.

6. Who are the intended readers of each of the three articles in this section? What differences in language and style do you see among the articles? How do these differences reflect the anticipated readership?

WRITING STEP BY STEP: ENGINEERING ONE'S OWN HAPPINESS

Do you think people can engineer their own happiness? Write an essay arguing your answer to this question.

A. Formulate a tentative thesis, or major claim, that clearly states your position on this issue.

B. Review your responses to the Preparing to Read, Responding to Readings, and Considering Content questions, and expand any thoughts that would help you in developing the arguments you intend to make.

C. List at least three reasons, or minor claims, to support your major claim.

D. Review your options for arranging an argument (pp. 292–293) and decide which best suits your topic and opinion. Make a sketch or outline based on your claims. Think of what people on the other side of the issue might say and be sure to include refutation at appropriate points in your argument.

E. Identify the types of evidence you have available or would need to gather to support your position. You might interview other people to gather evidence. Ask your instructor about using secondary sources.

F. Close by summarizing your main claims. You might conclude as Cynthia Crossen does by referring back to your introduction—with a twist or variation to round out your argument.

OTHER WRITING IDEAS

1. Use one of these quotations as the major claim for an essay:

   "Nothing can bring you happiness but yourself."
   —Ralph Waldo Emerson

   "Success is not the key to happiness. Happiness is the key to success."
   —Herman Pain

   "If you want to live a happy life, tie it to a goal, not to people or things."
   —Albert Einstein

   "The search for happiness is one of the chief sources of unhappiness."
   —Erick Hoffer

   Follow the guidelines in the Step by Step writing assignment to organize and develop your essay.

2. COLLABORATIVE WRITING. If money doesn't buy happiness, what does it buy? Get together with a group of classmates and brainstorm a list of answers to this question. Either as a group or on your own, write an essay that supports a major claim about the effects of money.

3. USING THE INTERNET. Do you think all lottery winners are as unlucky as those described in "The High Cost of Winning"? Search online to find examples of some fortunate lottery winners. Use the examples to write an article that supports a claim that winning the lottery can be a positive event.

4. WRITING ABOUT READING. Prepare a summary of Cynthia Crossen's article "Whether People Define Themselves as Happy Depends on the Era." Your goal is to communicate Crossen's main ideas to people who don't have access to the full article. Your summary should not be longer than 210 words. You will find guidelines for writing a summary at the end of Chapter 1, pp. 13–14.

GAINING WORD POWER

Writers sometimes make references to familiar or significant people, places, objects, or events from history, the Bible, literature and the arts, and even from popular culture. These references are called **allusions;** they help a writer to set the tone, heighten the meaning, or provide context without going into a long explanation. Identify and describe the following references from the articles in this section. Use a dictionary or other reference works to help you.

1. Benjamin Franklin
2. John Higginson
3. Alexis de Tocqueville
4. Jean Jacques Rousseau
5. The Maasai of Africa
6. Soviet-bloc countries
7. Paris Hilton
8. NASCAR
9. *The Sopranos*
10. NBC's *Dateline*

Can you explain why the writers mentioned these items? What did they add to your understanding or feeling about the material?

EDITING SKILLS: USING COLONS

Copy the following five passages exactly:

a. The idea that people can engineer their own happiness with the right combination of material and emotional goods has a corollary: Those who are unhappy have failed.
b. The Maasai of Africa have virtually no cash income: they have their cattle.
c. But some of our recent research suggests that at least some of the causal influence goes in the other direction: that cheerful people are likely to make more money than unhappy people.
d. Said Whittaker, whose blood-alcohol level registered 0.190, twice the legal limit: "I wasn't driving, absolutely wasn't driving."
e. Joseph Addison said there are three grand essentials to happiness: something to do, something to love, and something to hope for.

If you copied correctly, you put a colon (:) in each passage. Reread what you copied, and see whether you can come up with a rule about the use of the colon.

If you go back and reread the first part of each example, you'll probably notice that the colon comes after a complete sentence. The colon then introduces something that specifies or expands on the sentence before the colon. If you think of the colon as a verbal equal sign (=), you get the main relationship it suggests between the two parts.

As you see in examples c and e, the second part doesn't have to be a complete sentence; but if it is, you have the choice of using either a capital letter (as in example a) or a lowercase letter (as in example b) on the second sentence. It doesn't have to be a direct quotation, either. Neglecting to put a full sentence before a colon, when you are introducing a list (as in example e), is one of the most frequent mistakes in written English.

EXERCISE

Complete the following passages that include colons.

1. Sami has already bought her party supplies: _____.
2. Beau's next statement gave away his secret plans: _____.
3. The plans were not completely reasonable: _____.
4. _____: a paperback detective novel, a historical romance, and a Far Side cartoon.
5. _____: Austin cried only a little while.

Now edit the essay you just wrote, looking for places where you could have used a colon instead of a period or a semicolon. After consulting with your instructor, change the punctuation mark to a colon.

🌐 WEB SITES

http://peacecenter.berkeley.edu/greatergood/2009may/McMahon.php
This piece, "Happiness, the Hard Way," is based on a talk given in 2008 by Darrin McMahon, the author of *Happiness, A History*, which Cynthia Crossen quotes in her article in this section.

www.happiness-project.com/happiness_project/2008/09/happiness -int-1.html
This interview with Ed Diener and Robert Biswas-Diener about their book *Happiness: Unlocking the Mysteries of Psychological Wealth* was posted by Gretchen Rubin on her site, The Happiness Project.

Writing with Sources

Some writing projects will require you to go beyond personal knowledge and experience. At times, you may begin a paper and decide that you don't have enough information to cover the topic adequately or that you need additional support for your ideas. At other times, you may consult sources to explore a topic and decide how to approach it before you begin writing. You may also be assigned to write a research paper, one that will require the extensive use of sources.

USING SOURCES IN YOUR WRITING

Writers use sources to help them explain, develop, and strengthen their observations and opinions. That's what Brian Carter did with his essay "Almost a Winner" (see pages 288–290 in Chapter 9). Although Brian had worked out his own analysis of the causes for obsessive slot-machine playing, he wanted to find out what other people thought. So he went to the library to find material by experts who had published their findings on this form of gambling. After reading and taking notes from a number of books and articles, Brian revised his paper by incorporating facts and comments from several sources into his discussion. The revised, documented version of his essay appears on pages 363–365 at the end of this appendix.

The process for planning and developing an essay using sources will follow the same one described in Chapter 2 (pp. 16–23): to find ideas, devise a thesis, make a plan, compose a draft, improve the draft, target the readers, get feedback, and polish the final draft. You may not write a finished paper before looking at other sources, as Brian did, but you should begin with your own ideas. If you start with the sources themselves, you may end up presenting a summary of other writers' words and opinions instead of a discussion that clearly reflects your own thinking. The information you gather from sources should support your views, not replace them.

LOCATING SOURCES

Sources of information include books, magazine and newspaper articles, videos, interviews, government documents, Web site, and online publications. Your college library is the best place to find these resources, and you will almost surely conduct your initial search for sources on a computer. Most college libraries offer workshops to help students locate materials, conduct computer searches, use online databases, and navigate the Internet. If these courses are not required, take one anyway—you could save yourself hours of aimless wandering. Your library's information desk will provide you with schedules for tours and research tutorials.

Using the Online Catalog

Most libraries today list their holdings in a computerized *online public access catalog* (OPAC). The opening screen of the OPAC at the library Brian Carter used shows that he can search for books, journals and magazines, and other items owned by his library and by other libraries in the state. In electronic databases, such as InfoTrac and EBSCO, you can usually search for sources by author, title, and publication year and also by subject or keywords.

Subject searches focus only on the sources' contents and yield more limited, precise results. They work best when the descriptors (subject headings) conform to a database's directory of terms. For your library's catalog, the directory is the *Library of Congress Subject Headings (LCSH)*, which is usually available in printed form in the library's reference room. Keyword searches look through the entire database and are not dependent on preset subject heading. If you have determined your exact subject, you will want to begin with a subject search. A keyword search, on the other hand, is a good place to limit and refine your subject and discover specific descriptors. Remember that computers are unforgiving about spelling and typing errors. When your results are not what you expected, check the accuracy of the search terms you used.

To begin his search of the online catalog, Brian typed in the LSCH heading "slot machines" and selected "subject" in the "search by" menu. The results showed that his library did not have any books on this specific topic, but when he extended his search to include other libraries in his state's system, he found 11 possible entries. Because he lacked sufficient time to get these books through interlibrary loan, Brian used a more general subject heading instead. When he entered "gambling," he discovered 18 entries, most of which contained sublistings for related subtopics. He saw which books were available and where they were located in the library. Although he now had some material to begin his review of the topic, Brian felt he also needed to find out what was available in periodicals.

Using Indexes and Databases

Even though you might find valuable material in books to use in documenting your ideas and critical judgments, your paper will not be well researched unless you also find periodical articles relevant to your topic. Periodicals include newspapers, popular magazines, and scholarly journals. Because they are published frequently, periodicals often contain the most recent information on a topic. Popular magazines include articles of interest to the general public and are written in everyday, nontechnical language. Magazine articles mention the sources within the articles and seldom include bibliographies or footnotes. By contrast, scholarly journals are written by and for academics or expert researchers and require formal citations in bibliographies or footnotes. Journals rarely contain advertising, eye-catching artistic touches, or slick covers. Each journal is devoted to a specific academic subject, often a very narrow one.

Periodical sources can now be accessed electronically through online databases and text archives that your library subscribes to. The library homepage that Brian was using allowed him to move from the online catalog to a list of more than a hundred searchable indexes, bibliographies, and other electronic reference tools. The reference librarian recommended that Brian look first at two computerized indexes—*EBSCO Academic Search Elite* and *Infotrac Expanded Academic Index ASAP*—to find publication information on articles about slot machines because these databases cover periodicals in psychology and sociology. Other databases, such as *Article 1st* and *Wilson Select Plus*, deal with a wider range of more general subjects. Brief descriptions of the databases are often found on the library's homepage.

When Brian typed "slot machines" in the "find" box of the search screen of Academic Search Elite, he got 215 hits. The display also prompted him to narrow his results by subject and gave him several words and phrases to add to his search term. Brian entered the phrase "near miss," which reduced the list considerably. He could view these entries one at a time or print out the entire list. Each citation included the article title and the name, volume, date, and page number of the periodical; it also supplied the call number for any publications in his library. Many of the entries contained a brief summary of the article's content, and two included the full text of the article for him to read or print. He could also send this information to his home computer by email.

Brian browsed through these findings and printed the citations for several articles that looked promising. Because the library did not own a number of the periodicals, the librarian suggested requesting copies of the articles through interlibrary loan, but that would take several days. Another option was to consult a full-text database, such as *JSTOR (Journal Storage Project)* or *ProjectMUSE*, to see if the articles were available there. Brian discovered a promising article in *JSTOR* and printed it out.

These are some of the electronic tools that Brian used to search for possible sources. Your library may subscribe to many of the same indexes and databases, but you need to find out what's available and how to use them. You may also be able to access these resources from your home or other location through a proxy service that verifies your status as a registered library user.

Using the Internet

A number of useful online databases and text archives are accessible over the Internet. You can locate resources using any one of several different search engines—such as Netscape, Safari, Firefox, Google, Yahoo!, Ask.com, and Microsoft Explorer—catalog Web site in directories and allow you to conduct keyword searches.

You can also join electronic communities called *newsgroups*, through which members exchange information about a common interest or affiliation by posting questions and answers to online sites. Or you can become a member of an Internet discussion group, frequently called a *listserv*, whose subscribers use email to converse on a particular subject. Ask your instructor about using listservs and newsgroups as sources for your writing assignments.

If you need additional information about using the Web and the Internet, you might check out the Internet Detective (www.vts.intute.ac.uk/detective), a free online tutorial designed to help you develop the skills and critical thinking required for Internet research. You can also visit one of these useful reference sites:

A+ Writing Research Paper Guide	www.ipl.org/div/aplus
Searching the World Wide Web	http://owl.english.purdue.edu/owl/resource/558/01
Finding Information on the Internet	www.lib.berkeley.edu/TeachingLibGuides/Internet/FindInfo.html

EVALUATING SOURCES

With all the material available in print or on the Internet, the challenge isn't finding sources, but deciding how reliable they are. Just because an article or book appears in print or online doesn't mean that its opinions are credible or that its information is accurate.

Recognizing Bias

One of the most important goals of evaluating a source is to identify any bias in its treatment of a topic. The fact is that most writing is not neutral or objective and doesn't try to be. Authors and publications have political, social, economic, generational, and religious points of view that influence their presentation and determine what information they include—and exclude—especially when they deal with controversial subjects. These viewpoints alone do not make the sources unusable or untrustworthy, but you need to be aware of such potential biases and take them into account when deciding what to use and how to use it. For example, if you were to research the topic of home schooling, you might come across a periodical called *Growing without Schooling*. With a little investigation you would find that this publication is written by and for home schoolers. You might find a lot of valuable material in such a source, depending on your purpose and audience; but if you wanted something about the criticisms of home schooling, you would have to go to other sources.

Judging Online Sources

You should of course be concerned about the credibility of any source you use in your writing. You can generally rely on scholarly books and journal articles because they have been reviewed and edited, their authors are often recognized authorities, and their claims are documented. Popular books and periodicals aren't as reliable and sometimes have political biases, but the content has probably been reviewed and edited by publishers, editors, and librarians. Books are also reviewed after publication by specialists in the field, and magazines and journals frequently include letters to the editor from readers who question or support the articles' findings or conclusions.

Materials from the Internet are a different story. Anyone can create and post information and opinions on a Web site or in a newsgroup, and most postings are rarely reviewed for accuracy and completeness. When you use information from an electronic source, you want to be confident that it is reliable and that it comes from someone with the appropriate authority. Here are some guidelines for evaluating online materials:

- *Look for credentials.* What do you know about the people supplying the information? What's the basis of their expertise? Is the source also available in an established, conventional printed form?
- *Track down affiliations.* Who sponsors the online site? Is it a reputable group that you can easily identify? Is the information influenced by commercial or political sponsorship? Does the site include links to other reputable resources?
- *Analyze motives.* What purpose does the site serve? Many online postings are trying to buy or sell something; others are promoting a favorite cause. These may not be good sources for research.
- *Consider currency and stability.* Is the material updated regularly? Is there an archive for older information?
- *Confirm your information.* Can you find other sources to verify what you've found online? Ideally, you want to have several different kinds of sources to achieve a credible balance of research material.

For more details about evaluating online sources, you can visit one of these sites:

Evaluating Web Sites, a comprehensive and instructive guide to judging information resources for reliability and accuracy, at www.lesley.edu/library/guides/research/evaluating_web.html.

Evaluating Web Pages: Techniques to Apply & Questions to Ask, an online tutorial from the UC Berkeley Library, at www.lib.berkeley.edu/TeachingLib/Guides/Internet/Evaluate.html.

Finally, check with your instructor to determine the types of resources considered appropriate for your specific assignment.

WORKING WITH SOURCES

Once you have located the books and articles you want to read and assimilate, you can begin reading, taking notes, and synthesizing the material.

Taking Notes

Many writers use note cards for keeping track of the facts and opinions they find. If you decide to use cards, work out some system for recording information. Here are some suggestions:

1. Fill out a bibliography card every time you consult a new source and record all the details necessary for citing this source in your paper, including where to find the source again. Then put the author's last name, an abbreviated title, and the page number or numbers on all the note cards you use for this source.
2. Write only one idea or point on each card. This allows you to shuffle the cards as you figure out the precise organization of your paper.
3. Put subject headings on the cards—one or two words in the upper-right-hand corner to tell you what each note is about.
4. Summarize the ideas in your own words. If you think you might want to quote directly from the source, copy the author's exact words and enclose them in quotation marks.

Computers now come with a note card program, or you can purchase software for a note card system. You can use the computer note cards just as you would use index cards: title each card by topic, and then type your notes onto the card provided by the computer.

Using a Research Notebook

Another option is a double-entry research notebook where you summarize and analyze readings all in one location.

1. Divide a notebook or computer page vertically down the middle.
2. On the left side of the page, summarize your reading of the source material and write down the complete bibliographic data and URLs. Any exact words or phrases need to be placed within quotation marks.

3. On the right side of the page, comment on your sources, noting their importance to your topic and their relationship to other sources.

The response side of the divided notebook shows the evolution of your thinking, lets you articulate questions that arise as you read and process information and guide you toward a thesis for your paper. The system also helps you to avoid the cut-and-paste style of research writing because it encourages synthesis and analysis throughout the process. Finally, this record of your thoughts helps to identify which ideas are your own and which you picked up along the way—a key distinction that safeguards against inadvertent plagiarism and allows you to claim your own thoughts with confidence.

Using the Printout/Photocopy Option

If the time you can spend in the library is limited, you might want to print out an online article or photocopy portions of books in order to have these materials available to study at your convenience. In fact, you might find it easier to take notes from a printout than from a computer screen. You can underline or highlight key ideas, even color-coding these highlighted passages to fit different subtopics in your paper. You can also write comments or cross-references to other sources in the margins. It's still a good idea to put the information from printouts and photocopies on note cards or in your research notebook. This procedure forces you to summarize the material in your own words and makes it much easier to organize your ideas and sort the separate items into categories.

Summarizing, Paraphrasing, and Quoting

In most of your notes, you will be summarizing or paraphrasing your source materials, rather than quoting the author's exact words. In a **summary** you condense the main point of an argument or passage in your own words. A summary is useful when you want to capture the gist of an idea without including the background or supporting details. Compare this long sentence from an article about professional football with the summary that follows it.

ORIGINAL

In an effort to keep everyone buying tickets and watching television as far as possible into this elongated sixteen-game season, the NFL juggled its schedule so that strong teams faced the toughest tests and weaker members were able to kindle local hopes while playing fellow stragglers. [46 words]

SUMMARY

To keep fans interested through the long season, the NFL scheduled teams against others of similar strength. [17 words]

In a **paraphrase** you restate comments and ideas from a source, using approximately the same number of words as the original. Although written in your own words and style, a good paraphrase will reflect the author's point more clearly than a summary does. Here's a paraphrase of the passage about the NFL schedule:

> To keep fans coming to games and watching them on television throughout the long season, the NFL rigged the schedule so that the strong teams played each other and the weaker teams kept local fans interested by playing other weak teams. [41 words]

You will also find comments and observations that are so well expressed that you want to use the original wording rather than summarize or paraphrase it. Be sure to record the exact words of the original quotation within quotation marks, as well as the number of the page on which it appears.

Devising a Working Outline

As you are reading and taking notes, you should also be thinking about the organization of your points and ideas. Chances are the best arrangement won't emerge until you have consulted several sources. But as you collect more and more notes, leaf through your cards or printouts occasionally to see if you can arrange them into three or four main categories to form the major points in your discussion. The sooner you can get a plan worked out, the more efficient your efforts become. You can see exactly what you are looking for and avoid wasting time on sources that will prove irrelevant or unnecessary.

WRITING A FIRST DRAFT

If you have an earlier version of your paper, as Brian Carter did, then you are ready to look at your notes to see where the source material fits and how it affects what you have already written. If you don't have a preliminary draft, now is the time to collect your notes, your bibliography cards, your photocopied pages, your prewriting, your working outline, and anything else you need for composing a first draft. The actual drafting of the paper is a lot like writing a draft for any other paper (as described on pp. 20–23 in Chapter 2). But this time you will incorporate the material from note cards into your text and give credit to the original sources for any information and ideas you gathered from them.

Organizing Your Notes

The first thing to do is to read through your note cards. Then, using the headings that you put on the cards, group the ones with similar ideas together in stacks. If you photocopied most or all of your sources, write headings on the first page of each photocopy and sort the articles that way. Next, consult your working outline and arrange the stacks in the order that the headings appear there. As you write, the necessary information will be in front of you, ready to be incorporated into the draft of your paper.

If your stacks of cards or photocopies don't follow the outline but lie there in a confused, overlapping mess, all is not lost. You can still bring order out of chaos. Here are a few methods:

1. *Tinker with your outline.* It may seem like a step backward, but now that you have new information from your sources, the whole topic may look different. Look at the main headings and change any that don't seem to fit; add others that you have good material for but overlooked when you made the working outline.

2. *Put your note cards or photocopies into different groupings.* This process may suggest an organizing strategy that you wouldn't think of any other way.

3. *Set your notes aside and begin writing*—even if you begin in the middle of a thought. Force yourself, as in freewriting, to keep going, even if your paper seems repetitive, disorganized, and sketchy. Eventually, the writing will begin to take shape, giving you an idea about where to start your first draft.

4. *Explain your ideas to a friend who agrees to ask questions along the way.* Tape-record your discussion and see whether it suggests a sensible order of exposition.

Using Quotations and Paraphrases

You want to be selective when using the words and ideas of others in your writing. Your main goal is to present *your* thinking or advance *your* arguments, not simply to paste together other people's thoughts and words. You need to work them into your analysis and explain how they support your points. Take a look at this example from a paper about drive-in movie theaters:

> Why were these movie theaters so successful in the 1950s and 60s? As journalist Neal Karlen observes, "We had gone from Andy Hardy's front porch to the back seat of Dad's Chevy. In the fifties, nearly everybody had a car. No generation had ever had such opportunities to be alone together" (45–46). Drive-ins also provided cheap entertainment for large families. Mom and Dad had the front seat with a big tub of popcorn; we kids curled up with sleeping bags in the back. It was a treat to see a triple feature and stay out really late.

As you can see, the student writer answers her question about the popularity of drive-ins with a direct quotation from a source. She pursues the point further by adding several relevant observations taken from her own childhood experiences.

Integrating Sources

Whether you are quoting directly or simply paraphrasing someone else's ideas and observations, you should always give credit in the text of your paper to the person from whom you are borrowing—this process is called *documentation*. The MLA documentation style requires you to cite all sources *within* the paper. These in-text citations contain three important parts:

1. An introduction of the source, telling your reader that material from some authority is coming up, who or what the source is, and what the person's credentials are, if you know them.
2. The material from the source, quoted or paraphrased.
3. The parenthetical documentation, which tells your reader that your use of the source is over and gives the page number for the source of that particular material.

The passage above from the paper about drive-in movies illustrates the three steps in effectively integrating sources into your paper.

Here is another example from a research article on male athletes and sexual assault:

When we read of sexual assault cases involving athletes, they are, more often than not, participants in contact or combative sports. Players in these sports are encouraged to beat, dominate, and control the opponent. Little is known about a connection between on-the-field and off-the-field violence, but some observers wonder about the interpersonal effects of sports that teach athletes to use their bodies as instruments of force and domination (Messner 203). Some sport psychologists at the University of California have found that the more physically aggressive the athlete, the less mature his moral reasoning tended to be (Bredemeier 311). As reporter Jean Levy said in her book *Squeeze Play,* "You can't grow up if you spend your whole life perfecting the rhythms of childhood" (3).

In this paragraph, you see the writer's topic sentence (or main point), then a paraphrase from Messner's article to develop the topic, followed by a summary of Bredemeir's research and a quotation from Levy to nail down the point. You never confuse which is which, because this three-part citation system makes clear where all the ideas come from. More details about in-text citations are given in the explanation of the MLA documentation style later in this appendix (pp. 357–358).

Some writers make no attempt to work in direct quotations or provide complete citations of their sources in their first draft because pausing to do so interrupts the flow of their writing. They just jot down the name of the person who provided the information or idea; they go back later to provide attributions, fill in page numbers, and integrate exact quotations.

Using Attributions and Lead-ins

If you want your paper to read smoothly, pay particular attention to the way you introduce quotations and paraphrases. You need a ready supply of introductory phrases to slide the source material in gracefully—phrases like "As Sutherland points out," "Professor Weber notes," and "According to Dr. Carter." The first time you mention a source you should also consider providing brief background information to establish the source as relevant or important. These attributions help your readers to evaluate the source and to separate the source material from your remarks about it.

Don't drop quotations in without preparing your readers. Provide clear lead-ins, usually including the author's name, to connect the quotation to your text:

> Many fluent native speakers of English will claim they don't understand grammar. As Professor David Crystal points out, "Millions of people believe they are failures at grammar, say that they have forgotten it, or deny they know any grammar at all—in each case using their grammar convincingly to make their point" (191).

For variety, you may want to place the connecting phrase in the middle every so often, this way:

> The fundamental purpose of language is to communicate intelligibly. "But if thought corrupts language," warns George Orwell, "language can also corrupt thought" (38).

You don't always have to quote full sentences from your sources. You can quote only the telling phrases or key ideas of your authority, like this:

> Barbara Strang remarks that worrying about split infinitives is "one of the most tiresome pastimes" invented by 19th-century grammarians (95).

> The self-portraits of Frida Kahlo are bold and personal. Art critic Hayden Herrera describes them as "autobiography in paint" (xii).

But do introduce your quotations. Identifying the source before presenting the borrowed material helps your readers to know which ideas are yours and which come from sources.

AVOIDING PLAGIARISM

Research is a kind of conversation between writers, their sources, and others interested in the topic. One of the challenges for writers, then, is to clearly define their part in this broader conversation both accurately and ethically. The core principle here is *respect*: for the person whose ideas you are employing, for your own voice and credibility, and for your readers.

The failure to give proper credit to your sources is called **plagiarism.** It usually involves carelessly—or, far worse, deliberately—presenting the words or ideas of another writer as your own. Most universities have strict policies on academic dishonesty that require sanctions ranging from failing a paper, to assigning a failing grade for the course, to dismissal from the university.

You can avoid this dishonesty by using a moderate amount of care in taking notes. Put quotations marks around any passages, even brief phrases, that you copy word for word. Circle the quotation marks in red or highlight the quoted material in some way, as a reminder to give credit to the source.

You must also avoid the original wording if you decide to **paraphrase** your sources, rather than quoting directly. Changing a few words or rearranging the phrases is not enough: Such close paraphrasing is still considered plagiarism. The following examples may help you to see the difference between plagiarism and paraphrasing. The original passage comes from page 18 in the book *The Language Instinct* by Steven Pinker.

ORIGINAL PASSAGE

Language is not a cultural artifact that we learn the way we learn to tell time or how the federal government works. Instead, it is a distinct piece of the biological makeup of our brains. Language is a complex, specialized skill, which develops in the child spontaneously, without conscious effort or formal instruction.

PLAGIARISM

Humans do not learn language the way we learn to tell time or how the federal government works. Language is a part of the biological makeup of our brains, a complex skill that a child develops spontaneously, without conscious effort or formal instruction (Pinker 18).

PLAGIARISM

Humans do not learn language in the way we learn to count or understand how a computer works. Language is a part of our physical makeup, a complex, specialized skill that develops automatically, without conscious effort or formal instruction (Pinker 18).

ACCEPTABLE PARAPHRASE

Linguist Steven Pinker claims that human beings do not learn language in the way that we learn to count or how to use a computer. Language is a discrete part of our brain's structure; it's a sophisticated skill that children learn automatically without direct instruction (18).

COMBINED PARAPHRASE AND DIRECT QUOTATION

According to linguist Steven Pinker, humans do not learn language in the way we learn to count or understand how a computer works. Language is a discrete part of our brain's structure, "a complex, specialized skill" that develops automatically, "without conscious effort or formal instruction" (18).

DIRECT QUOTATION

"Language is not a cultural artifact that we learn the way we learn to tell time or how the federal government works," says linguist Steven Pinker. "Instead, it is a distinct piece of the biological makeup of our brains" (18).

Crediting Your Sources

The most obvious reason for acknowledging your sources is to avoid plagiarism. But there are less tangible, more important reasons for providing the details about your sources. Documentation will build your credibility, establish the background of your writing, enable your readers to follow up on your work, and give recognition to the people whose ideas and information you have used.

The conventions of writing with sources require that you document ideas and information that originate in someone else's work. All of the following materials should be accompanied by a reference to the original:

- Direct quotations
- Paraphrases and summaries
- Facts that are debatable or not widely known
- Statistics, graphs, charts, diagrams, figures, and other kinds of "hard evidence"
- Opinions, claims, or assertions of others, particularly when controversial or questionable

You don't need to document what is called "general knowledge"—that is, information that could be found in a variety of sources, particularly in an encyclopedia or dictionary—although you should use your own wording to convey these points. And you don't need to document your own thoughts, observations, and personal experiences. Sometimes, however, it is difficult to determine what falls into these last two categories. How do you know where your sources end and your own thinking begins? Which facts and ideas can you claim as your own and which ones came from your sources? One way to decide is to ask yourself, "Did I really know this information before I began looking at sources?"

Citing Sources Informally

A detailed, academic approach to citing sources is not always appropriate for some kinds of writing. Journalists, for example, routinely work source details into the text of an article, as seen in these examples from "The Trouble with Talent" by Kathy Seal (pp. 210–214):

> In fact, our reverence for innate intelligence has gone so far that many Americans believe people who work hard in school must lack ability. "Our idealization of a gifted person is someone so smart they don't have to try," says Sarah Graham of UCLA's Graduate School of Education.

> Columbia University psychologist Carol Dweck has conducted a fascinating series of studies over the past decade documenting the dangers of believing that geniuses are born rather than made.

> During a talk this past spring to the California Teachers Association, U.S. Secretary of Education Richard Riley pledged to work on setting national standards in education.

These references don't include the detailed, parenthetical citations that the MLA requires for academic papers, and the article doesn't include footnotes or a list of works cited. The author clearly knows the value of identifying her sources of information, but she also recognizes that a formal documentation style would not be appropriate for her audience and purpose. Several readings in this book contain informal citations. For your own writing, check with your instructor to see if citing sources informally is acceptable.

FORMATTING YOUR PAPER

The document format recommended by the *Handbook for Writers of Research Papers,* 7th ed., is fairly simple. But individual course requirements may vary from the MLA design, so check with your instructor before you begin preparing your final copy. Here are some features to examine:

Margins. Provide margins of at least one inch at the top, bottom, and both sides of the page.

Spacing and indentions. Double-space throughout, including quotations and the works cited page. Indent paragraphs one-half inch or five spaces.

Long prose quotations (five or more typed lines) and quotations of more than three lines of poetry should be double-spaced and indented one inch or ten spaces from the left margin.

Page numbers.   Number all pages, beginning on the first page. Put the numbers in the upper-right about one-half inch from the top. Place your last name before the page number in case the pages later become separated.

Heading.   The MLA does not require a separate title page. If your instructor asks you to use one, follow the format he or she provides. Otherwise, give your name and the date, plus any other information requested by your instructor (such as the title and number of the course), on the first page of your text. Place this heading an inch from the top of the page, aligned with the left margin.

Title.   Double-space after the heading and center the title of your paper. Do *not* underline or place your title in quotation marks, and don't set it in large type or capitalize all the words. Do capitalize the first and last words and all other words *except* articles (*a, an, the*), prepositions, coordinating conjunctions, and the *to* in infinitives. Double-space between your title and the first line of text.

Textual headings.   If you use headings within your paper to guide readers through the discussion, keep them as short as possible and make them specific to the material that follows. Do not boldface, italicize, or use bigger type or all capitals for these headings.

DOCUMENTING YOUR SOURCES: MLA STYLE

The documentation style of the Modern Language Association (MLA)—used in English, foreign languages, and some other humanities—requires that source citations be given in the text of the paper rather than in footnotes or endnotes. This in-text style of documentation involves parenthetical references.

Throughout this section, all titles of independently published works—books, plays, magazines, journals, Web site, online databases, television and radio programs, films, and works of art—are italicized. Titles of articles and other shorter works included in larger publications are punctuated with quotation marks and not italicized.

In-Text Citations

A. You will usually introduce the cited material, whether quoted or paraphrased, by mentioning the name of the author in your lead-in and then later giving the page number (or numbers) in parentheses. Put the parenthetical reference near the cited material, but preserve the flow of your writing by placing the citation where a pause would naturally occur, preferably at the end of the sentence, as in this example:

> Edmund Wilson tells us that the author of *Uncle Tom's Cabin* felt "the book had been written by God" (5).

B. Your readers can identify this source by consulting your Works Cited at the end of your paper. The entry for the source cited above would appear like this:

> Wilson, Edmund. *Patriotic Gore: Studies in the Literature of the American Civil War.* New York: Oxford UP, 1966. Print.

C. If you do not mention the author in your lead-in, include his or her last name in parentheses along with the page number, without an intervening comma, like this:

> One of the great all-time best-sellers, *Uncle Tom's Cabin* sold over 300,000 copies in America and more than 2 million copies world wide (Wilson 3).

D. If you are using a source written or edited by more than three people, use only the name of the first person listed, followed by "et al." (meaning "and others"), in your lead-in.

> Blair et al. observe that the fine arts were almost ignored by colonial writers (21).

Since *et* means "and," it isn't an abbreviation and therefore doesn't need a period.

E. If you refer to one of two or more works by the same author that are in your paper, put a comma after the author's last name and include a shortened title in the parenthetical reference.

> (Gould, *Mismeasure* 138).

Preparing the List of Works Cited

On a separate page at the end of the paper, alphabetize your Works Cited list for all sources mentioned in your paper. Format the list according to the these rules:

- Center Works Cited at the top of the page without underlining or boldface.
- Arrange your sources in alphabetical order by the last name of the author. If the author is not given in the source, alphabetize the source by the first main word in the title (excluding *A*, *An*, or *The*).
- Unless otherwise instructed by your teacher, double-space the entire list, both within and between entries.

- Use hanging indention: put the first line of each entry flush with the left margin, and indent any subsequent lines in the entry one-half inch.
- In both titles and subtitles, capitalize the first and last words and all other words *except* articles (*a, an, the*), prepositions, coordinating conjunctions, and the *to* in infinitives.
- Omit any use of the words *page, pages, line,* and *lines.* Do not even include abbreviations for these terms. Use numbers alone.

> Kinsley, Michael. "Continental Divide." *Time* 7 Jul. 1997: 89–91. Print.

- Shorten publishers' names: for example, use Prentice instead of Prentice Hall or Norton instead of W. W. Norton and Co. or Oxford UP instead of Oxford University Press or U of Illinois P instead of University of Illinois Press. See sample entries in the next section.
- For books, include the city of publication, usually given on the title page of the work cited. If you find two or more cities, use only the first.
- Abbreviate months as shown in the sample entries.
- Include the medium of publication—Web, Print, Film, DVD, etc.— for all sources.

Works Cited List: Sample Entries

The following models will help you write Works Cited entries for most of the sources you will use. If you use a source not illustrated in these examples, consult the more extensive list of sample entries found in the *MLA Handbook for Writers of Research Papers*, 7th ed., or ask your instructor for guidance.

The MLA now recommends including the medium of publication for all entries. Sources are divided into three categories: print, Web, and other common sources. Use *Print* for books, periodicals (magazine, journals, newspapers), and other printed materials. Use *Web* for any material you retrieved online. Other common sources include *Film, CD, DVD, Radio* or *Television program.* The medium of publication will usually be the last item in the citation. But when *Web* is the medium, the last item should be the date of access. The sample entries on the following pages provide plenty of examples.

Books

Book by One Author. Begin with the author's last name, followed by a comma and the full first name. Provide the full title of the book, including the subtitle. It should be italicized or underlined and capitalized. Follow with the city of publication and a shortened version of the publisher's name. End with the year of publication.

> Chused, Richard H. *Private Acts in Public Places: A Social History of Divorce.* Philadelphia: U of Pennsylvania P, 1994. Print.

Book by Two or Three Authors.   List the first author (following the order on the title page of the book) in the same way as for a single-author book. List subsequent authors, first name first, separating the individuals' names with commas.

> Anderson, Terry, and Donald Leal. *Free Market Environmentalism*. Boulder: Westview, 1991. Print.
>
> McCrum, William, William Cran, and Robert MacNeil. *The Story of English*. New York: Viking, 1986. Print.

Book by More than Three Authors.   List the first author in the same way as for a single-author book, followed by a comma and the abbreviation *et al.* ("and others").

> Medhurst, Martin J., et al. *Cold War Rhetoric: Strategy, Metaphor, and Ideology*. New York: Greenwood, 1990. Print.

Revised Edition

> Combs, Cindy C. *Terrorism in the Twenty-First Century*. 3rd ed. Upper Saddle River: Prentice, 2003. Print.

Edited Book or Anthology

> Wald, Catherine, ed. *The Resilient Writer: Tales of Rejection and Triumph from 23 Top Authors*. New York: Persea, 2005. Print.

Selection Within an Anthology

> Lamm, Nomy. "Fishnets, Feather Boas, and Fat." *Body Outlaws: Rewriting the Rules of Beauty and Body Image*. Ed. Ophira Edut. Emeryville: Seal P, 2003. 78–87. Print.

Chapter or Section of a Book

> Vowell, Sarah. "Rosa Parks, *C'est Moi*." *The Partly Cloudy Patriot*. New York: Simon, 2002. 119–24. Print.

Two or More Sources by the Same Author.   Use the author's name for only the first entry. For subsequent entries, use three hyphens followed by a period. List the entries in alphabetical order by title.

> Gould, Stephen Jay. *The Mismeasure of Man*. New York: Norton, 1981. Print.
>
> ---. *The Panda's Thumb: More Reflections in Natural History*. New York: Norton, 1980. Print.

Journals, Magazines, and Newspapers

Article from a Journal with Continuous Pagination Throughout the Whole Volume.   In some journals the page numbers in one issue pick up where the previous issue left off. After the journal title, give the volume number, followed by the year in parentheses, a colon, and the inclusive page numbers.

> English, Robert D. "Sources, Methods, and Competing Perspectives on the End of the Cold War." *Diplomatic History* 21 (1997): 283–94. Print.

Article from a Journal That Paginates Each Issue Separately.   Put a period after the volume number and add the issue number.

> Holtug, Nils. "Altering Humans: The Case For and Against Human Gene Therapy." *Cambridge Quarterly of Healthcare Ethics* 6.2 (1997): 157–60. Print.

Article from a Monthly or Bimonthly Magazine.   If an article begins in one place, such as pages 56 to 59, and is continued elsewhere, such as on pages 64 to 68 and 72 to 73, just write 56+ for the page numbers (do not write 56–72).

> Russo, Tom. "Lights, Camera, Data!" *Popular Mechanics* Jan. 2007: 56+ Print.

Article from a Weekly or Biweekly Magazine.   Place the number of the date before the month, followed by the year.

> Coghlan, Andy. "Warring Parents Harm Children as Much as Divorce." *New Scientist* 15 Jun. 1991: 24–28. Print.

Article in a Newspaper.   If the newspaper lists an edition, add a comma after the date and specify the edition.

> Weiner, Jon. "Vendetta: The Government's Secret War Against John Lennon." *Chicago Tribune* 5 Aug. 1984, final ed.: C1+. Print.

Letter to the Editor

> Kessler, Ralph. "Orwell Defended." Letter. *New York Times Book Review* 15 Dec. 1985: 26. Print.

Editorial

> "From Good News to Bad." Editorial. *Washington Post* 16 Jul. 1984: 10. Print.

Online Publications

Article from a Searchable Database.   If you retrieve source material from a full-text database, you need to indicate that you read it in electronic form. You will probably use a service to which your library subscribes, such as Academic Search Premier, JSTOR, Expanded Academic ASAP, ProQuest, Project Muse, Galenet, Lexis-Nexis. Most of the items in these databases were previously published in print. Give the print information first. If possible, give the inclusive page numbers or, when pagination is not continuous, the first page number and a plus sign; if page numbers are not available, use *n. pag.* Do *not* include the database URL or information about the library. Complete the citation by giving the name of the database (italicized), medium of publication (Web), and the date of access. Here are examples of entries for periodical publications retrieved from online databases:

Uhler, Walter C. "Gorbachev's Revolution." *The Nation* 31 Dec. 2001: 40–45. *Academic Search Elite.* Web. 3 April 2002.

Carey, Benedict. "Déjà Vu: If It All Seems Familiar, There May Be a Reason." *New York Times* 14 Sept. 2004: F1+. *LexisNexis.* Web. 28 Mar. 2007.

Articles Published Independently on the Web.   For articles that are available on independent Web sites—as opposed to articles accessed from an aggregate database—cite the author, title, and publication data for the printed version as usual; then give the number of pages, paragraphs, or other sections of the electronic version, if provided on the site. Conclude with the medium of publication (*Web*) and the date of access. Here are sample entries for articles on the Web:

Yeoman, Barry. "Into the Closet: Can Therapy Make Gay People Straight?" *Salon.com* 22 May 2000: n. pag. Web. 4 Oct. 2002.

Ebert, Roger. Review of *Real Women Have Curves,* dir. Patricia Cardoso. *Chicago Sun-Times Online* 25 Oct. 2002. Web. 2 Feb. 2003.

Daniel, Ralph Thomas. "The History of Western Music." *Britannica Online: Macropaedia.* 1995. Web. 14 June 2008.

"Key Facts about Avian Influenza (Bird Flu) and Avian Influenza A (H5N1) Virus." *Centers for Disease Control and Prevention.* 30 June 2006. Web. 12 March 2010.

SAMPLE STUDENT ESSAY WITH SOURCES

Brian Carter
Professor Day
English 145
18 January 2008

People, Pigeons, and Payoffs

In 2003 gambling casinos in the United States had three times more attendees than all Major League Baseball franchises combined, according to Professor Jeffrey Nealon (465). Most casino customers play slot machines, even though they would win more playing other games. As journalist Martin Merzer points out, the house advantage is far larger for slots, giving casinos at least 70 percent of their revenue from machines rather than from table games (1A). An observer in a casino might easily decide that most slots players are irrational at best, and insane at worst. Why do Americans shove $1 billion or more into slot machines every day (Merzer 1A)? What rational person purchases $20 worth of nickels to play a slot machine that has a maximum jackpot of $7.50? Why would someone play a machine and refuse to leave, even to go to the bathroom? What is it about slot machines that gives them the power to produce such potentially destructive effects?

The question is answered in any basic psychology class. B. F. Skinner, a psychologist who conducted experiments on the behavior of animals and humans, understood the dynamics of reinforcement. In a series of famous experiments, he showed that pigeons could quickly learn to peck a bar to get a pellet of food for each peck. If it took three bar pecks to produce a food pellet, the pigeons would keep pressing even faster. When reinforcements (like food) come at a constant rate, such as every three or five responses (pecks), this is called a fixed schedule. Skinner then made the reward occur on a variable, random schedule: a food pellet might drop on the 17th peck or the 10th peck, or even twice in a row. This produced even more energetic bar pecking compared to fixed schedules. Skinner also used a random schedule and then stopped dropping food pellets altogether, just to see how long the pigeons would continue to bar peck. He was astonished to see them peck for hours with no reward. Then, when it seemed like the pigeons were going to give up, dropping just one food pellet would cause them to begin bar pecking again, for hours (Domjan 163–74).

Slot machines operate on much the same principle. Their rewards are certainly random; a customer can go several plays without winning anything, but an occasional reinforcement will cause the player to keep going long into the night. One can see slot players as trapped pigeons in one of Skinner's laboratory experiments, conditioned to think they will receive another reward soon if they just keep playing.

The introduction of the computerized slot machine, which directly controlled the outcome of every spin of the wheels, further extended the psychological effects of reinforcement. By law, a slot machine is only required to show, accurately, which combination of wheel symbols pays which amounts—-for example, three cherries in a row pays $3, or four Cadillacs in a row pays $500. There is no law that says slot machines must display how likely it is for each winning row of symbols to show up. The odds are the ratio of no-pay tries to payoff tries, and these are astronomical.

Yet, the computer slot-machine companies introduced a scheme that would hook slot players more than ever before. All slot reel combinations either pay off or don't pay off. But with computerization, the slot manufacturers came up with the idea to include far more "near misses" in their nonpay combinations (Parke & Griffiths 407). In this setup a slot player would see two Cadillacs on the pay line but a third Cadillac just missing the line. Because slot machines display three lines on each try, the tempting third Cadillac would appear just above or just below the actual pay line, and these near misses would occur more often than they would by chance. The payouts of the machine would be the same mathematically as before. A near miss pays as much as a wide miss—that is, nothing. But this rigged system gave the illusion that the slot player was always getting close to the jackpot. Back in 1953 Skinner himself perceived the addictive effects of "almost winning the jackpot" (397). As addiction researchers Jonathan Parke and Mark Griffiths explain, "The player is not constantly losing but constantly nearly winning" (408). Put this little trick on top of the psychological influences already operating on slot players, and one can see why the casinos make sure customers get drinks and snacks without leaving their machines.

Luckily for the slot players, the Nevada Gaming Control Board banned the seductive near-miss practice in 1989 (Rose 1). The board ruled that slot machine reels *must* operate at random and cannot be fixed to show a higher than random rate of near misses. This ruling reinstated the status quo and returned slot players to mere pigeons, pumping money into a device that will surely bankrupt them if they play it long enough. The casinos didn't protest the gaming board's ruling. They still have the most powerful means of getting money from their customers: the psychology of reinforcement scheduling.

Carter 3

Works Cited

Domjan, Michael. *Domjan and Burkhard's The Principles of Learning and Behavior.* 2nd ed. Pacific Grove: Brooke/Cole, 1993. Print.

Merzer, Martin. "Slots Spin Big Dreams, Casino Profits." *Miami Herald* 6 March 2005:1A. Print.

Nealon, Jeffrey T. "Take Me Out to the Slot Machines: Reflections on Gambling and Contemporary American Culture." *South Atlantic Quarterly* 105 (2006): 465–474. *JSTOR*. Web. 8 March 2007.

Parke, Jonathan, and Mark Griffiths. "Gambling Addiction and the Evolution of the 'Near Miss.'" *Addiction Research and Theory* 12 (2004): 407–411. *Academic Search Premier*. Web. 7 March 2007.

Rose, I. Nelson. "Nevada Draws the Line at Near-Miss Slots." *Gambling and the Law: Monthly Format* 1989. Web. 7 March 2007.

Skinner, B. F. *Science and Human Behavior.* New York: Free Press, 1953. Print.

Credits

Isaac Asimov: "What Is Intelligence, Anyway?" copyright © Isaac Asimov. Reprinted by permission of the Estate of Isaac Asimov.

Russell Baker: "Learning to Write" from *Growing Up* by Russell Baker. Reprinted by permission of the McGraw-Hill Companies.

Dennis Baron: "The Noun Game—a Simple Grammar Lesson Leads to a Clash of Civilizations," by Dennis Baron from *The Web of Language*. Reprinted by permission of the author.

Anne Becker: "Hot or Not: Reality TV Can Be Harmful to Women" by Anne Becker from *Psychology Today,* March 1, 2003. Reprinted by permission of the publisher.

Elizabeth Berg: "My Heroes" by Elizabeth Berg from *Parents* Magazine. © 1992. Reprinted by permission of the author.

Suzanne Britt: "Neat People vs. Sloppy People" from *Show & Tell*, 1983. Reprinted by permission of the author.

Greg Crister: "Supersize Me" from *Fatland* by Greg Crister. Copyright © 2003 by Greg Crister. Reprinted by permission of Houghton Mifflin Harcourt Publishing Company. All rights reserved.

Cynthia Crossen: "Whether People Define Themselves as Happy Depends on the Era" by Cynthia Crossen. Copyright © 2006 by Dow Jones. Reprinted by permission.

Steve Daly: "The Man of a Thousand Faces" from *Entertainment Weekly*, January 26, 2007. Copyright TIME INC. Reprinted by permission. TIME is a registered trademark of Time Inc. All rights reserved.

Definition of "Unique" from *Webster's New World Dictionary and Thesaurus*, 2nd edition, by the Editors of Webster's New World Dictionaries and Charlton Laird. Copyright © 2002. Reproduced with permission of John Wiley & Sons, Inc.

Ed Diener: "Income and Happiness" from *Observer*, April 2005, Volume 18 No. 4. Association for Psychological Science. Reprinted by permission of the author.

James C. Dobson: "Two Mommies Is One Too Many" *TIME*, December 18, 2006, p. 123. Copyright TIME INC. Reprinted by permission. TIME is a registered trademark of Time Inc. All rights reserved.

Rita Dove: "Loose Ends" from *The Poet's World*, Library of Congress, Washington, D.C., © 1995 by Rita Dove. Reprinted by permission of the author.

David Elkind: "Types of Stress for Young People" from *All Grown Up and No Place to Go: Teenagers in Crisis* by David Elkind. Copyright © 1998 by David Elkind. Reprinted by permission of Da Capo Press, a member of the Perseus Books Group.

Facts on File: "Reality Television" © 2008 Infobase Publishing. In *Issues & Controversies on File*, January 11, 2008. Reprinted by permission of the publisher.

Carol Fleischman: "Shopping Can Be a Challenge with Curious Onlookers, Puzzled Clerks and a Guide Dog," *Buffalo News*, February 24, 1998. Reprinted with permission of Carol Fleischman.

Lilly Gonzalez: "Viva Spanglish!" *Texas Monthly*, Volume 29 no. 10 (October 2001), p. 50. Reprinted with permission of Texas Monthly.

Bob Greene: "Handled With Care" by Bob Greene is reprinted with the permission of Scribner, a Division of Simon & Schuster, Inc., and Sterling Lord Literistic from *American Beat* by Bob Greene. Copyright © 1983 by John Deadline Enterprises, Inc. All rights reserved.

Michael Hirschorn: "The Case for Reality TV" copyright 2007 The Atlantic.com as published in *The Atlantic Online*. Distributed by Tribune Media Services.

Oliver James: Excerpt from "Danger: Reality TV Can Rot Your Brain" from *They F*** You Up* by Oliver James. Copyright © 2002 by Oliver James. Reprinted by permission of Da Capo Press, a member of the Perseus Books Group and Bloomsbury Publishing Plc.

Tim Jones: "The Working Poor", from *Chicago Tribune*, April 25, 2004. Copyright © 2004 Chicago Tribune. All rights reserved. Used by permission and protected by the Copyright Laws of the United States. The printing, copying, redistribution or retransmission of the Material without express written permission is prohibited.

Index